The Failed Welfare Revolution

The Failed Welfare Revolution

AMERICA'S STRUGGLE OVER
GUARANTEED INCOME POLICY

Brian Steensland

PRINCETON UNIVERSITY PRESS

PRINCETON AND OXFORD

ML

Copyright © 2008 by Princeton University Press
Published by Princeton University Press, 41 William Street, Princeton, New Jersey 08540
In the United Kingdom: Princeton University Press, 3 Market Place,
Woodstock, Oxfordshire OX20 1SY
All Rights Reserved

Library of Congress Cataloging-in-Publication Data

Steensland, Brian, date.
The failed welfare revolution : America's struggle over guaranteed
income policy / Brian Steensland.
p.   cm.
Includes bibliographical references and index.
ISBN-13: 978-0-691-12714-9 (hardcover : alk. paper)
1. Public welfare—United States. 2. Guaranteed annual income—United States. I. Title.
HV95.S72. 2008
362.5′82—dc22   2007008734

British Library Cataloging-in-Publication Data is available

This book has been composed in Electra

Printed on acid-free paper. ∞

press.princeton.edu

Printed in the United States of America

10 9 8 7 6 5 4 3 2 1

For Shana, with love and affection

Contents

Preface

The Failed Welfare Revolution is about the rise and fall of an idea—the idea that the government should provide basic economic security for all Americans. I began this project intending to study America's changing views of poverty, inequality, and justice through the lens of debates over welfare reform legislation from the 1960s through the 1990s. In reading background materials, I ran across scattered references to guaranteed annual income plans. Though one such proposal nearly became law in the early 1970s, they received relatively scant coverage in the many books on American social welfare policy. The proposals captured my interest. Why had these proposals arisen and nearly passed into law? Why had the idea disappeared from the nation's collective memory? Did the idea hold any promise for the future? Given my interest in how people make sense of poverty in an affluent society, the struggle over guaranteed income policy also attracted me because of the candor with which members of the policy community debated, albeit briefly, such issues as the nature of poverty, the goals of welfare reform, and our collective obligations to one another.

As I delved more deeply into policy histories, I ran across a number of surprises. Guaranteed annual income plans were *the* welfare reform strategy of the late 1960s and 1970s. Three presidential administrations considered them, and they served as the centerpiece of welfare reform proposals under both Nixon and Carter. The plans also enjoyed an unexpectedly broad range of support. Though it was scarcely surprising that liberals liked the plans, many conservatives did too. (For example, former president George H. W. Bush voted for Nixon's plan as a Texas congressman and Donald Rumsfeld promoted it as the director of the Office of Economic Opportunity.) The politics of the plans also ran counter to a number of conventional expectations. Interest groups took unexpected positions on the plans; pressures from social movements mattered, but only to a point; elements of the American political system usually thought to obstruct policy innovation actually gave rise to such innovation; and government experts, whose role is often minimized in accounts of welfare policy development, turned out to play a highly significant role.

In reading through archival materials and media coverage from the era, I began to see that the cultural dimension of debates over guaranteed income plans could make sense of some of these puzzles and illuminate the failure of the plans. I realized that guaranteed income plans connoted a wide variety of meanings for different groups, and that there was frequently a contradiction between the substance and the symbolism of the plans (especially Nixon's). I also realized that guaranteed income plans failed because they challenged the cultural logic of American welfare policy, which is based on sorting the poor into different programs according to assessments of their "deservingness." In contrast, guaranteed income plans treated all the poor as deserving. These realizations came somewhat slowly to me because most existing scholarly perspectives on welfare state development lack the analytic tools to capture the significance of cultural factors such as the symbolic connotations of policy proposals or the moral boundaries policymakers reinforce through legislation. Therefore, the account in this book gives special consideration to cultural factors such as these while also showing their interrelationship with factors that are more typically emphasized in the welfare state literature, such as class struggle and institutional patterns of policymaking.

The importance of these cultural factors, I believe, goes well beyond debates among academics about the best ways to explain social policy development. The idea of providing basic economic security to all Americans (or even just American families) is not debated today, first and foremost, because it is *unthinkable*. It is currently beyond the pale of American political discourse. So too, of course, were other ideas once that we now hold dear, such as women's suffrage and equal rights for racial minorities. I invoke these comparisons not necessarily to cast positive light on guaranteed income policies by analogy, but to illustrate that the nature of the unthinkable changes. An idea is unthinkable when it does not fit with the dominant conceptual framework in society, a framework often bolstered by powerful groups and reinforced by institutional patterns.

The history the book recounts shows that American antipoverty policy is designed to stigmatize the poor who are deemed "undeserving" and mark them as morally different from the rest of society. This was part of the existing conceptual framework that guaranteed income plans challenged in the 1960s. Is this dominant conceptual framework valid? Are the poor really morally different from the rest of society? Is poverty their fault? Do they deserve to be stigmatized? Put positively, is providing economic security for the poor through government policy a worthwhile goal? These are questions that the nation has not debated for a generation. They are worthy of revisiting.

Acknowledging debts of gratitude is both one of the most enjoyable and most humbling parts of writing a book. I owe many people and institutions my thanks for their intellectual generosity, moral and financial support, and assistance in researching the project. I began this project as a graduate student at Princeton University, where Bob Wuthnow and Paul DiMaggio proved to be exemplary advisors, setting standards of generosity that I can only hope to approximate one day. Bob provided unstinting wisdom, intellectual guidance, and support throughout my graduate years, even as my research interests evolved considerably. Paul was a perpetual source of creative ideas, tough questions, and good humor. Frank Dobbin and Viviana Zelizer both gave me valuable feedback on the project at critical junctures, and I further benefited from conversations with Miguel Centeno, Michèle Lamont, Sara McLanahan, Paul Starr, and Bruce Western. Though I benefited in countless ways from my formal education at Princeton, I learned just as much from the fellow students whom I met there. For their friendship, good cheer, and more than occasional brilliance, special thanks to Courtney Bender, Bethany Bryson, Julian Dierkes, John Evans, Marion Fourcade-Gourinchas, Eszter Hargittai, Kieran Healy, Cynthia Hooper, Jackie Gordon, Erin Kelly, Jason Kaufman, Becky Pettit, Tania Rands Lyon, Kimberly Morgan, Mike Moody, Lynn Robinson, Jeannie Sowers, Steven Tepper, Margaret Usdansky, Brad Wilcox, and Kathrina Zippel.

The sociology department at Indiana University has been a wonderfully supportive and stimulating intellectual home for me since leaving Princeton. In their roles as departmental chair, Rob Robinson, Scott Long, and Tom Gieryn made sure that any delays in my book could not be blamed on too many onerous service obligations or a deficit of departmental resources. For valuable comments on my work at numerous stages I am indebted to many colleagues: Art Alderson, Clem Brooks, Tom Gieryn, David James, Patricia McManus, Rob Robinson, Pam Walters, and, especially, the incomparable members of the Junior Faculty "Working" Group—Elizabeth Armstrong, Tim Bartley, Tim Hallett, Ethan Michelson, Fabio Rojas, Quincy Stewart, Leah VanWey, and Melissa Wilde.

Outside these institutions I have been the beneficiary of considerable goodwill. At very early stages in the project, John Skrentny, Fred Block, Jill Quadagno, and Bill Gamson gave me valuable advice and assistance. Karl Widerquist invited me to participate in the Basic Income Guarantee network and introduced me to a number of colleagues with like-minded interests. Robert Harris gave me insights from his work as a policy analyst on guaranteed income plans in the 1960s and loaned me a treasure trove of government documents from his personal files. At the Nixon Project and the Jimmy Carter Library, a number of very competent and patient archivists helped me through a daunting maze of archival materials and gave me great advice on local dining and music. A number of people helped me collect and analyze the newspaper and periodicals data: Lauren Cusick, Jessica Hickok, Elaine Hsieh, Rob Laset, Andra Maniu, and Hilary Rubin. Without their assistance, the media analysis would not have been possible. Ariadna Philips helped organize the archival materials and Niki Hotchkiss collected valuable secondary data. For financial support at various stages of the project, I gratefully acknowledge assistance from the Princeton University Graduate School, the National Science Foundation, the Noah Cotsen Junior Teaching Fellowship, the Woodrow Wilson Foundation Summer Fellowship, the Center for the Study of Religion, the Center of Domestic and Comparative Policy Studies, and the Department of Sociology at Indiana University.

At conferences, workshops, and colloquia, I received valuable input that shaped my thinking on the project from Fred Block, Paul Burstein, Bruce Carruthers, Myra Marx Ferree, Chad Goldberg, Paul Lichterman, James Mahoney, Leslie McCall, Alice O'Connor, Monica Prasad, Ellen Reese, Robin Stryker, Ann Swidler, and Erik Olin Wright. For incisive written comments on the book's analytic framework, I thank Niki Beisel, Kieran Healy, Jeff Manza, and Ann Orloff. For invaluable commentary on the entire manuscript, I am indebted to Michael Katz, John Skrentny, and two anonymous reviewers. To whatever extent the book's arguments and insights cohere, much of the credit goes to the people mentioned above. The remaining weaknesses are of course my own.

I have enjoyed working with Tim Sullivan at Princeton University Press and thank him for his enthusiasm and judicious editorial guidance. I am also grateful to the University of Chicago Press for allowing me to integrate into the book portions of my article "Cultural Categories and the American Welfare State: The Case of Guaranteed Income Policy," *American Journal of Sociology* 111 (March 2006): 1273–1326.

I have been blessed throughout my life by love and affirmation from my parents, Mollie and David Steensland, and from my late grandmother, Maxine Sloat. I am deeply grateful to them. Finally, and closest to home, I owe a giant debt of gratitude to my wife, Shana Stump, for her support. She has not known me when I was not working on this project, so she more than anyone can share my joy in completing it. Because her passion inspires me, her humor cheers me, and her love sustains me, I happily dedicate the book to her.

Abbreviations

AFDC   Aid to Families with Dependent Children

DOL   Department of Labor

EITC   Earned Income Tax Credit

FAP   Family Assistance Plan

GAI   guaranteed annual income

HEW   Department of Health, Education and Welfare

NIT   negative income tax

NWRO   National Welfare Rights Organization

OEO   Office of Economic Opportunity

PBJI   Program for Better Jobs and Income

SSI   Supplemental Security Income

The Failed Welfare Revolution

Understanding the Failed Welfare Revolution

In the 1960s, a new idea for combating poverty emerged that promised a revolutionary change for American social welfare policy. Though the idea had a complex history, one of its main justifications was articulated by a commission appointed by President Johnson to evaluate the nation's antipoverty programs. The commission, which was made up primarily of business leaders and economists, issued a report in 1969 that urged making a sharp break with past approaches to fighting poverty. On the basis of its analysis, the commission believed that the existing welfare system was founded on the untenable premise that good jobs at adequate wages were available to all. Therefore it did not provide sufficient coverage for the poor who were left behind in an increasingly postindustrial economy. The report accordingly criticized the existing system for sorting the poor into different types of programs based on their ability or willingness to work. The report contended,

> Our economic and social structure virtually guarantees poverty for millions of Americans. . . . The simple fact is that most of the poor remain poor because access to income through work is currently beyond their reach. . . . There are not two distinct categories of poor—those who can work and those who cannot. Nor can the poor be divided into those who will work and those who will not. For many, the desire to work is strong, but the opportunities are not readily available.[1]

On these grounds the commission proposed replacing much of the current welfare system with a program that provided all Americans with a guaranteed annual income based solely on their economic need.

Guaranteed annual income programs broke sharply with past approaches to fighting poverty. Most important, they treated the unemployed and working poor in the same way. People who earned below a certain amount of income per year—whether because of unemployment or because they worked but were *still* poor—would receive cash benefits from the federal government to raise their annual income to a minimum level. The programs were innovative in other ways as well. They expanded eligibility for benefits from primarily single mothers with children to include two-parent families with a fully employed breadwinner. And they called for a comprehensive federal program to replace locally run programs that varied widely in their levels of support. All told, these changes marked a philosophical shift in which the government extended the right to basic economic security to the nation's poorest citizens for the first time. By the late 1960s both liberals and conservatives heralded the proposals as "a striking example of an idea whose time has come."[2]

From today's vantage point, it may seem strange that guaranteed annual income programs were ever seriously considered in the United States, since they run contrary to the nation's approach to welfare reform both before and after this era. So it may seem even more surprising that the strongest contender among these proposals nearly became law. President Nixon's Family Assistance Plan passed the House of Representatives by large majorities in both 1970 and 1971. Commentators at the time also expected it to pass in the more liberal Senate, but it never reached a full vote. Jimmy Carter made comprehensive welfare reform a major campaign issue in his bid for the presidency in 1976, and his administration took up guaranteed annual income plans once in office. This continuing consideration shows that the guaranteed income idea was not simply a product of "the 1960s." Carter's proposal fared less well than Nixon's and never reached the floor of Congress. This second failure of guaranteed annual income proposals marked their disappearance from the nation's legislative landscape and foreshadowed the diminishing prospect of a system that provides basic economic security for the nation's citizens.

The rise and fall of guaranteed annual income (GAI) proposals sheds light on the nation's provision for the poor in a number of ways. Perhaps most important, understanding the failure of these programs helps explain why the United States, while having one of the highest gross domestic product levels per capita in the world, lags considerably behind other advanced industrial democracies in rates of poverty reduction. Comparisons between these countries show that guaranteed income–style programs, such as family allowances, have proved to be among the most effective antipoverty measures available to policymakers.[3] More directly comparable evaluations of antipoverty measures in the United States and Canada show a similar pattern. Canada's more extensive incorporation of GAI-style programs during the 1970s and 1980s moved its poverty rates from nearly seven percentage points above that in the United States to four points below it.[4]

The history of GAI proposals is also significant because of its role in the evolution of U.S. social policy. These programs were the dominant welfare reform strategy of the late 1960s and 1970s, which was the transitional period between the liberal policy innovations of Lyndon Johnson's War on Poverty programs and the conservative reforms of the Reagan administration and beyond. Views of the welfare state clearly changed during this era. The struggle over GAI programs not only provides the primary lens through which this transition can be concretely understood, but in many ways, the strategies utilized during the debate over the plans actively produced, sometimes inadvertently, the intellectual and political groundwork for the subsequent conservative ascendancy.

From a more analytic perspective, examining why GAI plans became "the road not taken" can tell us as much, and in some ways more, about the nature of American antipoverty policy as examining episodes of successful legislative passage.[5] The proposals represent the boldest attempt to transform U.S. welfare policy in the twentieth century because they attacked the problem of poverty so directly.[6] Doing so called into question deeply held assumptions about the causes of poverty, the adequacy of the labor market, and the goals of welfare reform that are rarely debated in American society but that nonetheless guide policymaking. These assumptions are central to the cultural foundation of the American welfare state, but they are challenging to study because they usually go unspoken. The challenge posed by GAI proposals threw the impact of these assumptions on policy development into sharp relief, albeit for a brief period. This makes the struggle over GAI plans a valuable case for close examination, since it provides a rare window into the cultural processes that influence, and indeed constitute, policy development. As I will discuss later in the chapter, taking into account these types of cultural factors helps explain a number of puzzles about the politics of GAI plans that conventional perspectives on U.S. policy development have difficulty explaining.

Perhaps the most relevant puzzle is why GAI proposals disappeared, that is, why they are no longer considered by policymakers, even though many of the same problems that brought them to the public agenda in the 1960s and 1970s—low wages, economic restructuring, and inadequate welfare coverage—continue to be pressing concerns in contemporary America.[7] Guaranteed income plans are still consistent with goals held by both liberals and conservatives, as suggested by recent calls for these sorts of plans on both the political left and right.[8] Though there is a considerable amount of research on twentieth-century social welfare policy, little of it has focused on GAI policy.[9] Thus there is scant basis upon which to assess the significance and disappearance of these policies. This book traces the rise and fall of GAI proposals, illuminates the puzzling politics of the debates they launched, and finds that, despite their failure, the struggle over GAI proposals had a lasting impact on the American welfare state.

The book is oriented by three general arguments, which I briefly outline here and then elaborate in sections to follow. First, the main obstacle to GAI legislation was the cultural distinction that Americans draw between different categories of poor people. Put most simply, Americans have long considered some types of people, based on their perceived adherence to the work ethic, to be more worthy of government assistance than others. As the quote at the beginning of this chapter suggests, almost all welfare programs implemented before and after this episode have based the provision of government benefits on the *work capacity* of the poor. In contrast, the most significant feature of GAI programs was their provision of benefits based on *economic need* alone. The proposals placed all the categories of poor people in the same government program and treated them in the same way. This challenged the political, economic, and cultural status quo: it presumed that previously separate categories of the poor were morally equivalent to one another; it called into question existing definitions of "welfare"; it created a new category of government beneficiary (the "working poor"); and it rested on the premise that the labor market could not serve as the sole source of economic security for the nation's able-bodied citizens. After the failure of Nixon's proposal, legislators responded to the threats posed by GAI plans by creating new antipoverty programs—Supplemental Security Income and the Earned Income Tax Credit—that institutionally reinforced the categories that Nixon's plan had threatened to dismantle.

Second, GAI policy had multiple meanings attributed to it by various supporters. The proposals were ambiguous and underspecified when experts first advanced them.[10] Advocates from a number of ideological perspectives—libertarians, moderates, and socialists alike—all defined the plans as a promising way to alleviate poverty. Other stakeholders soon began to see the plans as a potential solution for other types of problems that were only tangentially related to poverty reduction, such as fiscal crises that beset state governments and administrative bloat within the government bureaucracy. These different policy meanings served as the basis for a diverse array of interests that propelled GAI proposals forward and, at least initially, masked the proposals' threat to the categorical logic of the existing welfare system. Understanding this multiplicity of policy meanings is essential for understanding how GAI plans arose on the policy agenda. As the debates over the next fifteen years foreclosed many of these ways of seeing GAI plans, their challenge to the status quo became clearer. This narrowing process can be seen both in the ecology of competing policy ideas among policymakers and in the ways in which GAI proposals were depicted in the media.

Third, as the discussion so far may suggest, the debates over GAI proposals did not simply reflect changing perceptions of poverty and the welfare state during this period; they were central in producing these changes. These changing perceptions, in turn, were the direct antecedent for the rise of conservative social policy reforms in the 1980s. Stated differently, Reagan's welfare state retrenchment was a much more direct product of the debate over GAI proposals than it was a reaction to Johnson's War on Poverty programs, to which it is more often seen as a response. Arguments for GAI proposals were based on new critiques of the existing welfare system and a new mode of expert analysis that focused on individual rather than social causes of poverty. The ascendant conservative movement appropriated these critiques and analytic innovations and effectively turned them against the welfare state in the 1970s. Guaranteed income proposals further served as the foil for critiques of an "entitlement" philosophy of welfare reform that directly paved the way for a new "paternalist" approach to welfare reform in the 1980s. Finally, the new Supplemental Security Income and Earned Income Tax Credit programs not only divided the poor by giving different categories of people different stakes in the welfare system, but they relieved some of the social pressure for comprehensive antipoverty reform that was present in the 1960s. These new programs isolated the most politically weak categories of the poor, making them highly vulnerable to the budget cutbacks that targeted the "undeserving" poor in the 1980s.

The account I advance in the book differs from conventional social scientific perspectives on welfare policy development, though it is indebted to the many insights they have generated. This difference stems in part from the book's main focus on the *idea* of providing Americans with a guaranteed annual income, rather than on a particular legislative episode. Yet it also reflects an effort to show the impact of cultural influences on welfare policy development in ways that are not typical, but that are essential for understanding the rise and fall of GAI proposals and, I would argue, policy development more generally. Broadly speaking, scholars typically emphasize the influence of two types of factors when seeking to explain patterns of policy development: the relative influence of various *stakeholder groups* such as business elites, government experts, and social movements; and the constraints on policy development imposed by U.S. *institutional arrangements*, such as federalism, sectionalism (regional differences), the congressional committee structure, and existing policy design.[11] These factors played important roles in the development and failure of GAI plans (though sometimes in unanticipated ways), and I discuss their impact throughout the book. Neither of these perspectives, however, is well equipped to examine how perceptions of worthiness attributed to different categories of poor people structured the entire debate over GAI proposals or how the varying meanings attributed to the proposals elucidate the puzzling patterns of support and opposition that the policies generated. My account highlights the importance of these factors and shows how they interact with more conventional factors—for instance, how perceptions of moral worthiness and stigma shaped the policy preferences of important stakeholders; how particular understandings of poverty and the poor gained prominence over others due to the nation's policymaking process; and how the pattern of preexisting public assistance programs constrained advocates of GAI plans when it came to framing these new proposals in culturally resonant ways. In the sections that follow, I discuss the contributions of existing perspectives to understanding the trajectory of GAI proposals, point out where they fall short, and elaborate on how they can be strengthened by paying more sustained attention to the cultural factors at play in welfare reform.

The debates over GAI proposals took place simultaneously in two important places: among members of the federal policymaking community and in the public sphere through the mass media. I examined the deliberation over the proposals in each domain, collecting government documents from the Nixon and Carter administrations and media coverage in newspapers and periodicals.[12] Comparing both expert deliberation and public discourse helps overcome a typical problem in policy studies, which is the difficulty of disentangling policy elites' "private" worldviews and "public" framing strategies.[13]

Furthermore, most studies of social policy focus mainly on elites, whether government bureaucrats, politicians, or interest groups. These groups are clearly crucial for shaping social policy. However, they do so within a broader public context that constrains their policy options and shapes their strategies of public persuasion. A full understanding of this episode requires looking at both how elite framing influenced public sentiments and how the "common knowledge" created by media accounts influenced decisions among policymakers.[14]

PERSPECTIVES ON AMERICAN SOCIAL POLICY DEVELOPMENT

Many Western nations experienced a process of rapid industrialization in the late nineteenth and early twentieth centuries that simultaneously increased their levels of economic development and disrupted traditional sources of economic security for their citizens. This industrialization process thus generated both the need for new sources of economic security and the fiscal means and administrative apparatus through which government could provide it, and it was during this period that the modern welfare state was born. As welfare states developed over the course of the twentieth century, they became central in defining the relationship between citizens and the state, regulating labor markets, and managing the social reproduction of the population.

There is a rich tradition in the social sciences devoted to understanding this process. Much of this research has sought to explain why the welfare states in Western industrial countries evolved in such different directions. Compared to the nations of Western Europe, for instance, social welfare policy in the United States is viewed as the most classically liberal—that is, oriented by its conformity to free market principles and norms of individualism. In contrast, Scandinavian social policy prioritizes solidarity and equality, and many other European welfare states, such as those in Germany and Italy, prioritize social stability and cultural traditionalism.[15] In light of these cross-national differences, scholars have offered a number of arguments to explain the relatively unique development of the U.S. welfare state. This body of work has made a deep contribution to our understanding of American social provision, especially by calling attention to the fact that the welfare state is a product of politics. What follows is a thumbnail sketch of some of the main lines of argument.

In the absence of a strong labor movement or socialist political party in the United States, social movements made up of poor and working-class citizens have been a significance force in social policy development. Especially notable in this regard are the 1930s and 1960s, decades characterized both by sustained popular protest and by landmark social legislation. Economic elites historically have been the main opposition to social policy expansion because of their fear that policy expansion will raise the costs of doing business. The political strength of big business coalitions in the United States, as compared to other nations, is a key reason for the more limited, market-based nature of the country's welfare system. Working somewhat independently from both social movements and economic elites, policy experts within and outside the government have, under the right conditions, been able to advance social reforms following their own political agendas.

Other factors that help explain the limited nature of U.S. social policy have more to do with the American political system than with the influence of particular stakeholders. A key factor is the weakness of the state itself, which lacks the centralized capacity necessary for policy innovation and significant intervention into labor market dynamics. Government power is instead diffused through a federal system in which state and local officials maintain authority over many aspects of policy development and implementation, particularly for means-tested programs. Political influence is diffused still further by constitutional checks and balances, but it is also concentrated in the hands of a few through the congressional committee system, the consequence being that a minority coalition can block legislation that the majority supports. Throughout the mid-twentieth century, southern political leaders did just that. They fought social welfare legislation that threatened to undermine their region's labor-intensive agricultural labor market or upset the southern system of racial domination by shifting power out of the hands of local officials and into those of federal policymakers or poor blacks. The overall weakness of the federal government combined with the political system's numerous veto points and the sustained opposition to welfare state expansion in the South together place substantial limits on American social policy development. One final constraint is that due to the sunk-costs of policy design, policy decisions that are made early on, such as during the New Deal, can have a lasting influence on subsequent policy development decades later.

As Edwin Amenta aptly characterizes it, these mainstream perspectives on U.S. welfare policy development draw from two traditions within classical sociological theory. Scholars who focus on business influence and social movements are informed by Marx's work on political economy, while studies focusing on state actors and institutional configurations draw from Weber's and Tocqueville's writings on bureaucracy and political institutions.[16] Neither of these orientations recognizes that systems of social provision are embedded in moral and symbolic orders (albeit contested ones) that shape their development. Therefore, existing perspectives suffer from a variety of blind spots that diminish their ability to incorporate the influence of factors such as moral categories, symbolic representations, and public discourse on policy development. In the remainder of this section, I discuss in greater detail what existing theoretical perspectives contribute to understanding the politics of GAI policy and where they fall short.

First, the social movement perspective argues that economically disenfranchised groups create pressure for welfare policy expansion by creating social disturbances. In response, political elites seek to restore stability by extending social provision along lines that are prefigured by existing institutional arrangements.[17] The 1960s were clearly marked by social disruption. This social movement perspective highlights the important role that multiple sources of social pressure—stemming from nonviolent civil rights activism, urban rioting in the mid-1960s, and welfare rights activism later in the decade—played in moving the issue of poverty to the top of the national agenda. Yet the presence of this pressure cannot account for the rise of GAI plans specifically—as compared to other antipoverty policy options—since the plans were not prefigured by existing social policy. The main policy outcome that the social movement perspective anticipates is the expansion of existing Aid to Families with Dependent Children (AFDC) rolls, which research has in fact shown to be positively associated with social unrest.[18] However, it does not anticipate either the sharp break in policy design that GAI represented or the continuing consideration of GAI proposals through the 1970s, which was a period of social quiescence among economically disadvantaged groups.

A second perspective focuses on the role of business interests in shaping policy development. According to the main arguments of this perspective, business coalitions have been key actors in opposing the expansion of national social policy because they have interests in limited government, low corporate taxes, and maintaining a compliant labor force.[19] This perspective points to the central role played by business groups during the debates over GAI plans, but it is also challenged because much of the business class—including many small business owners, corporate CEOs, and big business coalitions—supported GAI proposals. Business opposition came almost exclusively from the national office of the U.S. Chamber of Commerce. When such intracapitalist divisions occur, divergent policy preferences are typically explained in reference to varying economic interests based in different organizational environments or business sectors.[20] However, debates over the impact of GAI proposals on business spending and labor market processes were marked by a high degree of uncertainty, making the identification of straightforward economic interests difficult to calculate. Moreover, groups with the most ostensibly similar interests, such as the U.S. Chamber of Commerce and the National Federation of Independent Business, held different preferences. Policy memos circulated within the presidential administrations and the passage of alternative antipoverty legislation reveal that competing perceptions of the poor, which are ignored in existing accounts, contributed to the divergence of policy preferences among business groups.

A third perspective argues that policymaking elites within government have the potential to advance policy proposals according to their own agendas, rather than solely reflecting the interests of groups outside government, such as social movements or economic elites. The main conditions that contribute to this potential are a professional class of civil servants and the availability of fiscal resources.[21] This emphasis on state experts provides considerable explanatory leverage for the development of GAI proposals. GAI proposals had been considered by the Kennedy administration and subsequently dismissed as politically implausible. The institutional capacity of welfare experts increased at the outset of President Johnson's War on Poverty initiatives, and this increased capacity allowed for the uptake of new policy ideas.[22] For the next fifteen years, GAI proposals were advanced first and foremost by experts within the government bureaucracy. Yet as some critics have noted, this state-centered approach, particularly in its early formulations, offers relatively little guidance about the actual direction and content of expert reform.[23] In the absence of greater attention to the content of expert knowledge, particularly the dominant influences that shape elites' epistemic culture, this perspective lacks an account of why government experts initially favored GAI proposals over competing welfare reform alternatives or why they continued to favor it, against mounting opposition, in the years to follow.[24]

A fourth perspective argues that that institutional configurations of the U.S. state—especially sectionalism, federalism, and the congressional committee structure—shape social policy development.[25] Differences between the South and the rest of the country, especially those having to do with race relations and regional labor market dynamics, have created competing objectives for welfare reform between these regions. The influence of these regional differences has been further amplified by federal power-sharing arrangements that grant local authorities considerable control over public assistance programs and by the structure of the congressional committee system. It is certainly the case that sectionalism and federalism have been important influences in U.S. policy development in general. Yet in the case of GAI policy specifically, far from constraining policy development, the federal system of social provision— namely state-federal cost sharing—generated much of the pressure for reform and the porous nature of the political system expanded the constituency of GAI supporters. More broadly, commentators have noted that institutional constraints constitute a static framework in which other factors are required to explain temporal dynamics and causal processes in policymaking.[26] Institutional explanations often smuggle the interaction between institutional arrangements and cultural patterns—such as conservative ideology—into their empirical accounts while this interaction itself is seldom explicitly theorized.[27]

In the South, for instance, the mutual constitution of the regional labor market and beliefs about the poor held substantial consequences for Nixon's GAI proposal. The president's advisors thought that his plan would be popular in the South due to the fiscal dividends the region would reap, yet this is where the plan confronted some of its most forceful opposition. This opposition was not based on self-evident economic interests but on an interpretation of economic interests suffused with assumptions about the work ethic of black, low-wage workers. Since Nixon's advisors did not share these views of the poor, they calculated the effects of the plan in the South quite differently.

Institutionalists further argue that preexisting policy design channels policy development through "policy feedback" processes that allocate resources, shape incentives, and generate interpretive frameworks.[28] In general, this perspective has much to recommend it. Yet in practice, existing policy feedback arguments have focused on the *resource/incentive* dimension of policy feedback processes, while underplaying the *interpretive* feedback mechanisms—a mechanism that turns out to be central to the politics of GAI plans.[29] For instance, John Myles and Paul Pierson make a policy feedback argument in a comparative study of the failure of GAI proposals in the United States and their success in Canada during the same period.[30] The authors emphasize the importance of preexisting universal social policies in Canada that served as a "natural bridge" to new GAI policies and contend that GAI proposals failed in the United States in part because they lacked a similar programmatic bridge. These institutional legacies are clearly important. But what an examination of the actual debates over GAI policies shows is that supporters of GAI plans lacked a critical *symbolic* resource that a universal transfer program could have provided for defending a new type of social provision that did not distinguish between the deserving and undeserving poor, but that extended income benefits to a new category of recipient—fully employed workers—for the first time. This absence also helps explain a key difference between the U.S. and Canadian cases that Myles and Pierson argue is important but do not explain; namely, that GAI policy was so contentious in the United States because of its association with "welfare reform."

Existing perspectives on social policy development contribute a great deal to understanding the rise and fall of GAI plans. In particular, by evaluating the American welfare state from a historical and comparative perspective, this literature identifies some of the most important factors in explaining the contours of policy development in the nation. But these theories do not illuminate many important aspects of the debate over GAI plans. This is not solely due to the inexact fit between general theoretical claims and the historical specificity of a single case, but also due to the neglect of cultural analyses in the mainstream welfare state literature.

CULTURE, INSTITUTIONS, AND THE WELFARE STATE

To suggest that a society's culture influences its antipoverty policies perhaps seems uncontroversial. Yet social scientists typically dismiss this type of argument because of its association with a heavily criticized theoretical perspective that was prominent a generation ago. This "national values" approach conceptualized culture as a relatively coherent set of beliefs and values shared by a country's citizens.[31] If societies varied in their beliefs and values, they would, it stood to reason, produce different types of social policies. Social policy, in short, reflected a society's culture. In one of the classic studies from this perspective, Gaston Rimlinger argues that national values—particularly the extent of a country's embrace of classical liberalism—helped explain the divergent paths of welfare policy development taken by the United States, Britain, Germany, and Russia.[32] Critics responded in various ways to such arguments. They claimed that these approaches assumed an unrealistic level of cultural uniformity in heterogeneous societies; disregarded struggles for power and contention between competing stakeholders; and failed to specify the mechanisms through which values influence important aspects of policymaking, such as the timing, content, or fate of particular policies.[33] In evaluating these theories, for instance, Theda Skocpol queried, "Whose ideas and whose values? And ideas and values about what more precisely?"[34] Critics contended that these national values arguments were simply too vague to compete convincingly with other types of explanations.

More recent studies in a variety of policy domains address these criticisms by integrating insights from the "cultural turn" in the social sciences that began in the 1970s.[35] The most widespread advance is the recognition that policymakers and other stakeholders are guided by their interests, but that these interests are constituted by ideas. In other words, people do not simply have interests; they have ideas about their interests. This approach stands in contrast both to analyses that see policymaking as guided by values, such as individualism, and to analyses that view social policy as the end product of actors pursuing self-evident interests. Instead, scholars from this perspective seek to explain why, in a complex world of conflicting values, competing interests, and considerable uncertainty, some interests become more salient to people than others.[36] Most broadly, this orientation marks a shift from a narrow focus on *policy interests* to an expanded analysis of *policy meanings*, which entails looking at how actors define social problems, potential solutions, and the boundaries of political legitimacy.[37] This has led scholars to look at two types of ideas in particular: the policy paradigms that guide decision making among elites and the frames that actors employ to articulate and justify their policy positions amid competing claims.[38] The specification of these types of ideas, along with greater attention to contestation and mechanisms of influence, distinguishes this approach from what critics claim is an overly "anthropological" conception of culture in "national values" perspectives.

Another insight from the cultural turn, but one that has been insufficiently applied to policy studies, goes beyond the importance of ideas alone by grounding elements of culture more firmly in their institutional context. As William Sewell, Jr., argues, enduring institutions—such as social policy regimes—reproduce both social structure (such as patterns of relations and the distribution of material resources) *and* our subjective understandings of that structure. Furthermore, these structural patterns and subjective understandings mutually constitute one another.[39] Thus, for instance, a great deal of power in Western societies is based on private property holdings; this only makes sense, and appears legitimate, with the attendant notion of property rights. This view of institutions does not mean that culture is static or epiphenomenal and therefore has little causal influence.[40] Subjective understandings actively reproduce institutions. Moreover, when stakeholders alter interpretive understandings through definition work, they can profoundly transform social institutions. One example of this is the change in subjective perceptions, or "cognitive liberation," among black activists that Doug McAdam identifies as crucial for understanding the civil rights movement's challenge to longstanding structures of injustice in the American legal system.[41] Another example can be seen in the socially prescribed role of "wageworker" that characterizes employer-employee relations in a capitalist society. This is one of the most durable and powerful interpretive schemes in industrial societies, but its meaning, and thus its legitimacy, can be transformed through the definitional work contained in legal statutes, socialist tracts, union strikes, and so forth.[42]

The broader lessons derived from seeing institutions as mutually constituted as Sewell describes are threefold. Understanding the mutual constitution of cultural schemas and structural patterns through institutional reproduction allows us to account for cultural coherence in the face of social heterogeneity and fragmentation.[43] Moreover, when challenges to the existing institutional order emerge, such as challenges to an existing policy regime, they must overcome "institutional" obstacles that are both material and symbolic. Finally, interpretive change requires entrepreneurs who impose new schemas on existing social patterns, often by drawing these new understandings from other institutional realms.[44]

Seeing institutional patterns, such as policy design, in this manner sheds light on how social policies and cultural understandings impact one another over time. Drawing from the explanatory logic of "policy feedback" arguments, scholars have shown how policy decisions create interpretative feedbacks.[45] John Skrentny, for instance, has demonstrated how affirmative action programs for African Americans shaped policymakers' definitions of deservingness for arguably analogous minority groups, such as women, white ethnics, and the disabled.[46] Along similar lines, Nicholas Pedriana and Robin Stryker have shown how affirmative action legislation in the late 1960s provided symbolic resources for affirmative action supporters during subsequent debates over equal employment law.[47] Of course, the direction of influence between social policy and interpretation can also run in the opposite way. The dominant ideas that emerge in policy debates often provide the basis for new institutional arrangements. According to Judith Goldstein and Robert

Keohane, this is one of the main causal pathways through which culture influences policy development.[48] Once institutionalized, these ideas shape the definition of interests and this influence can last over generations, even when the original ideas are no longer widely held. This type of cultural influence is often neglected in studies of policy. Yet to use Ronald Jepperson and Ann Swidler's analogy, much as Marx viewed capital as "dead labor," policy design can be seen as something like "dead culture."[49] This process of embedding culture into the pattern of new institutions brings us full circle to Sewell's insight that institutions such as government social programs are mutually constituted by both social and symbolic relations.

These conceptual developments from the cultural turn, which I have sketched out at a general level, cast light on a number of key processes at play in the rise and fall of GAI proposals, as I will discuss in the following two sections. Most centrally, the plans faced obstacles that were simultaneously symbolic and grounded in the political economy of the labor market. These obstacles were not insurmountable, but successfully transforming the existing welfare regime required a new schema through which to understand American social provision, one that provided an alternative basis of worthiness that did not depend solely on labor market participation. Though such schemes were available, neither Nixon nor Carter advanced them, in part because existing patterns of social provision lacked symbolic resources for convincingly making this type of argument. Despite these obstacles, the multiple policy meanings attributed to the plans initially worked in their favor by masking the plan's threat to the status quo. After the failure of Nixon's plan, legislators created new programs that reinforced existing categories of worth.

CHALLENGING THE DISTINCTIONS BETWEEN POOR PEOPLE

The primary obstacle to GAI proposals proved to be the moral and programmatic distinctions drawn between poor people in American society. Based on perceived adherence to the work ethic and bolstered by Anglo-American individualism, the distinctions between "deserving" and "undeserving" constitute the cultural foundation of American social provision dating back to the colonial era.[50] Historically, these categorical distinctions have long been tied to labor market participation. Those who fall into the deserving category during a given historical period are not expected to work due to factors such as their age, sex, or family status. This classification pattern has clear affinities with the functional requirements of capitalism. The moral stigma attached to poverty and the meager benefits, if any, extended to undeserving populations have helped ensure a ready supply of cheap labor for business owners.[51] Yet the influence of these cultural distinctions on the development of antipoverty policy cannot be reduced solely to the instrumental maneuverings of the business class. In other words, they are not simply elements of ideology, as neo-Marxists may be wont to suggest. Their influence transcends direct class interests and is more accurately conceived as part of the nation's broader culture, albeit a contested culture and one that provides symbols and arguments that segments of the business class have effectively mobilized.[52]

The development of the modern welfare state in the 1930s further institutionalized these distinctions, though this was part of a more protracted differentiation process that only culminated decades later. Contributory social insurance programs, such as Old Age Insurance ("social security"), established the template for federal programs that served the deserving poor, and these programs were relatively generous and politically protected. Aid to Dependent Children ("welfare") initially served deserving widows, but it soon became the conduit for the more meager benefits provided to the undeserving poor through a set of politically vulnerable programs that varied widely by state.[53] A third category, the "working poor," included full-time workers who remained in poverty due to their low wages. Individuals in this group did not receive cash benefits from the government.

This three-part distinction between the deserving, undeserving, and working poor served as the basis of American social policy through the New Deal and postwar eras, but by the early 1960s a variety of groups began to call this distinction into question. The reigning economic orthodoxy of the postwar era stipulated that the main remedy for poverty was economic growth. From this perspective, if poverty was primarily caused by unemployment, then a stronger economy would lower rates of unemployment and alleviate poverty. However, increasing affluence combined with trends in industrial automation cast doubt on this formulation. Moreover, the southern civil rights movement exposed systemic forms of injustice in American society, such as job discrimination, that most Americans until then had disregarded, and it drew attention to the fact that blacks were especially vulnerable to industrial displacement.[54] These factors led experts to recognize a new kind of unemployment: *structural* unemployment. This was persistent unemployment among populations who were structurally disadvantaged in the economy because of such factors as age, race, educational attainment, geographical location, or family circumstance. According to this emerging view, the poverty experienced by many disadvantaged populations was beyond the assistance of economic growth and therefore had to be addressed in new ways. This marked the beginning of a significant shift within the government from attacking poverty with a growth-based employment approach to one based on direct income transfers that guaranteed the needy a minimum income.[55]

The defining feature of GAI proposals was their direct challenge to the categories upon which existing antipoverty policies were founded. The plans based social provision on the economic need of the poor rather than on their capacity to work, and thereby placed all three categories of the poor in the same government program on the basis of need alone. Proponents of GAI plans did not consider the poor morally deficient or otherwise living outside the mainstream of American values. Their poverty was viewed in circumstantial, not behavioral, terms. Therefore the poor did not deserve social stigma or programmatic separation from the broader population for the purposes of moral rehabilitation. Furthermore, the most favored type of GAI proposal, the negative income tax, not only blurred the lines between the deserving and undeserving poor but extended income benefits to the working poor for the first time. Until this point the working poor had not received cash assistance from the government. Thus the structure of GAI plans created a new category of government beneficiary: people who worked but were still poor.

Placing these formerly distinct social groups in the same program led to what Mary Douglas has described as *symbolic pollution,* a process in which the "impure" status of one group contaminates the "pure" status of another.[56] Neither experts nor the general public viewed the deserving poor, undeserving poor, and working poor as equivalent to one another, and in the absence of programmatic boundaries separating them, the morally tainted status of recipients receiving "welfare" benefits from AFDC contaminated the status of the other, more deserving categories of recipients in the program. This symbolic pollution, along with the drive to maintain distinctions between categories of poor people, affected the fate of GAI proposals in three ways.[57]

First, it influenced the way people *perceived* GAI programs. Perceptions of government programs are shaped by the cultural characterizations of the target populations they contain.[58] Since GAI plans contained the "welfare" population, both supporters and opponents of Nixon's proposal viewed it as a "welfare" plan, even though the majority of its benefits (up to 90 percent in some versions) went to "deserving" recipients. Because Nixon's plan was defined as a "welfare" proposal, even though it could have been defined otherwise, it then raised concerns about "welfare" spending, growing "welfare" caseloads, and other volatile political issues. Symbolic pollution also shaped the policy preferences of influential groups such as policy experts, business leaders, and the poor themselves. Conservative business leaders, for instance, opposed Nixon's plan even though it socialized the costs of low-wage labor. They feared stigmatizing the working poor with "welfare" benefits and the associated repercussions this stigma might have on the work ethic and labor market processes, even though state-of-the-art government studies suggested that there would be few negative labor market effects. Just as significantly, the working poor never lobbied on behalf of the program, even though they stood to gain from it economically. The plan did not make sense *culturally.* The working poor did not consider themselves to be "welfare" recipients; in fact, they actively distanced themselves from the label. Yet they were especially susceptible to being considered "welfare" recipients under Nixon's program due to the prior design of American social programs. Since the working poor had not previously received cash-based income maintenance from the government, there was no existing alternative status through which to define them as "non-welfare" recipients of income benefits.

Moral differentiation between categories of poor people, with its roots in the work ethic, was further reinforced by the strong racial dimension that welfare reform took on during this period and by gender-differentiated notions of worthiness.[59] Despite some high-profile incidents in which racial animus motivated welfare backlash in the 1950s and early 1960s, poverty was viewed throughout this period as a largely white phenomenon, and the moral differentiation between deserving and undeserving poor was between whites. Over the course of the next decade, views of poverty and welfare became racialized in American society for reasons including the shift in focus of the civil rights movement from legal equality to the fight for economic rights, the urban unrest that swept the country during the mid-1960s, and the distorted media depictions in the popular press that overrepresented blacks in stories about poverty, especially stories that contained negative portrayals of the poor.[60] By the early 1970s, despite the fact that blacks were neither the majority of the poor population nor the majority of people receiving public assistance, "welfare" and race had become largely synonymous in the public mind.[61]

While deservingness for men has long been based on labor market participation, for women it has historically been based on gendered expectations toward child rearing and sexual morality.[62] Beginning in 1967, however, policymakers increasingly used welfare reform to push single mothers into the labor market, even if their children were quite young. Work expectations began to factor into assessments of worthiness for women as well as men, though with less clear normative guidelines. By the Carter era, rates of female labor participation had increased to such a degree that conservatives and feminists alike were reconsidering whether expectations toward women's employment should be any different from men's unless unmarried mothers had preschool-aged children or younger. Yet beyond these changing work expectations, which began to approximate those of men, issues related to family structure and sexuality continued to define the boundaries of worthiness for women in distinctly gendered ways, as contestation during the Carter era revealed.

Second, the longstanding distinction between categories of the poor shaped the *language* people used to discuss GAI proposals. Opponents of Nixon's plan, for instance, mobilized language that presumed moral contamination between categories of the poor. Claims couched in this language were effective because they resonated with existing moral categories and pollution beliefs, and they capitalized on the uncertainty associated with erasing the existing policy boundaries. Nixon himself used public rhetoric that consistently reinforced moral distinctions between categories of the poor, even though his proposal outlined a completely new form of social provision that dissolved the existing categorical distinctions.[63] He sharply differentiated between the "work ethic" and the "welfare ethic," and between the "welfare rolls" and "payrolls," despite the fact that the structure of his plan created a continuum between "welfare" and work. Nixon also consistently referred to the "choice" not to work, which implied that the poor made different moral decisions (namely the wrong decisions) than did members of mainstream society, rather than acknowledging that poverty was a systemic problem.

In short, Nixon's language was categorical even though his proposal was not. Neither Nixon nor other administration officials provided the American public with a conceptual template for understanding the new type of social provision they proposed. This new template was available. Proponents ranging from liberal business groups to sympathetic government bureaucrats put forth alternative framing strategies along these lines. Yet neither Nixon nor his advisors ever took up the challenge. Doing so did not align with their broader political strategy, nor would this new rhetorical strategy have resonated with popular understandings without considerable definitional work. Open discussion of the fact that GAI plans were based on need and not work capacity would have entailed recognizing that the economy could not provide economic security for all able-bodied Americans. This recognition would have created the potential for a shared class-based identity among the unemployed and working poor rooted in their similarly disadvantaged economic circumstances.[64] In the absence of such a class-based identity, low-wage workers interpreted Nixon's proposal on the basis of existing racial, ethnic, or moral identities that placed distance between themselves and the "welfare" population.

Third, the distinction between categories of poor people served as the basis for *new institutions*—namely two new social programs for the deserving and working poor. Subsequent to the failure of Nixon's plan, policymakers enacted Supplemental Security Income (SSI) legislation, which was a GAI program for the aged, blind, and disabled. The programmatic separation of these groups from the undeserving poor was undertaken explicitly to protect them from the social stigma connoted by "welfare." The Earned Income Tax Credit (EITC), which was enacted in 1975, was a negative income tax plan for the working poor. Its design borrowed directly from Nixon's proposal, except that eligibility was restricted to people in the labor force. Therefore, it operated in accord with existing cultural categories of worth. Conservatives favored providing income supplements to the working poor under the EITC, even though it was precisely this type of income supplement that had been their main source of opposition to Nixon's GAI plan.

The contrast between their positions on these two pieces of legislation revealed that conservatives' influential opposition to Nixon's plan had not been based simply on the straightforward *economic* threat of income subsidies to low-income workers. Their opposition was based on the *cultural* threat of stigmatizing the working poor with "welfare" benefits that connoted dependency and the repercussions they feared this might have on workers' behavior.

These conservatives pursued their economic interests, but they did so in ways that were mediated by their subjective understandings of the poor and their perceptions of various types of government benefits.

One of the ironies of the struggle over Nixon's program was that the SSI and EITC legislation programmatically reinforced the categorical distinctions that GAI plans initially promised to dissolve. Thus when President Carter again took up a GAI proposal in 1977 he faced more challenging legislative and cultural terrain than had existed only a few years earlier. The discourse produced in the debates over Nixon's programs had reinforced the symbolic distinctions between categories of the poor, so it was even more difficult for most Americans to see the economic vulnerabilities shared by these groups. Moreover, SSI and the EITC created new constituencies in favor of keeping benefits in these programs, which produced greater political pressure to maintain the existing categorical distinctions between groups. These new programs also increased the number of technical obstacles to comprehensive reform strategies such as GAI plans. Thus by the late 1970s, the boundaries drawn between these different poor populations were symbolically and institutionally stronger than they had been a decade earlier. Any welfare reform plan that proposed to dissolve them faced a daunting challenge, one that the Carter administration could not surmount.

POLICY MEANINGS AND THE POLITICS OF GUARANTEED INCOME

Despite their challenge to cultural categories of worth, GAI plans garnered considerable support in the 1960s. This was due in part to the changing views of poverty, unemployment, and justice that weakened the normative basis of the existing categorical system. Yet an equally important reason for the rise of GAI plans was that a broad array of supporters favored them for very different, often contradictory reasons, some of which had little to do with poverty reduction. These multiple meanings, especially in the early years, obfuscated the ways in which GAI plans challenged the categorical nature of the existing system. Rather than seeing the prospects for GAI plans as doomed to failure from the start, just because the plans ultimately failed, the account I present here illuminates the factors that made them appear attractive initially and then explains why their promise diminished. Doing so situates GAI plans in a population of actors, interests, and meanings that evolved and winnowed considerably over time.[65]

Understanding how GAI plans aligned with or challenged policy experts' competing antipoverty paradigms is a key part of the story. The plans rose to prominence as part of a heated (and subsequently rare) debate over the causes of poverty, and it was through these debates that actors challenged the categorical nature of the existing system. Yet support for GAI proposals went beyond their potential to reduce poverty. The plans emerged during a period of social tumult. For influential stakeholders such as governors, big-city mayors, business coalitions, and civic groups, the plans came to be seen as a potential solution to a number of social problems. In other words, these stakeholders viewed GAI proposals not only as antipoverty policy but as urban policy, family policy, fiscal policy, and labor policy. Recognizing these multiple policy meanings helps us move beyond what Steven Teles calls the "consensus politics" view of welfare reform, one characterized by a shared understanding between actors of the meaning and consequences of pursuing particular policy options.[66] Tracing the multiple meanings refracted in GAI plans paints a more complex picture of policymaking, but only this approach can make sense of the plans' rapid rise to prominence and broad appeal.

Media depictions of GAI plans loosely tracked GAI plans' changing policy meanings over the 1960s and 1970s. As the debate progressed, the political discourse not only changed but narrowed, thus simplifying the terms of debate. During the 1960s, the policy discourse was marked by considerable heterogeneity. But over time it came to emphasize the fiscal and work-related aspects of the plans in ways that conferred greater legitimacy on the views of the plans' opponents. As an examination of the media coverage shows, a citizen reading about the plans during the Carter years would have taken away a very different picture of the stakes in debates over GAI plans than one reading the news a decade earlier. Just as important, some policy meanings, such as seeing GAI plans as a response to structural unemployment and low wages, were virtually absent from popular coverage, even though they had been prominent in policymaking discourse.

Antipoverty Paradigms and Social Problems

Government welfare experts played the most central and consistent role in advancing GAI plans. Though this lends support to perspectives on social policy development that emphasize the importance of state experts, proponents of this perspective have more typically focused on the conditions under which state actors can be independent from external societal influences than on the question of what motivates these actors to begin with. This has led some scholars to examine the content of experts' policy paradigms: the interpretative frameworks that define the nature of social problems and the solutions needed to address them.[67] These paradigms are typically tacit, but they are reflected in the specific legislative programs that experts and their political allies advance.[68] Deborah Stone extends this idea by arguing that a great deal of the political struggle involved in policymaking is generated by conflict between competing "causal stories" that allocate blame and responsibility for social problems.[69] Competition between causal stories can be fierce because they may distribute the burden of responsibility for reform quite differently. She further distinguishes between *problems*, which experts believe can and should be addressed through government policy, and *difficulties*, which are viewed as "natural" and therefore considered to be outside the realm of policy intervention. Stone contends that one of the driving dynamics of the political process is the attempt to convert difficulties into problems and vice versa, and an example she uses to illustrate this process comes from environmental policy. During the early phases of the environmental movement, activists tried to show that the deterioration of the environment was not a "natural" difficulty but the result of human actions that could and should be ameliorated through government regulation.

Competition between antipoverty paradigms was a central feature in the development of GAI plans, and the eventual success of one particular causal story naturalized some sources of poverty more than others. At the outset of the Nixon administration, proponents of four fundamentally different antipoverty paradigms, each of which contained a different causal story, competed for influence. (See chapter 3 for a more detailed discussion of these paradigms.) Three of these paradigms supported GAI plans. Proponents of an *economic citizenship* paradigm identified the economic system, especially structural unemployment and the wage structure, as the source of poverty. For proponents of this view, the objective of GAI policy was to alleviate poverty and provide citizens with basic income security. The *family stability* paradigm identified the social system, especially changing family structures within poor, typically black communities, as the source of poverty. Proponents of this view hoped that GAI policies would decrease poverty by providing additional support for maintaining two-parent families, since rates of marital breakup appeared to be correlated with poverty rates. The *laissez-faire* paradigm, which GAI supporters with a libertarian orientation invoked, identified the welfare system and its alleged perverse incentives against work as the root of the problem. Laissez-faire proponents felt that GAI plans would rationalize the welfare system by creating stronger incentives for labor market participation while also granting the poor greater freedom. The main opposition to GAI proposals within the administration came from officials who saw the behavior of the poor themselves as the primary cause of poverty and believed that welfare reform should rehabilitate the poor by exposing them to the discipline of the labor market. This *rehabilitation* paradigm argued that limiting eligibility for social provision and requiring recipients of government benefits to work would be the best path to eliminating poverty.

Over the next decade, a series of changes took place that contributed to the demise of GAI plans. These were a combination of what Peter Hall refers to as "first-order" and "second-order" changes within the field of policy knowledge.[70] First-order change refers to the changing definition of the social problems that concern policymakers. These are the most substantial type of policy change. Second-order change happens when the definition of a social problem remains constant but the policy instruments used to address the problem change.

Two subtle first-order changes reallocated the blame for poverty in ways that proved to be highly consequential. Among liberals who held a systemic view of poverty, the main split during the late 1960s was between people who viewed the labor market and people who viewed the welfare system as the primary problem. Over the following few years, the dominant causal story shifted to defining the welfare system as primarily responsible for poverty. This shifting orientation was not readily apparent, since both critics of the labor market and critics of the existing welfare system favored GAI plans. But it had important consequences. Defining the welfare system, rather than the labor market, as the main problem inadvertently established the groundwork for the conservative critique of the welfare state that emerged in the 1970s. The other first-order change happened among conservatives. By the early 1970s, the libertarian critique of the welfare system had lost influence to the rehabilitationist view. The remaining lines of battle then were between GAI supporters (primarily liberals though including some libertarians) who viewed the plans as a way to improve the welfare system and conservatives who sought to reform the poor themselves. The problems posed by structural unemployment and insufficient wages virtually vanished from the debate and the labor market became a "difficulty" beyond the realm of policy intervention through a GAI plan.

After the failure of Nixon's plan, two second-order changes occurred as well. Many of the remaining liberals who continued to criticize the inadequacies of the labor market shifted their policy preferences to public jobs programs instead of GAI plans. This split among liberals significantly weakened the legislative prospects for a GAI proposal during the Carter era. The opposite process happened among conservatives, who had been split between GAI supporters and opponents during the late 1960s but who subsequently united around an alternative welfare reform strategy. Laissez-faire conservatives shifted their allegiance, reluctantly in some cases, from GAI plans to the emerging "California-style" welfare reform strategies advanced by Governor Ronald Reagan. This type of plan was in keeping with the goals of rehabilitating the poor because it tightened welfare eligibility rules and contained strict work requirements. Though this approach ran at odds with some of the goals that libertarians sought, it did appear to remove the work disincentives in the existing system.

Aside from this contestation between proponents of competing antipoverty paradigms, other significant stakeholders initially supported GAI proposals because they viewed them as a potential solution to social problems not directly related to poverty.[71] These stakeholders' changing views or policy positions held further consequences for the proposals. Governors and big-city mayors supported Nixon's plan because rapidly mounting welfare expenditures were draining local treasuries. The FAP offered them much-needed fiscal relief because it included a full federal takeover of welfare payments that up until that time had been the obligation of state governments. But in 1972, amid the debate over the second version of the FAP, Nixon separated revenue-sharing legislation from his welfare proposal, which gave this group an alternative source of fiscal relief. After this point, support for Nixon's plan among governors and local leaders declined precipitously. Many business and civic leaders supported GAI plans for two reasons: to quell the urban unrest that beset many cities between 1964 and 1968, and to remove perceived work disincentives from the existing system. As unrest subsided after 1968, the push for GAI plans became less urgent for many of these groups, though some continued their advocacy through the end of the Nixon era. Yet social unrest alone did not motivate business moderates to support Nixon's plan. Along with many libertarians, they favored GAI plans because they promised to streamline government welfare administration while simultaneously removing perceived disincentives in the existing welfare system. However, these goals ran up against cultural categories of worth, which helps explain why even institutionally powerful players within the Nixon administration, such as the head of the Department of Labor, backed away from the plans. As the debates over the plans progressed, it became increasingly clear that the problem for libertarian supporters of Nixon's plan was that it granted increased personal autonomy and unconditional benefits to a population that was widely depicted as morally suspect.[72]

Opposition along these lines came from proponents of the rehabilitationist paradigm. This view had an influential set of sponsors behind it, including the U.S. Chamber of Commerce and some of Nixon's domestic advisors. One striking aspect of their opposition was its infusion with explicitly moral language. In contrast to government policy experts and moderate business groups, who typically couched their claims in the language of rationality and efficiency, the leaders of the chamber and their political allies argued that Nixon's plan would corrupt the work ethic of low-wage workers by rendering them dependent on the government. This moral impoverishment would damage the nation's economic productivity. These views were powerfully represented in Washington, since the chair of a key congressional committee viewed the corrupting influence of "welfare" in this way, as did many of his conservative allies in the South. These views of the poor served as the basis for "California-style" welfare reform, which these same conservatives quickly embraced.

Somewhat surprisingly, another source of opposition to Nixon's plan came from a group at the opposite end of the political spectrum: the National Welfare Rights Organization (NWRO). Welfare rights groups strongly favored GAI plans in principle, but they opposed Nixon's plan. A mix of economic and cultural factors drove this opposition. Since the NWRO's main constituency was unmarried mothers with children, their economic interests focused on raising benefits for the "welfare" poor rather than extending benefits to working poor families. Since the NWRO's membership was concentrated in the Northeast, where benefit levels were the highest in the country, the organization's leaders complained that the benefit levels in Nixon's plans were inadequate and persuaded some liberal members of Congress to support plans that more than tripled the benefit levels in Nixon's program. Their opposition was also based on Nixon's rhetoric, which often cast welfare recipients as lazy, undeserving, and degenerate. This rhetoric incensed activists, who were deeply suspicious of Nixon's motives; he had a history of using thinly veiled, race-based rhetoric to woo working-class voters into the Republican Party. Because the NWRO's leaders focused more on the FAP's benefit levels and Nixon's rhetoric than on the plan's substance, they showed little recognition that it was ultimately likely to benefit the poor because of its design. This stood in contrast to the views held by many conservatives, who understood the structural implications of Nixon's plan and vigorously opposed it for this reason.

From an entirely different perspective, proponents of the family stability paradigm lobbied on behalf of GAI plans throughout the early 1970s, but during the Carter era, results from a set of government experiments undercut these grounds for support. The experiments showed that GAI payments did little to reduce men's work effort, which had been the dominant concern for policymakers during the debate over Nixon's plan. Yet the most widely reported findings from the experiments showed that families who received GAI payments had substantially higher rates of marital dissolution than those who did not. Though the interpretation of these results was widely contested and their implications for the well-being of poor women were ambiguous, the findings about marital breakup were released during a period of mounting concern about the fate of the traditional family.[73] They delivered a fatal blow to arguments for GAI plans based in the family stability paradigm.

Framing GAI Plans in the Media

Coverage of GAI plans in the *New York Times* illustrates the competing ways in which the proposals were depicted and how the public discourse on the plans shifted over time.[74] Instead of containing elaborate policy paradigms, newspaper articles more typically contain fragments of policy meanings in the form of *policy frames*. These policy frames "promote a particular problem definition, causal interpretation, moral evaluation, and/or treatment recommendation" and make some aspects of a policy debate more salient to readers than others.[75] A social activist could frame GAI policies in terms of their impact on poverty reduction, a business leader might frame them in terms of their impact on work, and a senator might frame them in terms of their costs. Research shows that these types of frames influence the ways in which people

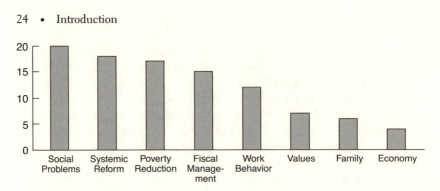

Figure 1. Percent of policy framing discourse, 1966–68.

make sense of complex policy issues and shape their policy preferences.[76] Thus examining patterns in policy framing both shows how spokespeople covered in the media sought to depict GAI policies and provides a picture of the dominant policy meanings that citizens had at their disposal for determining their views of GAI proposals.

News stories in the *New York Times* framed GAI plans in reference to eight broad frames: a *social problems* frame that drew attention to civic disturbances and social divisions based on race and class; a *systemic reform* frame that focused on improving the deficiencies of the existing welfare system; a *poverty reduction* frame that focused on alleviating poverty for individuals and families; a *fiscal management* frame that viewed welfare reform as a policy instrument to control government spending; a *work behavior* frame that focused on the attitudes and practices of the poor concerning work; a *values* frame that connected welfare reform to abstract values such as freedom, compassion, equality, and fairness; a *family* frame that emphasized the relationship between welfare reform and family structure; and an *economy* frame that linked poverty to the broader economic system.

During their first three years of media coverage, beginning in 1966, GAI plans were not associated with any one dominant meaning. News stories depicted GAI plans in diverse ways (see figure 1). The plans were most strongly linked to the social turbulence that characterized this period and to the problems that experts and activists identified with the existing welfare system. There was a clear focus on reducing poverty, but the plans were just as closely associated with managing state and local spending. Though the media coverage brought attention to the work ethic and work behavior of the poor, these issues did not dominate the national discussion by any means.

Notably, frames that discussed GAI plans in relation to the labor market and economy were nearly absent. Many government experts and business leaders initially supported GAI plans out of their concern over structural unemployment. They believed that the economy could not provide enough jobs at adequate wage levels to keep all Americans out of poverty. Yet this rationale was rarely discussed in the *New York Times*. Therefore, the adequacy of the labor market was rarely called into question, and one of the most prominent rationales for GAI proposals among policy experts was missing from public discourse. This meant that citizens lacked an important perspective with which to evaluate the merits of GAI plans and other welfare reform proposals.

A few months after President Nixon took office in 1969, it became clear that GAI plans were a frontrunner in his plan to overhaul the welfare system. From this point forward—through debate over two versions of Nixon's FAP and the Carter plan—the discourse surrounding GAI plans increasingly crystallized around a two main issues: government spending and the work behavior of the poor. Big-city mayors and many state governors viewed Nixon's plan as a means to garner federal funds for their mounting welfare expenditures. Opponents of the plans complained that they would only increase welfare spending. During the same period, concerns about work incentives, work requirements, and the work ethic increased, so much so that even supporters of GAI plans had to debate the proposals on these terms. In contrast, policy frames emphasizing poverty reduction and social divisions waned. The strong similarities between the debates over Nixon's second plan and the Carter proposal—despite the partisan differences between the two administrations—suggest that the terms of debate were well established and that discourse regarding government spending (both state and federal), welfare fraud and abuse, and the deficient work ethic of the poor was entrenched (see figure 2).

The dominant media frames reinforced cultural categories of worth, even if the language in the articles seldom used these categories explicitly. Frames that invoked concerns about the work behavior of the poor, as opposed to the functioning of the economy, both presupposed and validated the moral distinctions drawn between the deserving and undeserving poor. It cast the poor as impoverished due to their own moral deficiencies, which was the causal story embedded in the rehabilitation paradigm. Similarly, policy frames that depicted welfare reform as a means through which to limit government spending only made sense if the "welfare" poor were largely considered to be undeserving in the first place. This stood in direct contrast to the arguments made by proponents of the economic citizenship paradigm, who argued that people were often poor for reasons that had little to do with personal shortcomings. Some members of the Carter administration, including cabinet-level officials, tried to make this argument, but it received scant attention in the press.

In sum, although news stories on GAI plans never really contained elements of the causal story embedded in the economic citizenship paradigm, they did highlight issues related to poverty reduction and social divisions by class and race in the early years. Yet over time, media accounts increasingly told the causal story at the foundation of the rehabilitation paradigm. This

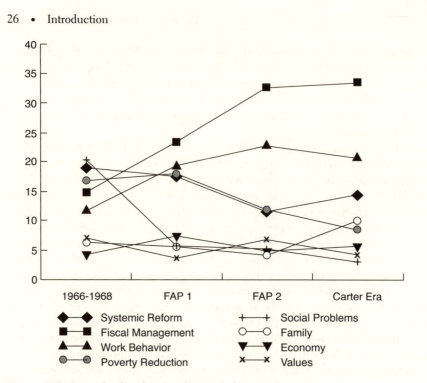

Figure 2. Percent of policy framing discourse, by period.

was a story about poverty in which the labor market was naturalized and therefore not considered blameworthy for the conditions of the poor. This transformed the market from being a "problem" amenable to human intervention, as it had been seen by many people in the 1960s, to a "difficulty" beyond the scope of policy intervention through a GAI plan.

BOOK OVERVIEW

The first six chapters of the book are organized chronologically. Chapter 1 discusses the emergence of GAI plans on the national agenda in the early 1960s. During this period, discussions of the idea were mainly restricted to policy experts, economists, legal scholars, and activists. Chapter 2 covers the years from 1966 to 1968, the period during which GAI proposals gained public attention and grew to be seen by many people as "inevitable." A major reason for this increasing support was the contention that GAI plans not only would address problems within the economy but that they could also address problems associated with the existing welfare system and with urban unrest. Chapter 3 examines the evolution of GAI plans during Nixon's first six months in office. Though Nixon surprised both his supporters and detractors by proposing guaranteed income legislation in August 1969, the debates and compromises that took place between the proponents of competing policy paradigms during this formulation period transformed both the substance and symbolism of Nixon's ultimate plan. Chapters 4 and 5 cover the four-year struggle over Nixon's proposal, the Family Assistance Plan. They reveal how the cultural distinction between the deserving and undeserving poor, and the symbolic pollution that resulted in blurring these categories, shaped stakeholders' policy preferences, presidential rhetoric, and public perceptions. After the failure of Nixon's plan, the creation of the SSI and EITC programs further reinforced the distinctions between categories of the poor by embedding them in the design of new legislation. Chapter 6 covers the consideration of GAI plans by the Carter administration. Many government experts continued to favor GAI legislation for its promise of income assistance based on need alone, while Carter favored the plans primarily for their promise of comprehensive reform. Carter's proposal, which many considered a diluted GAI plan, faced both familiar and new obstacles and never reached the floor of Congress.

The last two chapters offer assessments of different types. Chapter 7 traces some of the roots of welfare retrenchment during the 1980s back to the struggle over GAI plans during the preceding two decades and examines the future prospects for GAI plans in the United States. Despite the fact that there are compelling new justifications for this type of approach—such as providing income maintenance for nonmarket work like caregiving—the cultural threat implicit in any GAI proposal is still a central obstacle that supporters must confront more directly than they did during earlier periods. Chapter 8 outlines some insights for scholarship on the welfare state that can be drawn from examining the rise and fall of GAI plans.

CHAPTER ONE

The Rise of Guaranteed Annual Income

The New Deal era is typically viewed as the "big bang" of the American welfare state. President Roosevelt's legislation established the basic template of social provision that shaped federal policy development during the nation's pivotal episodes of reform, and it continues, however embattled, to exert considerable influence today. The idea of guaranteeing citizens a minimum annual income on the basis of need alone broke sharply with this New Deal template. This raises two related questions: Why did the idea arise in the first place? And why did the idea, which from today's vantage point appears quite liberal, garner early support from across the political spectrum?

The answer to the first question can be found by looking at the intersecting impact of influential stakeholders, changing cultural perceptions, and new government capacities. During the Kennedy era, experts inside and outside the government considered GAI plans because their views of work, opportunity, and justice were changing. Factors such as the country's postwar affluence, troubling patterns in unemployment, and concerns about technology in the workplace led to a reconsideration of the relationship between employment and income. The civil rights movement gave policy experts further cause to reevaluate the status quo. They increasingly recognized both the sources of systemic injustice in American society and that unemployment and industrial automation took a disproportionate toll on blacks. The consequence was the willingness, if not the imperative, among some experts and social commentators to think outside the dualities of existing antipoverty policy, since these new ideas and trends challenged the assumption that the able-bodied poor were responsible for their own impoverished condition and were therefore undeserving of government assistance. Despite these changes in thinking, however, GAI proposals received little traction within government policymaking circles during the Kennedy era because the institutional conditions within government were not auspicious. It was Johnson's War on Poverty initiatives that gave government experts the mandate, political autonomy, and organizational capacity conducive to fully developing GAI proposals as part of a broader plan to fight poverty.

Concerning the second question, a few factors contributed to the appeal of GAI plans across the ideological spectrum. The plans were new and ambiguous. They had few serious precedents and therefore were not already associated with any particular political party or ideological position. Their details were also underspecified. The term "guaranteed income" encompassed a variety of proposals that differed considerably in their eligibility criteria, delivery mechanisms, and benefit levels. The plans could be generous or stingy, universal or narrowly targeted. There were also different rationales for proposing GAI plans that aligned with competing causal stories about the sources of poverty. So in some cases, experts guided by different policy paradigms favored objectively similar plans. The two causal stories that played the most central role in the rise of the plans were those that saw either the deficiencies of the labor market or the deficiencies of the welfare system itself as the main source of poverty. People holding the latter view, at least during this early stage, further supported GAI plans because they promised to shrink the scope of the federal bureaucracy and the government's role in the labor market. Despite these differences in detail and rationale, however, the element all GAI proposals shared was their challenge to the symbolic and programmatic categories inscribed in the existing welfare system, since the plans were not based on work capacity but on economic need, family size, or both.

Consideration of GAI proposals was part of a broader effort to fight poverty, reform the welfare system, and expand rights and opportunities for blacks. While each of these issues received substantial attention during the early 1960s, GAI plans themselves received little. Prior to 1966, the idea was still limited largely to policy circles and discussions among experts. On the rare occasions that they did receive attention, the proposals were characterized as marginal and "far out," since the notion of guaranteeing citizens basic economic security was still beyond most people's imaginations.

The Seeds and the Soil

The Categorical Nature of American Welfare Policy

Since the early 1800s, both private charity and public social provision have categorized the poor based on social expectations that they work.[1] Prior to this period, there was little organized support for the poor. Family and community were largely responsible for caring for the needy. More institutional forms of poor support, such as poorhouses, developed during the nineteenth century alongside the social disruptions that accompanied the spread of capitalist enterprise and urbanization. Historians trace the roots of categorizing the poor within these new institutions to the increasing prevalence of wage labor coupled with already strong strands of Anglo-American individualism that emphasized self-reliance. Poorhouses reinforced the work ethic by restricting their provision to the "impotent" poor while the "able-bodied" were typically left to fend for themselves, mainly through greater participation in the labor market. The rise of "scientific charity" in the late 1800s, which sought to systematize public and private sector provision for the poor, further codified these distinctions. Reformers during this era worried that the poor might view relief—especially public relief—as an entitlement, so they sought to purge the "able-bodied" from poorhouses and to keep relief even for the deserving poor as a primarily private endeavor.[2]

A new wave of reform during the Progressive Era generated policy innovations that Roosevelt would incorporate into his subsequent New Deal legislation. Women's groups lobbied for mothers' pensions and by 1920 forty states had enacted them, despite opposition from charities that argued that support for these women should remain in the private sector.[3] Though these pensions were for the deserving poor (widows with children), their benefit levels varied from meager to generous because program administration was left up to individual states. In 1935, Roosevelt's Social Security Act used mothers' pensions as the model for the Aid to Dependent Children (ADC) program. As scholars have noted, the Social Security Act created programs that both reflected and reinforced existing distinctions between categories of people based on work expectations, race relations, gender ideology, and local labor market conditions.[4] ADC was no exception. Lawmakers anticipated that the program would generate little controversy because it was for a "deserving" category of recipient. Mothers with young children were expected to stay in the home and raise good citizens, so they merited government support. Furthermore, since Congress excluded agricultural, domestic, and casual workers from New Deal programs, the program functionally excluded most blacks. For these reasons, the structure of the ADC program was conservative in many ways. Yet it also marked a significant breakthrough. The program was the first federal recognition of single mothers as a deserving group worthy of social provision.[5]

By the late 1960s, the ADC program (which had been renamed Aid to Families with Dependent Children, or AFDC, in 1962) was the antipoverty program most closely identified with the increasingly pejorative term "welfare."[6] Two legislative changes after 1935 set the course for the program's transformation from being relatively uncontroversial to being embattled.[7] The first change took place in 1939, when another New Deal program, Old Age Insurance, expanded its eligibility criteria to include the most deserving portion of the existing ADC population: the wives and children of deceased workers who qualified for federal retirement benefits. The removal of this deserving group from the ADC rolls meant that the program's overall composition changed, and, after World War II, it began to serve increasing numbers of unwed mothers and racial minorities. It was during this postwar period that welfare backlash, particularly in the South, began on a limited scale. In 1962, Congress expanded the program by allowing states to provide benefits to two-parent families headed by unemployed men. This meant that *male* unemployment now became an issue addressed through the "welfare" system, which further heightened the program's stigmatized status. Able-bodied, unemployed men have always been the paradigmatic "undeserving" population. This change in the AFDC system foreshadowed the controversy over GAI proposals, since male unemployment was at the center of the debate over GAI plans.

In the postwar period, these categories still constituted the ideological foundation of the American welfare state. Because benefits for undeserving populations were administered locally rather than federally, the undeserving poor, if they were eligible for public assistance at all, received benefits that varied widely among states in their levels of support. Many considered these benefits to be grossly inadequate and existing eligibility standards to be too restrictive, especially during a period of postwar economic affluence. The emergence of GAI proposals in the early 1960s challenged the ideological core of this existing system.

The Origins of Guaranteed Annual Income

Though GAI legislation first appeared on the governmental agenda in the 1960s, the notion of having the government provide citizens with a basic minimum annual income developed alongside the modern welfare state during the interwar period, first in England and then in the United States. Historically, the idea has had many names, including state bonus, social dividend, social wage, citizenship income, and social credit. Some of the earliest published mentions, in the form of a state bonus, appeared in England in the years following World War I. Others proposed the idea during the 1930s in the midst of the Great Depression and the Keynesian revolution in economics. Social workers and social movement leaders in the United States advanced GAI plans as a challenge to Roosevelt's legislative agenda. In England, economists developed proposals for a "social dividend" that by the 1940s were held out as an alternative to the dominant welfare state paradigm outlined in the Beveridge Report.[8]

During this same period, the economists Milton Friedman and George Stigler (both future Nobel laureates) developed the idea of the negative income tax (NIT), which was the type of GAI plan that ultimately served as the basis for Nixon's proposal. While working at the Treasury Department, Friedman originally formulated the concept as a way to even out the tax penalty for fluctuations in earnings among low-income workers in order to make the tax system more equitable.[9] In 1946, Stigler published an article in the *American Economic Review* in which he proposed an NIT program as a more effective method of alleviating poverty than increases in the minimum wage. Though the specific recommendation took up only one paragraph of his argument (the majority was devoted to criticizing minimum wage increases), the article presaged many of the issues that would become pivotal in the debates over GAI proposals.[10]

The basic principles of the NIT were relatively simple. It extended the tax scale below a specified break-even point and filing units at income levels below this point would receive payments from the government instead of paying taxes. If a filing unit received no income, it would receive a "minimum income guarantee." As income levels increased up the scale from zero, government transfer payments would be reduced by some proportion of the earned income. This was the "negative tax rate." At the break-even point, the government payments ceased. Above the break-even point, the filing unit would be expected to pay taxes. For NIT rates less than 100 percent, as earned income rose, disposable income (earnings plus government payments) rose also. A tax rate of less than 100 percent preserved work incentives by some margin: the lower the rate, the stronger the incentives.

Stigler's main concern about income maintenance programs of any type was, in fact, work incentives. "Incomes of the poor," he contended, "cannot be increased without impairing incentives."[11] But he argued that this was not an insurmountable problem. He pointed out that the same essential tension between income levels and work incentives was inherent in progressive income taxes and estate taxes. Though the threat to incentives had also been a subject of debate when these earlier tax policies were initially considered, the trade-offs grew to be accepted. In contrast to programs that offered in-kind benefits to the poor, direct income transfers, such as the NIT, Stigler felt, were administratively simpler and allowed people to spend the money on what they wanted. Stigler proposed his solution accordingly.

> There is a great attractiveness in the proposal that we extend the personal income tax to the lowest income brackets with negative rates in those brackets. Such a scheme could achieve equality of treatment with what appears to be a (large) minimum of administrative machinery. If the negative rates are appropriately graduated, we may still retain some measure of incentive for a family to increase its income. We should no doubt encounter many perplexing difficulties in carrying out this plan, but they are problems which could not be avoided, even though they might be ignored by a less direct attack on poverty.[12]

Stigler's discussion was prescient. He hit on many of the themes that would recur as GAI proposals were later debated, including equality of treatment, work incentives, administrative simplicity, and freedom of choice. His recognition that a negative income tax would result in "equality of treatment" for the poor anticipated their threat to categories of worth, though little indicated that he realized how much of an obstacle this would actually be. He did recognize that an income-oriented antipoverty program as direct and transparent as an NIT would confront political problems that a more diffuse, service-oriented strategy might not. And the contrast he drew between the NIT and minimum wage increases also foreshadowed some of the reasons why some business leaders in the 1960s would favor GAI proposals. Some labor leaders, on the other hand, would be ambivalent about a program they feared might undermine union bargaining leverage in wage disputes.

Affluence and Technological Change

It would be about fifteen years before the next set of publications brought public attention to GAI proposals generally and to the NIT in particular. In the intervening years the nation enjoyed a period of unprecedented economic prosperity. Growth in the gross national product, real income, and standards of living were hallmarks of a new affluence in which most Americans enjoyed gains in discretionary income. Beyond just the necessities of life, most Americans, even those in the working class, could participate in the new postwar consumer culture.[13] However, as the general population flourished during the Eisenhower years, less noticeable changes caught the eye of some social commentators. Two trends that proved to be especially relevant to the development of GAI proposals were increasing levels of income inequality and perceived threats to skilled labor wrought by the changing nature of industry. These trends pointed to specific social conditions that policymakers would soon have to address. They also proved to be two aspects in a broader debate about the nature of social citizenship in an affluent nation: How much basic equality was required by a good society? And could income security be expected in the absence of employment?

The economist John Kenneth Galbraith was one of the most incisive commentators on the growing inequality in America. In his 1958 book, *The Affluent Society*, he self-consciously adopted the role of antagonist by discussing "unfashionable" topics such as poverty in the midst of optimistic and prosperous times.[14] One of the book's themes on this point was cultural lag: The American economy, he contended, enjoyed a type of prosperity unprecedented in world history, yet society's attitudes toward the poor had not yet advanced much beyond the eighteenth century. Widely shared ideas about the inevitability of poverty and the moral weaknesses of the poor, which had emerged under conditions of scarcity and privation in previous eras, required updating for a society in which it was possible for everyone to have their basic needs met.

More specifically, Galbraith argued that labor market participation and income security needed to be separated. As American productivity increased, and as the nature of the goods produced shifted from basic items to luxury goods, the importance of economic production resided less in what was being produced and more in the income that production work provided. In other words, jobs were important because they provided income, not because they produced goods. Yet jobs, he argued, were not available to everyone. Even if they were, full employment would lead to inflation as greater quantities of goods flooded the market and prices rose. "The solution," suggested Galbraith, "or more precisely part of it, is to have some reasonably satisfactory substitutes for production as a source of income. This would loosen the present nexus between production and income and enable us to take a more relaxed and rational view of output without subjecting individual members of the society to hardship."[15] In the original 1958 edition of the book, he proposed unemployment insurance at a rate near the average weekly wage as the policy recommendation. In subsequent editions, beginning in 1969, he proposed a negative income tax instead.[16]

Though poverty and inequality were Galbraith's chief focus, the changing nature of work preoccupied other social commentators, with trends in industrial automation driving much of the concern. Automation touched Americans in many job sectors—from longshoremen to coal miners to meatpackers—but the trends were most clear in places like the industrial North. For instance, Ford Motor Company, an industry leader in automation, set up an Automation Department in 1947 to help coordinate the reorganization of their manufacturing operations, and their competitors took up similar strategies in the following years. The effects of this move toward automation were often dramatic. At Ford's Cleveland plant, the number of workers it took to build 154 engine blocks in an hour dropped from 117 before the facilities were automated to 41 afterward. At another plant, employment fell from 85,000 in 1945 to 54,000 in 1954 to only 30,000 in 1960, all due to the various effects of automation.[17]

To some observers, such trends in automation signaled great societal progress, but for low-income, low-skill workers, they posed a threat. As Michael Harrington would soon write, "The poor, if they were given to theory, might argue [that] progress is misery."[18] The dangers of technological change not only were economic but were seen as moral as well. In her influential book *The Human Condition*, the philosopher Hannah Arendt expressed grave concerns about trends in automation, worrying that instead of resulting in greater freedom, technological "advances" would bring about a new form of spiritual impoverishment.[19] Despite such concerns, the effects of changes in the workplace remained largely in the realm of conjecture, and social forecasters worked as much on impression and anecdote as from hard statistics. It was difficult to anticipate the extent of the change that might result from automation and its technological handmaiden—the growing spread of computerization. The confluence of these two processes, in which the power of machines (automation) was coupled with the skill of machines (computers), became known as "cybernation," a term coined and promulgated by futurists Norbert Weiner and Donald Michael, but whose implications for GAI proposals were expanded on by Robert Theobald and his colleagues in a series of books, articles, and position papers.[20]

Guaranteed Income Proposals from the Left and Right

Theobald was an author and private-sector economist. Between 1961 and 1965, he wrote or edited three books that, when taken together, provided a social democratic rationale for GAI policy in the United States. In *The Challenge of Abundance* (1961), he took up many of the themes expounded on in Galbraith's earlier book, but with a more pronounced leftist twist. (Theobald, in fact, described *The Affluent Society* as "extraordinarily conservative.") Like Galbraith, he called for a new "economics of abundance" in which the highest social goal was to maximize individual freedom, which he defined as "the possibility to make meaningful choices."[21] Under conditions of abundance, he argued, it was immoral to deprive members of society of the means to make such choices, but this was the status of millions of poor Americans whose jobs were and would be threatened by the cybernetic revolution. The challenge, as Theobald described it, was that new ideas and institutions would have to develop alongside changes in work and the economy to ameliorate their effects.

Theobald's first book laid the groundwork for *Free Men and Free Markets* (1963), which outlined a GAI strategy that Theobald termed a "Basic Economic Security plan." The plan was premised on the belief that the prevailing socioeconomic system was outmoded by technological changes and the material abundance these changes had produced. Theobald called for a new set of principles that would break the existing link between income and work, and justify "due income" as a constitutional right. This idea of decoupling income from labor was an old idea, but in the recent age of affluence, it seemed newly possible. He proposed an income entitlement of $1,000 for adults and $600 for children in the form of a flat grant, giving a married family with two children a minimum income of $3,200 per year. At the time, the government generally considered the poverty line to be roughly $3,000, regardless of family size.[22] Under the Basic Economic Security plan, this income would replace many existing government programs, such as old-age insurance, unemployment compensation, and food stamps.[23] In the years to follow, Theobald edited a third book, titled *The Guaranteed Income* (1966), and gained a different audience for his ideas through media avenues such as *The Nation* and well-publicized reports. However, *Free Men and Free Markets* established the most well-developed social democratic rationale from which he and his collaborators would draw.

Theobald's proposal stood in sharp contrast to the primary income maintenance program in the existing welfare system, AFDC, both in terms of its benefit levels and eligibility criteria. Because AFDC benefit levels were set by the states and not the federal government, these levels varied widely. Most of them were significantly lower than those in Theobald's proposal. In 1968, a family of four in the lowest-paying state received $660 a year in benefits; the same family in the highest-paying state received $3,984.[24] In 1962, Congress had expanded the program by allowing states to provide benefits to families headed by unemployed but able-bodied men. Fewer than half of the states decided to implement this expansion (termed AFDC-UP), and even with it the eligibility requirements were stringent. Fewer than 100,000 families benefited from this expansion, leaving well over two million two-parent families living in poverty but excluded from the AFDC program.

During the same period that Theobald proposed his Basic Economic Security plan, Milton Friedman published perhaps the single most important book to enter the early debate over GAI policies, though from the opposite end of the political spectrum. *Capitalism and Freedom* (1962) represented a crystallization of Friedman's libertarian economic thought. Working over the course of the 1950s with colleagues at the University of Chicago such as George Stigler and Friedrich Hayek, Friedman developed a thoroughgoing economic philosophy in which the free enterprise system was heralded as the guarantor of the highest social good: individual freedom. The book chapter titled "The Alleviation of Poverty" was largely devoted to expanding the idea of the negative income tax that he and Stigler had developed in the 1940s.

Friedman did not provide a justification for alleviating poverty. He assumed its moral necessity and proceeded to spell out why the NIT would be the best means toward this goal. He contended that the benefits of an NIT strategy included its direct attack on poverty; benefits in a cash form; operation according to market principles (in contrast to the minimum wage, for which it had first been developed as an alternative); explicitness in fiscal and social costs; improved work incentives; and simpler administration. By implication, he suggested that the existing AFDC system was an uncoordinated set of inefficient and ineffective programs that interfered with the labor market and provided disincentives for work. Programmatically, he suggested that his new plan could be administered by the Internal Revenue Service and that the minimum income standard would be established by whatever amount of taxes society was "willing to impose on ourselves for the purpose."[25]

Friedman realized that the NIT was not without problems, the most serious of which he viewed as political.

> It establishes a system under which taxes are imposed on some to pay subsidies to others. And presumably, these others have a vote. There is always the danger that instead of being an arrangement under which the great majority tax themselves willingly to help an unfortunate minority, it will be converted into one under which a majority imposes taxes for its own benefit on an unwilling minority. Because this proposal makes the process so explicit, the danger is perhaps greater than with other measures. I see no solution to this problem except to rely on the self-restraint and good will of the electorate.[26]

Friedman's political concerns anticipated much to come in the debates over GAI. Negative income tax proposals would become politically contentious in terms of both their goals and their means. Friedman's plan aimed to alleviate the major symptom of poverty—the lack of money—rather than addressing some of the other historical aims of welfare programs, such as regulating the behavior of the poor. The freedom it gave the poor was in fact counter to behavioral regulation. The NIT also addressed the problem of poverty through the most direct method possible—cash transfers—rather than through services, such as job training, or in-kind benefits, such as public housing. This was politically dangerous for two reasons. First, it was an unveiled redistribution of income, something that has always been unpalatable in American society. Second, the NIT proposal created a tension between the desire to enhance the freedom of the poor and the desire to shape their behavior. Elsewhere in the book, Friedman noted that a major objection to free markets was freedom of choice, that is, allowing people to make their own decisions about what they want. As a result, when populations were not deemed responsible agents, market mechanisms that facilitate choice were often replaced by mechanisms that limit options and regulate behavior. Friedman argued that drawing this line was an unavoidable decision that societies had to make. Yet he characterized such paternalistic policies as mainly being applied to "madmen or children."[27] He underestimated the extent to which such views would be applied to the poor as well.

Friedman's main focus, as his book title suggests, was freedom, but his view of freedom differed considerably from the one advanced by Theobald. Each used a competing definition of freedom, ones that the philosopher Isaiah Berlin termed "positive freedom" and "negative freedom."[28] Positive freedom is based on the freedom to act, which in part means having the political and economic resources to attain commonly valued goals. If human arrangements, such as an economic system, prevent an individual's ability to attain such goals, then those arrangements limit positive freedom. Theobald's arguments were firmly rooted within this tradition, as he argued that only a right to a minimum income would guarantee this type of freedom in an emerging era of abundance and technological change. Berlin defined negative freedom, on the other hand, as the absence of coercion. It focuses on the unconstrained individual, and Friedman's laissez-faire view of human action and unencumbered free market economics was rooted in this view. Though Berlin himself favored an emphasis on negative freedom in response to the totalitarian threats of the postwar years, he argued that neither definition was ultimately more valid than the other and that conflict between them was an inevitable feature of social life. The tension between these two visions of freedom would underlie, albeit tacitly, much of the contestation over GAI plans in the coming years, particularly the debate over the desirability of expanding the number of people receiving government income assistance (did this enhance or undermine economic freedom?) and the normative connotation of receiving government benefits (should receiving benefits be stigmatizing or not?).

Race, Civil Rights, and Welfare Controversy

The emergence of GAI proposals took place concurrently with the nation's increasing attention to the civil rights movement. The movement's main goal in the 1950s was to end the legal segregation and commonplace brutality that upheld the racial power hierarchy in the South, and some of the milestones of the era were the 1954 U.S. Supreme Court ruling in *Brown v. Board of Education*, the 1956 Montgomery bus boycott, and the 1957 school desegregation battle in Little Rock, Arkansas.[29] With the sit-in movement and the Freedom Rides of the early 1960s, the movement garnered even greater exposure and media attention. By 1963, the year in which Martin Luther King, Jr., led the March on Washington, civil rights activists had broadened their goals, moved the struggle north, and begun a national movement for greater equality and justice.

Scholars disagree about the extent to which the War on Poverty—which Kennedy initiated shortly before his death and Johnson carried through to fruition—was a response to pressure from the civil rights movement. Some argue that Kennedy sought, albeit belatedly, to placate movement activists with legislative initiatives, while others contend that policymakers within the Kennedy and Johnson administrations pursued social reform independently from these pressures.[30] A tempered assessment suggests the importance of both social movement pressure and sympathetic state actors who channeled discontent through their own set of innovations. Furthermore, the civil rights movement not only applied pressure to the government but made moral arguments for social change. These arguments forced Americans to confront the woeful distance between their lofty national creed and their unjust practices and to rethink many aspects of the social system. This influence was based on consciousness-raising that reached into the highest levels of government and led to policymaking that was as much anticipatory as it was reactive.[31]

Given the disagreement over the role played by the civil rights movement in the emergence of the War on Poverty, despite the enormous amount of research on both subjects, it should come as little surprise that the movement's influence on the development of GAI plans is also somewhat ambiguous, at least in the early years.[32] Friedman's discussion of the negative income tax in *Capitalism and Freedom* did not mention racial inequality. But he devoted a separate chapter to racial discrimination in employment and education, so race relations was clearly an issue he had contemplated. Theobald's earliest arguments for GAI plans did not mention race either; however, by 1964 problems associated with black unemployment would be a dominant justification for Theobald's proposal. Thus, as Michael Brown has argued, it appears that 1963 marked a turning point in which associations between race and antipoverty policy began to grow stronger.[33] Although this association mainly pertained to the service-based antipoverty policies developed by the Johnson administration, it was also true for GAI proposals. A handful of social commentators and GAI proponents started to make direct arguments in favor of using GAI plans to ameliorate the economic injustices that many blacks suffered. Civil rights activists themselves did not make this argument for a few more years. For instance, the demands made by the leaders of the March on Washington in 1963 did not include calls for a GAI plan of any type. Instead, the marchers called for higher minimum wage levels, public works projects, and an end to labor market discrimination. These were elements of the conventional antipoverty repertoire of the era.[34] Guaranteed income plan innovations had yet to break into public consciousness. It would be only later that the plans were advanced by black leaders and more strongly associated with black activism in the public mind.

As historians point out, poverty was as likely to be considered a white phenomenon as a black one during this period.[35] President Kennedy's well-publicized campaign tour of poverty-stricken Appalachia is often seen as emblematic of the view that poverty was a rural and largely white problem. Yet the racial associations of public assistance programs were slowly changing, in part due to the shifting demographic composition of the AFDC rolls. A further concern that brought race and welfare together was interstate migration. There was a perception that poor blacks were moving from rural southern states to cities of the industrial North because northern states had more generous welfare programs.[36]

A well-publicized incident in Newburgh, New York, in 1961 symbolized the growing concerns about welfare migration and caught the attention of policymakers who would soon be making decisions about GAI policies.[37] In an effort to control rising welfare costs, the city council of Newburgh tried to implement a series of changes to their existing welfare programs, including regulations stipulating that able-bodied, employable men who refused to take city jobs could be refused benefits; that unwed mothers could be denied benefits if they had illegitimate children; that new applicants must prove they moved to Newburgh with existing offers of employment; and that all recipients, except the elderly and disabled, would only get three months of welfare assistance per year. The council's actions found a largely sympathetic audience among the city's population, whose attitudes were rooted in their views of welfare as an increasingly racial problem. The council's actions also resonated at the national level. One observer called the public debate about the controversy in Newburgh the most significant discussion about welfare in twenty-five years. Future Republican presidential candidate Barry Goldwater weighed in to support the council's actions, saying, "I don't like to see my taxes paid for children out of wedlock. I'm tired of professional chiselers walking up and down the streets who don't work and have no intention of working. I would like to see every city in the country adopt the plan."[38]

Beyond issues related to race, the commentary on the Newburgh incident was typical of the kind of attention poverty received during the period in two related ways. It showed that poverty was viewed as a local problem. Municipal or state government, rather than the federal government, was the focus of reform efforts. It also showed that poverty was viewed by most social commentators as an individual problem, resulting from personal deficits, such as laziness or irresponsibility, and not a large-scale, systemic problem. This began to change during the latter half of the Kennedy administration. Officials within the administration credited this renewed attention partially to the publication of Michael Harrington's *The Other America* in 1962 and a review essay of the book by social critic Dwight Macdonald the following year in the *New Yorker*.[39] The concerns raised in these publications merged with streams of thought gaining ascendancy within the government bureaucracy. On the crest of this wave of new attention, poverty became a national problem in two senses, both because it became widely acknowledged and because policymakers saw it as a problem falling under the jurisdiction of the federal government.

A NATIONAL PROBLEM

The "Other Americans"

Though few people seemed aware of it in 1960, about thirty-five million Americans, or one out of every five, lived in poverty. Harrington wanted to show that the scope of American poverty was much larger than most people realized and to explain why it was largely "invisible." Increasing levels of geographical mobility meant that the middle class did not interact with the poor as much as they had in former years, and a lack of political mobilization by the poor meant that their needs were not raised in public debate. Harrington wrote that the poor lived in "the other America" that "is hidden in a way that it never was before. Its millions are socially invisible to the rest of us."[40] He also wanted to show that this poverty was qualitatively different from the types of poverty that had preceded it. Following a theme elaborated on earlier by Galbraith, he argued that prosperity had left a substantial number of Americans behind and that they would be immune to the possible benefits of further economic growth. Worse still, this group would not be likely to muster the political clout necessary to bring about social change. During the Great Depression, poverty had been so widespread that society was forced to deal with "majority poverty." The policy innovations of the era were the result of political pressure from this majority. But by the 1960s, poverty had become a minority condition and thus one with lower chances of amelioration. In a theme that recurs throughout the book, he argued that it was worse to be poor in an affluent society than in one in which most of the populace was poor.

The causes of this invisible poverty were complicated, but Harrington repeatedly emphasized the effects of changing technology and racism. Like others before him, Harrington viewed automation in industry and mechanization in agriculture as displacing economically vulnerable workers, ranging from coal miners in Pennsylvania and assembly-line workers in Detroit to sharecroppers in the rural South and migrant farm workers in California. These "other Americans," he claimed, were "victims of the very inventions and machines that have provided a higher living standard for the rest of the society. They are upside-down in the economy, and for them greater productivity often means worse jobs; agricultural advance becomes hunger."[41] These effects, Harrington argued, were particularly harsh for blacks: "To belong to a racial minority is to be poor, but poor in a special way." Despite some advances in legal and political equality, there were systemic reasons for this situation. Blacks typically had the least seniority in the workplace and were consequently the first to be fired during hard times. Because they were also typically less skilled than their white peers, they found it more difficult to find a new job, particularly if they were over forty years old. He noted that one need not invoke direct discrimination to show how economic downturns would harm blacks more than whites. Yet, as Harrington further discussed in detail, discrimination and prejudice did exist, particularly in the South, where black families were repeatedly subjected to acts of violence for demanding equal opportunities in their communities. In short, he argued, "Negro poverty is unique in every way. It grows out of a long American history, and it expresses itself in a subculture that is built up on an interlocking base of economic and racial injustice."[42]

The interactions among technological changes, racial discrimination, and increasing isolation from middle-class society had created what Harrington referred to as a "culture of poverty": "Being poor is not one aspect of a person's life in this country; it is his life. Taken as a whole, poverty is a culture."[43] This culture was characterized by both a lack of connections to broader society and by the absence of mainstream aspirations. While Harrington viewed this culture as rooted in broad social conditions, such as discrimination and social isolation, and not inherent in poor communities, he also believed that this worldview deeply insinuated itself into a community. A change in these social conditions or in social policy would not necessarily have an immediate effect on the culture.

Harrington's perspective on the culture of poverty put him at odds with people such as Friedman, who viewed poverty as a monetary condition. According to a "monetary poverty" perspective, people were poor because they did not have enough money, not because they were culturally different from mainstream society. Harrington captured the crux of this distinction by relating an exchange (which is probably apocryphal) between F. Scott Fitzgerald and Ernest Hemingway. Fitzgerald is reported to have remarked, "The rich are different," to which Hemingway responded, "Yes, they have money."[44] Harrington suggested that Fitzgerald had the better of the exchange because the affluent indeed had different attitudes and worldviews from the rest of society. Harrington argued that this was even more true for the poor. The different perspectives taken by Harrington and Friedman were especially notable because "culture of poverty" arguments would soon be associated with conservatism while monetary poverty perspectives would be viewed as more liberal because they did not "blame the victim."[45] These competing understandings of monetary and cultural poverty would surface repeatedly in debates over GAI proposals.

Harrington's book contained few specific remedies for poverty. His aim was to place the problem on the national agenda rather than to outline detailed solutions. The following year, however, social critic Dwight Macdonald connected more explicit policy recommendations to Harrington's account of poverty in his review essay of the book in the *New Yorker*. Macdonald's review reflected Harrington's concerns with technological displacement, the racial dimension of poverty, and the importance of viewing "need" in relative and not absolute terms in a consumer economy. Yet most of all he emphasized that the source of poverty was located in an economic system that had left an impoverished and weakened minority poor behind and that only large-scale government intervention could provide a remedy. With the country's newfound affluence, Macdonald argued that "every citizen has a right to become or remain part of our society." This included a "reasonable standard of living" that did not depend on earnings.[46] Macdonald's essay was a cogent portrayal of the problem with a strongly argued case that some form of GAI policy was the solution. It was one of the first, highly visible calls for income security as a basic right of citizenship. The essay was read widely by the public and within the Kennedy administration, including by the president himself.[47]

The "Triple Revolution"

If Macdonald's *New Yorker* essay first put the issue of a citizen's right to adequate income in a high-profile publication, it was the release in the following year of a report titled "The Triple Revolution" that for the first time moved the issue to the center of debates in civil society, albeit briefly. In 1964, the Ad Hoc Committee on the Triple Revolution—a group of well-known scholars, writers, and other notables, including Robert Theobald and Michael Harrington—sent their report to the president, the minority and majority leaders of the both chambers of Congress, and to the secretary of labor.[48] The "triple revolution" they described in the report was made up of three separate but interrelated trends: the cybernation revolution, in which the increasing productive capacity of machines resulted in decreasing demand for human labor; the weaponry revolution, in which new weaponry could destroy human civilization but also be harnessed for lasting peace; and the human rights revolution, in which America's civil rights movement was a manifestation of a larger world movement to secure full rights of citizenship for formerly disempowered and excluded groups.

The report described trends in automation and industry with regard to unemployment that had concerned social commentators over the previous decade. Because of these changes, the report argued, the traditional approach to economic security—income through employment—was no longer enough. Furthermore, the report estimated than in the near future another six to eight million jobs would be lost. This job loss would have an especially dire impact on black Americans and their goal of full and equal participation in American society. As the report stated,

> The Negro claims, as a matter of simple justice, his full share in America's economic and social life; he sees adequate employment opportunities as a chief means of attaining this goal. . . . [Yet] the demand of the civil rights movement cannot be fulfilled within the present context of society. The Negro is trying to enter a social community and a tradition of work-and-income which are in the process of vanishing, even for the hitherto privileged white workers.[49]

The report stated that these large-scale changes forced society to reassess a series of historic questions: "What is man's role when he is not dependent upon his own activities for the material basis of life? What should be the basis of distributing individual access to national resources? Are there other proper claims on goods and services besides a job?"[50] The answer the committee outlined was for the government to recognize a citizen's right to an adequate income, or what would come to be labeled "welfare rights": "We urge, therefore, that society, through its appropriate legal and governmental institutions, undertake an unqualified commitment to provide every individual and every family with an adequate income as a matter of right."[51] This right to income was proposed within a larger context of social, political, and economic reforms in which the aim would be "the conscious and rational direction of economic life by planning institutions under democratic control."[52] This social democratic vision was fundamentally at odds with the noninterventionist, free-market system envisioned by conservative supporters of GAI plans such as Friedman and Stigler.

The Triple Revolution report garnered some publicity and generated virtually the only media coverage devoted to the GAI idea before 1966. The entire report was reproduced in *Advertising Age* accompanied by the caption: "Everyone in business and marketing should be informed of this far-out economic thinking." Well over fifty different magazines and newspapers contained news and editorial coverage of the report. A majority of the opinion coverage was negative, calling the report "nutty" or "utopian," or arguing that it was thinly veiled Marxism. However, few called into question the credentials or intentions of the report's authors.[53] The labor secretary, in an address to the United Auto Workers the day after the report's release, stated that the committee had done well in diagnosing some of the nation's problems, but that he disagreed completely with the solutions they proposed. "I don't believe that the world owes me a living," he declared, "and I don't believe it owes anybody else a living."[54] The concept of a guarantee to economic security had entered, however contentiously and briefly, into public debate.

GUARANTEED INCOME AND THE POVERTY EXPERTS

Structural Unemployment and the Income Strategy

Within the Kennedy administration, domestic poverty was not viewed as a pressing issue in need of special attention until 1963.[55] In the first two years of his presidency, Kennedy and his administration subscribed to the reigning economic orthodoxy of the era that assumed that poverty was best combated through increasing economic growth. To the extent that poverty remained beyond the reach of this growth, officials believed that it could be reduced though incremental reforms of the existing system. Another circumstance that illuminates the administration's disregard of the issue was that policy experts worked in a virtual data vacuum when it came to poverty-related issues. Henry Aaron, a former official at the Department of Health, Education, and Welfare (HEW), reported that "a complete bibliography of studies relating to poverty in the early 1960s ran to less than two pages" and that good data were not available until around 1965.[56] There were not even clear criteria for determining how many Americans were poor until the official poverty line was established in that year. Yet by 1963, malnutrition and homelessness had become more publicly visible as a result of research reports, television specials, the consciousness-raising efforts of the civil rights movement, and the work of writers such as Harrington and Macdonald. This course of events set the stage for the "rediscovery" of poverty among policymakers.

Up until this point, it was unemployment, rather than poverty per se, that had been the paramount domestic concern within the Kennedy administration. It inherited a shaky economy from the latter Eisenhower years and the affluence of the postwar era had seemingly stalled. The country experienced a sharp, though brief, recession in 1957–58 during which unemployment shot up to 7.5 percent, its highest level since the Great Depression. Another recession occurred in 1960 and unemployment never fully dropped again during Kennedy's tenure, staying above 5.5 percent. Perhaps even worse, the long-term jobless rates failed to drop, creating skepticism about the growth-centered approach to fighting poverty. Economists increasingly talked about a new type of unemployment: *structural* unemployment—persistent unemployment among populations who were structurally disadvantaged within the economy along dimensions such as age, race, geography, or family makeup. The administration found itself increasingly the target of criticism from left-liberal social commentators and civil rights leaders that it was not doing enough to assist people in such disadvantaged groups.[57]

This marked the beginning of a shift among many government economists, particularly within Kennedy's Council of Economic Advisors (CEA), from attacking poverty with an "employment approach" to an "income maintenance approach."[58] The poverty analysis of Robert Lampman exemplified this trend. Lampman, a CEA staffer and University of Wisconsin economist, had been a staunch defender of the growth-centered employment approach to poverty reduction in the 1950s. With contradictory evidence to the growth strategy mounting, Lampman was influential in formulating a synthesis of structuralist and growth-centered approaches that still looked to aggregate economic growth as the primary means to reduce poverty while also incorporating more targeted antipoverty programs for the most disadvantaged. Among these programs were manpower training, social services, and, importantly, the negative income tax.[59] Eventually, Lampman and James Tobin, another member of the CEA, became strong supporters of the NIT within the policy community. Armed with this new paradigm and a new set of policy proposals, Walter Heller, the chairman of the CEA, made the case to President Kennedy in 1963 that the fight against poverty required intervention by the federal government.[60] This set the stage for the federal government's substantial involvement in the years to come, but few economists within government at the time viewed GAI proposals as part of the solution. A CEA staffer remembered discussing it with colleagues during that period, but they collectively decided against it.[61] Yet the policy environment soon changed.

The War on Poverty: Innovation and Expanded State Capacity

On the day following Kennedy's assassination in November 1963, Heller met with newly sworn-in President Lyndon Johnson to brief him on what the CEA had been doing under Kennedy and what unfinished business remained. During the meeting, Heller told Johnson of Kennedy's plans to launch a large-scale attack on poverty. Johnson, who had been an active New Deal supporter in the 1930s and 1940s, and who had firsthand knowledge of poverty from his upbringing in west Texas, was reportedly enthusiastic about establishing antipoverty programs. To Heller's proposal, he responded, "That's my kind of program. . . . Move full speed ahead."[62] This was the birth of Johnson's War on Poverty initiatives, a set of federal, service-based programs designed to provide improved opportunities for the poor. Four programmatic areas were central to this effort: education, job training, civil rights, and juvenile delinquency.[63]

Guaranteed income strategies were antithetical to the philosophy of Johnson's programs. They provided benefits in cash—not services—and aimed at equalizing income—not opportunity. The differences between the War on Poverty programs and GAI proposals were, in fact, explicitly drawn. One of the earliest comprehensive antipoverty plans proposed stated, "[I]t is not permissible to view the War on Poverty merely as a program to provide money to the poor. Rather we emphasize altering society so poor people are able to raise *themselves* above the poverty level through their *own* efforts."[64] So it was with considerable irony that the initial development of GAI proposals within government took place in the administrative and intellectual center of Johnson's antipoverty efforts: the Office of Economic Opportunity.

In January 1964, Johnson gave his State of the Union message to a grieving nation. He assured Americans he would carry out Kennedy's unfinished legislative agenda, which included declaring "an unconditional war on poverty." In the following month, a report by the CEA outlined more detailed features of the program and Johnson appointed Sargent Shriver, a Kennedy in-law and the director of the Peace Corps, to head a task force to design the antipoverty program. By March, Shriver had submitted a bill for the legislation to Congress and it included the creation of a new office to spearhead the antipoverty program, the Office of Economic Opportunity (OEO), which he would direct. The goals of the OEO were twofold: to coordinate new and existing services and to provide more opportunity for the poor. (To emphasize the focus on opportunity, Johnson's persistent refrain in describing his programs was "a hand up, not a handout.") The main emphasis was placed on job training and education programs for youth, but the plans also contained major new initiatives like the Community Action Program, which was intended to empower the poor in their local communities. The sheer number of existing and potential programs required expanded efforts at coordination. The legislation called for the OEO to directly administer some programs—such as the Jobs Corps, Community Action, and VISTA (a domestic volunteer corps)—while supervising the administration of additional programs under the control of other agencies, namely HEW and the Department of Labor (DOL). The Economic Opportunity Act of 1964, which contained these elements, was passed by Congress in August and the OEO began functioning in earnest in November.

The OEO's explicit mandate was policy innovation, which had direct consequences for the development of GAI policies, as did a number of other organizational factors.[65] The first was the department's newness. Unlike related organizations, such as HEW and DOL, the OEO was not encumbered by preexisting layers of bureaucracy, nor was it committed to a set of preexisting programs or paradigms. The individuals who came to work there were young and brought new ideas to existing problems. Second was its budget, which was initially quite large: $750 million to be spent in the first six months in highly visible ways in order to show quick results to the public. People within the OEO knew they had the potential to put their ideas into practice. Third was Shriver's leadership style. He offered few guidelines for program development and administratively there was less coordination than in other agencies. Staffers described the atmosphere as "free-wheeling" and "chaotic." Fourth was the OEO's insulation from the pragmatic realities of legislative politics. There was little interaction between the policy analysts at the OEO and congressional and White House leadership. This insulated the development of policy ideas from the political and fiscal concerns that often constrained them as they emerged from agency staff members. All of these factors bolstered the OEO's independence from pressures both within the government and from the private sector. From this intellectual soil grew a number of new ideas about how to address social problems—including, for instance, Community Action, Head Start, Neighborhood Youth Corps, and VISTA—the idea of a GAI program being only one of them. These programs constituted the population of policy ideas from which GAI emerged during the next four years.

Evaluating Policy Alternatives

One of the key processes that determined the fate of these competing policy ideas was their evaluation and mutual comparison through systems analysis, a process that would ultimately favor GAI plans—and specifically the negative income tax—in the coming years. Systems analysis had been imported from the Rand Corporation by the Department of Defense in the early 1960s.[66] The specific program the defense agency implemented—the planning-programming-budgeting system (PPBS)—was credited with reorganizing and dramatically improving its operation and programming. This was viewed as a considerable feat since people regarded the Department of Defense as the government's most vast and unwieldy department. The essence of PPBS was first designing programs blind to their costs, then affixing costs to each program, rank ordering them by projected expenditures, and then evaluating them according to cost-benefit analysis. Costs could be measured in terms of manpower or time expended, but most often the metric was dollars. The objective was to select and implement the programs with the maximum positive difference between costs and benefits.

The OEO was the first federal agency outside the Department of Defense to employ the PPBS. In light of the OEO's administrative challenges, the complexity of poverty as a social condition, and the ambitious goals the office sought, systems analysis seemed well suited to the task. The program's use within the domestic bureaucracy was also in keeping with the cool imagery of behavioral analysis during the 1960s and the widespread confidence in social science's ability to address social problems. Not three years earlier, President Kennedy had articulated this confidence.

> Most of us are conditioned for many years to have a political viewpoint, Republican or Democrat—liberal, conservative, moderate. The fact of the matter is that most of the problems, or at least many of them, that we now face are technical problems, are administrative problems. They are very sophisticated judgments which do not lend themselves to the great sort of "passionate movements" which have stirred this country so often in the past.[67]

Indeed, through the end of the decade, party affiliation would pose few barriers to participation in poverty analysis. This nonpartisan ethos within the bureaucracy would prove to play a significant role in the emergence of GAI policy within the Nixon administration.

The use of systems analysis both relied on and reinforced trends in poverty analysis emphasizing quantification. Recent advances in survey techniques meant better data were available on extremely poor populations, who had previously been underrepresented in government data. Technological advances meant panel studies were more feasible, enabling researchers to gather longitudinal information on respondents at different points in their lives and under a variety of circumstances. And computer-processing capabilities meant that data could be arrayed in much more complicated ways than the two- or three-way static relationships that were typical of previous research. Patterns in the data could be teased out more effectively and this had implications for examining the complicated relationships among social characteristics such as age, race, sex, education, work experience, and region.[68]

Quantification and systems analysis were powerful tools that moved poverty research in beneficial directions, but they had important consequences for the definition of poverty, since the notion itself was in flux. Not only were there competing perspectives about whether poverty was a monetary or cultural condition, an additional debate concerned whether poverty was an absolute condition that could be precisely quantified based on income or wealth or whether it was really a relative condition based on social comparisons to other people, which was therefore more subjective and difficult to quantify. Over the course of the 1960s, largely as a result of quantification and cost-benefit analysis, poverty came to be defined by government experts in monetary and absolute terms.[69] Notably, this definition privileged income maintenance strategies over other types of antipoverty measures, such as community action, in part because they were more amenable to cost-benefit analysis. This pushed GAI plans toward the center of the OEO's initial policy agenda.

Shriver chose Joseph Kershaw to head the OEO's research department, where the PPBS was employed. Part of the conceptual apparatus borrowed from the Defense Department was the five-year plan. The goal of these plans was to evaluate a variety of programs in terms of their likely effectiveness and their optimal use of resources. This type of cost-benefit analysis was supposed to provide the most rational basis upon which a department's leader could make decisions and also sell his department's ideas politically. In 1965, Kershaw's office issued the first of these annual reports and interest in it ran high throughout government. Kershaw briefed Shriver as well as the vice president, the budget director, and the president's advisors. Importantly, however, these reports were intentionally not yet presented to members of Congress.[70]

The rationale for the OEO's programs illustrated the increasing rejection of the growth-based employment approach to fighting poverty and recognized the realities of structural unemployment.

> A healthy economy alone will not suffice. After the rapid economic growth of the Second World War ended, five million people *reentered* poverty. After the rapid growth of the Korean War ended, about three and a half million people *reentered* poverty. Rapid economic growth is essential to victory in the War on Poverty, but if the victory is to stick, fundamental change is equally necessary. . . . Our emphasis is on programs that complement and reinforce one another; on growth, structural [*sic*], and payment programs that fit together in an integrated War on Poverty.[71]

Toward this end, the Kershaw report contained a three-pronged attack on poverty that included public employment, community action, and GAI programs. This design was in part a manifestation of the emerging consensus that income programs needed to be separate from service programs.[72]

There was, however, a conflict between advocates of different types of GAI programs. Kershaw and his eventual successor, Robert Levine, supported the negative income tax as their favored type of GAI program. However, the report also contained references to another type of income maintenance program—a family allowance scheme—that Alvin Schorr, a staff member of the research office, and many other social workers favored over an NIT. Though both plans were GAI proposals, there were important differences between them.[73] Proponents of the NIT argued that if the main aim of income maintenance was the reduction of poverty, then income maintenance programs should be based on economic need alone. This meant no stigmatizing, work-related means tests for recipients but also that the programs should specifically be targeted to the neediest cases. The NIT fit this description and was consequently viewed as highly efficient in economists' terms. Supporters further contended that it would be simple to administer because the criteria—economic need—would be relatively straightforward to establish. The program could be administered through the IRS, which already coordinated tax payments and refunds to seventy-five million filing units.

The family allowance was a payment based on the number of children in a family, regardless of the family's income. Family allowance supporters pointed to the strong correlation between poverty and family size, and argued that income maintenance should focus on children. Families of the working and middle classes, they further argued, could also use income supplementation during their children's formative years. Importantly, supporters felt that such benefits to the middle class could create a broader political appeal for the programs. Moreover, since the program was not focused on need per se but on the number of children, the family allowance would diminish the social divisions between poor and non-poor that had become institutionalized in the existing welfare system. Proponents suggested that, given the nature of the criteria, it was their program and not the NIT that would have the simpler administrative apparatus. Most broadly, they pointed to the fact that almost all other countries of the industrialized West, including Canada, had family allowance programs of some kind. Though the consensus among these poverty experts was that some form of GAI program was needed, the debate over its specific program design—NIT versus family allowance—would continue.[74]

In 1966, the OEO planning staff submitted its second five-year plan and GAI programs appeared more prominently than they had the year before. The public jobs section was deemphasized largely because of declining unemployment rates. The escalation of the war in Vietnam had drawn many young men into the armed services, leaving their positions to be filled by less-skilled workers who might have been unemployed only a few years earlier. The report also downplayed community action programs. They had quickly come under attack from local political leaders because the political empowerment these programs sought to nurture within poor communities was being turned against local government itself in some high-profile instances. Thus, among existing antipoverty options, GAI plans were among the strongest contenders.[75] The planning staff continued to push the idea, as it had during the interim period between reports, and it started to be taken more seriously by people in the rest of government. Soon the idea would emerge from the confines of the policy community and enter into full-fledged debates over poverty and welfare in the nation.

CONCLUSION

Guaranteed annual income proposals emerged in a largely top-down fashion from government experts and academic economists in the early 1960s. The factors that contributed to the proposals' emergence included changing views of the economy and unemployment, increasing social affluence, renewed attention to poverty, social pressure and consciousness-raising efforts from the civil rights movement, and the increasing capacity for policy innovation as a result of the War on Poverty. Each played an important role. For instance, without changing conceptions of poverty and justice among policy experts, social pressure from the civil rights movement would likely have yielded reforms that were in keeping with the existing New Deal philosophy of social provision—public jobs, social services, and the like—and that worked within the existing categorical structure. Yet support for GAI proposals across ideological lines masked considerable disagreement—much of which was still latent—about their programmatic details and underlying justification. "Guaranteed income" was a promising but vague idea onto which people projected a variety of meanings. Some of this disagreement was based on contention over the details of the competing proposals, such as the differences between the negative income tax advanced by many economists, family allowances favored by social workers and sociologists, and universal flat grants advanced by leftists. Reflected in these disputes were competing ideas about the sources of poverty (whether it was a monetary or cultural condition), the nature of freedom (whether social policy should advance its negative or positive definitions), and the merits of targeted as opposed to universalistic social policy.

Despite the differences among the various GAI proposals, the common element they shared was their challenge to the classification scheme upon which the existing welfare system was based. Existing antipoverty policies distinguished between the deserving and undeserving poor, and the assumption underlying this distinction was that "undeserving" individuals were poor through some fault of their own and therefore needed the stigma of "welfare" and the fear of destitution to spur them into employment. Because GAI supporters believed that systemic factors of various types were largely responsible for poverty, it did not make sense to categorize the poor based on their moral worthiness. Notably, however, the proposals' supporters displayed little awareness of how powerful the distinctions between categories of the poor actually were. As GAI plans received more public scrutiny in the subsequent years, and as they became more strongly associated with claims to "welfare rights," the challenge these distinctions posed to economic security for all would become more apparent.

CHAPTER TWO

Guaranteed Annual Income Goes Public

The year 1966 represented a turning point in the politics of GAI policy. It was during this year that the idea entered into the broader public consciousness because government experts publicly placed it on the list of policy alternatives, business groups and economists lobbied on its behalf, and activists began to call for the right to economic security. Over the next few years the idea gained what many observers described as an air of inevitability. Part and parcel with this growing attention was a significant shift in the meaning of GAI proposals. For many proponents of GAI plans in the early 1960s, the main problems the plans addressed were structural unemployment, low wages, and the changing nature of work. These were problems located in the economy. During the latter half of the decade, however, poverty experts and others increasingly linked the plans with problems such as inadequate benefit levels, perverse incentive structures, punitive eligibility rules, and a lack of national standards. Though the debates over GAI were multifaceted, this change shifted the over-all attention from problems located within the economy to those within the welfare system itself.

Public consideration of GAI plans by government officials gave them a degree of legitimacy they had not previously enjoyed. One section of President Johnson's economic report to Congress in January 1966 argued for serious consideration of a negative income tax on the grounds that it "could be administered on a universal basis for all the poor and would be the most direct approach to reducing poverty."[1] This recommendation was the first public statement of support for GAI by a presidential administration and the announcement was picked up by major media outlets, such as *U.S. News and World Report*. Weeks later, a second government report urged Congress to give serious consideration to the GAI concept. A study undertaken by the National Commission on Technology, Automation, and Economic Progress proposed a three-part strategy to fight poverty, including a new approach to public assistance in the form of income maintenance. "In particular," the report stated, "we suggest that the Congress give serious thought to a 'minimum income allowance,' or 'negative income tax' program."[2] The report downplayed the effects of technology on unemployment, but called for a GAI program to eliminate means tests, increase work incentives, and minimize incentives for male desertion in the family, all of which were identified as problems with the current welfare system.

The shifting view of GAI policy as a means to deal with problems in the welfare system followed new lines of thinking developing in the policy community, particularly among the experts at the OEO and HEW. These experts continued to be primary players in advancing GAI plans and their focus was on the shortcomings of existing antipoverty programs. Guaranteed income plans were high on the list of alternatives to the status quo, including both the NIT and the family allowance. For reasons having to do with changes within the policy community itself, the NIT became the favored type of GAI proposal during this period. The prominence of the NIT reinforced a trend that was already underway in the evolution of antipoverty policy. While the existing AFDC program targeted women and children as its primary beneficiaries, GAI programs further targeted a new population: employable men. Because this marked an explicit departure from existing program objectives and raised a number of unexamined questions about the effects that income benefits might have on male recipients' work effort, the government launched a massive series of experimental pilot programs to test the effects of GAI plans.

Outside of government, business leaders, academic economists, organized social movements, and broader civic unrest all played a role in focusing attention on GAI policy. Drawing inspiration from the civil rights movement's legislative successes in 1964 and 1965, and civil rights leaders' more frequent calls for economic justice, a new movement emerged claiming the "right to welfare." Though this demand had multiple meanings, it directed attention to the deficiencies of the existing system and by the end of the decade had become roughly synonymous with GAI proposals. The protests undertaken by these welfare rights groups, along with the uncoordinated urban rioting that occurred between 1964 and 1968, pushed the issue of poverty reduction higher and higher on the nation's agenda. Partly as a result of this social instability, a number of business leaders and organizations coalesced around GAI plans as a promising way to alleviate urban unrest. They also favored the improved work incentives contained in the proposals. These views mirrored reasons for support among many economists. Both business leaders and economists favored GAI plans as a way of strengthening the American economy by facilitating the transition from public assistance programs to paid employment.

By the end of the Johnson administration, there was a wide range of support for GAI plans both within and outside government. As only a few commentators noted at the time, however, this support was based on divergent, and sometimes competing, visions of the social problems addressed by the proposals. This diversity of meanings also masked the challenge posed by GAI plans to the categorical nature of the existing system because issues aside from poverty reduction had become highly salient aspects of "welfare reform." Though leaders within the Johnson administration never threw their weight behind GAI proposals,

Johnson did appoint a presidential commission that would later announce its support for a GAI plan during the first year of the Nixon administration.

THE "RIGHT TO WELFARE"

The growing attention accorded to GAI proposals stemmed in part from their connection, beginning around 1966, with calls for "welfare rights." This connection, however, only emerged over the course of the decade. During the early 1960s, advocates of legal aid for the poor advanced a different and more prominent way of conceptualizing welfare rights that involved reforming the existing AFDC-based system.[3] This legal scholarship gradually dovetailed with arguments favoring the right to a guaranteed income, which was first publicly articulated by the Ad Hoc Committee on the Triple Revolution in 1964. Though the "right to welfare" meant a number of different things to different groups throughout the 1960s, eventually both poverty lawyers and social movement leaders converged on the notion that GAI plans were the best means to attain welfare rights.

Welfare Rights in Legal Scholarship

Poverty law had a long lineage dating back to the 1935 Social Security Act and the jurisprudence that developed in response to its statutes. The pronounced growth of poverty law in the 1960s had more immediate antecedents in the civil rights movement, the Ford Foundation's "gray areas" projects, the OEO's new legal services division, and the litigation strategies of local organizations such as Mobilization for Youth in New York City. The legal aims pursued by these groups on behalf of the poor included goals such as fair hearings, enforcement of statutory benefits, application of due process procedures, and retention of privacy rights.[4] An important turning point in the growth of the "welfare rights" concept within the legal community emerged from the developing nexus between the social work and legal professions. Central to the process was the work of Elizabeth Wickenden, a social worker and former New Deal alumna. In the early 1960s she coordinated efforts to involve lawyers in social welfare issues, having seen the successful litigation strategies of the civil rights movement. Perhaps most significantly she enlisted a young attorney, Charles Reich, soon to join the faculty at Yale Law School, to study the relationship between civil liberties and welfare statutes.[5] Reich published a series of influential papers in the mid-1960s that became foundational in the welfare rights lexicon.

Reich's article "The New Property" appeared in the *Yale Law Journal* and became the most frequently cited article ever to appear there.[6] Up until that time, welfare had been viewed mainly as largesse from the government—a gift to the poor to which they had no legal entitlement. In contrast, the newer line of reasoning adopted by legal advocates argued that welfare benefits were a statutory right once a recipient established eligibility and therefore that these benefits must be given out in accordance with constitutional protections, such as due process, equal protection, and the right to travel. Protections such as due process were an especially prominent concern for welfare recipients. They were a safeguard against the contested practice of "midnight searches" used by social workers and other officials to monitor whether female welfare recipients, who in most states had to be single, were cohabitating with men. According to existing court decisions, beneficiaries of public assistance enjoyed due process protection only if the state threatened an individual's "life, liberty, or property." If welfare payments were not defined as falling into one of these three categories, recipients had a difficult time obtaining protection.[7]

Reich's article squarely addressed these issues. He framed his article by noting the increasingly vast role of the state in providing for the well-being of citizens. The state, he argued, provided many forms of valued goods (jobs, income and benefits, occupational licenses, contracts and subsidies) that "were taking the place of traditional forms of wealth—forms which are held as private property. . . . The wealth of more and more Americans depends upon a relationship to government."[8] The law, according to Reich, had not sufficiently responded to these changing circumstances. What was needed was a new zone of privacy beyond which neither government nor private interests could reach. For the poor, as for others, government largesse needed to be viewed as a right.

> The concept of right is most urgently needed with respect to benefits like unemployment compensation, public assistance, and old age insurance. These benefits are based upon the recognition that misfortune and deprivation are often caused by forces beyond the control of the individual, such as technological change, variation in demand for goods, or wars. The aim of these benefits is to preserve the self-sufficiency of the individual, to rehabilitate him where necessary, and to allow him to be a valuable member of a family and a community; in theory they represent part of the individual's rightful share in the commonwealth. Only by making such benefits into rights can the welfare state achieve its goal of providing a secure minimum basis for individual well-being and dignity in a society where each man cannot be wholly master of his own destiny.[9]

Reich's article neatly synthesized within a legal framework views of the structural sources of poverty and the necessity of positive freedom articulated by Galbraith, Harrington, the Triple Revolution report, and others, and affixed to it a solution that defined welfare benefits as a right equivalent to other forms of private property. It circulated widely and became a key tool in legal efforts on behalf of welfare recipients.

The Welfare Rights Movement

A somewhat different notion of welfare rights developed in the social movement activities of New York–based welfare rights groups and later the National Welfare Rights Organization (NWRO). The legal team at Mobilization for Youth had been influential poverty advocates in New York City in the early 1960s. But a sharp strategic shift took place around 1966, when Columbia University social scientists Richard Cloward and Francis Fox Piven published an article in *The Nation* titled "A Strategy to End Poverty" and convinced a former staffer at the Congress of Racial Equality (CORE), George Wiley, to form a new organization to implement the plan they had outlined.

Cloward and Piven's article opened by stating their desire to bring together civil rights organizations, antipoverty groups, and the poor in a strategy to generate a political crisis that would result in GAI legislation. Their focus was the New York City welfare system and the key to the strategy was placing fiscal strains on this system. This, they argued, would be accomplished by mobilizing the poor along two fronts. First, there were many recipients who received benefits that were far short of the total amount to which they were legitimately due by law. Those recipients, together with lawyers and social workers, would push to receive full benefits. Second, half of the people eligible for public assistance in New York City were not on the welfare rolls at all. Therefore, they would organize a registration drive to move these hundreds of thousands of people onto the rolls. The end product of their strategy would be an enormous financial strain placed on local coffers. If this strategy were replicated in cities across America, they contended, it would disrupt big-city Democratic coalitions. To avoid party upheaval, the Democratic presidential administration would be forced to advance a federal solution to poverty. The legislative result, they hoped, would be a GAI policy.[10]

Their article did indeed serve as a blueprint for social activism in the immediate years to follow.[11] However, it is instructive here to examine the article for the multiple ways in which "welfare rights" and "guaranteed income" were mentioned, because this usage is characteristic of the terms' overlapping meanings in broader discourse throughout the 1960s. Three prominent meanings were ascribed to welfare rights. The first was the meaning primarily used by the poverty lawyers, such as Reich. Under statutory law, welfare recipients were entitled to certain benefits and constitutional protections, which they were often not granted. Subsidiary claims were that such benefits should be unconditional and provided at adequate levels. Second, as Cloward and Piven observed, a large number of individuals and families who were eligible for public assistance under existing rules were not receiving benefits of any type. These people had a right to receive government assistance, but needed to be encouraged to actively seek them out. Third, the authors claimed, the right to adequate income needed to be granted to all the poor, even those outside the current eligibility standards, such as unemployed fathers in intact families, the working poor, childless couples, and single individuals.

These meanings of welfare rights were clearly different and they were employed by various groups over the course of the late 1960s. Yet a significant end product of this multiplicity of meanings was a unified-sounding call for the right to welfare. The first meaning, *procedural and adequacy rights*, focused on people currently within the welfare system but only receiving partial benefits and protections; the second, *eligibility rights*, focused on individuals who were eligible under current law but not receiving benefits; and the third, *income security rights*, focused on groups who were neither receiving nor eligible under existing programs for benefits. Activists often invoked these different definitions of welfare rights without fully specifying their meanings. It was this multifaceted understanding of welfare rights that gave the concept its power during the period. A variety of groups and activists were able to rally around the concept and make a coherent-sounding call for reform, even though the idea itself was not well specified.[12]

The third understanding of welfare rights typically led to discussions of GAI policy because welfare rights in the broadest sense required a comprehensive overhaul of the existing system and GAI policies were a means of doing so. However, during the mid-1960s, few people outside the policy community understood the range of options, all of which were described as "guaranteed income" policies. Cloward and Piven, for instance, stated directly that their long-term aim was a GAI policy, but they did not specify any particular programmatic form.

> Several ways have been proposed for redistributing income through the federal government. It is not our purpose here to assess the relative merits of these plans, which are still undergoing debate and clarification. Whatever mechanism is eventually adopted, however, it must include certain features if it is not merely to perpetuate in a new guise the present evils of the public welfare system. First, adequate income levels must be assured. . . . Second, the right to income must be guaranteed, or the oppression of the welfare poor will not be eliminated.[13]

The NWRO was the most visible organization during the second half of the 1960s to push for welfare rights of various types, and its formation was inspired by the Cloward and Piven strategy. The NWRO was founded by George Wiley, a former faculty member at Syracuse University who left the university in 1964 to join CORE in New York City as associate national director. Wiley quit his position with CORE in 1966 amid growing disagreements over its aims. Unlike many in CORE, Wiley felt that the goals of the organization should be redirected toward economic issues rather than primarily racial ones. A movement focusing on economic issues could be more racially integrated and work more effectively on behalf of all poor people. The Cloward and

Piven strategy provided the blueprint. After a year as the leader of an interim organization called the Poverty/Rights Action Center that organized a series of highly publicized welfare marches and demonstrations, Wiley convened the inaugural convention of the NWRO in August 1967.[14]

The first of the organization's four stated goals was: "Adequate Income: a system that guarantees enough money for all Americans to live dignified lives above the level of poverty."[15] Wiley had first been exposed to the idea of a guaranteed income system in 1965 through interaction with CORE's research committee, which included Cloward and Robert Theobald, among other scholars. Over the next few years, the practical goals of the NWRO would vary considerably—within and between the three aforementioned under-standings of welfare rights—and there was internal disagreement among the ranks of the leadership and members. A significant factor in determining which types of rights would be pursued was the level of government at which efforts were focused. In 1967–68, most of the efforts were local, in part because Wiley was concerned with building organizational membership, which was most effective if recipients' immediate (and largely local) concerns could be addressed through mobilization. In these campaigns, procedural and eligibil-ity rights were central. After the NWRO achieved a series of initial successes in 1967, New York City implemented a number of changes, including a flat grant for "special needs," that confounded many of the NWRO's short-term goals because the changes removed the targets of reform.[16] In response, the NWRO's attention shifted to the national level at precisely the time that Nixon would propose his version of a GAI bill.

The Welfare System and Its Alternatives

During this period, policy experts at the OEO and HEW continued to develop and evaluate GAI plans, though with few references to "welfare rights." As the analyses progressed, their views of the problems addressed by GAI proposals increasingly shifted from those located in the economy to problems with the welfare system itself. Subjecting the welfare system to scrutiny was in fact part of their mandate. Before the creation of the OEO, the institutional capacity for such governmental self-scrutiny was limited, but the stated objective of the OEO was to evaluate, coordinate, and improve the nation's antipoverty efforts. Implementation of the PPBS further bolstered this capacity because it provided a methodology for comparing antipoverty alternatives through cost-benefit analysis. Research by the OEO and the agencies it oversaw (such as HEW) provided the raw materials for a new type of welfare-critical discourse aimed at existing antipoverty programs that had little precedent. As expert attention shifted to the shortcomings of the current system, four problems stood out. The first was inadequate coverage of the poor population, which was the main concern articulated by welfare rights groups. The remaining three had to do with behavioral incentives that the new poverty economists believed were built into the welfare system itself: work disincentives, incentives for marital breakup, and incentives for migration from low- to high-benefit states. Though the extent of the problems associated with these incentives was never clear, the experts' concerns about them weighed heavily in the calculus of evaluating new antipoverty proposals such as GAI plans.

The Problem of Incentives

In 1966, HEW experts wrote an influential research report showing that the current system fell woefully short of the government's goal of ending poverty. Sixty percent of the people living in poverty did not receive benefits from public assistance or social insurance programs. Of all the subpopulations of poor individuals, children fared the worst. The authors argued that modifying existing programs would not help most of the poor and that comprehensive restructuring was necessary.[17] This conclusion resonated with another report, titled "Having the Power, We Have the Duty," that was submitted to the secretary of HEW around the same time. The basic problem with the current system, the report argued, was that it provided too few benefits to too few people. The nation could well afford to provide modest but adequate income to all, but it failed to do so.[18] These ideas about seeking better coverage for the poor gained in currency. A growing number of experts viewed the welfare system as inadequate and they proceeded toward the ambitious objective of eliminating poverty in America through overhauling the nation's social welfare programs.

Yet three other problems, some more and some less directly related to poverty reduction, also commanded a great deal of attention among poverty analysts in government, and these had to do with the welfare system's incentives structure. The first problem was related to work and it became the overwhelming concern in the coming debates over GAI plans. Poverty analysts, who increasingly had backgrounds in economics, knew that work disincentives existed in the AFDC program. Analysts differed on how to best move the unemployed poor into the labor market—some focused on reducing disincentives to work while others emphasized work requirements—yet concerns about labor force participation were paramount in deliberations over welfare reform. Using an incentive-based approach, the HEW report was one of a number of critiques of the existing system that recommended that earnings disregards, which exempted some earnings from the benefit reduction schedule, and lower marginal tax rates needed to be implemented so that government beneficiaries could keep more of their earned income. Otherwise, with what was essentially a 100 percent tax on earnings, recipients would have little motivation to enter the labor market because they would not fare any better financially. The problem for government analysts was that there was very little data on how people responded to the work incentives contained in social programs.[19]

The experts felt that it was essential to know the answers to these questions, especially as they related to employable men. So in 1967, the OEO began developing what was then considered the largest social experiment ever undertaken by the federal government, the Graduated Work Incentive Experiment in New Jersey. The aim of the experiment was to assess the effects of various types of GAI programs—which were based on the negative income tax—on work behavior.[20] Because of the new emphasis on social scientific analysis within government, poverty analysts believed they could only lobby for a GAI plan if they were armed with such data. The population chosen for the experiment was restricted to low-income families containing an employable man between the ages of eighteen and fifty-eight. Most families were black or Hispanic. This focus on men was a clear indication that the greatest concern among experts was the labor market participation of poor, minority men in intact families. This marked a signal shift in the objectives of public assistance programs, since AFDC benefits had heretofore been given mainly to women and their children in single-parent households.

Beyond the work issue, a second problem to which poverty analysts devoted considerable attention was marital instability. The AFDC system originated during the 1930s as a largely state-administered program for women with children who were widowed or otherwise without a breadwinner. In 1962, legislative amendments referred to as AFDC-Unemployed Parent (AFDC-UP) opened the opportunity for states also to give benefits to families in which the father was present but chronically unemployed. However, by the mid-1960s, fewer than half the states had implemented this policy. Poverty analysts believed that this was a serious design flaw in the program. In the states without AFDC-UP, the incentive structure meant that women receiving welfare benefits would lose them if they decided to get married, even if their husband experienced employment problems. It also meant that poor mothers living with the fathers of their children would be eligible for benefits only if the man left the household. Based on the limited data available, researchers knew that the number of single-parent families on welfare had been increasing, along with out-of-wedlock births, over the course of the 1960s, and data suggested that poverty was highly correlated with living in single-parent families. The government's poverty analysts believed that if disincentives for marriage were removed from the system, more families would stay together (or get together in the first place) and that poverty would decrease as a result.[21]

The third issue that concerned the analysts was interstate migration, and its associated fiscal problems, because similar incentives existed for poor families to move from states with low benefit levels to those with higher ones. This had been the major source of concern underlying the welfare controversy in

Newburgh earlier in the decade. Because of AFDC's original federal-state partnership design in the 1930s, benefit levels had been left to the determination of the individual states and these levels varied widely, often being lower in the South than the North by a factor of five. Since the 1940s, there had been a steady flow of poor, mainly black families from the rural South to the urban North as the development of agricultural machinery replaced much of the work formerly done by low-wage, low-skill laborers.[22] State officials in the urban North believed that the migration to their states was caused in part by higher levels of benefits. Certainly the welfare rolls were growing, which created a fiscal strain on state and local coffers. Signs of backlash among white taxpayers were apparent, since it seemed that most of the new welfare recipients were black, and influential governors and big-city mayors were demanding help from the federal government. Their main proposal was the creation of national benefits standards by which each state would have to abide. One of the selling points of GAI plans, as they developed within the OEO and HEW, was that they contained such standards.

The diagnoses of the work, family instability, and interstate migration problems were based on economists' recognition that incentives for undesirable behavior on the part of welfare recipients existed in the present system. However, there was no solid evidence that these incentives actually affected recipients' actions and were therefore causally accountable for the patterns in work, marriage and childbearing, and migration behavior that concerned the analysts. On the issue of work incentives, this is why the OEO undertook the negative income tax experiments. In the area of family instability, Alice Rivlin, the assistant secretary of PPBS planning at HEW during this period, was blunt in her retrospective account of policy development during this era: "It was clear that these monetary incentives existed. It was not clear how many families actually responded to them. The number of broken families was rising, but there was no evidence to show how much, if any, of the rise was due to the perverse incentives built into the welfare system."[23] Indeed, the historian James T. Patterson argues that although the correlation between family instability and poverty was strong, more evidence suggested that the causal influence ran in the opposite direction than believed by the poverty analysts at the time: "the main reason for family breakup among the poor . . . was not welfare but poverty itself."[24]

On the subject of interstate migration, Robert Levine, the director of PPBS systems analysis at the OEO, was equally clear that economists' behavioral assumptions were driving policy development. In his retrospective account of the period, he wrote,

It is sometimes contended that people move from low-welfare states like Mississippi to high ones like New York and California in order to receive public assistance. Aside from occasional anecdotes this has never been demonstrated; most migrants are those who move reluctantly in search of jobs, not relief. . . . Nonetheless, the differences between the low- and high-welfare-payment states are striking and perhaps "ought" (in the economists' amoral usage of the word) to induce movement.[25]

From these accounts it is clear that proposals for reforming antipoverty policy developed in an atmosphere of widespread uncertainty about cause and effect. Experts developed programmatic ideas based less on data and more according to anecdote, intuition, and especially behavioral paradigms—that is, beliefs about how people behaved.[26] These beliefs were rooted in a rational action paradigm that served as the basis of econometric analysis.[27] Trends in quantification and systems analysis further reinforced the types of causal attributions made by welfare experts, most of which involved the role of the disincentives in the welfare system itself influencing the behavior of the poor.

Three Competing Policy Alternatives

On the basis of these analyses and assumptions, three major welfare reform strategies competed for prominence within the offices of the OEO and HEW. One was an incremental approach to improving AFDC. It included national standards for benefits and mandatory implementation of AFDC-UP. Another was an NIT scheme of the type that the OEO was testing in the New Jersey experiments. (Among supporters of the NIT, there were further debates about whether the program should cover all poor individuals or just poor families.) A third option was the family allowance. The main difference between it and a family-oriented NIT system was that its benefits would be given to families regardless of their income level.[28] Each policy held different consequences for the changing meaning of "welfare," since they each expanded eligibility to different populations of recipients. So it is worthwhile to examine why one reform strategy triumphed over the others.

Three sets of factors contributed to GAI programs' generally being favored over incremental reform and to the NIT being favored over the family allowance: the participants involved, research and development processes within the administration, and the broader political context. A marked shift occurred in the mid-1960s in the composition of antipoverty experts who worked within the federal government. Prior to the mid-1960s, most of the experts had been social workers who carried on the social service orientation established by the policies enacted during the New Deal. But after 1966, the year HEW issued the service-oriented report "Having the Power, We Have the Duty," the influence social workers exerted on policy development declined as economists played an increasingly central role.[29] Social workers tended to favor either incremental modification of the existing service-based system (in which they played a central role) or the family allowance, because of its emphasis on children, its universal coverage, and its simplicity. Economists, on the other hand, favored the NIT. Though its details and implementation were more complicated, they understood it.[30] The NIT was efficient, in economists' terms, and its presumed efficacy was based on economic maximizing, the domain assumption of economics. Moreover, it was innovative, and the mandate among these experts, especially at the OEO, was innovation. Developing an NIT program allowed them to apply their particular econometric skills.[31] The balance of influence tilted further in favor of econometric modeling when Shriver left the OEO early in 1968. Along with him left many experts who had favored programs such as the empowerment strategy of the community action programs and in their place entered economists who focused on cost-benefit analysis.[32]

This suggests the second set of factors, those having to do with the new research and development processes used at the OEO and HEW. The most significant was the use of the PPBS. In 1965, implementation of PPBS had been a significant factor in the initial development of the NIT and family allowance because one of the basic precepts of the PPBS was that programs should first be developed blind to their costs. Both of these programs were more expensive than the existing welfare programs and, based on their costs, would likely have faced more daunting obstacles to being seriously considered in the absence of the new PPBS guidelines. The next step was to rank order the alternatives according to their expense and then subject them to a series of cost-benefit analyses. This required data, computational power, and simulation models, which poverty analysts did not begin to have available until about 1966. It was at this second stage that the NIT fared far better than the family allowance.[33] Cost-benefit analysis favored measures that were commensurable. Money, being the most fungible unit—unlike things such as dignity, motivation, empowerment, or the subjective feelings of full citizenship—became the favored measure. Since poverty had come to be defined in absolute monetary terms, this meant that both program costs and recipients' benefits were measured monetarily. The NIT, because it was income tested, proved more efficient, less "wasteful," and less expensive than the family allowance. It was the most direct way of alleviating poverty. The main objectives of family allowances, such as improving child well-being and mitigating social divisions by race and class, were outcomes less amenable to measurement and analysis. The result was that the PPBS, though it was technically an evaluative *means*, ended up prescribing poverty analysts' *ends*, according to how capable they were of measuring and comparing them.[34]

The final set of factors that affected the viability of the alternatives was the political feasibility of the proposals, and nothing recommended the NIT more than its promise to improve work incentives. The poverty analysts, though they were insulated from immediate political pressures, knew that conservatives in both parties would want programs that bolstered the work ethic. The NIT fared better by this yardstick than either the family allowance or the proposed improvements to the existing system. Costs were an additional factor. Proposals for an NIT estimated its costs at roughly $5 billion, while costs for a family allowance were estimated between $6 and $14 billion. With the escalation of the war in Vietnam, the federal budget for domestic spending contracted sharply, as indicated, for instance, by Johnson's unpopular 1967 proposal for a surcharge on corporate and individual income taxes.[35]

The politics of the black family posed a further obstacle to the family allowance. The third rail of social policy in the late 1960s was the relationship among race, poverty, and family structure. Daniel Patrick Moynihan had been one of the earliest advocates of the family allowance, proposing such a plan during his tenure as an assistant secretary at the Department of Labor during the early Johnson years. In 1965, he wrote a government report titled *The Negro Family: The Case for National Action* (known as the Moynihan Report) that set off a storm of controversy.[36] In the report, Moynihan argued that black communities were deteriorating and that the cause was the breakdown of traditional family structures, as suggested by trends such as increasing rates of out-of-wedlock births and growing numbers of female-headed households. The root cause of the breakdown, he contended, was black male unemployment and he proposed the large-scale expansion of federal jobs programs in response. The spark of the controversy, however, was Moynihan's description of the black family as being caught in "a tangle of pathology," including its matriarchal structure, the "crushing burden on the Negro male," and the production of delinquent children.[37] Aside from the fierce reaction to this characterization from the political left by both blacks and whites, this portrait of the black family raised the fear that family allowances would create further incentives for population growth in black communities. The use of the family allowance in European countries was in fact motivated by such pronatalist reasoning.[38] The controversy over the Moynihan Report had a chilling effect on policymakers' willingness to intervene directly in the area of the black family for a nearly a generation.[39] In the coming years, the black family would still occupy a central place in welfare reform thinking but would be dealt with in more circumspect ways.

BUSINESS LEADERS AND ECONOMISTS WEIGH IN

The Chamber of Commerce Symposium

As deliberation among government experts proceeded, business leaders and professional economists also debated the goals and implications of GAI policy. In December 1966, the national office of the U.S. Chamber of Commerce convened the National Symposium on Guaranteed Income at which five prominent speakers were invited to discuss GAI proposals: Robert Theobald,

Milton Friedman, James Tobin (professor of economics at Yale), Henry Hazlitt (journalist and author), and Thomas Curtis (Republican member of the House of Representatives). The *New Republic* reported that the attention devoted to GAI plans by the chamber signaled that this "crazy" idea was beginning to be seen as respectable.[40]

The symposium was notable for two reasons. The U.S. Chamber of Commerce was well-known as a bastion of conservative economic ideology, so an evenhanded consideration of GAI policy illustrates that support from conservative economists, such as Friedman, was not an anomaly and that the idea was not summarily dismissed as "too liberal." At this point, the idea was ideologically ambiguous. In addition, the symposium foreshadowed many issues in the debates to come. In his prefatory remarks, the chamber's executive vice president noted the novelty of GAI, its far-reaching importance, its perceived inevitability as a legislative item, and the fact that the chamber held no policy position on the issue.

> [Guaranteed income] is being advanced not only by the so-called new liberals, the new reformers, but also by some of those who can be described as liberals in the traditional sense. . . . This proposal is a new type of thinking, or at least a comparatively new kind of thinking for America. It is a sort of startling idea to think of getting paid whether you are working or not. It catches the imagination. And it arouses emotions, of course. Up until now it [has not been] a legislative issue. But sooner or later, it will be.
>
> . . . [B]ecause the guaranteed income proposal is so new and so different, and because we, as yet, know so little about it—about where it might lead economically, socially, or politically—the business community as represented by the National Chamber has no policy position on this proposal.[41]

Three of the participants—Theobald, Tobin, and Friedman—argued in favor of GAI plans. Their discussions, however, illustrated the multiple understandings of the idea, both in regard to policy details, relation to welfare rights, and policy justification. Theobald presented what he termed a radical vision of welfare reform, Tobin discussed a politically liberal one (similar in many ways to the understandings of guaranteed income at the OEO), and Friedman presented the libertarian vision of his NIT.

First, the participants did not support the same types of GAI proposals. Theobald presented his version of a flat income grant that would go to all citizens. Tobin and Friedman, in contrast, proposed versions of an NIT. One of the main distinctions they drew between the NIT and Theobald's flat grant was the NIT's retention of work incentives. Friedman further argued that an NIT could be viewed as either liberal or conservative, depending on the break-even point (the earnings cutoff under which a filing unit paid no taxes) and the guaranteed income (the minimum income a filing unit was guaranteed under the system). The higher these amounts were set, the more liberal a program would look, even though the delivery mechanism, the NIT itself, would remain the same.

Second, they discussed the relationship between rights and the welfare system in markedly different ways, particularly on the issue of whether the current system already contained a right to income security or whether GAI was a substantial break with the past. Theobald contended that "the guaranteed income concept states that each individual or family should receive a set level of income as an absolute right" and that this marked a revolutionary shift in economic and social thinking because it broke the traditional linkage between work and income.[42] He emphasized GAI as a way of ensuring income rights. Tobin disagreed: "I don't think we should regard the idea as a radical departure, since it was some 30 years ago or more that the United States finally faced up to the fact that it would be a government responsibility, in the last analysis, to see that people have at least a minimum subsistence if they didn't have any other way."[43] He also argued that many of the poor did not in fact have access to minimum subsistence because the current system did not adequately deal with procedural and eligibility rights. Friedman went farther in opposing Theobald than Tobin: "The elementary and basic fact is that we now have in this country a guaranteed income. There can be no two minds about that. The fact is that we now have a collection of governmental programs that guarantee individuals in this country a level of consumption below which they will not be permitted to fall. . . . The problem is that it's a terrible system."[44]

Third, the three participants, not surprisingly, justified their proposals on different grounds. For Theobald, a GAI plan was necessary because the full-employment paradigm on which the existing welfare system was based was in crisis. Most people agreed that employment levels could not dip below 4 percent because of inflationary pressures, but this left millions of people in poverty. Moreover, technological change and the lack of skill among minority groups made things worse. Automation would decrease the availability of low-wage jobs while the population of young black men was becoming less equipped to fill the jobs that remained in the labor market. While Theobald's rationale rested on a structural unemployment argument, Tobin's and Friedman's rationales utilized the emerging criticisms of the existing welfare system: it was inadequate in coverage; it did not adequately provide for the people it did cover; the administration of the system was unwieldy and costly; and it provided disincentives to work, to save, and to remain in families. Friedman objected to Theobald's characterization of the economy, agreed with Tobin on the failings of the current system, and added that it undercut private charity and represented an "intolerable degree of interference by the government with the personal lives of individuals."[45] Politically, Friedman noted, the NIT provided opponents of the existing system with an alternative system of welfare provision to propose in its place. Both Tobin and Friedman cited evidence that if much of the current system were fully replaced by an NIT program, the costs of an NIT would only be moderately higher than existing government outlays, but that the new system would be far more administratively effective.

The remaining two participants—Hazlitt and Curtis—criticized the existing system but also argued against the guaranteed income concept. Both made arguments that would become prominent in the coming years and, tellingly, both invoked distinctions between the deserving and undeserving poor. Hazlitt objected to GAI plans on both economic and moral grounds. He contended that a guaranteed income system would be too expensive and detrimental to work incentives. There would be no one "willing to take a smelly job or any low-paid job."[46] This argument was diametrically opposed to Tobin's and was based on a different understanding of what constituted a "guaranteed income" and its policy details. In Hazlitt's view, the existing system *did not* already offer an income guarantee. He further argued that a GAI program would damage national domestic output, intolerably expand the reach of government, and result in an immoral redistribution of wealth. All of these criticisms were premised on a vision of the poor that viewed them as shiftless, unworthy citizens who "could refuse to seek or take a job" and might easily "throw the handout money away at the races, or spend it on prostitutes or whiskey, cigarettes, marijuana, heroin or what not."[47] Clearly Hazlitt viewed the poor as outside the mainstream American value system. Therefore it was not surprising that he opposed Friedman's laissez-faire approach to providing freedom for the poor to do with the money as they wished.

Curtis provided a slightly more moderate account of his criticisms, explicitly grounding it within the culture of poverty thesis. He, too, did not view the poor as sharing in the values of mainstream society. Poverty, he argued, was not simply the economic problem that Friedman's presentation implied. Therefore a solution based on income transfers would not address the central problem. In fact, he felt that it would have the opposite effect of perpetuating poverty. A GAI program would have other problems as well. According to Curtis, it would slow economic growth by removing incentives to work and save, it would be difficult to administer, and it would further divide society between those who held middle-class values and those who lived within the "subculture of poverty."[48] These arguments suggested that the disagreement between supporters and opponents of GAI plans were fundamental.

Business Leaders, Civic Unrest, and Work Incentives

As proposals for a negative income tax received more public attention over the next two years, the business community became increasingly involved in the deliberation process and many business leaders came to support NIT proposals. In what became an influential gathering, New York governor Nelson Rockefeller convened a group of national business leaders in 1967 to discuss "new approaches to public welfare in the United States" as part of the one-hundredth anniversary of the state's Board of Social Welfare.[49] Rockefeller said that he assembled business leaders to discuss welfare policy because he believed the private sector was the nation's source of ingenuity and that the social upheaval facing the country called for such innovative thinking. The participants, known as the Arden House group, consisted of heads of such organizations as Xerox, Metropolitan Life Insurance, the New York Stock Exchange, Inland Steel, Mobile Oil, and the Ford Motor Company. After a year of deliberation they issued a position paper favoring a GAI program among other policy recommendations.[50]

The problem, as the report emphasized, was that despite almost full employment, nearly thirty million Americans were classified as poor, only eight million of whom received public assistance. This fostered civic unrest and urban blight, and "unless our country, including the northern cities, solves the problem of the slum areas, the nation stands in danger of being torn apart."[51] The report recommended a negative income tax plan because it accomplished a number of objectives: it combined financial assistance with a national minimum standard; it contained strong work incentives; and its administration through the IRS would be more efficient and effective than the current welfare delivery system. These reasons matched those outlined by economists such as Milton Friedman and James Tobin.

The backdrop for the Arden House report, as its language suggested, was heightened concern about social turmoil. A wave of urban riots swept the country between 1964 and 1968, beginning with major urban disruptions in Harlem and Watts. In 1966 there were thirty-eight riots. In the following year, the urban unrest reached its height: during the first nine months of the year there were 164 riots, the most destructive of which happened in Newark and Detroit.[52] The unrest in these two cities lasted for nearly a week. As Detroit burned, a leader of the emerging Black Power movement threatened more of the same in the absence of a national response to black outrage: "If America don't come around, we're going to burn it down."[53] The violence continued into 1968, following the assassination of Martin Luther King, Jr., as Baltimore, Chicago, and Washington each saw major outbreaks of burning, rioting, and looting.

This urban disruption, along with the responses it engendered, strengthened the association between black insurgency and GAI plans. Shortly after King's death, civil rights leaders proceeded with his plan to mount a large-scale march on Washington as part of the Poor People's Campaign to alleviate poverty. Fifty thousand protesters showed up in June to hear Ralph Abernathy, the new leader of King's movement, invoke Old Testament imagery and declare that the movement would "plague the Pharaohs of this nation with plague after plague until they agree to give us meaningful jobs and a guaranteed annual income."[54] During the same period, the Kerner Commission, which had been appointed by President Johnson to study the origins of the civic disruptions, issued a highly publicized report that contained recommendations for preventing further violence. The report began on a dire note, stating that its most basic conclusion was that "the nation is moving toward two societies, one black, one white—separate and unequal."[55] According to the commission's analysis, the major sources of urban unrest included rampant racial discrimination and chronic underemployment in the black community. As part of its package of policy responses, it outlined guidelines for a comprehensive overhaul of existing antipoverty programs. The report said that the government's long-range objective should be a GAI plan that provided a basic floor of economic security for all Americans based on need alone.[56]

Above and beyond these concerns about urban unrest, the realization that must have come to business leaders, such as those who participated in the Arden House conference, was that implementation of a GAI plan appeared to align with their economic interests. As George Stigler had first noted in the 1950s, an NIT administered to both the unemployed and employed poor was a wage supplement that provided an alternative to the minimum wage, which was unpopular throughout the business community. Moreover, income maintenance programs such as the NIT recognized that low-wage work was inevitable, but they socialized the costs of low-wage work without the risks of inflation that economists worried would come with wage increases. Because the NIT was a cash-based system, as opposed to being service-based, it worked according to market principles that business leaders felt were more effective at distributing goods and services. It empowered consumers. And because of its graduated benefits scale, it provided work incentives that were lacking in the current system, thereby promising to bring more people into the labor force.[57]

The Arden House group ended up being influential beyond its original purposes for a number of reasons. First, the report's recommendation for an NIT plan was discussed prominently in the *New York Times*, placing the plans once again squarely in the public eye. Second, Nelson Rockefeller would come to play a substantial role in the development and politics of Nixon's GAI proposal a year later, and he and his staff gained considerable background knowledge on the issue of welfare and income maintenance through their involvement in the meeting. Third, leaders from the business community were likewise informed about the details of GAI policy and many made their views clear to Nixon in other venues. Fourth, Daniel Patrick Moynihan, among other experts, was involved with the Arden House group as an expert consultant on poverty issues, and he became one of the chief advocates of GAI proposals in Nixon's White House. He was able to assure Nixon of business support for his plan. Fifth, the Committee on Economic Development (CED) devoted its public policy forum in 1968 to the issue of welfare policy. The CED relied heavily on the recommendations of the Arden House report and it reconvened many members of the Arden House steering committee to meet with the CED trustees and other participants. Sixth, and finally, the steering committee shared its data and recommendations with a commission that President Johnson appointed to study the issue of income maintenance in depth. This commission would end up proposing a very similar set of policy recommendations in its final report.

Economists Publicly Support GAI Plans

A month after the media coverage of the Arden House report, over 1,200 economists publicly made the case that proposals for a GAI plan were economically sound, fiscally feasible, and socially desirable. In May 1968, this group endorsed a statement calling for a "national system of income guarantees and supplements." It further mentioned that similar proposals had been adopted by the Poor People's Campaign, the Arden House group, and the Kerner Commission. Coverage of the statement included a front-page article in the *New York Times*.[58] The sponsors of the statement were among the most well respected and widely known economists in the country—Paul Samuelson (MIT), John Kenneth Galbraith (Harvard), James Tobin (Yale), Harold Watts (Wisconsin), and Robert Lampman (Wisconsin)—and the signers were drawn from 125 colleges and universities. The statement described the current system as inefficient, inadequate, unfair, and punitive, and it proposed two main criteria for a new system: welfare benefits should be conditioned on need and family size; and incentives should be present for work, savings, job training, and family formation. The costs for such a plan, they stated, would be "substantial but well within the nation's economic and fiscal capacity."[59] The authors did not specify any particular type of guaranteed income plan, but a number of the most well-known signatories were on record as supporters of NIT plans and the stated emphasis on improving work incentives suggested the same.[60]

THE JOHNSON ADMINISTRATION DEFERS

During the mid-1960s, business coalitions, social unrest, fiscal strains, and pressure from welfare rights groups pushed welfare reform, and thus GAI proposals, toward the top of the domestic policy agenda. Yet a number of factors undercut support for GAI policies within the Johnson administration: the political undercurrents exposed by the midterm elections of 1966, perceptions of budgetary pressures due to the escalation of the Vietnam conflict, a debate in 1967 over amendments to the Social Security Act, and cross-cutting pressures within the Democratic Party. The 1966 midterm elections dampened the fortunes of the Democratic Party and Great Society liberalism. After this point, the popular support Johnson had enjoyed during his first couple of years in office waned considerably.[61] Republicans picked up three governorships, three Senate seats, and forty-seven seats in the House of Representatives. Some commentators viewed this as a reaction to Johnson's Great Society programs, particularly to the perception that the administration devoted too much money and attention to programs that seemed to benefit primarily racial minorities. This apparent backlash coupled racial antagonisms with concern about the economy. The country was experiencing growing inflationary pressures and rising interest rates. Concerns over racial integration, such as open housing policies, were mounting in cities across the country, and the rhetoric of keeping the streets safe euphemistically referred to the increasing incidents of black urban rioting, some of which required intervention by the National Guard and the U.S. Army. By the autumn of 1967, polls showed that Johnson had the lowest presidential approval ratings since Truman during the Korean War.[62] This did not suggest propitious timing for an untried and potentially controversial welfare reform proposal.

Vietnam and its drain on the federal budget contributed to this state of affairs. By 1966, more than 500,000 Americans were involved in the conflict in Vietnam and spending was increasing rapidly. The cost of fighting skyrocketed to $20 billion and the federal deficit, instead of being $1.8 billion, as was widely reported, was actually $9 billion. Foreign spending dramatically undercut Johnson's confidence in his ability to finance his domestic agenda. The reality of this trade-off, however, was more complex. On the one hand, it was true that antipoverty spending had been high during 1964–65, only to be subsequently cut as war spending increased. On the other hand, the Vietnam War did not limit spending on social welfare programs as much as people felt that it would at the time. Between 1965 and 1976, expenditures on social welfare programs rose at an annual rate of 7.2 percent (in constant dollars), as opposed to 4.2 percent between 1950 and 1965. Such spending was 7.7 percent of the GNP in 1960 and 16 percent by 1974. These expenditures, however, went mainly toward non-means-tested programs, such as Social Security and Medicare, and in-kind public assistance programs, like Medicaid. Means-tested income transfer programs, such as the existing AFDC system, were less popular and thus more susceptible to fiscal constraints. In sum, the impact of Vietnam spending was to aggravate growing animosity toward welfare spending on the poor, but the constraints were as much ideological as fiscal.[63]

A congressional struggle over antipoverty legislation in 1967 established the template for debates over Nixon's GAI program two years later. The shift in the country's mood, along with changing governmental leadership, had resulted in a congressional culture that was increasingly antagonistic toward the poor. This was first made apparent in a series of 1967 legislative actions concerning crime and housing.[64] More important, the same held true for welfare legislation, as illustrated in the debates over the 1967 Social Security amendments, the centerpiece of which was the Work Incentive Program (WIN). The WIN program was a congressional response to concerns about the rising number of people on the welfare rolls and about fears that the current welfare system dampened the motivation to work. Between 1960 and 1967, the number of people receiving AFDC had almost doubled and politicians at the state level, where AFDC was financed and administered, complained that their monetary outlays were becoming intolerably high. The WIN proposal included a number of different features for reforming welfare that involved both incentives and coercion.

The incentives were increased day care funding to help mothers enter into the workforce and an "earnings disregard" that allowed recipients to keep the first $30 of each paycheck plus a third of the remaining amount above $30. Proponents hoped that the earnings disregards would provide greater work incentives because recipients would be able to keep more of their paychecks. The coercive element was a work requirement—or "workfare" as opponents began to call it—that stipulated that most welfare beneficiaries would lose their benefits if they failed to participate in work or training programs without "good cause." However, the addition of the work stipulation, a product of concerns about the work ethic and a permissive welfare system, was directly at odds with the original intentions of the AFDC system, which aimed to help mothers stay at home to raise their children. WIN demanded that recipients work, and thus it represented the beginning of a significant philosophical shift in the way in which Americans thought about the functions of welfare, particularly for women. It also illustrated the growing sense among some members of Congress that many mothers receiving AFDC benefits were not fully deserving of government assistance.[65]

The NWRO, which mainly included black, female AFDC recipients, reacted sharply to the Work Incentive Program, calling it "WIP" (its more accurate acronym) in reference to both the work orientation of the amendments and to evoke the imagery of the slave driver's whip. Due in considerable part to the NWRO's involvement, the politics of the legislation took on racial overtones. During the spring and summer there had been a series of civil disturbances by black protesters, including destructive rioting in Detroit and Newark. The NWRO brought similar, though more mild, strategies of disruption and protest to the debates over WIN, marking the first of such strategies to be used in fights over a federal welfare bill. Within this volatile context, some members of Congress reacted with equivalent, racially coded vehemence, including one senator in a congressional hearing who infamously referred to the disruptive NWRO representatives there to testify as "female broodmares" bearing out-of-wedlock children at the expense of taxpayers. The confrontation over WIN established a precedent for animosity between the NWRO and Congress (and, to a lesser extent, the White House) that would repeat itself during the debates over Nixon's proposal. The NWRO would strongly oppose the Nixon plan, calling it inadequate, regressive, and racist, and the tone of this opposition had its immediate roots in the feelings of distrust and animosity that developed in the struggle over the 1967 amendments.[66]

Soon after the debate over the WIN amendments, President Johnson appointed a commission to study comprehensive welfare reform strategies. In January 1968, he created the President's Commission on Income Maintenance after over a year's delay in his public promise to appoint such a group. The commission would later announce its support of a GAI proposal just months after Nixon announced his own GAI plan in 1969, and the members of the commission's research team developed close ties with the policy experts in the Nixon administration. The appointment of this commission was the only step Johnson took toward a GAI policy, one that was, by all accounts, taken with reluctance.[67]

Despite strong interest within the government bureaucracy, Johnson and high-level administration officials had reasons to oppose GAI policy. Johnson had studiously ignored the recommendations of the Kerner Commission, which included calls for a GAI plan, because he interpreted them as a repudiation of his War on Poverty programs.[68] The income-based approach to public assistance found in GAI plans was philosophically at odds with the service-based approach of the Great Society, which in turn was rooted in the New Deal programs of the 1930s. Wilbur Cohen, Johnson's secretary at HEW in 1968, was likewise committed to existing New Deal approaches. So while many lower-level experts within the agency supported GAI plans, the agency's leader did not. If political support for GAI policy was not forthcoming from HEW, it was unclear where it would be found within the administration. It was unlikely to be at the OEO, despite that fact that GAI plans had more interest there than anywhere else in Washington, as exemplified by the agency's massive efforts to field the NIT experiments. The office had been embattled since 1966, largely because of opposition to Community Action, Legal Services, and other "empowerment" programs that became the flashpoints for controversy.[69] As a result of these various battles, the OEO's leadership lacked additional political capital to expend on GAI legislation.

Few core Democratic interest groups supported GAI policy. The centrality of the social service strategy within the War on Poverty meant that social workers, public interest attorneys, and many government bureaucrats held a vested interest in maintaining the current system. In many versions of GAI proposals, especially those espoused by conservatives, one of the express objectives of the plan was to eradicate the social work and social service bureaucracy from the public assistance system. Labor leaders were not receptive to the proposals because they feared GAI programs would institutionalize low wage levels and undermine their collective bargaining power. Segments of the civil rights movement, such as the Poor People's Campaign, supported the principles of a GAI plan. However, since 1966 the Johnson administration had been trying to distance itself from its close association with the interests of black America. Many welfare recipients themselves, such as the members of the NWRO, experienced a sense of betrayal at the hands of congressional Democrats in Congress with the passage of the 1967 Social Security amendments, so this strained relations between GAI's main constituents and a likely set of political allies.[70]

Guaranteed income policies played only a limited role in the politics of the 1968 presidential campaign. In the spring of that year, President Johnson decided not to run for reelection, which opened up the field for Democratic presidential contenders. Senator Hubert Humphrey, a liberal from Minnesota, eventually emerged as the party's candidate. He had been an early advocate of civil rights long before it became a nationally popular issue, yet he kept the aims of civil rights leaders, who increasingly called for GAI programs, at a greater distance during the campaign as he positioned himself nationally for the presidential race.[71] The NWRO called for a $4,000 guaranteed income floor at a Democratic platform meeting, but received only a very measured response.[72] Richard Nixon, the Republican nominee, explicitly opposed the idea of a guaranteed income while on the campaign trail, saying, "I do not see a reasonable prospect that I will recommend . . . a guaranteed annual income or a negative income tax."[73] And for George Wallace, the independent party candidate from Alabama, the idea of a GAI policy that might empower poor blacks in the South was unthinkable.

In November 1968, Nixon won by a very narrow margin over Humphrey—by less than one percentage point in the popular vote—even though he had run ahead of him by up to twenty-four points during the campaign.[74] Nixon ran a strong campaign against Johnson's Great Society liberalism, but his slender victory convinced him not to abandon Johnson's programmatic commitments but instead refashion them with his own ideas and rhetoric. Nixon saw himself as a conservative who could embrace liberal policies, if they suited his ends.[75] Part of this thinking was illustrated by his attraction a year later to the argument outlined in Richard Scammon and Ben Wattenberg's book, *The Real Majority*.[76] The authors claimed that New Deal liberalism was not dead. In fact, it was still the reigning domestic doctrine, but it had nevertheless been sullied through recent associations with welfarism, antiwar protest, black militancy, and leniency on crime. The next successful political coalition, they contended, would distance itself from these connotations and focus on white, middle America. This argument had particular resonance after a presidential campaign in which Wallace, a southern racist, had received nearly 13 percent of the popular vote. What was unforeseeable at the time was that Nixon would soon advocate a GAI plan. But his efforts to sell it as a policy to assist the white working class, the "forgotten Americans," would indelibly color the perceptions of GAI, and welfare reform more generally, in the years to come.

"An Idea Whose Time Has Come"?: Public Discourse on GAI Plans

In June 1968, when the presidential campaign was in full swing, Paul Samuelson wrote in one of his *Newsweek* columns that the political prospects for NIT proposals looked good. Any proposal, he argued, that commanded support from both Milton Friedman and John Kenneth Galbraith "must have a lot going for it." After describing the outlines of such proposals and making the case that Congress was likely to take one up in the near future, he closed his column with a quote from Victor Hugo: "Stronger than all the armies in the world . . . is an idea whose time has come."[77] Samuelson, one of the most prominent economists in the country, had signed the open letter in support of GAI proposals weeks earlier, so his sympathy for the idea was clear. But he was not alone in his assessment that GAI plans appeared to be on the path to legislative inevitability. Remarking on support for GAI proposals from across the political spectrum, the editors at the *New Republic* concurred, noting that the United States was the only Western industrial nation without an income maintenance program for families. Both *U.S. News and World Report* and *Newsweek* ran evenhanded stories on the pros and cons of NIT plans. Each compared liberal and conservative versions of the proposals, and *Newsweek* concluded by quoting Galbraith's statement that "it only takes three years for a good idea to become a human right."[78]

Indeed, a mere three years earlier GAI plans had been scarcely mentioned in public discourse but now the idea was presented as all but inevitable. To the average American, the change must have been sudden. News stories in the *New York Times* (as reported in the introductory chapter) presented a fragmented picture of GAI plans during this period, one that reflected the multiple ways in which various groups framed the proposals. What images of GAI proposals did magazine stories, which contain more in-depth commentary and sustained argument, create in the public mind?

One pronounced absence in the magazine coverage was the mainstream critique of the "economic growth" strategy for fighting poverty that had led experts to develop GAI plans in the first place. Experts within Kennedy's Council of Economic Advisors and Johnson's antipoverty agencies had proposed GAI policies in light of their realization that some segments of the poor would never be likely to climb out of poverty through economic growth alone and that many *employed* persons still lived in poverty because existing wage levels in many job sectors were too low to pull them out. This was also the argument made by the members of the Arden House group. But this principal rationale for GAI proposals rarely appeared in the news media, including the weekly news magazines, and when it did, it was seldom voiced by temperate-sounding commentators, such as the government economists or business leaders who held this view.

Instead, when such views received press coverage at all, they came from people or groups on the margins of the mainstream. Robert Theobald was one such person. In 1967, he published an article in the *New Republic* provocatively titled "The Goal of Full Unemployment."[79] Reprising his arguments from earlier in the decade, he heralded a new postindustrial economic order and argued that it required a new set of social policies. Drawing attention to the urban unrest of the recent years, he argued that overall economic growth had not improved the employment situation in Watts, the site of one of the decade's most violent civil disturbances in 1965. The implication was that GAI policy could quell the continuing unrest in the nation's cities. Another marginal voice came from the welfare rights movement. The NWRO generated a fair bit of coverage in 1966 and 1967, and the "right to welfare" discourse provided a broad umbrella rubric under which to discuss the GAI idea, as exemplified in a three-part series of opinion columns in the *New York Times*.[80] This coverage of the NWRO contained some of the same criticisms of the existing labor market as those enumerated by respected poverty experts. Yet the provenance of these claims from marginalized social movements coupled with their claims for economic entitlements produced media coverage that emphasized "rights" rather than problems with the labor market or wage structure.[81]

Two themes in articles on GAI policy that *did* sit squarely in the political mainstream were criticisms of the existing welfare system and a focus on work behavior (rather than labor market conditions). In regard to critiques of the existing system, there was a shift during this period from an emphasis on adequacy to a focus on perverse effects. The balance of early coverage of problems with the existing welfare system emphasized problems mainly from the recipients' point of view: inadequate coverage, meager benefit levels, oppressive amounts of surveillance, social stigma, and the like. These were the sorts of claims that poverty lawyers levied against the system and that welfare rights activists sought to bring to the public's attention. However, by the time that GAI proposals appeared "inevitable" in 1968, most of the problems associated with the existing system were linked either to the perverse incentive structures that government experts argued were present in the existing AFDC program or to problems associated with welfare activism itself, such as expansion of welfare caseloads and rising welfare costs. This shifted the locus of attention from systemic problems in coverage and implementation to the individual behavior of the poor—namely, their response to various types of incentives—and the problems associated with the demands they placed on local welfare provision.

The second theme to appear in much of the coverage was work. During this period, both supporters and opponents of GAI proposals framed their positions in reference to how GAI plans would affect the work behavior of the poor. James Tobin and Leon Keyserling each made the case for a GAI program on the basis of its effects on work effort. Tobin preferred the NIT over family allowance proposals because it contained stronger work incentives. Keyserling advocated a GAI program for the unemployable that could be coupled with a guaranteed jobs program for those able to work.[82] In contrast, Henry Hazlitt reprised the arguments he made in his U.S. Chamber of Commerce talk in the *National Review*, contending that it was immoral to give government money to able-bodied people capable of working and that a GAI plan would destroy work incentives and thereby threaten the economy.[83] An article in *U.S. News and World Report* that was critical of the existing system implied that a growing number of recipients simply did not want to work. The lead sentence read, "Living on handouts at tax-payers' expense has become a way of life for many Americans," and the article identified GAI plans as the next step in such "welfarism." The article buried a quote from a Johnson administration official who reported that only 1 percent of current welfare recipients were able-bodied men.[84]

A short *Newsweek* story in July 1968 on GAI proposals tried to sum up the state of affairs. It began,

> To an American steeped in the ethic of an honest wage for an honest day's work, the notion of a guarantee of income for each citizen—worker and shirker alike—has always seemed repugnant. Why give the shiftless and lazy a free ride? Yet, the unrest of the ghettos, the inadequacies of the welfare system, and the failure to mount an effective jobs program for the hardcore unemployed have created a new ethic of necessity. At the moment, the concept of a guaranteed income is enjoying an astonishing vogue.[85]

This opening succinctly highlighted the sense of social crisis and the perceived failures of the existing system. Notably, the distinction between workers and "shirkers," or between the deserving and undeserving poor, suggested that GAI plans would give "shirkers" a free ride rather than address problems in the labor market. This framing ignored ample evidence that the poor were willing to work but that structural unemployment was a considerable problem and that most welfare recipients were not able-bodied men.

In the face of these problems, why did GAI policies now seem to be the best answer? Friedman provided the most tenable explanation in one of his *Newsweek* columns.

> The widespread interest is remarkable. But the appearance of growing agreement—of support for a negative income tax by the right and the left, by businessmen and professors, by Republicans and Democrats—is highly misleading. In large part it reflects the use of the same term to describe very different plans.[86]

Friedman's column went on to show how differences in the details of NIT plans—regarding the minimum income guarantee level, the break-even point, the presence of a work requirement, the scope of coverage, and the programs such a plan was proposed to replace—held vastly different consequences for the redistribution of wealth, the streamlining of government, the emphasis placed on work effort, and many other issues. In other words, these details determined the ideological affinities of GAI plans. In the following year, the introduction of GAI legislation would force supporters to compete with each other over the specification of these types of details, thus cracking the veneer of agreement that existed in 1968.

Conclusion

Two somewhat distinct processes help account for the air of inevitability associated with GAI plans by 1968. First, poverty analysts within key governmental agencies continued to forge ahead with NIT plans, launching a series of experiments to assess their impact on labor market behavior and family structure, even though Johnson and other administration officials failed to lend their support to the plans. The social unrest of the era, including both uncoordinated civil disturbances and coordinated movement activism, pushed antipoverty policy, and therefore GAI proposals, higher on the nation's agenda. Taken together, this meant that both sympathetic government actors with resources and grassroots mobilization played an important role in the continuing rise of the proposals. Second, the number of problems connected to GAI plans expanded once the idea entered into public consciousness. Prior to this period, most GAI supporters favored the plans because they addressed labor market problems or the inadequacy of existing public assistance programs. However, increasing public attention to GAI plans resulted in new associations. Experts drew attention to perverse incentives for laziness, family breakup, and interstate migration present in the design of the existing AFDC program; activists created a new lexicon of "welfare rights"; and the federal takeover of public assistance costs contained in most GAI proposals looked like a way for states to deal with their mounting welfare costs. The prospects for GAI plans looked favorable because the plans meant different things to different people.

Notably, as GAI proposals received more attention from a wider public audience, they were consistently defined as "welfare" plans, even though they did not contain only the AFDC, or "welfare," population. As the media coverage suggested, this worked to the proposals' advantage in the short term, as frustration with the existing system ran higher and higher and "welfare reform" seemed imperative. Nixon encountered this frustration early on in office, leading him to advance his own version of a GAI program quite unexpectedly. Yet in the longer term, the focus on problems in the welfare system deflected attention from the structural problems in the economy that had earlier concerned government experts. This laid the foundation for more conservative proposals to address what many saw as the mounting welfare crisis.

CHAPTER THREE

The Origins and Transformation of the Nixon Plan

When Richard Nixon took office in January 1969, few people could have predicted that seven months later he would propose a guaranteed annual income (GAI) program. Nixon's proposal was surprising because little foreshadowed it. On the campaign trail for president a year earlier, he had explicitly opposed GAI plans and Nixon's political party, the Republican Party, was not associated with domestic programs for the poor. Given this background, the first question this chapter will address is, why did the Nixon administration come to propose a GAI policy? Though Nixon surprised both his supporters and detractors with his proposal, it differed from the GAI plans developed during the Johnson years. These differences played a central role in his plan's political fortunes once he publicly announced it. So the second question this chapter addresses is, how and why were both the substance and symbolism of GAI policy transformed during the first six months of Nixon's presidency? To answer both of these questions I examine the internal debates over Nixon's plan within the presidential administration to reconstruct perceptions of the plan by the policymakers who fought over and shaped its development.

Neither Nixon nor the Republican Party was associated with the "reform-oriented" characteristics that would lead to expectations that the Nixon administration would launch a major, comprehensive antipoverty policy overhaul that increased government spending and extended benefits to new recipients.[1] However, Nixon faced a number of pressures for reform. The urban riots of the previous years had created a great deal of concern among many groups about social turmoil and unrest. The administration had, of course, not yet realized that the worst of the unrest was already behind them. Welfare rights activists also created civil disturbances, but the main consequence of their activism was growth in the AFDC rolls and thus increasing antipoverty expenditures. The institutional design of the AFDC program meant that state governments bore the bulk of these costs. So in contrast to conventional expectations that American federalism inhibits welfare state growth, in this case it created pressure for federal expansion. State and local leaders wanted a full federal takeover of program payments. Furthermore, the porous nature of the policy development process meant that a variety of stakeholder groups, such as business coalitions and civic organizations, in conjunction with local government officials, effectively applied pressure on Nixon to address what was increasingly referred to as the "welfare mess." These groups lobbied for reform because they associated it with fiscal policy and urban policy as much as with antipoverty policy.

Despite the considerable pressures that the Nixon administration felt to address problems in the AFDC system, the adoption of a GAI proposal was not inevitable. There was considerable disagreement within the administration about the direction that policy change should take. The first proposal for reform that Nixon's advisors advanced called for incremental changes only. Similarly, the presidential advisor who ultimately became the strongest advocate for GAI plans within the administration did not initially favor them. It was government experts retained from the Johnson administration who put a GAI proposal into the mix of policy options shortly after Nixon took office. Once on the agenda, GAI proposals became fiercely contested within the administration. Opponents tried repeatedly to sabotage the idea in favor of programs that cut costs and tightened eligibility requirements.

The stakes in these debates were high and the issues under consideration were discussed with an unusual degree of candor and intensity because the country's traditional welfare philosophy had rarely been so directly challenged. The debate was notable for a few reasons—the breadth of issues raised by comprehensive welfare reform, the range of government officials involved in the debate, and the sense of urgency with which reform was undertaken. The central issue was the meaning of "welfare" itself. Guaranteed income proposals erased the existing symbolic and programmatic boundaries between the "welfare" population receiving AFDC and populations either receiving other types of benefits or no benefits at all, such as the working poor. This raised a host of questions. Would new government benefits for the working poor under a GAI program render them in a state of dependency? Would these payments be "welfare" payments? Should receiving government benefits be stigmatizing for the recipient? Should Nixon's GAI program be considered a "welfare" program or was it a new type of social provision altogether? These questions stemmed from the symbolic pollution entailed by placing categories of people with different moral statuses in the same program. The nature of these questions threw the definition of "welfare" wide open.

Additional dimensions of the debate were also relevant. These concerned issues regarding the causes of poverty, the main problems with the existing system, the primary goal of reform, the economic rationality of the poor, and the definition of poverty as either a monetary or cultural phenomenon. The debate over these issues might have been straightforward to understand politically had there been only two groups with distinct and opposing viewpoints fighting over reform. But such was not the case. There were four policy paradigms within the administration, and they had cross-cutting and overlapping premises and perspectives (see table 1). Three of these paradigms favored GAI policies while one opposed them. Each represented a different overarching vision of welfare reform's meaning and goals.[2]

TABLE 1
Competing Welfare Reform Paradigms

	Economic citizenship	Family stability	Laissez-faire	Rehabilitation
Position on GAI policy	support	support	support	oppose
Locus of problem	labor market	social system	welfare system	individual behavior
Existing welfare system	inadequate	destructive	irrational	permissive
Primary reform goal	income security	family stability	labor market participation	rehabilitation
Attribution of rationality	weak	weak	strong	inconsistent
Definition of poverty	monetary	cultural	monetary	cultural
Ideological affinity	liberal	moderate/ neoconservative	libertarian/ conservative	conservative
Exemplar	OEO experts	Moynihan	Shultz	Burns

The first was an *economic citizenship* paradigm, which was the perspective that underpinned the original formulation of NIT policies early in the Johnson administration at the OEO. As discussed in previous chapters, the early advocates of GAI policy viewed it as a way to ameliorate the effects of structural unemployment and inadequate wage levels. Such a program would provide economic security for those who could not attain it solely through their labor market participation. The economic citizenship model took both radical and moderate forms: the radical form was advanced by people such as Robert Theobald who intended GAI policy to pave the way toward the decommodification of labor; the moderate form was illustrated by the experts within the Johnson administration who viewed the NIT as the most efficient and effective way to ensure income maintenance for all. Both the radical and moderate versions viewed poverty as a monetary condition, viewed the existing welfare system as inadequate, and defined the ultimate goal of welfare restructuring as ending poverty.

A second source of support for GAI was a *family stability* paradigm. This was rooted in the culture of poverty perspective and viewed the social system— particularly family instability—as the proximate source of poverty. (Some experts who held this viewpoint further considered unemployment to be the source of family breakdown, but they viewed the family as the locus of welfare policy intervention.) Family instability was further exacerbated by incentives for marital breakup in the existing system. From this perspective, the main goal of welfare reform was to improve families' economic conditions and remove incentives for having children out of wedlock and for fathers to abandon their children. This perspective in some ways struck a middle ground between those who located the source of problems within the economic system and those who focused on problems of individual behavior. Because of their primary concerns about parental stability and needy children, individuals from this perspective typically favored family allowances over NIT programs.

A third source of support for GAI plans came from a *laissez-faire* perspective. This was based on a monetary definition of poverty and held that the most effective way to end poverty was through a direct income transfer program that contained work incentives. Adherents of this view opposed work requirements because they were coercive. Welfare recipients were viewed as rational actors and the welfare system itself was held to be the primary source of poverty because of its irrational incentives structure. This was a libertarian-conservative orientation and it laid little blame for poverty at the feet of welfare recipients themselves; they were seen as simply reacting rationally to a perverse set of incentives—mainly the incentive not to work. The goal of welfare reform was therefore to restructure these incentives with the aim of moving welfare participants into the labor market.

The fourth was a *rehabilitation* perspective. Unlike the other three perspectives, individuals who held this view *opposed* GAI policies because they felt these policies did not aim to rehabilitate welfare recipients. In this view, the poor did not share mainstream values such as the work ethic and individual responsibility, nor did the existing welfare system or GAI proposals reinforce these values. Both were seen as too permissive. Since the deviant behavior of the poor in this view was not rooted in the structure of the economic, social, or welfare systems but was inherent in the character of the poor themselves, advocates of rehabilitationist reform called for policies aimed at behavior modification. Their favored programs contained compulsory measures that instilled the "appropriate" work and family ethics in the poor.

Each of these paradigms contained a causal story that located the sources of poverty in a different place. The three that favored GAI plans also favored erasing the boundaries between the deserving and undeserving poor, though for different reasons. For proponents of the economic citizenship and family stability paradigms, erasing these boundaries was intentional. For proponents of the laissez-faire paradigm, it was a secondary byproduct of a more rational program design. Opponents of GAI plans, on the other hand, wanted the categorical distinctions drawn between poor people and the stigma that reinforced these distinctions strictly maintained.

Somewhat remarkably, GAI proposals did not evoke strong ideological reactions from most administration officials, with a few notable exceptions, during the early months of consideration. Early critics who opposed it did so for pragmatic rather than ideological reasons. It took active claims-making on the part of the plan's fiercest opponents to link the boundary transgression contained in Nixon's plan to high stakes outcomes such as concerns about damaging the nation's economic productivity. These claims, premised on beliefs about symbolic pollution, were influential because they resonated with the existing template of categorical welfare provision. Over the course of the summer, policy entrepreneurs on all sides of the debate worked hard to define the ideological affinities and political implications of GAI proposals.

This maneuvering resulted in two changes in the policy's aims that held significant implications for Nixon's plan. The first concerned the population GAI plans intended to benefit. This target population shifted, both symbolically and in program design, from unemployed blacks to working poor whites. This shift occurred because of diminishing concerns about racial violence, the unintended consequences of program development, and a political strategy aimed at appealing to ethnic, working-class whites. The second shift was a move away from exclusive reliance on work incentives toward reliance on compulsory work requirements to channel people into the labor force. This change was a concession to conservative opponents of the Nixon plan within the administration. The result of these two changes was a final proposal that contained internal contradictions between substance and symbolism. On one hand, the majority of the benefits in Nixon's August proposal were aimed at the nation's working poor, who were largely white. However, Nixon's rhetoric repeatedly contained derogatory references to the deficient morality of welfare recipients who, in the minds of most Americans, were stereotypically black. This contradiction meant that neither working-class whites nor unemployed blacks—most of whom would have materially benefited from the program—had strong reasons to support the plan: the white working class did not want to receive stigmatized "welfare" benefits and black recipients considered the plan demeaning and punitive.

The "Welfare Mess"

To understand how Nixon came to propose a GAI plan, it is important to recognize his administration's intellectual legacy from the Johnson administration. Through the retention and subsequent influence of Johnson-era policy experts, this legacy directly shaped the development of Nixon's plan. Two groups—the Task Force on Public Welfare and the newly created White House office of the Urban Affairs Council—played early roles in the welfare reform process. As antipoverty plans continued to develop, the administration drew on expertise within the Department of Health, Education, and Welfare

(HEW). The admixture of ideas from these three groups set the early stage for the GAI proposal that eventually emerged.

The Initial Policy Recommendation: Incremental Reform

Five days after his election in November 1968, President-elect Nixon appointed the Task Force on Public Welfare, which was headed by Richard Nathan. The mandate of the task force was to prepare a briefing paper that would serve as a guide for poverty-related policymaking in the new White House. Nathan was a research associate at the Brookings Institution, a former member of the Kerner Commission on civil disorders, and had most recently served as chairman of Nixon's preelection task force on intergovernmental fiscal relations. The rest of the committee was staffed by a mix of Democrats and moderate Republicans. Nathan's previous governmental experiences led him to view welfare reform primarily from a fiscal perspective, which subsequently influenced the recommendations of his group.[3]

Nathan submitted his committee's recommendations at the end of December. The task force favored incremental reforms to the existing system rather than complete overhaul. The report enumerated many of the criticisms that had already been lodged against the AFDC program, but it focused heavily on two, calling the wide variation in assistance levels among states a "major weakness in public welfare" and saying that incentives for family breakup was one of the system's "basic deficiencies." As part of their solution, the task force recommended establishing national benefits and eligibility standards, federalizing welfare payments, and mandating state participation in AFDC-UP, an optional program designed to give benefits to two-parent families in which the father was unemployed. This latter recommendation, it was hoped, would decrease the incidence of marital breakup. The report noted that its recommendations contained elements that resembled revenue-sharing plans to allocate federal money to the states (a relatively new issue to which Nathan had devoted considerable time during the presidential campaign) and that welfare reform should be considered in relation to such programs.[4] The report concluded by stating that some members of the panel felt that its recommendations would not achieve the government's goals of family stability, work incentives, and efficiency, and that other measures might be required in the future, possibly a negative income tax or a family allowance. These latter recommendations, however, were not viewed as likely options for the new Republican administration.[5]

The man charged with directing antipoverty policy for the administration was Robert Finch, secretary of HEW. He favored Nathan's plan for reform and commended the report to the president.[6] Despite what may have appeared to the report's authors as a set of modest proposals, Finch viewed them as establishing a bold direction in social policy. The report recommended making welfare a fully federal obligation for the first time, a move that ran counter to historical Republican social welfare priorities. According to the report, this would increase federal welfare spending by up to $1.4 billion a year. However, Finch viewed these proposals as good politics. The Nathan plan would give far greater benefits to the poor in the South, would lessen fiscal pressures on all state and local governments, and would decrease incentives for poor, unskilled workers in the South to migrate north, thereby pleasing northerners as well. In doing so, the proposal would also respond to protests lodged recently by the Poor People's Campaign against the great disparities between welfare benefits in the northern and southern states. In January 1969, news of the Nathan plan leaked to the press. Despite the administration's concern over how the proposal would be received, most of the coverage was favorable.

Welfare Reform as Urban Policy

While the Nathan recommendations percolated down the administrative ranks at HEW, the White House set up antipoverty efforts elsewhere as well. President Nixon's first executive act was establishing the Urban Affairs Council (UAC). The UAC was to be the domestic policy analog to the role served by the National Security Council in foreign affairs. Its charge was to develop a "national urban policy" and its membership was wide-ranging, including the president, the vice president, the attorney general, and the secretaries of agriculture, commerce, labor, housing and urban development, transportation, and health, education, and welfare.[7]

As the title of the council and its mandate suggested, in 1969 the nation's domestic problems were reducible in many ways to its urban problems—including those pertaining to poverty, violence, education, housing, and local budgets. Most prominent of these was racial strife. There had been a steep and steady increase in the number of civil disturbances between 1964 and 1968, and in its early months, the administration came under growing pressure from business groups to address the problems of the cities. When asked, city leaders said their main concerns were unemployment and welfare.[8] Consequently, welfare reform became a chief goal of the UAC and it was viewed through a distinctly urban lens. To be sure, as the Nathan report had discussed, there was a fiscal component of urban problems. One of the UAC's main points in its first report was that "a primary objective of federal urban policy must be to restore the fiscal stability of urban government."[9] However, more important, welfare was viewed as a cultural issue—encompassing matters such as race relations and family instability—by its executive secretary, Daniel Patrick Moynihan.

Moynihan brought an eclectic set of experiences to the job.[10] While working for the Johnson administration, he had been one of the early advocates of the family allowance and had written a controversial government report on the status of the black family (see chapter 2). In 1966, he served on a poverty task force for New York City mayor John Lindsay and in 1967 he was a consultant to Governor Nelson Rockefeller's Arden House steering committee on public welfare. This combination of experiences had consequences for his role in the UAC and his subsequent support for a GAI policy. Prior examination of the welfare system had led Moynihan to advocate its complete replacement with a family allowance; preparation of the Moynihan Report had prompted him to think about the relationships among unemployment, family structure, race, and the inner city; and work with the Lindsay and Rockefeller groups inclined him to project solutions for poverty problems onto the special case of New York City. All these factors would converge in the coming months.

In a series of early memos to the president and his administration, Moynihan painted a complicated, and sometimes contradictory, picture of what was happening in the nation's cities with regard to what Nixon would call the "welfare mess." Moynihan made the case that the cities were near the brink of irreparable breakdown. Distinguishing himself from "structuralist" thinkers (a label that included both Marxists and those in the monetary poverty camp), he argued that the crisis of the cities was "more a moral and cultural crisis than a material one. Indeed it is frequently the former that produces the latter."[11] Much of this breakdown, he contended, was due to the lack of "private sub-systems of authority" that could control members of society. A primary subsystem of authority was the family, and, as he had claimed in the Moynihan Report, the family structure in black communities (the majority community in many urban areas) was deteriorating. This breakdown, coupled with poverty and isolation, produced racial strife and constituted the "single most serious problem of the American city today."[12]

New York City was the crucible in which many of these trends were the most visible. In mid-January, Nixon read a front-page *New York Times* story containing allegations of fraud and abuse in the New York City welfare system, which he believed was characteristic of the welfare system nationally. He wrote a memo to four of his cabinet and White House staff members (including Finch and Moynihan) asking them for input on what he viewed as the pressing problem of welfare reform.[13] Moynihan recommended a set of incremental reforms that looked markedly similar to the major components of the Nathan plan: national standards and the federal requirement that all states allow families with unemployed male heads to receive welfare benefits. Most of all, Moynihan wanted to impress upon Nixon that something had to be done about the current system. In light of the accusations of fraud about which Nixon had expressed concern, Moynihan felt the system itself was even worse: "The more one knows about welfare, the more horrible it becomes: but not because of cheating, rather because the system destroys those who receive it, and corrupts those who dispense it."[14] Since writing the Moynihan Report, he had come to view the source of the problem with the black family as not only with the cultural elements he had described in the report, but also as rooted in the welfare system itself. During his tenure in the administration, Moynihan consistently equivocated on whether the sources of the poverty problem lay within the social system of the black community or the welfare system. Though he would sometimes emphasize the latter for politically expedient reasons, his overriding logic focused on ameliorating the dysfunctions of the black family through increasing income maintenance for families and employment opportunities for black men.

Johnson-Era Experts Introduce the Guaranteed Income Option

After receiving a sympathetic hearing from Finch and Moynihan, Nathan's incremental reform plan encountered its first opposition in early February. At a meeting of the UAC welfare subcommittee—which included Finch, George Shultz (secretary of labor), Clifford Hardin (secretary of agriculture), Maurice Stans (secretary of commerce), and Attorney General John Mitchell—the plan provoked sharp questioning and resistance. Though the committee did not reject the plan outright, the members wanted more details at a subsequent meeting. Nathan, who had become assistant director of the Bureau of the Budget, decided to set up a sub-cabinet task force of welfare experts to strengthen the proposal. The task force would be a joint HEW and Budget Bureau endeavor.[15]

Unbeknownst to Nathan, his attempt to save his plan by establishing this task force would have the opposite effect: it would not only doom his plan but give rise to a GAI policy within the administration. This was largely due to the composition of the welfare experts who constituted his new task force. During the previous eight years, poverty expertise had been institutionally and ideologically rooted in the Democratic Party. The social scientific approach to welfare policy was a product of work within Kennedy's CEA and Johnson's antipoverty programs, and it had hardly existed prior to 1960.[16] Outside government, poverty experts were mainly academics of a liberal persuasion with distributionist concerns. (Conservatives would not create a solid base of expertise on social policy until the early 1970s.) Therefore, when Nathan and Finch assembled their teams of welfare experts, there were few choices aside from those who were politically liberal (or at least moderate), many of whom had served in either HEW or the OEO under Johnson. This was precisely where the idea of GAI policy had been incubating.

These experts defined the GAI plan they would eventually advance as "modest," even though it was the first such plan ever to be seriously considered by any presidential administration. Nathan's sub-cabinet task force on welfare was headed by John Veneman, a liberal Republican, who joined HEW as undersecretary.[17] Providing assistance to Veneman were two others whose participation was crucial in the emergence of a GAI plan: Tom Joe and Worth Bateman. Joe, an expert on welfare in his own right, was critical of the Nathan plan because he believed that not enough money would actually be received by the poor; instead, money would mainly go to alleviate state fiscal pressures. Bateman was an outgoing HEW official from the Johnson administration who was helping Joe conduct an overall review of policy issues facing Finch and the department. Bateman was familiar with the Nathan report and likewise critical of it. He submitted a paper to Joe describing his criticisms. He felt that the inequity of treatment between male- and female-headed households would result in marital breakup and that the plan discriminated against the working poor, who might end up earning less income than would people receiving government benefits. A better proposal, he suggested, would be "a modest new program which is income tested but provides supplementary income to all families with children. The program could be staged in a way which could result in some State savings. (This is a Negative Income Tax plan for families with children, but it could be called by a different name.)"[18] Joe presented the Bateman paper, along with a number of other policy papers, to Finch and Veneman in the middle of February. In Bateman's characterization, the NIT appeared as a technical fix rather than an ideological coup.

Veneman subsequently appointed Bateman as the head of the technical team on the welfare task force. Though it was not clear whether Veneman read his discussion of the NIT, Bateman proceeded with plans to draft an NIT proposal and enlisted another former Johnson poverty expert, James Lyday, who had been the OEO's primary draftsman of NIT plans. In consultation with other former Johnson staffers they drafted the outlines of an NIT program. Other members of Veneman's subcommittee task force worked on their original aim of trying to strengthen the incremental Nathan plan. Throughout February, the work of the task force proceeded along these two different tracks: one focusing on modifying the current system according to the Nathan plan, the other focusing on structural reform of the welfare system based on an NIT program.

While these plans proceeded in Veneman's subcommittee task force, a different type of opposition to the Nathan plan, spearheaded by Arthur Burns, took shape. Burns, a former head of the CEA under Eisenhower, was one of Nixon's counsels on domestic policy, though he would soon be appointed chairman of the Federal Reserve Board. Over the course of the summer to come, he became one of the chief opponents of GAI proposals of any type, but now he was criticizing the much more moderate Nathan plan. His objections to both plans were based on similar grounds: concerns about spending, business confidence, and inflation. These political and economic concerns were reinforced by a pronounced ideological aversion to welfare, which he found antithetical to the functioning of the free market economy and the values of individualism.

These pragmatic and ideological concerns were repeatedly reflected in Burns's negative interpretation of the growing welfare rolls. In a memo to Nixon criticizing the Nathan plan and the proposal for national standards, he wrote, "Our welfare system is in serious trouble. The desire to do something—such as setting up national standards—should be resisted until we have a clearer idea of what the results may be. . . . The American people . . . want and expect you to provide the leadership toward effective reform—that is, a reduction in the number on welfare rolls."[19] In the following weeks Burns would develop a welfare reform alternative that sought to achieve these goals. It became the rival plan to Nixon's nascent GAI proposal.

As Bateman and Lyday developed their plan, their first crucial hurdle was gaining support from Veneman. To their relief, he was in favor. Joe attributed Veneman's support to his prior experience with overhauling the Medicaid system in California. As was the case with the medical system for the poor, he saw many of the problems with welfare as rooted in systemic flaws, so rather than accepting the Nathan proposal, which modified the existing system, he was receptive to more fundamental change.[20] The next step up the administrative ladder was Secretary Finch, and Veneman assisted Bateman and Lyday in selling him the proposal.

Finch's main concern was how to justify adding an estimated six million people to the welfare rolls, but he saw value in debating the merits of the plan. He appreciated the fairness with which the proposed system would treat working families, both by providing cash supplements to their work-derived earnings and by treating intact families the same as single-headed households. For him, efforts to improve work incentives and family stability were paramount for any proposed program. Lewis Butler, one of the participants in the decision making at HEW with Finch, recalled that the Bateman-Lyday plan simply seemed sensible—a technical fix for problems everyone realized were pressing: "Among most of us, I don't think it was thought of as a big deal."[21] In the technical worldview of the experts, a negative income tax appeared to be an effective solution to the welfare problem with few ideological drawbacks.

Moynihan Provides Further Support for Comprehensive Change

Moynihan was unaware of the Bateman-Lyday NIT plan until just before it was presented at the UAC meeting. But he had inadvertently prepared the groundwork for its presentation to the president through a series of memos to Nixon in which he further outlined the details of existing urban problems and the weaknesses of the existing system. Nixon was particularly intrigued by a tangential discussion in an early Moynihan memo about the decreasing correlation between unemployment rates and welfare caseloads: prior to the mid-1960s that correlation had been solid—a decrease in unemployment rates correlated strongly with a decrease in the number of people on welfare. Since the mid-1960s, Moynihan argued, this correlation had disappeared. Nixon wanted him to explain what had happened.[22]

In response, Moynihan outlined four reasons for the increase in welfare caseloads: (1) increasing acceptance rates of welfare applicants; (2) an increase in the number of unmarried mothers receiving welfare benefits (a growing percentage of whom were black); (3) changes in federal law that increased eligibility; and (4) a demographic shift to metropolitan areas.[23] In sum, he stated, "The bulk of the AFDC recipients are now made up of persons not associated with husbands or fathers with an attachment to the labor market. They are drawn from a population that is rapidly growing in size. As a result, changes in the labor market no longer affect the number of AFDC recipients."[24] Though this summary statement did not necessarily follow from his four previous points (since, for instance, AFDC recipients had always been primarily single mothers), it did reaffirm findings from studies of structural unemployment noted by Kennedy's CEA a decade earlier: the condition of some of the poor was impervious to improvements in the labor market. This was particularly true for women in female-headed households who for various reasons, such as lack of training or child care, had difficultly finding employment. Moynihan linked structural unemployment more directly to the rise of female-headed households than it had been in the past, and this later became one of his chief rationales for supporting a GAI policy. The one policy recommendation that Moynihan closed with was an argument for national welfare standards. Such standards would stem the tide of the migration from the South and thereby prevent further expansion of the urban "subculture."[25]

Nixon pressed further and asked Moynihan about attitudes toward welfare and whether they had changed. Moynihan responded that attitudes might have indeed changed, based on a combination of the growth in government programs of all kinds, social movement activism, and societal permissiveness. Citing survey findings, he said that the country at large and individuals themselves held contradictory attitudes toward welfare programs, favoring assistance toward the truly needy on one hand but also favoring self-reliance on the other. Evidence also showed that most people on welfare had not been on it before, which belied the prevalent fear of long-term and intergenerational welfare dependency. He closed by reiterating his call for national welfare standards to prevent the further growth of welfare rolls in the major metropolitan cities.[26]

Two additional things stood out in this memo. First, in Moynihan's series of recommendations, he did not directly mention, or even allude to, a GAI proposal, since at this point he was not aware that GAI was a policy option under consideration. However, he was identifying for Nixon the problems that other experts would soon argue that GAI policies could address. Second, he included a discussion of race. He cited evidence from surveys that showed that both whites and blacks viewed welfare as supporting mainly black families.[27] Moreover, Moynihan himself equated welfare reform with "the whole effort the nation is making to respond to the needs of the black urban lower class." In Moynihan's mind, as in the mind of many Americans, welfare reform had become associated with a black subculture of poverty.

Nixon's Decision in Favor of a GAI Plan

The situation among poor urban blacks was certainly on the minds of business leaders at the time, and they let their concerns about the country's urban problems be known to the president. Three weeks after Nixon took office the U.S. Chamber of Commerce enumerated many of its urban concerns for the president and offered the services of a free, full-time staff person to help the administration work on issues relating to the "urban crisis."[28] Two days after the UAC meeting on March 24 at which the Bateman-Lyday NIT plan was discussed, the U.S. Chamber of Commerce sponsored a national "town hall" meeting telecast via closed circuit to twenty thousand business leaders in twenty-six cities across the country. UAC members discussed their views of social problems and fielded questions from the viewing audience. Nixon read a critical AP news account of the event the next day, which claimed the meeting "proved that the Urban Affairs Council members have been in office for far too short a time to do much more than size up the vast problems of the cities."[29] This was part of growing coverage from the press that claimed that Nixon focused too much of the administration's early energies on foreign affairs and needed to develop a strong domestic agenda.

In response, Nixon asked Burns, Finch, and Moynihan to each prepare domestic policy papers for him to review over the first weekend of April, during his Easter weekend trip to Florida, so he could begin to make decisions on domestic programs. Burns's outline for domestic policy named inflation as the nation's most pressing problem, yet devoted the most discussion to urban issues. Notably, in proposing ways to address these problems, he did not mention welfare reform at all. He did, however, propose that revenue-sharing programs be enacted to relieve some of the fiscal problems in the cities.[30] For Burns, urban problems could be addressed by fiscal policy, a strategy that would be no less present when he turned his attention more directly to welfare in the coming months.

Burns's policy outline stood in stark contrast to those from Finch and Moynihan, who not only discussed the need for welfare reform in general but specifically broached the topic of the Bateman-Lyday GAI plan, now known to supporters as the Family Security System (FSS). Though it had been discussed by the UAC the previous week, there was a great deal of contention over the merits of the program and how to proceed. This acrimony did not prevent Finch from saying that Nixon should make welfare reform "the keystone of the domestic program," that the FSS would "appeal to state and local governments and taxpayers" because of the fiscal relief it contained, and that it "should appeal to many conservatives, since it provides incentives for work and family stability."[31] Moynihan, like Burns, framed his support for the FSS in the context of rising inflation, but argued that Nixon's recent promise of budget cuts allowed room for proposing legislative alternatives to the programs that were going to be cut back. Greatly overselling the efficacy of the FSS and underestimating its costs, he argued to Nixon that "for two weeks' growth in the Gross National Product you can all but eliminate family poverty in America. And make history."[32] Using almost the same words as had Finch, Moynihan argued that the "entire basis" for the FSS was "the provision of these new incentives for family stability and work."[33]

Moynihan's argument contained contradictions that reflected wider confusion within the administration about how to view the "welfare" rolls. He consistently described the growth in the welfare rolls as a problem and suggested that welfare reform should address it. Yet he favored a plan that would expand the number of people receiving government benefits. In his view, the existing system was racially divisive. Current recipients were, at least in major cities, more likely to be black and thus the program's administrative structure pitted black welfare recipients against white taxpayers who paid for the program. Since FSS benefits would also go to working people, who were more likely to be white, the divisions between these two groups would be mitigated.[34] Public assistance would no longer be "a black program": it would include people across racial and class-based divisions. What he failed to recognize, or at least discuss in his memoranda, was that that a major selling point of the FSS—providing benefits to poor people who worked— would also greatly expand the number of people on the rolls. This was a trend that most experts, including Moynihan, were on record as wanting to reverse. The contradiction was unavoidable as long as FSS payments were considered "welfare" payments. This would become a pronounced sticking point in welfare deliberations during the summer. During the spring, however, it went largely unrecognized.

Over Easter weekend, Nixon read through his domestic policy briefs and met with his three domestic advisors personally. He heard Finch's and Moynihan's justifications for the FSS and surprised Burns by not dismissing the possibility of the program out of hand. When Burns protested, Nixon responded that he had a problem—the urban problem—and that if Burns did not like the FSS solution, he should develop an alternative.[35] Nixon did not make any firm decisions that weekend, but ten days later he confidentially told his advisor John Ehrlichman that though he did not want Finch or Moynihan to know it yet, he had decided to go forward with the FSS and wanted a plan drafted and ready by the following week.[36] Nixon had agreed to proceed with the unreconstructed Johnson-era negative income tax plan.

The Escalating Debate over Guaranteed Income

Oppositional Claims-Making and Symbolic Pollution

Though Nixon's decision to proceed with the FSS was not yet known throughout the administration, a counteroffensive against it was already being launched. By mid-April, it was clear to both supporters and opponents that the FSS was the frontrunner for the administration's welfare reform proposal. The president felt that he had to do something about welfare soon and the FSS was the plan many of his welfare experts advocated. It was in this context that Burns and one of his main advisors, Martin Anderson, launched a fierce attack. They could read between the lines of the technical policy descriptions and perceive the outlines of something they found abhorrent: a plan that gave the poor an income by right and extended "welfare" to employed workers. Their attack on Nixon's GAI proposal reverberated loudly within the administration, ultimately to considerable effect. The welfare reform system that Nixon proposed later that summer was different in significant details from the FSS plan of mid-April as a result. More significant, the Nixon administration's *rhetorical* framing of the welfare proposal was strongly influenced by the concerns raised by Burns and Anderson in their attempts to thwart GAI proposals altogether.

Anderson was an economist at Columbia University and a close associate of Burns, and he mounted a clever attack on the FSS by the use of analogy. On the same day that Nixon secretly decided to proceed with the FSS, Anderson submitted a paper to the president titled "A Short History of a 'Family Security System,'" which consisted exclusively of six pages of quoted excerpts from Karl Polanyi's classic book, *The Great Transformation*.[37] In the book, Polanyi described the Speenhamland Law of 1795, which was the origin of the English poor laws that established the basis for Anglo-American government assistance to the poor. Yet the Speenhamland Law, critics felt, made the poor worse off, not better off, by harming the work ethic instead of strengthening it. As a result of such criticisms, the English poor laws were amended in 1834. Anderson quoted at length Polanyi's account of these criticisms, painting a picture in which the Speenhamland regime damaged productivity, drove down wages, demoralized workers, and threatened the capitalist order.

> It introduced no less a social and economic innovation than "the right to live," and until abolished in 1834, it effectively prevented the establishment of a competitive labor market.
>
> ... To later generations nothing could have been more patent than the mutual incompatibility of institutions like the wage system and "the right to live," or, in other words, than the impossibility of a functioning capitalist order as long as wages were subsidized from public funds.

... Only when a grave deterioration of the productive capacities of the masses resulted—a veritable calamity which was obstructing the progress of machine civilization—did the necessity of abolishing the unconditional right of the poor to relief impose itself upon the consciousness of the community.

... The outcome was merely the pauperization of the masses, who almost lost their human shape in the process.[38]

Anderson's rhetorical strategy was adept. The sharp contrast between work (the "wage system") and welfare ("the right to live") clearly reinforced the distinction between the deserving and undeserving poor. Moreover, the reference to wage subsidies threatening the capitalist order showed how radical the notion of income supplements for the working poor seemed to opponents of the FSS at the time, since income-based benefits for workers heretofore did not exist. The epigraph of Anderson's memo was Santayana's well-known quote, "Those who cannot remember the past are condemned to repeat it." The implication was that the FSS, by subsidizing wages and establishing economic security as a right, would present the same economic and moral threat to America's free market system as had the Speenhamland Law to that of England.[39]

Nixon was disturbed by Anderson's memo and asked members of his administration to address the issues that it raised. Moynihan, Shultz (secretary of labor) and Paul McCracken (chairman of the CEA) responded to the president by defending the FSS, and in doing so broached some of the work-related issues that would arise repeatedly in debates over GAI proposals, namely those involving work incentives, work requirements, wage levels, and job training.[40] All three men argued that Speenhamland was not similar to the FSS because the tax rates on recipients' earnings with the Speenhamland Law were 100 percent, while they were 50 percent under the negative income tax rate in the FSS. McCracken noted that, based on preliminary results from the OEO's negative income tax experiments in New Jersey, a tax rate at this level did not appear to damage the work ethic. Shultz wrote that the history of Speenhamland showed the damaging effects of coupling an income maintenance plan with work requirements. The FSS, as yet, did not contain such requirements. Shultz, a proponent of the laissez-faire paradigm, wrote, "The lesson is clear. Welfare programs must maintain a principle of free choice with respect to labor force participation in order to avoid the dual evils of crushing work incentives and removing effective wage competition."[41] Finally, each writer noted that in contrast to Anderson's claim that Speenhamland was analogous to the FSS, it was actually much more similar to the existing AFDC program—with its 100 percent tax rate and work requirements implemented in 1967. To their minds, this provided further evidence, from Anderson himself no less, that the current system indeed needed to be dismantled and replaced with something that resembled the FSS.

In contrast to Anderson's sidelong historical critique of the FSS, Burns mounted a full-frontal attack by designing a competing plan. On April 21, he presented to Nixon a forty-one-page policy paper titled "Investing in Human Dignity" that outlined his proposal.[42] Though his strategy was different from Anderson's, the overarching concerns were similar. He framed his proposal by discussing the increase in welfare caseloads that had occurred in recent years. Yet even more troubling than this trend during times of fiscal strain, Burns argued, was the moral affront represented by the FSS. It represented a shift in welfare policy away from assistance based on disability-related deprivation and toward income as a matter of right: "The principal significance of this trend is that we are shifting from the historic emphasis on helping the poor to become self-supporting members of the active labor force. Instead, conditions are being created under which the poor find it increasingly acceptable to stay on welfare rolls."[43] The reference to "historical emphasis on helping the poor" was noteworthy in this context because Burns expressed concerns about alleviating poverty only once in the entire document, noting that welfare benefits were too low in the South. Rather, the "major effort" in welfare reform, according to his analysis, was getting "welfare recipients off the rolls to the maximum extent feasible."[44] Reducing the welfare rolls, not reducing rates of poverty, was for Burns the central objective.

As with Anderson, Burns's concerns involved much more than the budget; they encompassed morality, national productivity, and the behavior of the poor: "The single most important issue raised by the FSS is its effect on economic and cultural values. . . . Giving people an income as a matter of 'right' is a significantly different thing from extending assistance with the understanding that they will strive toward self-support to the extent of their capabilities. . . . It seems inescapable that more and more people would make the purely rational decision to remain idle rather than work, especially so in the case of individuals possessing only low-level skills."[45] Burns's emphasis on economically rational behavior would stand in contrast to arguments he made elsewhere in the GAI debates that were based on the premise that welfare recipients were behaviorally deviant (i.e., nonrational) and required rehabilitation. He held mutually incompatible images of the poor, though his emphasis on their deviance from mainstream cultural norms was dominant.

Three other aspects of Burns's views were notable. First, his opposition to the FSS was based on defining it as a "welfare" program, even though it included other populations, such as the working poor, who were not AFDC recipients. On this basis, he defined all of its recipients as "welfare" recipients and its costs as increases in "welfare" costs. Second was Burns's view of dignity. Throughout his campaign against the FSS, he contended that dignity was derived from work; the FSS deprived people of their dignity because it would prevent them from working. In the closing words of his paper, he said that the main merit of his plan was that it helped people "free themselves from dependency on welfare. As suggested at numerous points in this report, the achievement of human dignity should be the primary goal of welfare re-form."[46] This view of dignity was directly at odds with that held by members of the NRWO and others (recounted in chapter 2) who defined dignity as the absence of coercive measures designed to make people undertake demeaning labor against their will. These competing understandings of the sources of individual dignity harkened back to the opposing definitions of liberty out-lined in the early 1960s by Milton Friedman and Robert Theobald.

Third, disagreements about rights were also central in the GAI debates. Both Burns and Anderson strenuously opposed the "right" to a basic income on ideological grounds, a right they felt the FSS would ensure. However, the debate over rights hinged not only on the desirability of the *principle* of a right to a minimum income but also on how to recognize one *in practice*. Burns and Anderson clearly saw the right to income embodied in the FSS system. By extension, they believed that the FSS would undercut the free enterprise system by weakening the work ethic. In contrast, people such as Friedman and Moynihan argued that the existing system *already* assured welfare benefits as a matter of right, albeit "a legal entitlement that society has nevertheless managed to stigmatize."[47] Similarly, Melvin Laird, Nixon's secretary of de-fense, would argue that the administration "should move from the present [AFDC] system which is really nothing more than a guaranteed income wel-fare program to a work incentives welfare program" such as the FSS.[48] These disagreements demonstrated that definitions of "welfare rights" were funda-mentally contested.

In lieu of the FSS, Burns proposed a plan similar to the one contained in the Nathan report, one that modified the existing AFDC system to include minimum national standards and the extension of AFDC-UP. His two most significant deviations from the Nathan plan, and those with the largest long-term impact, were a proposal to link welfare reform and revenue sharing and a requirement that even the mothers of young children should be ex-pected to work for their benefits. He proposed that revenue-sharing legislation, which was being developed concurrently within the administration, could require that states maintain specific minimum welfare standards in order to receive their full amount of money. Integrating the two systems—revenue sharing and welfare—in this fashion would lower the states' welfare-related outlays without a substantial increase in federal expenditure, since revenue-sharing legislation was being considered by the administration anyway. Though the Nathan report had suggested legislation in this direction, Burns's proposal for the first time articulated its advantages and how it might be done. Because of the range of political interests involved, as the debates over GAI progressed, this fiscal dimension of welfare reform would affect debates and legislative outcomes considerably.

Burns's recommendation requiring single mothers of young children to seek employment proved to be a considerable sticking point in the coming months and highlights his overarching concern about work. To facilitate mothers' entry into the workplace, Burns included plans to increase job training for women and create a network of federally funded children's day care centers. This recommendation was antithetical to Moynihan's family-oriented focus for welfare reform. Not only did the Burns proposal not provide incentives for family stability, it would require that single mothers enter the labor force rather than "properly" socializing their young children and providing a stabilizing presence in urban communities.

Division and Pragmatic Opposition within the Administration

As he had with Anderson's "Speenhamland" memo, Nixon solicited the opinions of his cabinet members on the Burns plan in comparison to the FSS. Robert Mayo (budget director), Spiro Agnew (vice president), and David Kennedy (secretary of the treasury) responded with pragmatic concerns about the FSS and modest support for the Burns plan. Each articulated the recognition that something needed to be done with the welfare system.[49] Mayo, for instance, argued that welfare reform was "the most important challenge facing the administration," and Agnew recognized "the need that a radical and innovative departure be employed by the administration with respect to welfare." They felt the administration had to propose *something*. They supported the idea of national standards and recognized the appeal of linking those to welfare standards with stipulations contained in the revenue-sharing legislation under consideration. Mayo and Kennedy unsurprisingly, given their administrative positions, expressed concerns about the costs and budgetary effects of the FSS. Like Agnew, they supported the Burns plan in the short term, since its consequences were clearer and recommended thinking about the FSS in the long term, once the findings from the NIT experiments were analyzed and the costs of the various components were estimated more thoroughly. One marked commonality that the three cabinet members shared was their tempered consideration of the FSS. Their reservations about the program were not based on ideology. None shared the moral concerns that Burns and Anderson expressed, which suggests that the plan had not yet been widely associated with an ideological or partisan position.

The primary opposition to Burns's proposal came from Finch, Nixon's secretary at HEW. In a detailed, sixteen-page response, Finch critiqued Burns's position on factual, political, and ideological grounds.[50] He argued that Burns overlooked many of the reasons that the welfare rolls were increasing, particularly the root causes of the increase, which he claimed lay in marital breakup and illegitimacy. According to Finch, Burns's plan, like the AFDC system that it built upon, would only maintain the system of incentives that produced these problems, while the systemic changes proposed in the FSS would remove them.

Work, Welfare, and the Politics of Definition

Another major difference between the two proposals concerned work incentives and the working poor. Finch wrote, "Specifically, the major point of difference is whether the working poor should be included. I think they should, and as I have stated earlier, this is not a move toward a guaranteed income. Rather, it attempts to remove the perverse consequences of our present system whereby the working man can earn less money than the welfare recipient."[51] Beyond its practical consequences, Finch argued that the inclusion of the working poor could have significant political advantages: "To include the working poor is not a basically 'leftish' or liberal initiative, but rather an essentially conservative move which, while appealing to liberals, is rooted in the concept of making work as rewarding as welfare in a system which in many states has reversed the incentives."[52] Finch was among the first to make a strong and explicit case to Nixon for including the working poor. Notably, his rationale was to improve work incentives for the unemployed by making work itself more attractive than welfare benefits. The implied target population for this aspect of the FSS was *unemployed black* men. This rationale was in contrast to another that emerged in the months to follow that targeted *employed white* men.

In arguing that the inclusion of the working poor was a basically conservative reform, as opposed to a liberal one, Finch was an early participant in the "definitional work" that would increasingly characterize the politics of GAI proposals. Amid the complex and often uncertain politics of welfare reform, such efforts sought to define the meaning of the FSS.

A further dimension of this definitional work was constructing the meaning of being "on welfare" and the normative implication of increases or decreases in AFDC caseloads. As Finch explained it, the current increase in AFDC caseloads that conservatives found so problematic could either mean a "liberalization" of eligibility standards, as Burns contended, or that more people were eligible, for whatever reason, and that the government should not shirk its duty to these citizens if the cases were legitimate. Finch argued that to rely on stigma to discourage benefits that were legitimately owed to recipients, as Burns suggested, was bad government. A related issue was whether the working poor who would be incorporated into the FSS system were considered "on welfare" or whether the connotation of receiving this new category of benefits would, or should, be considered altogether different. Finch's comments indicated that new categories of thought would be required to accompany the new institutional categories that the FSS contained, since existing policy did not provide an alternative label for income benefits for workers. These concerns about the necessity of simultaneous change in both programmatic structure and cultural understanding came to be prescient, though few supporters of the FSS, particularly among the president's close advisors, devoted sustained efforts to this cultural dimension of reform.

Experts at HEW, following Finch's lead, went to work on defining the FSS as favorably as possible, composing a list of fifteen questions and answers about the FSS and the existing welfare system that responded to some of the FSS plan's most widespread criticisms.[53] They sent this document to John Ehrlichman, one of Nixon's chief counsels, who was serving as the intermediary between the competing factions within the administration and the president. Three of the initial questions concerned definitional issues. The first claimed that there was widespread "confusion of labels" about GAI programs. They reasserted Finch's point that whether a plan provided a "guaranteed income" depended on the work stipulation attached to it. This was just as true for the current AFDC system or the Burns plan as it was for the FSS. Notably, in a response to a separate question on the desirability of whether work requirements should be compulsory or not, they said that "it is unlikely that empirical evidence can be developed to settle the issue one way or another," implying that political imperatives and policy paradigms would remain as determinants in settling the issues.[54] Second, they argued that the coverage of the working poor within the FSS had no bearing on the issue of "guaranteed income." The income supplements, in their view, corrected for the perverse incentives of the present system in which non–working poor were helped while the working poor were excluded. Third, they responded to the question of whether the FSS was a negative income tax, a term that opponents, such as Anderson, had used derisively. They said that "again there is a problem with labels."[55] They contended that simply because programs were structured to decrease benefits as wages increased did not make them an NIT. This structure was present in the current AFDC system as well as in the administration's food stamp proposal. Using a narrow definition of an NIT, they argued that the FSS was not one because its benefits did not apply to everyone universally and because it was not administered through the IRS.

Continuing Questions and Uncertainty

Solid support for the FSS within the administration was less readily found. This was in large part because the goals of welfare reform remained unclear to many participants. The murky nature of these objectives appeared with the most force at the CEA, which had undertaken an ongoing technical evaluation of the FSS and Burns plans. McCracken, frustrated by trying to evaluate the policy without a clear sense of welfare reform's goals, articulated three key questions that remained unanswered by the administration.

- Do we simply want to reform the existing welfare system, focusing on families now eligible for AFDC, or should we move more generally toward income maintenance—helping all the poor?
- Related to this, do we want to leave out of our income maintenance system the family of a working man who can't earn income even up to the poverty line? They are, in a real sense, the "deserving poor."
- Do we want to force welfare mothers to work by making benefits conditional on work or training, or do we want to induce them to work by letting them keep some of their earnings?[56]

McCracken's questions asked how committed the Nixon administration was to comprehensive reform in efforts toward poverty reduction, whether the government should be responsible for supplementing an insufficient wage structure, and whether women in female-headed households should be expected to work, even if they had young children. Each was a significant question—bearing on either categories of deservingness or the administration's emphasis on work and family—and McCracken contended that without answers, the administration could not proceed with an integrated plan.

Despite the absence of answers, the CEA forged ahead with its evaluations and focused most of its analyses on four issues: state-level fiscal problems, national standards, family stability, and work incentives.[57] On March 29, McCracken submitted a preliminary report to Nixon comparing the FSS to the Burns plan. According to early analyses, both plans contained elements that established national standards and relieved state fiscal pressures for relatively similar additional costs: Burns's plan at a cost of $2.5 billion and the FSS at either $2.0 or $2.9 billion depending on coverage. At the higher level of coverage, the FSS would include twice as many people as the Burns plan, since it included the working poor. Beyond this, there were two main differences. First, the Burns plan contained incentives for family breakup while the FSS contained incentives for family cohesion. Second, the FSS contained lower marginal tax rates than the Burns plan (50 percent as compared to 67 percent), which translated into stronger work incentives in the FSS. The report added, however, that the actual effects of these differences were unknown. To offset its weaker work incentives, the Burns plan contained work requirements.

Two days later, McCracken submitted to Nixon the full report from the Technical Subcommittee of the Task Force on the Family Security System.[58] The subcommittee included people from a range of departments and offices: HEW, labor, budget, treasury, the OEO, the UAC, the CEA, and the White House staff, and it contained both supporters and opponents of the FSS. Significantly, the report compared *three* alternative proposals—the FSS (in two versions), the Burns plan, and a third plan called the Universal Security Sys-

tem (USS), which essentially expanded the FSS to include "virtually all people." By revised estimates, the plans' costs were estimated to be the following:
Burns, $1.9 billion; FSS-low, $2.3 billion; FSS-high, $3.2 billion; and USS,
$3.1 billion. The technical report was based on the premise that the three
proposals shared the same basic objectives: a decent level of income support;
reduction over time in the number of households on welfare; and incentives
for families to stay together. The USS plan, the report noted, was included
"for comparison purposes" and it recognized the government's responsibility
for the economic security of all the poor, not only families with children. It
was closer to the objectives of advocates of the economic citizenship paradigm.
The inclusion of this plan, even if solely for a point of comparison, was remarkable, considering that only five months earlier the Nathan report, which only
modified the existing system, had been considered by its authors to be the most
expansive welfare reform strategy possible for the administration to undertake.

During the same period that the subcommittee was finalizing its report,
Nixon belatedly heard from three other members of his cabinet on their views
of the comparison between the FSS and the Burns plan.[59] Unlike previous
evaluations of the two plans, these discussions emphasized the *political* implications of the two plans as much as they dealt with programmatic issues and
technical details. Stans (secretary of commerce) shared many of Burns's and
Anderson's concerns that the FSS would undermine the self-reliance of the
American people. He further repudiated the idea of a right to an income.
Extrapolating these views to the public at large, he argued that taxpayers,
especially those who had supported Nixon in 1968, would oppose giving
people money as a matter of right. Charls Walker, undersecretary of the treasury, likewise supported the Burns plan. He felt that the political damage of
proposing the FSS would come not from the public but from the elite level.
He contended that the FSS would divide the Republican Party, and that
state and local leaders would prefer the revenue-sharing and national
standards elements contained in the Burns plan. Laird (secretary of defense)
prefaced his recommendations to Nixon by acknowledging the significance
of the welfare decisions at hand: "I am aware of the incredible complexity of
the present system and the volatility of the welfare issue in the political arena.
There is no question in my mind that we stand in a virtual crossroads situation
today."[60] Like Stans and Walker, he could not throw his support behind the
FSS, at least not at the present time. He felt that it launched too sharp a break
with the past without clear knowledge of the consequences. Moreover, he
felt that it was not politically palatable. However, he did not like the Burns
plan either. In his view, it affirmed the discredited philosophy and administrative mechanisms of the current system. He proposed an incrementalist approach to welfare reform based on the formation of additional study groups
with perhaps the adoption of a work-related negative income tax (such as the
FSS) in the long run.

All three members of the administration reacted to the ideological over-tones they perceived in the FSS, though in different ways, once again demon-strating the multifaceted perceptions of the existing and proposed systems. Walker and Stans objected to the affirmation of the right to welfare they saw in the FSS. Laird saw the opposite. He considered the current AFDC system to be an entitlement program that consisted of a guaranteed income, while the FSS was a "work incentive welfare program," albeit structured as a nega-tive income tax. This ambiguity concerning how to think about the various proposals partly depended on what kind of work stipulation was attached to the proposals. As Finch had tried to point out to the administration, "Whether or not we move further in the direction of a 'guaranteed income' depends not on anything which is built into the FSS, but on whether—under any system—people will lose their benefits if they refuse a bona fide work or training oppor-tunity. FSS can be constructed with or without a compulsory work aspect."[61] As both opponents and supporters of the FSS began to realize, there remained a considerable amount of definitional work to do on both sides of the issue.

An Emerging Consensus?

While the policy experts at HEW worked on these definitional issues, the analysts at the CEA continued the technical comparisons of the Burns plan and the FSS.[62] At the end of May, McCracken submitted to Nixon a memo proposing the "possible resolution of the welfare controversy."[63] He wrote that upon further examination, when the Burns and FSS plans were considered in conjunction with upcoming changes in AFDC regulations and the admin-istration's recent food stamps proposal, the competing plans did not contain as many differences as early comparisons had indicated. Two significant differ-ences between the plans remained, and those concerned family stability and the working poor. The AFDC-UP option, in which benefits could be paid to families in which both parents were unemployed, was only used in a minority of states (in the remaining states, benefits could only go to the female-headed households), and the Burns plan would do nothing to change this. McCracken, like most other experts, believed that without the AFDC-UP modification, there remained considerable incentives for family breakup. Sec-ond, the Burns plan contained no coverage for the working poor while the FSS did. McCracken recommended going forward along the essential lines of the Burns plan while mandating that all the states adopt AFDC-UP, which would cover families with two unemployed parents. This would leave the issue of the working poor, and Nixon could appoint a task force to study this issue and make a report later in the year.

Up until this point, everyone involved in the welfare debates had viewed Burns and Moynihan as starkly at odds in their positions on welfare reform. So their follow-up comments to Nixon on the McCracken evaluation were remarkable: both indicated that they agreed with almost everything McCracken said, though each had some caveats. It was these caveats that served as the sticking points in the final months leading up to Nixon's announcement. Burns isolated two sources of disagreement: work requirements and the working poor. He felt that McCracken did not go far enough in the direction of work requirements, which had been left out of his recommendations. Burns considered such requirements an essential element of any welfare reform plan. On the subject of the working poor, he indicated that he had been giving thought to programs that could benefit the working poor, and he would report back to Nixon on the matter in a follow-up memo. In light of his earlier views on benefits going to the working poor, this was a tentative, and temporary, move toward compromise.[64] Moynihan argued that the main issues for consideration were not technical—based on the remaining differences between the two programs—but political. Not wanting to let go of any aspect of the FSS, including the working poor component, he pressed Nixon to move forward for strategic reasons. He cited evidence from New York City and fifteen different state-level general assistance programs that work supplements would not harm the work incentives of those already in the labor force. Therefore, he argued, Nixon should proceed with the part of the plan to assist the working poor. Employing his familiar strategy of urging Nixon to propose a distinctly *Nixonian* plan, Moynihan highlighted the fact that a number of other organizations were pressing some type of welfare reform proposal—the Urban League, the Urban Coalition, the U.S. Chamber of Commerce, and social work organizations—and that Nixon needed to set the agenda before they did. On the issue of welfare, Moynihan argued, Nixon could be an opinion leader, setting the agenda that others could follow. Finally, he argued that a plan like the FSS was inevitable: "This is an idea whose time has come."[65]

The apparent near agreement between Burns and Moynihan would evaporate in the final months of welfare planning as the deadline for Nixon's announcement drew near. The main sticking point was whether to include the working poor in a welfare reform strategy. Administration officials debated the political and programmatic merits of including this group and grappled with how to conceptualize a new type of social policy that included both the working poor and existing AFDC recipients. During this same period, Secretary of Labor George Shultz, who had largely been on the sidelines of the welfare debate, advanced a third "compromise" proposal that modified the FSS.

ANTICIPATING THE PUBLIC REACTION

At the end of May, Donald Rumsfeld, the director of the OEO, shared with Nixon his opinion of a Burns memo on urban problems. His comments raised a series of issues that foreshadowed an important dimension of the coming debates.[66] Burns had made the case that Nixon's domestic programs needed to tackle problems that affected everyone, not just minorities or the poor. Rumsfeld agreed in part, but also argued that these two types of policies were not so easily distinguished. Programs for the poor and for minorities did, in fact, benefit everyone in the long run. Evidence suggested, for example, that crime would drop as the poor gained access to employment, housing, and educational opportunities. Unlike Burns, Rumsfeld felt that the administration should pursue both types of policies. The crux of his memo raised a question that touched on issues of race, class, and politics: Should the administration push for programs that would mainly benefit minorities and the poor, in the hope of co-opting traditional Democratic issues, or should it focus on its Republican constituents, thereby bolstering its political base?

This question cut a large swath across the domestic agenda and it become more relevant to welfare reform as thinking shifted from policy formulation to political strategy. Central to this shift was Burns's mounting concern about a backlash from the white, ethnic working class against "liberal" programs that they felt unfairly privileged the needs of poor minority groups. Burns was strategic in the way he introduced this concern to Nixon. He submitted a memo summarizing a recent article about the possibilities of such a backlash, and in his cover letter linked this possible backlash to the politics of Nixon's welfare proposal and other domestic programs.[67]

White Working-Class Backlash

The article, written by Pete Hamill and published in *New York* magazine, was titled "The Revolt of the White Lower Middle Class." Burns characterized the article with a few highly evocative, extended quotes. In one, a man complained about working full-time, and even overtime, and having no extra money, and then opening the papers to find that "some fat welfare bitch" is demanding a credit card at Korvette's (a local department store): "I work for a living and I can't get a credit card at Korvette's." In another, a man complained about "niggers . . . who take the welfare and sit out on the stoop drinkin' cheap wine and throwin' the bottles in the street. They take money outta my paycheck and they just turn it over to some lazy son of a bitch who won't work. I gotta carry him on my back." Hamill concluded that "the working class white is actually in a revolt against taxes, joyless work, the double standards and short memories of professional politicians, hypocrisy, and what he considers the debasement of the American dream. Any politician who leaves the white man out of the political equation does so at his own risk."[68]

In his commentary, Burns argued that white working-class men had not seen their positions improving in recent years and they blamed "the government, intellectuals and Negroes for this condition. The bitterness of the urban white worker, who feels he is supporting Negroes on relief as a result of the machinations of vote-hungry politicians, is a social and political fact of first-rate importance." Regarding welfare, he said that "people on welfare must be subject (wherever applicable) to a strict work requirement. Any reform of the welfare program which guarantees an income to people who refuse to work or otherwise improve their conditions by their own effort (which is what the so-called Family Security System would do) will enhance the growing bitterness of the white lower middle class and may lead to disaster."[69]

In a message to Ehrlichman regarding Burns's comments, Nixon wrote, "John—Shultz, Finch, Moynihan et al. should consider the implications and find an answer."[70] The answer that would emerge in the following two months was constructing the FSS, both in programmatic detail and public rhetoric, as a program to appeal mainly to the (majority white) working poor—a goal considerably removed from the aims that originally gave rise to guaranteed income plans and then placed them on the Nixon agenda.

Clearly by this point GAI policy was fraught with racial overtones. Not only did concern about white backlash confront Nixon and his advisors, but so too did pressures pushing in the opposite direction from civil rights leaders, and the administration realized that it had to recognize their concerns as well. Early on during the policy formulation process, in an effort to diffuse criticisms coming from the Poor People's Campaign, the White House had arranged for the movement's leader, Ralph Abernathy, to meet with members of the UAC to discuss some of his domestic ideas.[71] Yet despite early hopes that a guaranteed income policy could be seen as a more "color-blind" program than AFDC, the administration realized this would be an uphill struggle. Burns reported Gallup poll results to Nixon showing that most of the public did not favor GAI policies and, further, that opinion was divided across racial lines. Blacks favored GAI programs two to one, while the opposite was true among white respondents.[72] Finch, like other FSS supporters, viewed the FSS as a program that could diminish the racial divisiveness of the current system. He hoped that by including the working poor—a group with a much higher proportion of whites than the unemployed categories covered under AFDC—the program would blur the racial and class-based divisions that the current system both reflected and reinforced.[73]

In the early summer, Nixon took a more central role in welfare decisions than he had earlier, and the possibilities of white working-class backlash raised by Burns appeared to preoccupy him more than the other issues involved in the reform process. Apparently in response to Burns's memo and another article on white backlash that had recently appeared in *The Nation*, Nixon directed the White House to circulate a three-page report titled "The Working Poor" to all the cabinet officials involved with welfare reform. The report made many of the same points as Hamill's article, saying that racial and class divisions were near a "boiling point" and that it could be "a long, *white*-hot summer."[74] It estimated that the working poor, defined as those earning between $5,000 and $10,000 a year, were the majority of the nation's workforce. One national leader was quoted as saying that "unless the problems of lower income white ethnics are solved, all black progress will be lost because they'll turn to Wallace."[75]

Discussions of these problems were not coming from the media only, nor did the problem of white backlash exist mainly among southerners. In the middle of June, Nixon read a letter that caught his attention from a public official on Long Island who expressed deep concerns that "serious political damage will result from Administration sponsorship of income maintenance payments unrelated to work or need."[76] The writer recounted a recent incident in which a substantial amount of money raised in pledges during a community fund drive had been retracted by donors once it became clear that some of the money would go to seven Community Action programs in the community. From one company alone, three thousand workers had withdrawn their pledges. According to the writer, "This was an amazing reaction which demonstrated to me that the sensitivity of low and middle income workers to 'giveaways' is particularly acute right now. I'm inclined to think the so-called negative income tax is bad politics, bad economics and bad psychology any time, but I'm sure the country is not ready to start down that road now."[77]

Burns received a copy of the letter and forwarded it to Nixon to make sure he had seen it. Shortly afterward, Burns responded to Shultz's new recommendations for the FSS, once again emphasizing the political necessity of explicit work requirements, not simply work incentives as Shultz had proposed: "We need a strong work requirement—something which is not currently embodied in law—rather than monetary incentives to persuade people to do something they should be doing anyway."[78] He promised that he would give Nixon a new welfare reform plan within two weeks, a plan that would contain what he considered the most important elements of welfare reform: revenue sharing, AFDC-UP, work requirements, job training, day care, a ceiling on welfare grants, and fiscal incentives for states to curb welfare rolls.[79]

Despite the growing attention to the large number of people who worked full-time yet remained poor, there was virtually no critique of labor market functioning within the White House. The "working poor" memo that Nixon circulated among his staffers and cabinet leaders closed with a quote from Andrew Greeley, who was the director of the National Opinion Research Center. In explaining the perceived backlash of the white working class, he said that "in today's mechanized society the working poor is the group that feels the most vulnerable and impotent, which is why they strike out at the blacks rather than attack the root causes of their own problems."[80] The reference to "mechanized society" suggested that the root causes Greeley referred to were labor market dynamics. This focus recalled the structural unemployment concerns of GAI proponents earlier in the decade. The notable aspect of welfare reform debates during the Nixon era was the virtual absence of discussions that located the problem of poverty in the economic system.

The Shultz Plan and the Laissez-faire Paradigm

On June 10, one of Nixon's closest advisors, George Shultz, entered the fray with his own welfare reform proposal, which was firmly rooted in the laissez-faire paradigm. It built upon the structure of the FSS plan, and the administration would soon adopt his recommendations. (This resulting new plan was often referred to as the FSS-Shultz plan, though hereafter it will be referred to as simply the FSS since the structure was similar.) Shultz's plan was notable for its substantial increase in costs, its open discussion of the effects of policy design on human behavior, and his explicit presumption of rational economic maximizing on the part of the poor.[81]

Shultz's proposal was motivated by the goal of moving people from welfare to work. In this, his goal was similar to that of Burns. However, unlike Burns, he viewed the source of the problem as AFDC itself, which created a system of perverse incentives that resulted in unintended and undesirable behavioral consequences. Accordingly, it was the system, not the individual, that needed to be the focus of reform. With his focus on labor market participation, Shultz recommended actions to facilitate the entry of mothers into the labor force— for instance, by including stronger training programs and greater emphasis on child-care facilities. He argued that existing reform proposals overlooked the costs to recipients of going to work and therefore advocated an "earnings disregard" in which part of every paycheck would be exempted from taxes or earnings reductions. This would further strengthen incentives to work by making initial entry into the labor force less costly. Though his main concern was work, he strongly opposed work requirements because he felt they interfered with freedom of choice and would ultimately have harmful labor market repercussions. With the inclusion of his earnings disregard, the additional costs of improved training and child-care programs, and a recalibrated estimate of how many people might leave their existing jobs to sign up for training programs, he estimated that his changes to the FSS would cost an additional $2.2 billion.

Like many of Nixon's other advisors, Shultz was forthright in expressing how complicated reforming the welfare system was. Yet this complexity, he believed, was mitigated by the economically rational behavior of the poor. His proposal was built on the assumption that the behavior of the poor could be shaped by the structure of economic incentives: "The prospects for success in this attempt hinge on the effects of human behavior in such basic matters as working, marriage, rearing of children and family dissolution. Many of the most powerful forces involved are virtually invisible; but one, the ability to understand and the desire to follow economic self-interest, is clear and clearly related to movement from welfare to work." Such rationality on the part of the poor, in his view, made it especially important to make sure that incentives were structured correctly: "While the system may appear complicated in Washington, we can be sure that the individual [recipient] will be able to figure it out in actual operation. He must, and can, make rational decisions affecting his economic interests."[82]

Shultz's characterization of the poor as driven largely by economic rationality had direct programmatic consequences. It led him to advocate a coercion-free welfare program that used completely different mechanisms than did the Burns plan, even though he shared some of Burns's concrete goals. The contrast between his approach and Burns's approach was stark: incentives, freedom, and trust versus requirements, monitoring, and suspicion.

As Shultz's memo highlighted, value judgments about human nature played a central role in welfare policy design. The memo, running thirty-two pages, was an exemplary piece of meticulous analysis. Yet on the point of economic maximizing, he could only sketch out hypothetical examples of how the poor might behave under particular circumstances.[83] No evidence was provided in support of the major premise on which his plan was based. Shultz, Burns, and Moynihan each held different perceptions regarding the behavior of the poor, and, given the dearth of solid data of any type at this point, there was little evidence to either support or contradict their views. These behavioral assumptions played a significant role in policy development.

Business Groups, Governors, and Mayors Weigh In

To the extent that poverty problems were located in the wage structure, the government could either subsidize wages, as the FSS would do, or increase wages through minimum wage legislation. This was the choice presented in Stigler's first discussion of the negative income tax in the 1950s. Officials within the Nixon administration were in fact thinking about relaxing the minimum wage, or doing away with it completely, in tandem with FSS legislation.[84] If the latter, the dual effect of this legislative action, when coupled with the FSS, would be to socialize the costs of wage subsidies while privatizing the benefits of low wages.

In all likelihood, this accounted for at least part of the business support the FSS received during the summer. Other factors included business leaders' favorable disposition toward the administration's focus on work incentives and concerns about safety and civic order.[85] Much of this support was solicited by Moynihan, who kept Nixon informed of the favorable leanings of business. Moynihan consulted with many of the same leaders who had participated in the Arden House meetings in 1967–68, and they reported that Nixon was on the right track, particularly if work incentives were strengthened more than those in the current system. Arjay Miller, the CEO of Ford, went so far as to say that if Nixon could end the conflict in Vietnam and pass the FSS legislation, the Republicans would become the majority party in the country.[86] As news of the plan traveled, many business leaders sent Nixon telegrams and letters in favor of the bill; economic organizations, such as the Committee on Economic Development, lent their support to the program; *Business Week* magazine gave the FSS its editorial blessing; and the National Association of Manufacturers issued a position paper that favored a bill similar to the FSS.[87]

Pressure to do something was growing, not only from the business community but from state and local leaders. Since the early months of the administration, state governors, led by Nelson Rockefeller, had pressured officials to undertake ways of alleviating the mounting fiscal strains in states in the industrial North. Big-city mayors applied similar pressures. John Lindsay of New York City lobbied Nixon for the federal government to take over all welfare payments, saying that the economic survival of big cities was at stake.[88] As discussions such as these increasingly linked welfare reform with revenue sharing, local officials began to see welfare reform through a distinctly fiscal lens. The pressures on the Nixon administration were difficult to negotiate, however, because the coalition of northern state and city leaders who brought the most pressure to bear on it also stood to gain the *least* from the existing FSS plan, since the inclusion of national standards would mean bringing the benefit levels in southern states up to those of the North, rather than directly helping the northern states and cities. Despite these substantial benefits for the South, southern leaders did not lobby Nixon officials on the bill.

Work, Rehabilitation, and Viewing the FSS as "Welfare"

As pressure for reform continued to mount, Ehrlichman and Shultz developed a set of goals and guidelines that the administration would use to direct its last month of policy development.[89] Significantly, explicit discussions of urban disorder, family stability, interstate migration, and other social problems that were initially associated with GAI proposals were not part of the guidelines. These concerns had receded to the background. Of the nine programmatic criteria, six related in some way to work, including the necessity of a work package in the plan; a name for the program that connoted work; stronger overall work incentives; and child-care provisions so that women could work. The three other guidelines noted that costs should be secondary (the program costs would not be taken from the current fiscal year), stated that the program would eliminate social workers' "snooping," and argued that the younger generations should be kept off of welfare. Programmatically, these guidelines worked largely within the laissez-faire welfare reform paradigm, though the language regarding incentives sounded increasingly like what others described as work requirements.

Burns's continuing opposition to the FSS was relentless. During the same period that Ehrlichman and Shultz drafted their guidelines, he wrote a series of memos that criticized the FSS plan and outlined a final version of his own proposal. Nixon had in fact asked him to draw up a proposal that included most of the details of the FSS but also included work requirements. In the preliminary memo to his proposal, Burns complimented Nixon on his decision to include work requirements, but also took the opportunity to assail the FSS on a number of grounds, including its costs, its politics, and its effects.[90] When outlining his own proposal, he argued that welfare programs should be organized fundamentally around the concept of rehabilitation.[91] Inextricably linked to this perspective was his belief that the number of people on the welfare rolls should not increase. Concerns about the size of the rolls brought up the question of the working poor and whether to include them in the program. Toward the end of his proposal, he addressed this issue.

> The agitation for income guarantees and the like is coming from intellectuals who have not considered sufficiently what may happen to the moral fiber of America when many millions of people, many of whom do not consider themselves poor, are suddenly thrust by law onto the welfare rolls. If I am right in thinking that the basic aim of welfare reform should be to rehabilitate people, then the gains to be achieved through work and rehabilitation—on which I have been insisting—may be nullified by placing millions of self-reliant working people in a state of dependency.[92]

Here was the clearest statement of the rehabilitation paradigm. Burns located the source of the problem in the individual welfare recipient, who was in need of rehabilitation. Such rehabilitation would come through work. By this account, an increase in the rolls would mean a failure of the system because it fostered the conditions in which more rehabilitation was necessary.

More significant, however, was his equation of receiving income supplements, as the working poor would under the FSS, with being in a state of "dependency." This helped explain why he opposed income supplements to the working poor, even though he thought Nixon's welfare reform proposal needed to appeal to the white working class. What would please low-income workers more than a program in which they received money from the government in recognition of their work efforts?

The key to Burns's logic was concern about dependency and stigma. In his view, the working poor would be rendered "dependent" once they began receiving government benefits. The logic of this analysis depended on perceptions of moral contamination—that is, defining the FSS as a welfare program and then extrapolating the negative effects that the receipt of "welfare" payments would have on those who were already in the workforce. He was further convinced that the working poor themselves would see these payments as "welfare" payments and that they would reject any program that connoted this stigma.

Burns was not alone in his opposition to the FSS. By July, other important opponents to the plan included Bryce Harlow, Mayo, Kennedy, and McCracken; however, their opposition was more pragmatic than ideological. They did not react as much to the philosophy of the program as much as to its costs, timing, political liabilities, and unknown consequences. Because Nixon had promised to cut spending by $3 billion, some of his advisors believed it would be difficult to propose a program as expensive as the FSS. Politically, the timing was inopportune because the White House was also trying to push through other difficult legislation.[93] McCracken and the CEA analysts supported the possibility of enacting a plan like Burns's in the short term and then possibly proposing legislation like the FSS as a follow-up, once the effects of such programs were more well documented.[94] The fact that detractors of the FSS did not form a unified front weakened their opposition.

The Economic Citizenship Paradigm and Counterframing against Burns

Meanwhile supporters of the FSS devised counterframes that directly responded to the concerns of Burns and the other critics, especially on the issue of defining "welfare." A HEW report tried to present the big picture and clarify the different views of being "on welfare" that were implicit in the competing proposals.[95] The report argued that the new FSS gave the administration an overarching "vision" for its entire domestic agenda. It was a move away from in-kind services and toward cash programs that emphasized individual choice and empowerment. On the issue of adding millions to the welfare rolls, the report took Burns's claim head-on by giving Nixon a new framework with which to present his proposal.

> It is improper to consider the working poor, who will get wage supplements under the Shultz plan, as being added to the welfare rolls. These are not welfare recipients—they are not dependent persons who are living on the dole. It would be equally illogical to add to the welfare rolls all those persons who are receiving wage supplements under social security, veterans' benefits, food stamps, or unemployment insurance. This is a *new* category—it is a *new* Federal program of wage supplementation to the working poor—and the whole point is that these people are not thought of as welfare recipients.[96]

The document closed with the following argument about the inclusion of the working poor.

> It is important to recognize that the Shultz plan is by far the best approach we can take to deal with the "forgotten man"—the low income wage earner

in the $2,000 to $4,100 category. We can really do something for these people under this program, and it should have a tremendous beneficial political impact to [*sic*] the administration.[97]

The HEW report presented Nixon with an alternative vision of social provision and offered him a new way to discuss government support for the poor that steered away from the language of "welfare." The working poor would not be "welfare" recipients under the FSS scheme and their inclusion in the proposal, the report contended, could play to Nixon's advantage politically.

At the end of July, less than two weeks before Nixon's scheduled welfare announcement, supporters of the economic citizenship paradigm tried one more time to insert their proposal into the mix of welfare alternatives, since their vision of GAI plans had slowly been whittled away over the course of the summer. James Lyday, at the OEO, wrote an evaluative report that compared the original FSS, the new FSS-Shultz plan, and an "alternative" plan that he favored.[98] Though Lyday's alternative was not quite as comprehensive as the universal plan (the USS) that had been evaluated earlier, it was the most generous in benefit levels and most expansive in coverage to be discussed during the summer months. It had a larger income disregard rate and a higher income floor ($1,750) than did the Shultz plan. The bigger disregard would allow people to keep more of their initial income. The higher income floor would transfer more money to "those most in need" at the very bottom of the income ladder—those with little or no alternative sources of income. Though this plan had a higher net cost, it also covered 113,000 more families than did the Shultz plan. Thus, though the plan was not universal—it did not cover childless couples and single people—it covered the great majority of poor families in the country. Rumsfeld, Lyday's boss at the OEO, submitted Lyday's evaluation of the three plans to Ehrlichman, saying that it was based on the most recent data available. However, there was no further discussion of Lyday's alternative as the welfare reform planning went into its final days.

Selling a Plan for the Working Poor?

Foremost on the administration's agenda by this point was how to sell the Nixon plan to the public, whatever its final details looked like. By the middle of July, it was clear that one of the main themes the White House would emphasize was work—in particular, the plan's assistance to the working poor. Nixon himself had made this explicit. Moynihan described to Nixon a family allowance being considered in New York State that the *New York Times* characterized as a measure to aid "the working poor." Moynihan continued: "This phrase is appearing more and more frequently in both the press and in political discourse, as the problem it describes is increasingly understood to be of critical dimensions—and one that cannot logically or humanely be ignored by those who seek to address the problem of black, non-working, abject poverty."[99] Implicit in Moynihan's commentary was the view that "welfare" was for unemployed blacks, while a program that also assisted the working poor was categorically different. In the margins of the memo, Nixon circled the words "the working poor" and wrote *"excellent theme."* His advisor wrote to Moynihan to let him know that Nixon favored the working poor theme.[100]

Attempts to name Nixon's proposal suggested some of the difficulties in conceptualizing a program that did not work within the traditional categories of social provision. William Safire, one of Nixon's main speechwriters, led the effort to name the new welfare program along with naming the overall domestic package the president would announce with his welfare program—a package including revenue sharing, manpower training, and a reorganization of the OEO. In correspondence with Ehrlichman, Safire noted that coming up with a name for a program that included both aid to dependent families with no income and income supplements for the working poor was a difficult task. For the income supplement program, Safire recommended such names as Base Pay, Take-Home Supplement, and Paylift. As his ideas for naming the whole package progressed, he leaned toward Fair Share.[101] Writing to Ehrlichman, he noted, "Liberals will say it's about time people got their fair share. Conservatives will say they hope no one gets more than their fair share. States will say their fair share should be much higher, but cannot complain that any other State is getting more than their fair share of what goes to all States."[102]

Nixon liked Fair Share and indicated that he would use it in his address. Burns complained that Fair Share echoed Truman's Fair Deal domestic program moniker and that it also suggested redistribution. Instead, he proposed Full Opportunity System. In line with his focus on rehabilitation, he wrote that "the term 'Full Opportunity System' suggests a key role for the individual, while the term 'Fair Share System' may suggest a key role for the government."[103] Ultimately neither name was adopted. Two days before Nixon's address, the administration still could not decide on the name for either the welfare program or the domestic package. Two of the three favorite names for the welfare proposal emphasized work: Work Incentive Assistance and Workfare. The third was Family Assistance System.[104] By the day of Nixon's address, the White House had still not decided on a name and Nixon referred to the program in his speech as the Family Assistance System, which later became the Family Assistance Plan.

Final Objections to Nixon's Proposal

In the closing days before the announcement, critics of the proposal within the administration mounted their final attempt to change the president's mind. Their criticisms of the FSS raised two main points: concerns about costs and concerns about adding what was estimated to be thirteen million people to the "welfare" rolls. Unsurprisingly, the cost concerns were most forcefully articulated by Kennedy, Nixon's secretary of the treasury. Kennedy supported the Burns plan because it would reduce the number of people on the rolls, would cost less than the FSS (about $2.5 billion compared to the FSS at nearly $5 billion), and would still fulfill Nixon's pledges for welfare reform and revenue sharing. He argued that Nixon needed to make across-the-board cuts to programs, including defense, and this would make it difficult enough to afford the Burns plan, much less the FSS. Welfare spending at this level would leave virtually no additional money for other programs that Nixon desired. The president, he was afraid, would lose credibility on fiscal responsibility if he proposed the FSS.

Vice President Agnew and Burns also brought up the increase in "welfare" rolls. Agnew, who said he spoke for many within the administration, saw the FSS as a threat to the free enterprise system and, moreover, as pandering to the working poor. He argued it would bring "the addictive philosophy of welfare to those who are presently self-reliant."[105] Though he said the plan had arisen from the need to appeal to those just above the existing welfare payment lines, he felt that adding thirteen million people to the rolls would create a new class of "working poor," that is, those just above the new cutoff point. In his view, there would always be people just above the ceiling of welfare benefits who would be dissatisfied with the system. He further questioned the political viability of the plan. According to Agnew, it would "not be a political winner and will not attract low income groups to the Republican Party."[106]

Burns concurred: "Who will benefit? As the full implications of this proposal unfold, it becomes clear that FSS focuses primarily on the working poor. Over 90 percent of the $4 to $5 billion cost will be devoted to supplementing the incomes of the working poor."[107] He said that the FSS was really two programs—FSS-Welfare (which replaced AFDC) and FSS-Working Poor. The thirteen million new recipients in the working poor category, Burns argued, would receive immediate wage supplements and then "be virtually caught in a trap from which they have little financial incentive to move."[108] He tried to persuade Nixon that the consequence would be a vast number of workers with no incentive for self-improvement. In sum, Agnew and Burns, along with others, argued that adding the working poor to the rolls was objectionable on fiscal, economic, political, and moral grounds.

State governors raised different objections to the FSS in the days leading up to the announcement. In the middle of July, Governor Rockefeller had informed Nixon that he would be forced to oppose the FSS, even if he agreed with it in principle, because New York State would not receive any fiscal relief under the current plan. In his opinion, the FSS only benefited those states, such as many in the South, that had previously spent very little on the poor. He asked Nixon to revise the plan so it did not "discriminate" against more generous states.[109] Toward the end of the month, Ehrlichman and other

White House staff decided to meet with Rockefeller and other influential governors.[110]

At the meeting, the governors expressed unanimous dissatisfaction with the plan. Most important, they said there was not enough money for relatively generous northern states and that the plan appeared to be an attempt to court the favor of those in the South. The states with large welfare bills needed more money and revenue sharing, they argued, was not going to be enough. There were additional concerns expressed as well. The governor of Ohio did not think the Republican Party should help the working poor and considered the work incentives in the plan "phony." The governor of Massachusetts claimed that people were fed up with welfare. The governor of Maryland argued that welfare was a federal responsibility and that the government should take over even more public assistance programs than it had proposed. And Ronald Reagan, the California governor and the only non-northern governor present, argued just the opposite—that the states should have total control over welfare administration.[111] Ultimately this pressure from the governors resulted in the addition of the "50-90" provision of Nixon's plan, in which each state would be required to spend at least 50 percent of its current welfare expenditures, while no state would be required to spend more than 90 percent of expenditures under the current system.

Framing Nixon's Plan

On August 6, two days before the scheduled announcement of his domestic program, Nixon held a cabinet meeting at Camp David to go over the final details. The administration's briefing team opened the discussion of welfare reform by enumerating the failures of the current system—family breakup, interstate inequities, and so forth. They included as a failure the dramatic increase in the AFDC caseload, without noting the apparent contradiction that the proposed FSS would dramatically increase the number of people receiving cash benefits from the government by many millions of people. Nixon closed the discussion by pitching reform as an attempt to address the current "welfare mess." Though he was aware of criticisms of the plan, he encouraged the assembled members of the administration to focus the public's attention on the merits of the new reform package. Regarding the name of his plan, everyone agreed that its current, working title, the Family Security Plan, needed to be changed in order to emphasize the plan's strong work requirements and the provision of work incentives and job training.[112]

The new proposal would cover all poor families, both "dependent" and "working poor," including working poor families headed by a man. Baseline benefits for a family of four would be $1,600 per year, with an earnings disregard of $720 annually per family. So that benefits would not be reduced for any family currently on AFDC, states would be required to pay benefits equal to the difference between the proposed minimum standard and the state's present level. However, all states would receive federal assistance and none would be required to supplement the incomes of the working poor. A work requirement would stipulate that the unemployed poor in the "employable" category were required to register for training or employment placement, or else lose a portion of their family benefits. Training and day care programs were included in the plan and it would be administered by the Social Security Administration. Fiscal relief for the states would follow the 50-90 plan the governors had lobbied for, along with the additional revenue-sharing funds. The total cost of the program was $5 billion, with $2.2 billion going to the poor, $1.7 billion going to the states, $600 million going toward job training and day care, and another $500 million for additional expenses.[113]

In the final two days, Ehrlichman honed the public presentation of the plan. In reviewing a draft of the president's welfare speech, he noted that it needed to make a stronger statement that Nixon was not proposing a GAI program. However, the program was, he argued, a brand-new approach to fixing the "welfare mess." Ehrlichman emphasized that the speech should stress a phrase about moving people "off the welfare rolls and onto payrolls." To anticipate criticisms of the costs, he noted that the president should emphasize that the program would not begin until the 1971 fiscal year, when the administration projected that funds would be available. Most significant, he wrote that rhetorically the welfare speech had to be explicitly targeted at taxpayers and the working poor, and not at current AFDC recipients, blacks, or the unemployed.[114]

This signaled the final transformation of GAI programs over the six-month development period within the Nixon administration. The FSS was not targeted to assist unemployed blacks or even largely to replace the current AFDC system with a better program for the unemployed poor. Though the plan did not propose to make existing AFDC recipients any worse off, the great majority of the new expenditures would go to the working poor, who were largely white. Despite the packaging, however, the proposal was still revolutionary. It provided benefits to two-parent families. It guaranteed all families a minimum income. And, most important, it provided benefits to the unemployed and employed poor within the same program, thereby erasing the existing distinctions between different categories of poor people.

Yet one would never have known these things from listening to Nixon's address. In his welfare speech, which introduced his newly renamed Family Assistance Plan, Nixon said the nation faced a crisis, "an urban crisis, a social crisis, a crisis in the confidence in the capacity of the government to do its job. . . . Nowhere has the failure of government been more tragically apparent than in its efforts to help the poor, and especially in its system of public welfare."[115] He enumerated the administration's criticisms of the existing system and outlined his new approach, following Ehrlichman's lead.

This new approach aims at helping the American people do more for themselves. It aims at getting everyone able to work off welfare rolls and onto payrolls. It aims at ending the unfairness in a system that has become unfair to the welfare recipient, unfair to the working poor, and unfair to the taxpayer.

The president recognized that the current system "has been bitterly resented by the man who works," and Nixon harkened back to the theme of work again and again. (A liberal critic wrote that Nixon "offered the poor the Protestant Ethic warmed over.")[116] He said that the new system rested on three principles: equal treatment across the states, a work requirement, and work incentives. He said that the government recognized for the first time that it had an equal obligation to the working poor as it had to the non–working poor. "But what of the others—those who can work but choose not to? Well, the answer is very simple." The answer was work requirements.

In defense of the considerable expense of the program, he argued that the program was an investment, a " 'start-up cost' in turning around our dangerous decline into welfarism." He added,

> In the final analysis, we cannot talk our way out of poverty; we cannot legislate our way out of poverty; but this nation can work itself out of poverty. What this nation needs now is not more welfare, but more "workfare." The task of this Government, the great task of our people, is to provide the training for work, the incentive to work, the opportunity to work, the reward for work. Together, these measures are a first, long step in that direction. For those in the welfare system today, or struggling to fight their way out of poverty, these measures offer a way to independence through the dignity of work.

Finally, Nixon distanced his program from what critics would call a guaranteed annual income program.

> This national floor under income for working or dependent families is not a "guaranteed income." Under the guaranteed income proposal, everyone would be assured a minimum income, regardless of how much he was capable of earning, regardless of what his needs were, regardless of whether or not he was willing to work. No, during the Presidential campaign last year I opposed such a plan. I oppose it now, and I will continue to oppose it. And this is the reason. A guaranteed income would undermine the incentive to work; the family assistance plan that I propose increases the incentive to work. A guaranteed income establishes a right without any responsibilities; family assistance recognizes a need and establishes a responsibility. It provides help to those in need, and in turn requires that those who receive help work to the extent of their capabilities. There is no reason why one person should be taxed so that another can choose to live idly.

Nixon's rhetorical efforts to reposition his GAI plan within the rehabilitation paradigm contained four central ironies. First, Nixon repeatedly referred to unemployment as a "choice," even though the plan he proposed had originated within the Johnson administration in response to structural views of unemployment. Second, he bemoaned the country's decline into "welfarism," even though his program proposed to add thirteen million recipients to the government rolls. Third, 90 percent of the expenditures in Nixon's program were directed at the working poor, yet Nixon denigrated the character of people who received government benefits. Fourth, Nixon argued that he wanted to move people from the "welfare rolls" to the "payrolls," even though the majority of the recipients in this program would have been simultaneously located on both. The plan, in fact, was recognition that the "payrolls" themselves did not provide economic security for many Americans. In these ways, Nixon's rhetoric reinforced the categorical distinctions between poor people that his program actually blurred. Nixon was proposing a new kind of social provision to the American public, but he did not offer them a new conceptual framework through which to understand it. This set the stage for the coming debate over GAI policies.

CONCLUSION

If Nixon struggled in his welfare speech to distance his plan from a "guaranteed income" program, it was largely because he had never intended to propose one. He assumed office knowing he would have to contend with the many issues collectively known as the "welfare mess": urban unrest, racial tensions, rising welfare caseloads, interstate migration, family instability, the lack of national standards, and fiscal crises in state and local governments. Despite the pressures these issues placed on the administration, guaranteed income plans were not an inevitable response. Nixon ended up advancing a GAI proposal because a cadre of government experts convinced him that it was a promising way to deal with these problems. The plan could carve out a new direction for domestic social policy in ways that might appeal to new constituents. Despite the bold break with existing policy design that the FSS represented, few of the administration's policy experts, with a few significant exceptions, associated it with strong ideological or partisan overtones in the early months of deliberation.

Though the FSS eventually encountered opposition based on a variety of concerns, the inclusion of the working poor within the Nixon administration's "welfare" package proved to be the most contentious and problematic element of the plan as it developed over the course of the summer. The plan included income supplements for the working poor to reward participation in the labor market and to ensure that employment always paid more than receiving welfare benefits while unemployed. Yet this created a cultural problem. Everyone viewed the working poor and the "welfare" poor as categorically different from one another. Nixon's speechwriter realized this as he struggled to come up with a name for a plan that encompassed both these groups. Burns captured this most succinctly by claiming that Nixon's proposal really contained two different programs, FSS-Welfare and FSS-Working Poor. This perspective was shared by many others—Moynihan, Ehrlichman, Finch, Safire, and Agnew— both supporters and opponents alike. In other words, they all shared the same cognitive template that distinguished between different categories of poor people. The disagreement within the administration involved not how they perceived these groups, but whether it was desirable to blur the distinction between these groups through the structure of Nixon's new plan or reinforce it through Burns's alternative proposal.

The consequences did not speak for themselves. It took active claims-making on the part of opponents such as Burns and Anderson to construe the FSS as threatening the existing economic order. They warned against giving income supplements to the working poor because doing so would trap workers in a state of dependency from which they could not escape. These claims were based on symbolic pollution—that is, on seeing even income supplements for the working poor as "welfare" benefits that would corrupt the work ethic of employed recipients. The institutional structure of the welfare state made the working poor especially vulnerable to being labeled "welfare" recipients, since existing social policy did not provide any alternative status through which to understand them as government beneficiaries of income maintenance. Burns, along with other conservatives, was convinced that even members of the working class themselves would define the benefits contained in Nixon's program as "welfare" benefits and resist the associated stigma.

Concerns about an unconditional entitlement to a minimum income accounted for the inclusion of work requirements in the final plan that Nixon announced to the country. These requirements were antithetical to Shultz's laissez-faire justification for his own GAI proposal, which relied solely on work incentives, as well as to the economic citizenship approach to reform, which did not assume that the work behavior of the poor was the problem at all. Yet fears of a racially motivated public backlash against the plan impelled Nixon to append work requirements to his program. The contradictory messages that the plan's programmatic details and public symbolism projected helps account for the confusing political dynamics that ensued once Nixon's proposal went public.

CHAPTER FOUR

Nixon's Family Assistance Plan Stalls

After Nixon announced his Family Assistance Plan (FAP) in August 1969, the administration sought to curry public favor for the plan and guide it through Congress. Frustration with the existing system ran high and the initial public reaction to the FAP was positive. During the early months of consideration, the meaning of Nixon's proposal was widely debated and its legislative prospects were far from clear. One could have supposed—as people did—that the FAP would receive support from Democrats because it was an expansion of welfare state protection, from Republicans because it was associated with Milton Friedman and had been proposed by a president from their own party, from the southern states because they stood to receive the greatest fiscal benefit from the legislation, from the working class because they would receive income supplements on top of their earned income, and from welfare rights groups because they had been calling for this type of legislation. The reality turned out to be more complex. One contemporaneous commentator, noting the surprising policy stances taken by many groups, observed that the debate over the FAP "revealed a state of ideological anarchy."[1] In the spring of 1970, the FAP passed in the House of Representatives by a large majority and headed into the Senate, which was considered the more liberal chamber of Congress. However, the plan stalled in a Senate committee for the rest of the year. This meant that new legislation needed to be proposed at the start of the 1971 congressional session. This chapter traces the debate over Nixon's first version of the FAP, which extended through the end of 1970.

Understanding the trajectory of Nixon's legislation requires looking at the interplay between cultural conceptions of the poor, the policy preferences and legislative influence of various stakeholder groups, and the broader institutional context in which the policy debates took place. The distinction between the deserving and undeserving poor defined the cultural context for the whole debate. While administration officials had developed an alternative template for understanding poverty and social provision during the lead-up to Nixon's announcement, neither the president nor members of his administration utilized this new template. Instead, their language hewed closely to dominant understandings of poverty and American social policy. On the basis of the administration's rehabilitationist framing, the proposal received a considerable amount of conservative support. However, the fact that the design of the plan actually blurred the distinction between deserving and undeserving poor had far-reaching consequences. Because the tainted moral status of the AFDC population contaminated perceptions of the whole program, Nixon's plan was defined as a "welfare" plan and its costs were defined as "welfare" costs.[2] The fact that the FAP's benefits, even those for employed recipients, were characterized as "welfare" benefits subsequently shaped the interests of important stakeholders, such as the U.S. Chamber of Commerce and the working poor themselves. And though costs alone were never an insurmountable obstacle for GAI plans, because politicians and the public construed them as "welfare" costs, increases in such expenditures were highly contentious, especially since by this time "welfare" and welfare rights had become closely associated with black activism.

The interest group environment was complicated, as many commentators noted, due in large part to the contradictions between the plan's substance and symbolism. State and local leaders were a potent source of support for the FAP, despite a number of criticisms, because they viewed the plan as a way of obtaining fiscal relief from the federal government. Moderate business leaders and organizations, who did not consider the poor to be responsible for their own poverty, favored the plan for reasons having to do with urban unrest, enlightened self-interest, and a sense of social justice. In direct contrast, many conservative small business owners favored Nixon's plan because they were swayed by his rhetoric about dependency and the importance of the work ethic. They were convinced that the plan was "tough on welfare." The NWRO strongly supported the principles of GAI plans. Yet they opposed Nixon's specific legislation. In part, this was due to concessions he had made to state leaders and conservatives that resulted in lower benefits and stricter work requirements for the unemployed poor. The NWRO's demands, however, far exceeded those considered by any policymaker. Its leaders called for benefit levels that more than tripled those contained in Nixon's legislation. Tensions between welfare rights groups and the administration were further exacerbated by Nixon's persistent use of rhetoric that cast the poor in a negative light in an attempt to appeal to working-class voters. Throughout consideration of the legislation, labor unions, working-class citizens, and left-liberal opinion leaders remained disengaged from the debate.

One of the most influential sources of opposition came from the U.S. Chamber of Commerce. Strikingly, the chamber's primary rationale for opposing Nixon's plan was not based on its increased benefit levels for the "welfare" poor currently receiving AFDC, even though opposing these types of increases was a longstanding practice of the chamber's. Their opposition was based instead on the plan's wage supplements to the working poor, which the chamber felt would threaten the nation's economic productivity and render the working poor in a state of dependency. This claim reproduced Martin Anderson's earlier concern that a GAI plan would have the same deleterious effects on the nation's economic system as the Speenhamland Act had had on England's. Extending stigmatized "welfare" benefits to fully employed households threatened the economic interests of low-wage employers, though this threat depended on particular assumptions about the poor that were widely contested.

Regional differences between the South and the rest of the country exerted considerable influence on the development of Nixon's plan, and the influence of these differences was further magnified by the policymaking process in Congress. The policy preferences of blacks, Democrats, and business groups were each split along regional lines. For blacks, this mainly had to do with the vast differences in existing AFDC benefit levels between northern and southern states. Poor blacks in the South stood to gain much more from the FAP than did poor blacks in the Northeast. Democrats and business groups in the South viewed Nixon's plan in fundamentally different ways than did their northern counterparts because of the complex interplay between labor market dynamics, race relations, and views of the poor that were particular to the region. Concerns about work, which were heightened by race-based stereotyping and animosity, led these groups to oppose the plan on economic grounds. Just as important were the political implications of the plan. The white southern establishment feared that Nixon's plan would equalize power between the races. These views were disproportionately influential in Congress because the legislative process channeled decision-making power on most antipoverty policy through the Senate Finance Committee, which was chaired by a conservative southern Democrat. He and other conservatives on the committee sharply distinguished between the deserving and undeserving poor, and their overwhelming objective was not to alleviate poverty but to decrease welfare caseloads and put the poor to work. This congressional bottleneck posed a persistent obstacle to Nixon's legislation. Yet at the outset of debate over the FAP, these obstacles seemed surmountable to the Nixon administration if handled in the right manner.

Despite the fact that few groups were wholly enthusiastic about Nixon's proposal, a host of concerns propelled it forward. Everyone wanted welfare reform and the FAP seemed like one of the few viable alternatives to the status quo. Many moderates, and even some conservatives, argued that a vote against the Nixon plan was a vote for the status quo. Given concerns about fiscal strains, family stability, interstate migration, and other issues that constituted the "welfare mess," few people wanted to keep things as they were, even though concerns about civil unrest had begun to subside. One of the striking things about the debate as it unfolded was the relative inattention to the issue of poverty. Despite the fact that GAI proposals had emerged directly from concerns about poverty reduction, little of the public discourse reflected this objective. By 1970, the dominant set of problems to be addressed by welfare reform had shifted from poverty reduction to work behavior, program costs, revenue sharing, and the deficiencies of the welfare system itself.

THE INITIAL REACTION

Nixon understood the importance of crafting his messages for media consumption and was consummately strategic in this regard. One of his aides reported that Nixon could "think like an editor" when it came to packaging his ideas and programs.[3] In the days preceding his welfare announcement, Nixon got to work framing his plan. He assured key leaders in Congress that he would emphasize its work requirement and revenue-sharing aspects. The leaders expressed concerns that Nixon's legislation contained a guaranteed income component, but he assured them that it would not.[4] Nixon's emphasis on work and revenue sharing, as well as the carefully crafted rhetorical description of his legislation, accounts for the favorable public reaction that the FAP initially received between August and the first House vote on the bill in the spring of 1970. Instead of promoting new ways of thinking about poverty and the role of government along the lines articulated by early proponents of GAI plans, Nixon capitalized on prevailing understandings and stereotypes.

In the days following Nixon's announcement, the White House left nothing to chance. The administration mobilized briefing teams to visit the editorial offices of both the big-city newspapers and those located in the country's hinterlands. Daniel Patrick Moynihan, Robert Finch, and other welfare experts appeared on the weekend television news shows. The public relations staff described a "sell and re-sell" strategy in which they carefully selected aspects of the legislation to highlight with various constituencies, such as minority groups and business leaders.[5]

These efforts appeared to reap dividends as the White House began to tabulate its analyses of press coverage. A preliminary assessment of over four hundred editorials showed that more than 90 percent of them favored Nixon's plan. The most popular aspect of the plan was the merging of work requirements with the general income maintenance scheme. Most of the editorials couched their praise in the argument that the existing welfare system was a "colossal failure," an indication that the mounting criticisms of the existing system from policy experts and Nixon's antiwelfare rhetoric had persuaded the country of the desperate need for reforming the system. The most prevalent reservation among the editorials was that Nixon might not be able to achieve the objectives he outlined for the country. The few editorials that opposed the plan criticized it as a continuation of the existing welfare state that would further increase welfare costs and add to the number of people on the rolls.[6] This critique, of course, depended on seeing the FAP as a "welfare" plan. A more detailed follow-up analysis undertaken by the White House a month later confirmed these trends in editorial support, but noted that despite this continuing support, editorialists and columnists had begun to express reservations and objections as time passed, particularly in regard to the plan's workability.[7]

Letters written to the White House further affirmed the administration's view that it had strong support to proceed with the program. In the three days following Nixon's announcement, the FAP received positive comments by a ratio of over ten to one.[8] In the following month, the trend largely continued. From a total of more than 2,700 letters and telegrams, over 80 percent expressed unqualified approval, and another 10 percent approved, though with reservations and suggestions for improvement. In examining the results, one of Nixon's aides noted the fact that most of the letters came from "usually noncommunicative middle-class Americans who have not written to the President before" and who had likewise sent correspondence to their members of Congress favoring the plan.[9] Nixon had apparently raised themes in his speech that resonated with these citizens, one of which was undoubtedly his emphasis on work. Public opinion polls by the Gallup and Harris organizations showed support for Nixon's plan, particularly when the survey questions emphasized work incentives. Some Gallup polls showed support as high as 65 percent.[10]

Race and the South

Support for the FAP was not evenly distributed geographically, however, and Nixon recognized this. In particular, he understood the challenges that regionalism and race would present to his plan. He asked Ehrlichman, "What kind of people in the South" currently receive welfare? Ehrlichman, understanding the racial coding of his question, responded with an analysis of welfare recipients broken down by race and family structure. In the southern states, roughly half the families receiving benefits were black. Of the black families, two-thirds were female-headed households; among white families, the percentage of female-headed households was under 50 percent. The FAP would triple the number of families receiving government assistance in the South, and 60 percent of the additional families would be white.[11] Despite this boon to southern whites, initial support in the South was considerably weaker than it was throughout the rest of the country. This would prove to be a crucial fact as the legislation wended its way through Congress. The role of the South in shaping federal antipoverty policy, such as during the debates over Roosevelt's New Deal legislation, has always been considerable, and the politics of the FAP proved to be no exception.[12]

Immediately after Nixon's announcement, the White House launched initiatives to emphasize the benefits of the FAP in the South. In a memo to the state chairmen of the National Committee of Southern States, the administration highlighted the program's selling points, emphasizing both the fiscal assistance the bill provided and the strong work requirements. The memo continued: "If this is handled properly, you ought to be able to get some of the traditional Democrat votes loosened up and capture some votes that went the third party route in 1968."[13] This objective was part of Nixon's broader "southern strategy," an effort to pry away from the Democratic Party the southern white voters who had been attracted to George Wallace's segregationist 1968 presidential campaign.[14] Administration officials touring the region immediately after Nixon's announcement looked forward to considerable support in the South, particularly because of the well-received emphasis Nixon had placed on the work features of the plan.[15]

However, the Nixon administration faced an uphill battle in the South. The southern economy, due to its labor-intensive agricultural base, had long depended on a low-wage labor market. Historically this meant hostility toward any type of policy that was construed as placing upward pressure on wages. Thus southern business interests played a longstanding and central role in fighting federal social policy.[16] Even largely state-run antipoverty efforts were subject to more hostility in the South than they were elsewhere. Some of the earliest backlashes against AFDC in the 1950s occurred in southern states like Georgia, where the influence of agribusiness, race antagonisms, and fiscal pressures combined to create potent antiwelfare sentiments. The link between welfare backlash and local labor market conditions became especially apparent in many southern states during the planting and harvesting seasons, when local welfare agencies cut off their benefits altogether in order to expand the pool of low-wage laborers available to plantation owners.[17]

Nixon's plan thus raised these same types of concerns about labor market defection, as was well documented in a widely read *Fortune* magazine article titled "The Looming Money Revolution Down South."[18] On the possible consequences of the FAP, it quoted Georgia representative Phillip Landrum as saying, "There's not going to be anybody left to roll these wheelbarrows and press these shirts. They're all going to be on welfare."[19] The southern conservative quoted in the article took a clearly rehabilitationist view of the aims of welfare reform. Georgia's governor argued that welfare programs needed to be made more demeaning rather than more liberal: "Able-bodied men or women who could work, but refuse job after job in order to draw a welfare check should be made to feel like the bums they are."[20] Though the article did not say so explicitly, one of the concerns among southern politicians and business interests was that Nixon's legislation, by increasing welfare benefits, would increase the "reservation wage"—the wage at which people find it more attractive to work than remain unemployed.[21] This could force employers to raise wage levels, which would cut into their profit margins and could make the South a less attractive destination for businesses that sought to locate in states with a cheap, nonunionized labor force. This had been the source of opposition to raising traditional "welfare" benefits under the AFDC system.

Yet the FAP was not the same as the AFDC program. It also contained income supplements for the working poor. This meant that even if the base reservation wage were raised by the higher benefit levels given to the unemployed poor, employers would not necessarily be pressured to raise their own wage levels because the government would step in to provide income supplements. This, at least, was what government officials believed. The article quoted a HEW official who argued that work defection would not be a problem, even in the absence of work requirements: "Everything we have been able to learn indicates that when people have the work habit, and the great majority do, it is very strongly held. Even if there were no work requirement in the bill, I would expect the tractor operator to keep on driving the tractor and the maid to keep on cleaning house—so long as they keep all or most of what they earn."[22] Following lines of thought among many policy experts in Washington, this official viewed the poor as sharing the mainstream work ethic and assumed that negative effects on labor market dynamics would not be a problem as long as income through employment was more economically rewarding than government benefits alone. Based on this analysis, the article's author seemed to share these sentiments. He noted that "work will not be a novel experience for the majority of the family heads covered by the bill . . . 67 percent of them are already working at low-wage jobs." Especially in light of the work stipulations contained in the bill, he contended that the "practical effect, in most cases, will be to confirm these family heads in the jobs they already hold, while providing a bonus in the form of a family assistance check."[23]

Thus concerns about work were clearly at the heart of the debate over the FAP in the South, but the perceived threat to the southern labor market was based to a considerable extent on the way one viewed the poor themselves. Did the poor value work and the opportunity to better themselves and their families, or were they shiftless opportunists who would take any opening to opt out of the labor market? It was here that racial stereotypes intersected with concerns about work. And particularly in the South, views of the poor were inextricably premised on racial stereotypes that reinforced a racial caste system that had only recently been challenged. Racial animus lay just beneath the surface of the backlash against welfare in the post–New Deal period. Many "race-blind" policies had disproportionately adverse consequences for blacks.[24] Throughout the 1960s, southern politicians were on record calling black welfare recipients slothful and lazy and equating poor black "welfare" mothers with breeding animals.[25]

Despite disagreements over the work behavior of the poor, the consequence of the FAP that nearly everyone agreed on was that it would equalize earnings between men and women and blacks and whites at the bottom of the wage scale.[26] Because it placed a safety net underneath the household earnings of *all* the poor, this type of income equalization threatened to transform the balance of political power between blacks and whites. Greater economic security would translate into greater political power. Blacks in the South had long been subjected to threats and physical violence when they had become too involved in the political process. They were also systematically excluded from the welfare system when they engaged in civil rights activities or tried to register to vote. Despite the civil rights legislation of the mid-1960s, blacks were still profoundly underrepresented in the political process.[27] The *Fortune* article reported that "a guaranteed income, under a federal program with national standards fairly administered, could go a long way to lift black fears of voting and speaking out. The day of black government may be speeded in the hundreds of small towns and dozens of counties where blacks are in the majority."[28] As one black interviewee bluntly assessed the FAP's possible consequences, "I know a lot of white people who will be told to go to hell."[29] Given these implications, black activists expressed skepticism that the white power structure would permit the effective implementation and operation of Nixon's legislation.

Poor whites in the South were conspicuously absent from the debates over the FAP in the South. They were, as Sherlock Homes might put it, the dog that did not bark. The Nixon administration had structured the FAP so that the working poor would receive more benefits than the "welfare" poor, and as government studies made clear, poor whites in the South stood to gain considerably more than did poor blacks. Had poor whites placed pressure on southern politicians to pass the legislation, one possible outcome could have been a weakening of the national standards criteria contained in the bill. Since both wage and benefit levels were so much lower in southern states than in the rest of the country, weakening these standards could have dampened upward pressure on wages, to the extent it existed, while still providing improved income assistance to white workers. So why did the white working poor not express their support for the legislation? In the absence of much evidence it is hard to know. A likely reason is that they simply did not recognize that the FAP would work in their favor. Nixon's plan was seen as a "welfare" plan, and the president characterized it as a bold move to end the problem of welfare dependency. The dominant rhetoric surrounding the bill, both nationally and especially as used by administration officials in the South, emphasized work requirements and rehabilitation. So it would be unsurprising if the white working poor never realized that the legislation was also in their material interest. Moreover, white southern politicians had scant incentive to alert them to the fact.

The FAP presented a complex set of choices for people in the South. White and black communities had reasons to both support and oppose the plan. White officials realized the FAP would bring an infusion of federal dollars into an underfunded system, the spending of which would be left up to the discretion of local authorities. Moreover, over half of the poor who would be newly covered by the FAP were white. These were the benefits that the Nixon's administration emphasized to southern leaders. In the everyday calculus of elected officials, these merits would have appeared compelling. But the downside for white leaders was that many beneficiaries would be black and this might further alter the political and economic dynamics in a region that was still profoundly struggling to cope with the changes wrought by the civil rights movement. White politicians were also skeptical that the work requirements contained in the FAP could be adequately enforced. Blacks, on the other hand, favored the aspects of the bill that would reconfigure power and influence in the region. However, they distrusted both Nixon and white southern politicians and considered the work requirements racist. Further, most of the information that southern black leaders received about the FAP came from blacks in the North, who distrusted Nixon even more and argued that the benefit levels in the bill were far from adequate. Due to the large differences between AFDC benefit levels in the North and South, blacks in these regions had interests that were considerably at odds.

Black Leadership and the NWRO

Nixon had never been on good terms with the black community. One of his first meetings with national black leaders—arranged by Moynihan and including Ralph Abernathy, George Wiley, and others—went disastrously. According to one of Nixon's advisors, Nixon's guests criticized him so harshly on racial issues that he broke off the meeting in frustration, told them that the country's priorities were foreign policy and ending the Vietnam War, and then stormed out of the room. The black leaders duly reported to the press that Nixon did not care about impoverished blacks. Nixon considered the meeting one of the major mistakes of his first year in office.[30] This strained relationship worked to his disadvantage when trying to sell the FAP to black leaders. They were especially critical of his rhetoric about welfare dependency and all it implied about the black community. Almost all the politically active black groups were located in the North and they recognized that most of the benefits would go to the South. In fact, as congressional hearings would show, some northern welfare recipients might be slightly worse off under the FAP than they were under the existing system. Thus, black journalists reacted coolly to the FAP and public opinion polls showed less support among blacks than whites.[31]

Among black leaders, opinion on the FAP was split and no one fully embraced the plan without reservations. Whitney Young, leader of the National Urban League, issued a reserved statement directly following Nixon's announcement saying that the FAP was a step in the right direction, primarily because it recognized a number of problems that had previously gone unrecognized. He called for additional funds to be devoted to the program, but said that the FAP was a palatable opening gambit, considering the generally punitive mood the public seemed to be in.[32] To the extent that black leaders, such as Young, viewed the FAP favorably, it was probably because Moynihan actively cultivated their support prior to Nixon's announcement.[33] Yet throughout the congressional debates over the FAP, the black community's support was never more than ambivalent. The exception was the NWRO, one of the most publicly visible organizations in the welfare debates, which railed against the FAP from the beginning. In the weeks following Nixon's announcement, George Wiley, the organization's leader, argued that the benefit levels of the FAP legislation were insufficient and suggested there might be rioting in the streets as a consequence. These threats against the administration were reiterated in places like California, where welfare activists labeled Nixon an "enemy of the poor" and called for actions to improve the situation of welfare recipients by "any means necessary."[34]

Views of the FAP by the leadership of the NWRO only became more critical over time.[35] While they always viewed the benefit levels in the FAP as inadequate, they initially treated the legislation as a useful point of departure for negotiations. The organization's early slogan was "Up the Nixon plan!" which both suggested their hostile view of the administration and their assessment that the benefit levels were far too low. As time went on and the content of the FAP was modified by congressional committees in ways the organization considered increasingly threatening to existing recipients, the group's organizing slogan became "Zap FAP!" "NWRO's response," Wiley claimed, "must be to escalate the 'welfare crisis' which forced Nixon to make his token proposals," and therefore create further pressure for Nixon and Congress to increase benefit levels.[36]

Because the NWRO had been campaigning since 1967 for a welfare recipient's "right to income," the organization's opposition to the Nixon plan might be puzzling on its face. However, the organization's leaders distrusted Nixon because they recognized his attempt to appeal to the racially prejudiced constituency that had voted for Wallace in 1968.[37] In addition, Nixon emphasized the work requirements of the bill and emphatically argued that the FAP was not a guaranteed income because of these requirements. The NWRO leadership focused more on Nixon's rhetoric than the programmatic advances the plan promised through its design. Like their counterparts in the South, they were skeptical of the plan because of their suspicion of those in power.

The NWRO's opposition also had a more pragmatic element. It concerned the FAP's benefit levels and illustrates the gendered nature of the plan. With its emphasis on work incentives, the bill primarily targeted employed or employable men. The main goal of the FAP was to maintain and encourage male participation in the low-wage labor market. The administration viewed the FAP's income supplements as a key selling point. However, the NWRO was made up primarily of unemployed mothers receiving AFDC. So they focused on the FAP's minimum guaranteed income of $1,600 that would go to women outside the labor market rather than focusing on the new benefits that would go to the working poor. As the debates over the FAP wore on, the NWRO would advocate legislation with a minimum income floor of up to

$6,500, which was based on the Bureau of Labor Statistics' standard-of-living measure, legislation that entailed an enormous increase in program costs.[38]

Business Opposition: The U.S. Chamber of Commerce

Another set of stakeholder groups that played a significant role in the debates over Nixon's plan was the business community, especially the U.S. Chamber of Commerce, the National Association of Manufacturers (NAM), and the Council for Economic Development (CED). These groups received much more attention from the Nixon administration than groups like the NWRO because they were traditional Republican constituents. In the final analysis, the business community was divided over Nixon's plan. The leaders of the U.S. Chamber of Commerce strenuously opposed the FAP, while most other business groups supported it.

The administration's chief focus among all the groups that opposed the FAP was the U.S. Chamber of Commerce. Aside from the chamber's lobbying power, this concern also reflected Nixon's interest in the views of "Main Street" over those of Wall Street.[39] The White House took great pains to stay in contact with the Chamber of Commerce throughout the debate over FAP, to cultivate the points of agreement between the chamber and the administration, and to mobilize a countervailing business response on the points of disagreement. In the months immediately following Nixon's announcement, the chamber did not direct much of its attention to the administration's welfare proposal. Instead their lobbying efforts focused on domestic issues such as manpower training, housing construction, crime control, and vocational education. During the winter of 1970, as the bill's prospects looked increasingly favorable, the chamber's priorities changed. It announced its opposition to the FAP and made defeating the bill its highest legislative priority.[40]

This opposition from the national office was out of step with the views of members of local branches of the Chamber of Commerce. Internal polling showed that 86 percent of local business leaders who were affiliated with the chamber *supported* the FAP. Nevertheless, in the days preceding the first vote of the full House on the FAP, the chamber's national office placed ads in the *Washington Post, Wall Street Journal, New York Times,* and other papers detailing its opposition to the legislation. This media strategy was accompanied by lobbying visits to members of Congress in key states.[41]

The U.S. Chamber of Commerce had consistently opposed the expansion of governmental social provision, especially if it threatened to undermine the low-wage labor market. Yet rather than opposing the FAP on the basis of its guaranteed minimum income for the unemployed poor—which could facilitate the ability of the poor to opt out of the labor market altogether—the main reason the leadership of the chamber opposed the FAP was the bill's inclusion of the working poor.[42] In its "Special Report on Welfare" mailed out to thirty thousand of its action committee members, the chamber contended that FAP legislation targeted three different groups—those receiving categorical assistance, such as the blind, aged, and disabled; those currently receiving AFDC benefits; and the working poor. The report stated that if the FAP covered only the first two groups, the chamber would have far fewer criticisms of the bill. However, the inclusion of the working poor was objectionable on a number of grounds. Most fundamentally, as the report stated, "As long as welfare is restricted to families where the family breadwinner is incapacitated, unemployed, or just not there, there is a more or less realistic measuring rod . . . [but] a system under which everyone is guaranteed a minimum income would do incalculable damage to an economic system that is built on an incentive system. . . . It is this provision that packs the greatest economic wallop."[43] Like many southerners, the chamber's leadership believed that workers would cease seeking advancement because their incentives would be weakened by the FAP benefits. A further concern was that workers might not register for new training opportunities that could upgrade their skills. While the chamber articulated other concerns—such as doubts that the FAP could mitigate rates of family breakup and interstate migration—the concern about the working poor dominated their criticisms of the plan.

A month later, the chamber's executive vice president wrote to Nixon to reiterate the organization's opposition to the FAP. The great majority of the three-page letter was devoted to objections to providing income supplements to the working poor.

> We do not believe that adding them to the welfare rolls is a solution to the basic welfare problem. . . . We believe that work incentives and personal initiatives would be weakened by such a program. . . . We believe that in its total effect, this part of the program—paying welfare to fully employed father families—would impair the nation's productivity.[44]

A few things stand out in the opposition to the FAP articulated by the Chamber of Commerce. First, the chamber viewed the plan as providing benefits to fundamentally different categories of people. Second, the organization's primary concern about payments to the working poor once again showed how radical this type of income supplementation program appeared to the plan's opponents. Third, both the special report and the personal correspondence to Nixon repeatedly referred to such payments as "welfare" payments. Following lines of reasoning that had been expressed by Arthur Burns, Anderson, and others, these opponents feared that such "welfare" payments would harm workers' work ethic by rendering them "dependent." Fourth, both the special report and the correspondence noted how little was actually known about the possible effects of a GAI program on the behavior of the poor, either in terms of affecting family stability or of its impact on work effort.[45] Therefore, the impact of income supplements on the working poor—and thus the impact of the FAP on the economic interests of business—remained a speculative matter based on existing preconceptions. The need for more research on these issues had in fact prompted the OEO to launch a series of experiments to assess the impact of GAI plans on work effort and family structure in the late 1960s, but few data were yet available at the outset of the debate over Nixon's plan. The earliest and most tentative findings from the OEO experiments, announced during the same month that the chamber launched its legislative offensive, had found "no evidence that work effort declined among those receiving income support payments."[46]

Business Support from across the Ideological Spectrum

The White House launched a strategy to counter the opposition from the Chamber of Commerce with support from others in the business community. This included coordinating the lobbying efforts and publicizing the views of NAM, the CED, the National Federation of Independent Business, and a coalition of national business leaders organized by the Urban Coalition.[47] Even before Nixon's welfare announcement in August 1969, NAM had issued a report favoring the idea of a negative income tax plan.[48] Once the details of the administration's plans became clear, they threw their lobbying efforts behind it. In direct contrast to the Chamber of Commerce, NAM believed that the legislation strengthened the link between work and income by substantially improving the working incentives beyond those contained in AFDC. They also viewed the FAP as more equitable and humane. As the first House vote in the spring drew near, however, NAM officials contacted the White House to let them know that the association had done enough in support of the FAP and that they would be cooling their lobbying efforts. The reason they cited was their hesitancy to take on the Chamber of Commerce directly in their lobbying efforts. Yet as the chamber conducted its final push in the campaign to influence the House vote, the NAM leadership agreed to openly support the plan and contact members of the House to lobby in favor of the FAP if it looked like their support would assist in the bill's passage.

The CED also supported the FAP. In contrast to the U.S. Chamber of Commerce, which had low organizational barriers to entry, the CED was an elite organization of a few hundred businessmen and educators that had originally developed in response to the conservatism of the chamber.[49] During the Johnson years, the members of the CED and the Arden House steering committee shared information on public assistance programs and spoke at each other's gatherings. As the legislative wrangling in the House gathered steam in early 1970, the CED issued a report just prior to the House vote that strongly supported the FAP as a productive first step in welfare reform. It was viewed as only a first step because the CED's report made recommendations that were more liberal than Nixon's plan and quite similar to those made by the Arden House report two years earlier.[50] (The CED report noted that many of its trustees participated in the Arden House meetings.) The benefit levels were higher and their plan covered all the poor, including childless couples and single people, not only families. The sole criteria for public assistance would be need.

The CED report, which was covered in the press, was one of the last public statements of the economic citizenship rationale for GAI policy, one in which the alleviation of poverty was the express and overriding goal of reform and the causes of poverty were located in the functioning of the economic system. The report opened by stating that the existing New Deal–era welfare system was inadequate for the country's current economic and social milieu. It continued,

> The long sustained prosperity of the United States over the past quarter of a century or more, leading to a greater affluence for more people than has ever been experienced in world history, has not eliminated poverty and extreme deprivation. . . . The poor today in the United States are largely those unequipped by reason of some disability—age, sickness or other physical incapacity, lack of education or training, discrimination because of race, or some other circumstance over which they have no control—to find gainful employment either in the private or the public sectors of the economy, even though the jobs are available. To the diminished number of Americans who endure the harsh realities of deprivation, their plight is nonetheless real.[51]

This rationale contrasted sharply with the reasons for support articulated by members of another business organization, the National Federation of Independent Business. The organization issued a press release in March 1970 that began, "If the support of independent businessmen of the administration's welfare reform proposal continues, a reappraisal of who and what is conservative or liberal may be necessary."[52] The press release reported that the nation's independent businessmen supported the FAP by margins of 59 percent in favor, 31 percent opposed, and 10 percent undecided. (Despite the majority support for Nixon's plan, the percentage in support of the plan here was *lower* than that found in the chamber's internal polling of its membership, which had been 86 percent.) Interestingly, the results from the National Federation showed little regional variation, even in the South and in other conservative states. A month later, after the Chamber of Commerce had begun its anti-FAP campaign, support at the National Federation remained high—in fact one percentage point higher than the previous level. The results were based on over 25,000 survey responses. A report presenting these findings also included some of the additional responses that were written in by respondents. These shed light on the reasoning underlying these businessmen's support. Typical comments, as quoted by the press release, were the following:

A Minnesota realtor says, "Welfare is something I think is very important. However, I am fed up with the present system that allows able-bodied people to sit on their hind ends. Let's get a program to train these people to support themselves."

A Tennessee garage owner says, "Welfare is one of the most abused programs we have. We have tried to get some of the big strong fellows to work too many times. They have refused because their families were getting welfare and food stamps."

A Wisconsin water service operator with six employees says, "In my opinion, please help the welfare people, but stop giving it to them. Training is a wonderful thing, but they can do unskilled jobs."

The owner of a Wisconsin photographic studio expresses a viewpoint of many who write with the following: "People who draw welfare should not be permitted to vote."[53]

Comparing Policy Preferences between Business Groups

These quotes reveal that support among small business owners for Nixon's welfare proposal was emphatically not located within the economic citizenship paradigm, as was the case at the CED. Rather the National Federation's support was squarely located within the rehabilitation paradigm that Burns had characterized so well during the debates within the administration. However, instead of opposing the FAP as Burns had, the respondents supported the program. The reasons, it appears, were that these businessmen had been convinced by Nixon's depiction of the current system as irreparably broken and in need of reform, and by his presentation of the FAP as embodying a new system that emphasized work, rehabilitation, and self-improvement. Thus both the federation's members and the CED supported Nixon's plan, but for diametrically opposed reasons.

The other puzzling contrast within the business community was the opposing positions taken by the U.S. Chamber of Commerce and NAM. During the New Deal and postwar era, these two business groups took largely similar positions on social welfare policy. But during the early 1960s, the composition of NAM's executive committee began to draw more from the big business community. Prior to that period it had drawn more from the ranks of small- and medium-sized firms, and many of the members of NAM's upper echelons had been members of ultraconservative organizations, such as the John Birch Society.[54] The changing composition of NAM's leadership suggests not only shifting economic interests, based on firm size or industry sector, but a change in ideological outlook among NAM leaders as well. Since the effects of the FAP on work effort were as yet unknown, as parties on all sides attested, these ideological differences may explain the variation in the stances taken by the two groups.

A survey of big business leaders from the period suggests as much. Academic researchers fielded a survey in 1971 to evaluate the attitudes of business elites toward welfare reform and redistributive attitudes.[55] While the results showed wide variation in elites' economic attitudes, the main finding was a strong tendency toward centrism, which the study's author found was grounded in Keynesian moderation. More specifically, the study asked the businessmen about their attitudes toward Nixon's Family Assistance Plan. Almost two-thirds of the respondents—63 percent—indicated that they favored the legislation. Another question on the survey strongly suggests that this policy preference was not based on a conservative view of the plan, as it had been among the members of the National Federation of Independent Business, but on a more liberal perspective. When asked if "too much is done for the poor in this country," 81 percent of the respondents disagreed. Based on other questions in the survey, the author suggested that these pro-welfare attitudes were based on a set of interrelated factors, including the respondents' education, geographical and cultural origins, and participation and membership in policy planning organizations and networks. In short, the findings from the study suggest that a combination of shifting cultural dispositions and social networks may have been the distinguishing factors that explain the divergent policy positions taken by NAM and the U.S. Chamber of Commerce. Moynihan's own account of these different business positions made a consonant point. He observed that "cultural divergences" between the leadership of various business coalitions "routinely override similar economic interests."[56] And subsequent studies of policy preference formation among business groups provide further evidence that participation in policy networks influence corporate preferences in directions different from those suggested by "self-evident" economic interests.[57]

The Urban Coalition and Organized Labor

While these business organizations coordinated their lobbying and public relations efforts internally, the Urban Coalition simultaneously nurtured support from other disparate business interests. The Urban Coalition had formed in 1967 in response to the urban unrest that beset the nation and it had become a prominent left-liberal voice in Washington. It held a respected place in the debates over welfare reform because its leader, John Gardner, had been secretary of HEW under Johnson and was also a former head of the Carnegie Corporation and a Republican.[58] Gardner became a strong advocate for the FAP and he threw the weight of his organization, which derived largely from the prestige of its members in the business community, behind the bill. In testimony before the House Ways and Means Committee, he emphasized that if the legislation passed, "the Federal government will for the first time in history accept responsibility for providing a minimum level of payment throughout the Nation and for financing it. I would have been very proud had I been able to establish that principle during my tenure as Secretary of Health, Education and Welfare. It is an historic step."[59] By the time the legislation reached the floor of the House, Gardner had rallied over one hundred business leaders as signatories for a letter to each member of the House in support of the program. Some of these businessmen further agreed to contact their congressional representatives directly and to write to the U.S. Chamber of Commerce to voice their displeasure with its opposition to the bill.[60]

Organized labor played a minimal role in the debates over the FAP. Historically, union leaders believed that benefits for workers should be sought mainly through collective bargaining agreements rather than through social policy. On these grounds, labor fought Social Security legislation and the minimum wage when they were originally proposed. In the 1960s, labor leaders preferred guaranteed jobs over GAI proposals and did not favor any kind of program that removed the link between benefits and labor market participation.[61] In this, they found themselves sharing more affinities with the U.S. Chamber of Commerce than with moderate business groups. Nor were labor leaders, much like George Wiley at the NWRO, enthusiastic about legislation that undercut their own role as chief negotiator of benefits for their constituencies.[62] If nothing else, their reason for existence was to maintain wage levels and the FAP threatened to diminish this control.

One of the oddities of Nixon's domestic politics was his cultivation of George Meany, the leader of the AFL-CIO.[63] In Nixon's quest for a political realignment following the 1968 elections, he sought an alliance with Meany and organized labor. It was this relationship that probably led to the understated support for the FAP signaled by the AFL-CIO, despite its many possible reasons for opposition. On a personal level, Meany had stated that he was opposed to the bill but supported it publicly because it was "socially progressive." However, Meany also felt that most of the rank and file members opposed the bill because "it provides help for those unwilling to work."[64] As the vote in the House of Representatives approached in April 1970, the executive committee of the AFL-CIO, which Meany headed, "quietly endorsed" the FAP.[65] This silent support would characterize the role of the AFL-CIO in the years ahead. They made it known that they did not oppose the bill. However, because the AFL-CIO was one of the most effective lobbying machines in the country, commentators recognized this inaction as the political equivalent of damning the legislation with faint praise.

State and Local Leaders and Civic Groups

Governors and local political leaders were much more enthusiastic in their support, despite their persistent attempts to further modify the legislation to their benefit. The overwhelming reason for their support was the FAP's promise of fiscal relief. A secondary reason was the hope that improving the plight of unemployed or underemployed minorities in urban areas would subdue the continuing threat of civil unrest. Under the "50–90 agreement," states were not required to spend more than 90 percent of their current welfare spending, and some states could cut welfare expenditures by up to 50 percent. The White House was careful to highlight these savings in the fact sheets it circulated to local leaders. These summaries showed that overall, of the projected $5 billion that the FAP would cost, $1.7 billion would go directly to relief for state and local governments (as opposed to going toward cash assistance for the poor).[66] When big-city mayors met with the administration to discuss urban problems, they expressed fears of "riots, confrontations, and burnings" that they felt threatened to explode in their cities. As much as they, like the governors, appreciated the fiscal relief Nixon's plan promised, they believed the legislation would also cool the mood on the streets. For similar reasons, the National Association of Counties gave a "ringing endorsement" to the congressional leadership.[67]

Nelson Rockefeller was one of the witnesses in the congressional hearings on the FAP, and he strongly endorsed the proposal, calling it the "most significant federal domestic legislation put forward in a generation."[68] This enthusiasm, however, did not prevent him from describing the FAP as a "workable first step" in which much more was needed to relieve state fiscal pressures. For years Rockefeller had been saying that New York stood to benefit least from reform legislation, relative to other states, because of its already high levels of spending. Bringing the rest of the country up to its standards would do New York itself little good. He did not hesitate to make the same point to members of the House. Leading up to the House vote, Governor Ronald Reagan of California—one of the nation's most conservative Republican governors, in contrast to Rockefeller's northern liberalism—also told the administration he would probably support the bill, despite reservations.[69] He was not alone among conservatives. Ideological diversity among the governors did not prevent them from converging on the view that Nixon's welfare reforms would greatly benefit their states' fiscal situations. The president was under considerable pressure to keep them satisfied, especially because many of the governors were national players in party politics and because they were the legislation's most dependable source of support.

Other groups weighed in on the FAP as well. The League of Women Voters supported the bill, saying it was equitable and efficient, even though they, like many liberal groups, pushed for higher benefits. In a pattern that became familiar, many other liberal groups initially supported the FAP but then retracted their support as the debates continued. Americans for Democratic Action, a prominent liberal activist organization, was one of these groups; others included the National Council of Churches and other liberal Protestant groups. Roman Catholic and Jewish groups, on the other hand, supported the FAP throughout the legislative battle, despite some strong reservations. In the words of the chief lobbyist for the American Jewish Committee, it would be a shame if fellow liberals "let the best be the enemy of the good," a phrase that not only became widely repeated but also took on poignancy for supporters of the FAP as they saw one liberal group after another abandon the legislation in favor of proposals with higher benefits and less punitive work stipulations.[70]

THE HOUSE OF REPRESENTATIVES

The Legislative Prospects

When Nixon took office, Republicans had not held the presidency in eight years and did not have majority control of either chamber of Congress. In some respects this played to Nixon's obvious disadvantage. President Johnson, for instance, had been able to push through the Great Society legislation in 1964–65 in large part because of cooperation from the majority Democrats in Congress. Yet commentators did not perceive Nixon's situation as an insurmountable challenge. Since 1952, Nixon had been known as a coalition builder just as likely to ally himself with conservative Democrats as with members of his own party. The fact that there was a Democratic Congress also meant that Nixon was able to take political risks, knowing that he would have the opportunity to blame failures on the legislative branch.[71]

The FAP posed a specific set of challenges because it had developed with little input from members of Congress. Negative income tax plans had been designed by economists whose focus was the alleviation of poverty. During the Johnson years they spent little time contemplating the political viability of the plans, nor did they have much contact with legislators who could sensitize them to the symbolic politics of welfare legislation. Likewise Nixon's own administration formulated the FAP during its first six months with virtually no input from members of Congress. To be sure, Nixon's advisors, such as Agnew and Burns, were keenly aware of the politics of welfare reform and they alerted him to potential drawbacks and dangers. Yet as the day of Nixon's welfare announcement in August approached, members of Congress who caught wind of the plan expressed considerable anger and frustration that they had not been consulted during the policy formulation process.[72] This dissatisfaction was the backdrop against which Nixon sent his legislation to Congress in October 1969.

The legislation, the "Family Assistance Act of 1969," contained the following basic elements:

- eligibility for both "dependent families" (defined as being headed by either a woman or unemployed man) and "working families" (defined as families headed by a man employed full-time)

- basic federal benefits of $1,600 for a family of four—$500 for the first two family members and $300 for each additional family member (up to a seven-person family)
- under the negative income tax scale, families of four with earnings up to $3,920 would be eligible for benefit payments
- all families would be allowed a $60/month "earnings disregard," with additional earnings taxed at a rate of 50 percent
- state supplemental benefits equal to the difference between the proposed federal minimum and the state's existing benefit level
- required registration with the Employment Service for all unemployed but eligible beneficiaries
- a reduction of family benefits if recipients refused to accept suitable employment or register for job training
- expanded access to child-care facilities
- federal administration by the Social Security Administration within HEW
- estimated cost of $4 billion (plus an additional $1 billion through an integrated revenue-sharing program)[73]

Because it was a tax bill, the legislation had to originate in the House Ways and Means Committee, which was responsible for drafting revenue legislation. Its status as a tax bill also distinguished the FAP legislation from most of the antipoverty programs of the Great Society era, which were subject to annual appropriations. This meant that the FAP was the most serious test of congressional commitment to comprehensive welfare reform since the New Deal because it would be a permanent statute financed automatically by the treasury.[74]

There were reasons to be optimistic about the FAP's legislative future. Moynihan reminded members of the administration that revolutionary legislation like Social Security and workers' compensation had faced equally steep uphill battles in their day but had since become staunchly protected elements of America's welfare state. The Ways and Means Committee, the first hurdle, was likely to be sympathetic, since the membership included a number of representatives from states with AFDC-related concerns. If the legislation made it through the full House, it might find an even more receptive audience in the more liberal Senate.[75]

More immediately, Moynihan reported to the president that he had met with the head of the Johnson-era President's Commission on Income Maintenance, Ben Heineman, and that it appeared that the commission was going to recommend a GAI program similar to the FAP. Moynihan felt strongly that the public announcement of the Heineman commission's recommendations later in the fall would give the FAP an extra boost of legitimacy, since a similar plan would have essentially been proposed by both Republican and Democratic administrations. And indeed, when Heineman announced his commission's recommendations in November, he described the Nixon plan as "a gigantic step forward—pioneering and courageous."[76] Though it was impossible to know in advance, the Heineman report would not receive nearly as much attention as other government reports on related issues, such as the Kerner Commission's report on civil unrest or Moynihan's own report on the black family, and therefore its recommendations would not provide much of an added boost to Nixon's plan.

The House Hearings: Concerns about Work and "Welfare" Costs

Two weeks after Nixon sent the FAP to Congress, the Ways and Means Committee held eighteen days of hearings on the administration's bill, which combined the FAP with Social Security amendments that included benefit increases and future automatic adjustments for higher living costs. These amendments were politically pressing at the moment, with inflationary pressures causing increasing concern among the public. The Social Security amendments received most of the attention at the hearings, but a number of expert witnesses were called in to testify on the FAP and the members of the House appeared receptive, knowing there was pressure from across the political spectrum to do something about the welfare situation.[77]

The administration brought in Finch, George Shultz, and other welfare experts from HEW and the Department of Labor to testify, and they proceeded to engage in the definitional work required to shape the public image of the proposal. Finch stressed the administration's selling points of the FAP: the provision of national standards, equity to the working poor, strengthening of work incentives, bolstering incentives for family stability, and fiscal relief for the states. Shultz, the secretary of labor, introduced his testimony by framing it in reference to the issue of work: "This is not a proposal for a guaranteed minimum income. Work is a major feature of the program."[78] An undersecretary at HEW explained that the FAP was building on and strengthening the work incentives and work requirements of the WIN legislation in 1967, a description that framed the FAP as a continuation of legislation that the Ways and Means Committee itself had proposed and enacted. Administration experts discussed the emerging first wave of results from the OEO's negative income tax experiments and reported no apparent reduction in work effort. Governors and mayors testified on the necessity of fiscal relief that the FAP provided. Despite some tough questions about the plan's integration with other social programs and its effects on out-of-wedlock births and desertion, the hearings did not appear to pose any insuperable challenges to the legislation's progress.

During the hearings, which ended in mid-November, a number of the president's staff suggested that Nixon speak personally with the chairman of the Ways and Means Committee, Wilbur Mills, a moderate Democrat from Arkansas and one of the most powerful men in Washington.[79] Though he was a southerner, Mills did not feel strongly about the FAP either way. Having been involved in welfare policymaking before, he understood the issues and saw the need for reform. Yet he had concerns, especially concerning the work aspects of the bill: How would "suitable employment" be defined, if recipients were not to turn it down under the work requirements? What would happen to cheap labor? Would jobs be available after recipients went through training? Could all the trainable welfare mothers be placed in jobs? Moreover, Nixon's staff felt, Mills needed to be reassured of the administration's commitment to the bill, since he would have to work hard to get it through the House.[80]

Such calls for increased presidential involvement would recur throughout the debates over the FAP. Rumors circulated that Nixon had informed his staff not to devote any White House influence to the legislation, that he was not aware of what the legislation really contained, and that he did not care.[81] These perceptions threatened to damage the bill, particularly among conservative Republicans, who would vote for the bill only reluctantly out of party loyalty but not if they did not believe that Nixon really wanted the legislation passed. Contrasting with these rumors was substantial evidence to the contrary: Nixon's closest domestic advisor described welfare reform as one of the domestic programs the president cared most about; Nixon described welfare reform as his number one domestic priority in his 1970 State of the Union address; and reams of paper and thousands of man-hours within the White House were expended in an attempt to shepherd the legislation through Congress.[82] Still, the rumor dogged the program throughout Nixon's presidency.

As Mills's questions about the FAP suggested, a primary lens through which most people, particularly members of Congress and interest groups, viewed the proposal was its relation to work. Though Mills was ambivalent about the FAP in many respects, he liked the work requirement and he knew it would resonate with many members of Congress and with voters.[83] Other legislators and interest groups opposed the FAP because of its work requirement, but they were in the minority. As the debates began in earnest in the new session of Congress in 1970, administration staffers believed that the work component of the legislation, one of its strongest selling points, was being lost. They believed that this could be redressed rhetorically, and symbolically, by changing the spokespeople whom the White House directed to discuss welfare reform. One staffer put it this way:

> It is important, by the way, that the issue be taken out of its current exclusively HEW orbit; the Congress is beginning to believe it's all welfare and very little workfare. Congressman Byrnes [the minority leader in Ways and Means] is ardently pleading for far more prominent involvement of Secretary of Labor Shultz, and less prominence for Finch [at HEW].[84]

Elsewhere, another staff member expressed similar concerns about his office's interactions with members of Congress.

We've heard too much about 13 million more on the rolls and "more checks going out." Our editorial support is deteriorating and we must have a more effective follow-up on the work aspects which were developed so well in the President's TV speech.[85]

Nixon's own rhetoric had set a tone that resonated both in public and within Congress, but the administration's ability to capitalize on it appeared to be weakening over time.

Aside from mobilizing Shultz, the White House also called on the OEO to further publicize its findings from the NIT experiments, which contained benefits similar to those in the FAP. At a White House press conference held in February, the OEO's director, Donald Rumsfeld, emphasized that the results were very preliminary; the experiments were not scheduled to conclude for over two more years. He described the biggest hurdle to the FAP in Congress as beliefs about its negative effects on work. Based on the OEO's findings, he said, such concerns appeared to be unwarranted. He stated that "there is no evidence work effort declined among those receiving income support payments." If anything, findings suggested that the program increased the work effort of participants receiving these payments. Rumsfeld clarified that the FAP was different in some respects from the OEO's program, in that it contained work requirements and included a child-care component. Therefore, if anything, the OEO's results underestimated the FAP's potential efficacy.[86] Despite these efforts, the White House worried that the public did not know enough about the legislation, especially its work component, because the media was focusing mainly on the growth in costs and the increasing number of people on the welfare rolls.[87]

These White House concerns were well grounded. The *New York Times* coverage of the FAP leading up to the House vote did frame the FAP more in terms of its fiscal elements than in any other way, though frames emphasizing work ran a close second.[88] Concerns about rising costs and increasing AFDC caseloads, along with references to municipal fiscal crises, dominated news stories, but these frames frequently favored the FAP because they cast such a negative light on the existing system. In contrast, the fiscal frame that was most commonly used to oppose the FAP was the allegation that it would add between ten and thirteen million new people to the "welfare" rolls. Stories that framed the FAP in reference to work most often highlighted that the FAP's benefit structure would include the working poor. These benefits commanded such media attention because they were a driving concern among legislators and interest groups. Adding thirteen million people to the "welfare" rolls, especially when they were employed, was not viewed as providing an economic boost for people who were already playing by society's rules. Rather, it was viewed as exacerbating the already pressing problem of dependency. Critics of Nixon's plan did not view it as a new type of social provision distinct from "welfare."

Nor did the administration provide the public with a new way to think about it. In fact, Nixon's rhetorical strategy for selling his plan made matters worse by vilifying the existing welfare system and repeatedly implying that welfare recipients were morally inferior to the mainstream of society who understood the value of work. This cynical strategy accounted for much of the support of the plan among the general public, because of the emphasis on the work ethic. But it also undercut the FAP's political viability because it hampered the administration's ability to distinguish the FAP as something other than a plan to further increase the "welfare" rolls.

Despite its lack of public forthrightness, the administration understood that the FAP blurred the distinction between the deserving and the undeserving poor and that it was in fact a new type of social provision. In a memo to Nixon, Moynihan articulated the benefits of the FAP in contrast to the existing system.

> The far more important truth is that [replacing AFDC with the FAP] goes from a dependent to a non-dependent system of income maintenance. I.e., receiving assistance is not conditioned upon being dependent; the working poor receive it as well as the non-working poor. Thus the great stigma of welfare is removed.[89]

Moynihan's characterization showed that he wanted to change the overall perception of public assistance and he felt the FAP could do just that. He hoped that placing the deserving and undeserving poor together in the same program would cleanse the program of its negative connotations. In this sense, he was one of the few within the administration who recognized both the dilemma and strategic potential of symbolic pollution. He hoped that the "worthy" status of the working poor would purify the whole program.

But Nixon could not, or would not, deploy language that worked toward this end. On one of the only occasions that he publicly challenged the categories contained in existing social programs he was quickly chastened by his advisors. In a speech following the Ways and Means Committee hearings, Nixon described the selling point of the FAP as residing in its noncategorical design, saying, "it would put cash into the hands of families because they are poor, rather than because they fit certain categories."[90] Upon hearing about this speech, Burns immediately sent an impassioned memo to Ehrlichman asking for a clarification, since Nixon's statement looked like the "classic definition of a guaranteed income." Burns had received queries regarding whether the president had changed his earlier position toward these types of programs, or whether he was "simply using strong rhetoric to make his point."[91] Ehrlichman understood the political significance of these distinctions and suggested to Burns that the president had not meant his statements to be taken literally.[92]

Family and Fiscal Concerns

At the end of January, a well-publicized congressional staff report criticized Nixon's plan along different lines—its possible effects on family desertion. The House hearings during the previous fall had opened up this line of criticism, in particular in questioning by Congresswoman Martha Griffiths, who asked about the FAP's effects on out-of-wedlock births and marital stability. At the time, the administration was unequipped to give very thorough answers. Moynihan later admitted as much to the president, saying that despite the fact that family stability had been a "central issue of social policy for a decade now . . . HEW and OEO have not got five cents' worth of information on the subject."[93] The program had been designed based on experts' assumptions about recipients' responses to incentives, but now the House committee wanted facts.

The new report said there was little evidence that the FAP would reduce family instability. On the contrary, using different assumptions, it was just as likely that the new plan would increase fatherhood desertion. Fathers could abdicate responsibility for family caretaking if they saw that the government would do it for them. Or perhaps worse, a father might take the legislation as a sign that the government felt him officially incapable of supporting his family. These criticisms were equally as conjectural as the administration's arguments in favor of the plan. Yet to the extent that the FAP was framed as a means to stabilize the structure of poor families and decrease rates of desertion, the congressional report was a substantial blow.[94]

In February, the Ways and Means Committee moved the bill along toward a vote, making one significant change in the process. It was essentially a trade-off between relief for the states and relief for the poor. In lieu of the 50–90 rule, which was a key fiscal relief element, the committee substituted legislation that would give the northeastern states additional savings and likely mean that eight southern states would be relieved of their public welfare payments altogether. No states would lose any fiscal relief as a result of this substitution because it raised the overall costs of the legislation. To bring the costs back into balance, the committee also substituted a 100 percent tax rate on unearned income for a previously proposed rate of 50 percent, thus decreasing the amount of money the poor could keep for themselves. Both the committee and the administration recognized the trade-off and accepted it as a political necessity.[95] Yet this was one of a number of occasions during which the administration's trade-offs to increase support from state and local leaders decreased the likelihood that the poor themselves, particularly welfare rights activists in the Northeast, would support the plan due to its shrinking overall benefit levels.

The Ways and Means Committee approved the FAP on March 5 by a vote of 21–3 and reported it to the House a week later as H.R. 16311 ("Family

Assistance Act of 1970"). The strong majority vote in the committee, however, belied considerably weaker sentiments toward the bill. Liberals were concerned that it would not improve the situation of the poor, since so much of the money went to the states. Conservatives worried that they were approving a guaranteed income because the work and training requirements were unenforceable and because they feared there were not enough jobs available for eligible recipients. Mills was among the members who were more hesitant, but he ended up sponsoring the bill because he believed the present system was ineffective and there were few viable alternatives.[96]

The Full House Vote: Mixed Signals between Substance and Symbolism

Though the FAP was expected to pass the full House, the five-week period leading up to the vote developed into a lobbying frenzy coordinated by the White House. Nixon made phone calls to members of the House, and the vice president and other cabinet members made speeches in which they mainly emphasized the work component of the bill. All the key business groups—the U.S. Chamber of Commerce, NAM, the CED, and the Urban Coalition's business leaders—mobilized their influence on the legislation. The AFL-CIO executive committee issued its "quiet endorsement." Some key governors, such as Reagan, reversed their positions and opposed the bill; others, particularly those in the urban North, spoke on its behalf. The National Association of Counties sided with the northern governors. Mills's congressional study group, though still concerned about the problems it had identified in its report, decided to endorse the FAP upon further consideration.[97]

Perhaps the most incisive commentary during this period came from the editors at the *National Review,* a conservative political magazine. The commentary was all the more notable because the editors reversed their stance toward the legislation. Immediately following Nixon's announcement, the editors had applauded the proposal, but now they opposed it. Their initial support had been in large part due to the libertarian promise of GAI plans to do away with the existing welfare system, which they considered inefficient and ineffective. However, six months later they felt it was relatively clear that the FAP would add to the number of people in the federal welfare bureaucracy. They feared the bill's potential for growth in size and costs. Most of all, they objected to benefits going to the working poor. Like the Chamber of Commerce, the editors worried that the employed poor who received money would abdicate their responsibilities to their families and permit welfare to become "a way of life." Noting the discrepancies between the administration's framing of the plan in contrast to its actual design, the *National Review* contended that "the conservatives were getting the rhetoric while the liberals got the action."[98]

The editors at the *National Review* perceived such a threat in the structure of Nixon's plan that the magazine published seven different stories on the FAP during the months leading up to the House vote, most of which either opposed the legislation outright or urged the president to tighten work requirements and strengthen work incentives. In contrast, the liberal *New Republic* only ran two (largely supportive) stories on the FAP and the leftist *Nation* ran none at all. The FAP clearly provoked more concern on the part of conservatives, due to its program design, than excitement on the part of liberals or leftists.

The contradiction between the symbolism and substance of the FAP noted by the *National Review* illuminated many of the odd dynamics that had unfolded in the six months after Nixon's welfare announcement and that continued to unfold in the House.[99] During the floor debates, Mills tried to downplay the symbolic elements of the bill by saying that the FAP was not a GAI program at all. In contrast, he said, the existing system was one and it was failing. For him, approval from the House was not meant to be an ideological coup but a pragmatic improvement over the discredited AFDC system. Some conservatives shared this position, implicitly accepting Nixon's rhetorical cloaking of the bill. Other conservatives looked at the legislation and, like the *National Review*, saw nothing less than a full-scale threat. William Colmer, a southern Democrat in his nineteenth term, objected strenuously.

> Unquestionably, it is the most controversial, it is the most important, it is the most complex and disturbing piece of legislation that I have had occasion to consider in my whole career here as a member of this body. I am very much disturbed by this bill. I am very much disturbed about the threat it poses to our system of government, to our way of life.[100]

Liberals were equally divided. John Conyers, Jr., a black representative from Detroit, voted against the bill because he believed welfare should be an entitlement and felt that the FAP did not ensure this right to income security. Martha Griffiths, an authority on welfare legislation and a critical voice during the House hearings, said the legislation was a realistic step toward progressive reform. On April 16, the House passed H.R. 16311, including the intact FAP legislation, by a wide margin—243–155. Two weeks later it was taken up by the Senate Finance Committee.[101]

The Senate

The Legislative Prospects

When the president first sent the FAP to Congress, many commentators viewed Mills's Ways and Means Committee and the full vote in the House as the main obstacles to the proposal. The Senate itself was generally considered to be more liberal than the House and Nixon's plan could be seen as a liberal bill because it increased social spending on the poor and expanded antipoverty coverage. Opinion was mixed on the bill's odds in the Senate Finance Committee, where the legislation would start. While many in the administration viewed the committee as a challenge, some commentators assumed that Nixon could count on most of the Republican votes out of party loyalty and count on votes from half of the Democrats—those from the more liberal northern states who liked the principles of the FAP.[102]

The view that the Senate would prove receptive to the FAP turned out to be inaccurate because a potent mix of ideological and institutional factors militated against it. The influence of conservative ideology within the Senate was amplified by the Senate's committee structure, which concentrated a great deal of power over social welfare spending in the Finance Committee. For a generation the committee had been dominated by conservative southern Democrats. This influence had been on prominent display during the mid-twentieth century, when southern conservatives in the committee thwarted civil rights legislation.[103] The influence of the committee structure was well-known to Nixon and his advisors, so it was with a sense of anxiety and uncertainty that they took up a dialogue with the members of the Finance Committee. All seven of the committee's Republican members were conservatives and six of them came from rural states west of the Mississippi in which welfare concerns did not figure prominently. The remaining Republican, John Williams, was from Delaware. Three of the committee's ten Democrats were southerners whose voting records appealed to the American Conservative Union.[104] Only two were northerners—Eugene McCarthy from Minnesota and Abraham Ribicoff from Connecticut. There was virtually no urban representation on the entire committee. All in all, the committee was conservative, rural, and non-northern—an inhospitable environment for GAI policy.

However, at the outset, the prospects seemed reasonably favorable. The chairman of the committee was Senator Russell Long, a Democrat from Louisiana. His father, Huey Long, had also been a Louisiana senator and was a populist crusader for the poor. Russell Long shared some of these same populist sentiments, though he was considerably more conservative economically. In the months leading up to the House vote, Long signaled to the White House that he favored the FAP, though with reservations about the work component and the provision of benefits for the working poor. The senior Republican on the committee, John Williams, stated at the outset that he would oppose the bill, largely because he felt the plan could not deliver on its promises. But he also informed the administration that he considered the legislation likely to pass anyway, despite his opposition. Ribicoff was one of the few liberals on the committee, and though he wanted to improve it, he favored the Nixon plan. He had been secretary of HEW during the Johnson administration and was the committee's most knowledgeable member on welfare issues.

In the days following the House's approval of the bill, he publicized fourteen amendments he would add to the legislation in order to liberalize it.[105]

The "Notch Effect" and Concerns about Malfeasance

When Moynihan met with Ribicoff about the amendments, they discussed costs, party politics, and some of the committee's concerns about the bill. Ribicoff realized that the legislation was somewhat constrained by budgetary concerns and that his amendments would add more expense to Nixon's plan. At this early stage of debate in the Senate, he was not sure how much support his amendments would receive among fellow liberals or how much opposition they would draw from conservatives. Ribicoff did say that the conservatives on the committee were "getting a bit nervous" about the bill and that only a Republican president could get the conservative Republicans to endorse the legislation. The committee's shared concerns pertained to administrative issues. For instance, because of the FAP's integration with state benefits, unemployed recipients in some states might make more money than they would with a low-paying job. This problem contradicted one of the main promises of Nixon's proposal—that the new program would always make it more worthwhile to be working than to be on welfare.[106] This weakness soon became the first thread pulled in the unraveling of Senate support for the FAP.

At the end of April, the Finance Committee began hearings on the FAP and the plan ran into immediate problems.[107] Senator Williams was the instigator. Well before the hearings, Williams had expressed his strong opposition to the bill, which seemed to be based on criticism of the program's administration. In preparation for the hearings, Williams, who was known to be concerned with matters of government efficacy, asked HEW to prepare a series of charts that showed the benefit schedule of the FAP and how these benefits meshed with those of other public assistance programs. Specifically, he asked for a chart showing the value of FAP benefits combined with a family's additional benefits from public housing, food stamps, and Medicaid. In his critique of the FAP, he counted these benefits as equivalent to cash and considered them "spendable income." Based on the data from the charts, he argued hypothetically that if a family increased their earned income from $720 to $5,560 under certain conditions, they would lose a total of $19 in spendable income because of the way in which the FAP interacted with other government benefits.

This was what tax experts called a "notch effect": a point on a benefit schedule at which a beneficiary would experience a net loss if he or she earned one more dollar. When Williams confronted HEW officials with this phenomenon in the hearings, they were not able to justify it, to which Williams responded that a welfare beneficiary would be "better off just to spit in the boss's face to guard against a pay raise."[108] This was exactly the kind of situation that both southern low-wage employers and the U.S. Chamber of Commerce leadership had feared—that the FAP would reduce incentives for hard work, promotions, and training. The notch effect also called into question one of the basic premises of the FAP, namely that under its provisions, no recipient would be better off on welfare than working. Notably, these notch effects were theoretical, just as economists' view of incentives for interstate migration had been. There was no evidence that government beneficiaries would recognize the existence of these notches, much less act on their pattern of incentives. Moreover, the analysis showed that notch effects applied to very few potential recipients. Yet Williams's critique so resonated with existing concerns about the shiftless nature of the poor that Chairman Long suspended the hearings indefinitely until the administration could revise its legislation to address Williams's concerns.

The administration agreed to revise the bill, but soon after reviewing the issues Williams had raised, the welfare experts in the administration realized that they would only be able to partially address them in the short term. Moynihan recognized that under the conditions that Williams specified, if recipients could "manage to get on all the right programs" there were incentives not to work, even though "only a tiny fraction of persons get themselves into such favored situations." However, Moynihan argued that the FAP needed to be viewed as the beginning of a long process of welfare reform, in part because some of the returns on the program were long-term benefits, and in part because the FAP's integration with the other programs involved reforming these other systems and taking up their own idiosyncratic politics. Moynihan asked Nixon to use his influence with his fellow Republicans to convince them that the FAP was the first step in a series of reforms that the welfare system required.[109]

Continuing Concerns about Work and "Welfare"

The conservatives on the committee made it clear that their main concerns were welfare costs, the addition of thirteen million people to the welfare rolls, the fact that many claimed that the FAP assured a "right to welfare," and the addition of the working poor to the welfare rolls. Nixon's staff advised him to be candid with the conservatives and recognize their discomfort with each of these issues, but they also said that each criticism had to be rebutted. Nixon had to emphasize the indirect and mounting costs of governmental inaction and the fact that the FAP was projected to decrease in costs after its initial outlay. He needed to stress that making the working poor eligible for government assistance reversed the current policy that often made it more worthwhile to be on welfare than to work. And the president needed to convince the congressmen that the FAP actually strengthened the link between work and income, as opposed to the existing system, which essentially consisted of fifty separate, state-run guaranteed income programs. Aside from these programmatic considerations, Nixon's staff further recommended that in his meetings with the senators he emphasize the political considerations of supporting the bill—that a big victory on welfare reform would help them in the 1970 and 1972 elections, and that, since there were few alternatives to his plan, a vote against the FAP would be a vote in favor of the existing system, which people across the political spectrum viewed as intolerable.[110]

As Nixon's advisors assessed the bill's prospects in the committee, they felt that it faced a tough yet surmountable set of challenges. Some of the opposition, for instance from Williams and Republican senator Carl Curtis of Nebraska, seemed unmovable for reasons having to do with work and costs. However, Moynihan and others felt that the remaining Republicans could be swayed by party loyalty, but only if they were convinced that Nixon really wanted the legislation. Sectional interests also directly played into this opposition. In assessing the bill's prospects, Moynihan said that though Long seemed like he could be swayed to support the FAP, he wanted "even more draconian work requirements." But two of the other southern Democrats on the committee were "probably irreversibly opposed." Moynihan further speculated about the reason underlying the opposition: "They seem to realize what the bill would mean to the South. (It would very likely mean the end of those political dynasties built on poverty and racial division.)"[111]

After the administration submitted its revised proposal to the Senate, Long resumed the hearings in late July 1970. Elliot Richardson, the new secretary of HEW, presented the new plan to the committee.[112] As Richardson described it, the administration had been able to take care of the notch problem, but the trade-off had been a reduction in the work incentives. While it was still true that under the FAP alone, the marginal tax rate on earnings was 50 percent, when combined with the benefits from other programs, the tax rate increased up to 67 percent. This reduced work incentives somewhat because recipients were able to keep less of their income as their earnings increased. Richardson explained why this was so: there was an inherent tension in welfare reform among adequacy of benefits, strength of work incentives, and program costs. He showed how fixing the notches had weakened incentives at low wage levels, and explained that the only way around this dilemma was to extend the cutoff ceiling (the income level at which a person could not receive benefits) to very high income levels, which would add millions more to the rolls and increase costs exponentially.

Nevertheless, Williams and Long both reacted negatively to the new proposal, this time focusing on the weakened work incentives. They argued that the changes decreased the likelihood that an unemployed mother receiving welfare benefits would go to work for the minimum wage. They complained that Richardson's analysis was "just flowery explanations."[113] Their objections were rooted in rehabilitationist views of the poor that had permeated discussions of welfare reform since the mid-1960s. Furthermore, these objections hinged on viewing the primary objective of welfare reform as improving incentives to work.

Work was indeed a concern of Long's—both that it should be rewarded for those actively in the labor force and that it should be enforced for those who were not. Even after all the criticisms of the Nixon plan, he still told administration officials that he would probably support the legislation. His main concern, as he expressed throughout the hearings, was sufficient work incentives for those who were unemployed. He had taken part in passing the WIN amendments in 1967, which contained incentives and requirements of their own, but which had also been plagued with problems since then that had rendered the incentives ineffective. He was enamored, however, with the FAP's proposal to supplement the incomes of the working poor, and soon after the hearings opened he told a reporter that the FAP, or "a bill to help the working poor," would become law in the current session of Congress.[114] Unfortunately for the administration, as the drawbacks of the bill became more salient to Long, he devoted more attention to crafting his own legislation that would help the working poor alone.

Other conservatives on the Finance Committee shared Long's concerns about work incentives. Jack Miller, a Republican from Iowa, was on the fence regarding the bill and his major concern was that the marginal tax rates on earnings were too high, thereby decreasing incentives to work. To others, the inclusion of the working poor in the program was anathema. Curtis was the most hostile member of the committee next to Williams, and he particularly opposed giving benefits to the working poor because such benefits would demean their "sterling character." This was a clear expression of concern about what the stigma of "welfare" benefits would do to employed workers. The rest of the conservatives were not explicit with the administration about their opposition to the program, but Nixon's staff believed they were most concerned about the cost and caseload increases.[115]

Between July and early September, the Senate held eighteen days of hearings. By the end of this period it was clear that the members of the Finance Committee were considering three different kinds of changes to the legislation. The administration needed to decide in what areas it was willing to compromise. Ribicoff wanted to delay the effective date of the FAP and instead run three pilot programs to test the elements of the FAP. Nearly all of the members of the committee wanted to add provisions that required the creation of public sector jobs. This would ensure that welfare recipients had employment available once they completed job training. Long accepted the idea that the working poor needed government assistance through wage subsidies. Yet rather than providing the working poor directly with government subsidies, he wanted to subsidize employers who in turn would raise wages.[116]

The administration estimated that it had sixty votes in favor of the FAP in the Senate, so it was eager to surmount the obstacles to the legislation posed by the Finance Committee. Nixon's staff agreed that they were open to negotiations on the issue of the pilot projects, even though they felt they were both ill conceived and redundant to the OEO's experiments. On the issue of jobs, administration officials were not philosophically opposed to creating public sector jobs and were therefore willing to be accommodating, but they felt the key to the FAP's success would be placement in the private job market. Beyond that, they adamantly opposed guaranteeing employment for recipients after training because that would make the government the employer of last resort. Nixon's staff pronounced Long's plan for subsidizing employers "completely unacceptable" for economic, political, and administrative reasons. However, they saw the necessity of accommodating him in some way, so they advanced the possibility of either providing a short-term transitional subsidy to employers that would function in a similar way to job training or creating a pilot project to test Long's plan.[117]

After the Senate closed the hearings on H.R. 16311, the administration worked on finalizing its version of the FAP. The plan's supporters had to balance the commitments that were embedded in the original legislation with three competing concerns: internal dissent within the administration, evaluations of the public mood, and the pressures for change coming from the Senate committee. Moynihan had worried over the course of the summer about the influence of the administration's leaders on the legislation. He feared that most members of the cabinet and the White House congressional liaisons opposed the plan, and that their lack of enthusiasm would harm the bill's chances.[118] He continued to be concerned through the fall. After a meeting with George Meany of the AFL-CIO, in which the labor leader expressed his personal opposition to the plan, even while supporting it publicly, one of Nixon's staff members wrote that his longtime doubts about the FAP had been confirmed.

> I feel very strongly that the Family Assistance Plan is counter-productive politically to our efforts with the average middle-class working man and the labor movement. I think in this area Meany's personal feelings are particularly significant. I realize we can't abandon it, but we can soft pedal our position between now and November.[119]

Working in favor of reform was the fact that AFDC rolls had continued their steep rate of increase during the period between Nixon's welfare announcement and the negotiations with the Senate: the number of recipients had risen from 6.7 million to 8.6 million. Studies showed that in the year preceding July 30, 1970, three states had experienced 50 percent increases in their welfare rolls, while another ten states saw their rolls increase by over a third.[120] This continuing rise in the number of people receiving welfare sharpened the need for some kind of reform.

In the shorter term, the administration had to appease the members of the committee. As amendments to the core of the bill, they added an income supplementation pilot program for Long, an additional NIT experiment for the working poor for Senator Wallace Bennett, a provision for public service jobs for Ribicoff, and other additional changes, such as replacing food stamps with cash assistance, and strengthening the work incentives and "suitable employment" provisions. By making these changes, Nixon's advisors projected the bill would receive support from three of the seven Republicans and six of the ten Democrats, which would give them a majority of the full committee.[121] On October 13, the administration submitted its second revision of the legislation to Congress.

The NWRO Hearings: Race, Gender, and Work

A month later, in the days preceding the Finance Committee's vote on the legislation, the NWRO held hearings of its own on the FAP. The hearings were "unofficial," but they took place in a Senate building and Senator McCarthy, one of the most liberal members of the committee, conducted them. The objective of the hearings was to testify against the FAP's work requirements and argue that its benefit levels were too low. George Wiley, the leader of the NWRO, appeared on the scene in a colorful dashiki and ran the proceedings for ten senators whom McCarthy had assembled.[122]

The tone over the two days of hearings was combative. Testimony by Beulah Sanders, the NWRO's vice chairman in New York City, against the work requirements was typical.

> You can't force me to work! You'd better give me something better than I'm getting on welfare. I ain't taking it. . . . I heard that Senator Long said as long as he can't get his laundry done he's going to put welfare recipients to work. . . . Those days are gone forever! We ain't gonna clean it![123]

Testimony was punctuated with the call and response of assembled NWRO members, shouting, "That's telling them!" and "Hear that!" As one observer described the scene, "It was as though after decades of treatment as 'house slaves,' black women had turned upon the plantation aristocrats in proud and open revolt."[124]

If the hearings exposed latent racial antagonisms and diametrically opposed visions of rights and work held by the NWRO and conservative senators, they also suggested more pragmatic reasons the NWRO opposed Nixon's legislation: its members were in fact women with children and they had learned how to work the discretionary aspects of the existing system. Since the early days of the negative income tax idea, the main target population for the program in the minds of most government experts was employed or employable men. This was explicit in the design of the OEO's negative income tax experiments in New Jersey. Once the Nixon administration decided to proceed with a GAI proposal, the plan's design shifted even further toward assisting the poor who were already in the labor force. Thus the majority of the FAP's cost increases went to the working poor, not the poor who were eligible for AFDC benefits. The development of the negative income tax since the mid-1960s had not emphasized increasing benefits for single women with young children, nor was this a constituency that the Nixon administration sought to win over. This is why the benefit levels contained in the FAP failed to garner support from members of the NWRO.

The NWRO's collective experience, legal acumen, and political clout also enabled many of its members to obtain "special needs" payments in addition to their regular welfare payments (see chapter 2). One witness at the hearing, the chairperson of the NWRO's national legislative committee, lived in Connecticut with her three children and testified that her benefits would be cut substantially under Nixon's program. She went on to explain that her current benefits, including special needs payments, amounted to over $4,800, almost one-third over the poverty level. (This exceeded the amount a person working full-time for 50 percent more than the minimum wage would take home.) In place of the $1,600 minimum for a family of four guaranteed by the Nixon plan, the NWRO wanted a minimum of $5,500.

Contemporary observers claimed that these hearings turned potentially supportive liberals against the FAP.[125] The day after the NWRO hearings, the Senate Finance Committee voted 10–6 against the FAP. Three liberal senators voted with the majority. On December 11, with three weeks remaining in the 91st Congress, the Finance Committee submitted a bill to the Senate that contained the Social Security amendments and a number of other unrelated measures. On the floor, Ribicoff and Bennett tried to add a liberalized version of the FAP as an amendment to the Social Security provisions. After a long filibuster and a floor fight in which the Ribicoff-Bennett amendment was first supported, Long offered a motion to delete their amendment from the bill and the motion carried. On December 31, the House refused to go to a conference committee even on the Social Security measure, and thus both the FAP and the Social Security bill died with the closing of the 91st Congress.

During the same month, legislation known as the Talmadge amendment passed in Congress by an overwhelming majority. The Talmadge amendment required that mothers receiving welfare benefits register for work when their children reached school age, and that the Department of Labor create a program for public service jobs for women who could not find work in the private market. They would receive no further compensation for their work beyond their regular welfare checks. When he signed the bill on December 28, Nixon praised its "workfare" component while additionally vowing he would return to the welfare reform issue in the next session of Congress.[126] Both Nixon's allusion to "workfare" and the easy passage of legislation emphasizing work, in contrast to an expansion of the welfare state, anticipated the politics of GAI policy in 1971–72.

CONCLUSION

Nixon's legislation generated a great deal of controversy and debate. Because it was a new type of antipoverty program, the public needed a new way of thinking about poverty and the government's role in providing economic security for its citizens. New conceptual frameworks were available, but neither Nixon nor officials within his administration used them publicly and therefore the FAP was interpreted along lines established by past social programs. This left the working poor especially vulnerable to being tainted by their inclusion in the same program as AFDC recipients, since there was no existing alternative status through which to understand their receipt of income benefits. Negative reactions to adding thirteen million people to the "welfare" rolls and to billions of dollars in additional "welfare" spending depended on defining the working poor as "welfare" recipients. This prevailing understanding of the program translated into concerns about the work behavior of the fully employed poor, whom conservatives felt would be rendered in a state of dependency upon receiving welfare.

Somewhat surprisingly, given the original intent of GAI proposals, the unemployed poor never rallied on behalf of Nixon's plan and the most politically organized welfare recipients—the members of the NWRO—actively opposed it. This odd state of affairs had its roots in the numerous compromises and strategic decisions that Nixon and his advisors made over the course of developing the plan, most of which were a response to threats perceived in the noncategorical nature of the plan's design. Conservatives worried about the work ethic of the unemployed poor, so Nixon eventually decided to add work requirements to his proposal in an attempt to gain conservatives' support. To mask the fact that the plan did not differentiate between categories of beneficiaries, Nixon persistently employed categorical language to describe the poor and argued that his plan would help fight the problem of dependency. To appeal to working-class ethnics and stave off a potential welfare backlash, Nixon shifted the benefits structure so that the bulk of the new spending went to the working poor rather than toward further improving benefits for the unemployed, who were mainly single mothers with children. And to maintain support from governors and big-city mayors, who supported the plan largely for its promise of fiscal relief, Nixon made trade-offs that increased the revenue stream to states and cities but decreased overall benefits for the needy. Though most of the unemployed poor would have benefited financially from Nixon's

plan, without these comprises it would have been considerably better. Moreover, because of the emphasis on work requirements and the administration's
rhetorical cloaking of the plan, the unemployed poor had reason to be skeptical of the FAP's ultimate value.

While the contradictions between the FAP's substance and symbolism help
explain the puzzling mix of policy positions taken by many interest groups
and lawmakers, the differences between the South and the rest of the country
also shaped the plan's prospects. The complex interplay among conservative
ideology, local labor market dynamics, and race relations made the South
particularly inhospitable to Nixon's plan. Southern politicians clearly viewed
the behavior of the poor differently than did the northern policy experts who
formulated GAI plans. Because the regional agricultural economy relied so
heavily on low-wage labor, a policy perceived as possibly undermining the
local labor market received fierce resistance, even though state-of-the-art government research showed little reason to expect job defection. On top of these
work-related concerns, it seemed clear to most southern policymakers that the
FAP would further extend the redistribution of power to blacks in the region
that earlier civil rights legislation had put in motion.

Media coverage of GAI plans changed substantially after Nixon's announcement. By the end of 1970, when the Senate Finance Committee allowed the legislation to stall, frames emphasizing the fiscal and work dimensions of the bill accounted for over half of all the policy frames in the *New
York Times*. A parallel trend occurred in magazine coverage. This meant that
many of the problems that GAI plans originally sought to address—poverty,
social divisions, low wage levels, and unemployment—had dropped out of
public deliberation to a considerable degree. Yet the FAP was still seen by
many in a positive light because it promised to replace and improve the beleaguered existing system. Because GAI plans were viewed as the main alternative to the status quo, Nixon rejoined the battle over the FAP in 1971. Yet his
revised legislation would not remain the only welfare reform option for long.

CHAPTER FIVE

Defeat and Its Policy Legacy

As a new session of Congress began in 1971, it was unclear how welfare reform would proceed. Nixon had promised to revisit the idea, but the FAP experienced enough difficulties to call into question whether a GAI policy would still be the vehicle for reform. Yet Nixon left little doubt about his intentions. In his State of the Union address, he announced he would call on the new Congress to complete much of the unfinished business of the previous year. The "most important" piece of this agenda was welfare reform, placing "a floor under the income of every family with children in America."[1] This was clearly a continuation of the FAP's program design. In keeping with the priority that Nixon gave to welfare reform, when the House Ways and Means Committee later reported out the bill containing a new, revised FAP proposal, the committee assigned it the symbolically important name H.R. 1, designating it the first order of business for the new Congress. Though the legislation passed the floor vote in the House by a wide margin, it once again came under attack in the Senate Finance Committee, with lawmakers there proposing both more conservative and more liberal alternatives for reform. The FAP died in committee at the end of 1972, so it never received a full floor vote in the Senate. In the wake of the bill's failure, however, two further pieces of antipoverty legislation did pass. These achieved some of the original aims of Nixon's proposal but they also programmatically reinforced the distinction between the deserving and undeserving poor. This chapter examines the failure of Nixon's revised FAP and its legislative legacy.

Nixon's revised legislation contained a number of concessions to its conservative critics, yet it still challenged existing categorical distinctions between poor people by placing all its beneficiaries in the same program. As before, this meant that the morally tainted status of AFDC recipients contaminated the status of the entire program. The costs were still seen as "welfare" costs and the working poor were still seen as "welfare" recipients. As debate over the FAP entered into 1972 and he sought to distinguish himself from Democratic presidential candidate George McGovern, Nixon amplified his categorical rhetoric even further. While McGovern briefly supported a GAI plan in the form of a basic income grant to all Americans, he quickly backed away from that proposal in response to sharp criticism. In the end, he advanced an antipoverty plan that was more categorical than Nixon's own. This is further indication of the influence exerted by categories of worth, since McGovern was beholden to completely different constituents than was Nixon. During the presidential campaign, welfare reform became a crystallizing symbol for racial and economic ideologies in a more wide-ranging political fight. Increasingly fractious racial politics permeated many domestic issues, such as debates over school desegregation and busing.[2] To the extent that blacks came to be seen as the default group receiving welfare benefits, the increasing antagonism between blacks and whites exacerbated polarization over welfare reform.[3]

During this second round of debate, the competing antipoverty paradigms that generated so much conflict early on during the policy development process came into direct conflict once again. One marked difference between the debate over Nixon's first FAP plan and the revised one was the emergence of alternative reform proposals. The conflict in the Senate revolved around contention between the FAP and two more ideologically "pure" bills that were based on the economic citizenship and rehabilitation paradigms. Furthermore, the administration, through Nixon's secretary of labor, tried to defend the remaining laissez-faire components of the plan against the conservative push for more "workfare." Even during this second round of debate there were moderate Republicans who upheld a version of GAI plans that was consistent with Milton Friedman's initial rationale, though their influence by this point was considerably diminished.

Among stakeholders who supported GAI plans, government experts held a weakened position. After becoming marginalized within the administration, Moynihan left his position at the Urban Affairs Council to return to academia, so his crucial role as a policy entrepreneur within the White House no longer existed. Nixon essentially removed the OEO from the policymaking process through a formal reorganization of the agency (which was soon to be phased out of existence completely), and he shifted responsibility for the FAP's public relations strategy away from HEW because of the agency's associations with "welfare" and not work. Thus experts within these two agencies were not in positions to frame the FAP in terms of poverty reduction, social divisions, or the inadequacies of the existing wage structure, or to challenge with disconfirming evidence the pervasive claims that GAI plans threatened the work ethic. State and local leaders were perhaps the most influential remaining advocates for Nixon's plan, but the president drastically undermined this source of support when he split off fiscal relief measures to the states from his welfare reform legislation. Once governors had access to revenue streams through other channels, their support dropped precipitously. Support from moderate business groups faded since the urban unrest that had prompted their sense of urgency now lay two years in the past. Different economic problems faced the country. Business groups had issues such as wage and price control policy and a potential recession to address.[4]

Meanwhile, opposition continued from both liberal and conservative groups, primarily as a result of the mismatch between the programmatic details of the plan and the rhetoric surrounding it, and the regional differences between the South and the rest of the country. The clash between the substance and the symbolism of the plan meant that while stakeholders could find grounds for support, they could also find grounds for opposition. Given the lack of clarity about Nixon's own motives and the uncertainty about the actual implementation and effects of the plan, many groups seemed to base their policy stances on their worst-case scenario. This was most clearly illustrated in the continuing conflict over the plan's work requirements, which most conservatives believed were unenforceable and many liberals considered tantamount to slavery. Sectional differences also divided many groups. The wide variation in existing AFDC benefit levels in the North and South meant that northern blacks, many of whom saw little benefit to Nixon's plan, opposed the bill while many southern black leaders favored it. While some white liberals argued that the FAP should be supported solely because it would redistribute more political power in the South to blacks, many others ended up opposing Nixon's plan in favor of alternative proposals that contained higher benefits for the unemployed poor and no work requirements.

Most of the conservative opposition was channeled through the Senate Finance Committee, which had the institutional leverage to challenge the FAP. Among most of these committee members, including both southern Democrats and conservative Republicans, concerns about rehabilitating the poor predominated. They clearly viewed the poor as lacking the appropriate work ethic, and their arguments recapitulated those made by southern white politicians and the U.S. Chamber of Commerce during the debate over Nixon's first bill. Yet by this time it was not only conservatives in the South who opposed the FAP. Senator Russell Long, the committee's chairman, formulated his alternative legislation with the assistance of an advisor of Governor Reagan's. This collaboration brought "California-style" welfare reform to Washington, where it would become the primary alternative to GAI proposals.

In the years following the FAP's defeat, Congress also passed into law two pieces of antipoverty legislation that extended benefits to populations that had previously been contained in Nixon's plan. The easy passage of both of these policies highlights the structuring role that categories of worth play in policy development, since both policies worked within these categories. Supplemental Security Income (SSI) provided a federally guaranteed income to the blind, aged, and disabled. Nixon and members of Congress explicitly contrasted the deservingness of this group with the inferior status of recipients receiving "welfare." The Earned Income Tax Credit (EITC) was based on the design of the negative income tax, but it provided benefits only for the working poor. Its passage showed that the adamant conservative criticism of the FAP was not, as conservatives repeatedly claimed, based on the plan's economic threat of giving income supplements to the working poor, since the EITC did exactly that. Conservatives did not believe that the working poor would suddenly be rendered dependent by EITC payments. Rather, conservative opposition to the FAP had been based on the incompatibility of simultaneously giving the working poor nonstigmatizing benefits labeled as something other than "welfare" and retaining the less generous and stigmatizing benefits targeted at the unemployed poor in order to rehabilitate their work ethic. The subsequent creation of SSI and the EITC foreclosed the immediate possibility that AFDC recipients could be folded into a broader, more politically protected antipoverty program that also served "deserving" populations. The consequence was that the unworthy "welfare" poor receiving AFDC became further isolated, symbolically and programmatically, within the overall system of American social provision, thereby making them more vulnerable to future cutbacks.

The Family Assistance Plan, Round Two

In the middle of January, Martin Anderson, one of the FAP's arch opponents in the White House, proposed a welfare reform alternative he claimed would be more palatable to the Senate. Anderson's plan contained considerably stronger work requirements and it completely dropped coverage for the working poor.[5] Yet Nixon's State of the Union address days later showed that the president planned to press forward with his GAI proposal despite the opposition in the Senate. Two issues dominated this second round of debates over GAI policy. As the content of Anderson's alternative proposal suggested, concerns about work remained foremost. Conservatives doubted that the original FAP legislation contained strong enough work requirements and they wanted them strengthened. Moreover, they opposed the idea of extending government benefits to the working poor. In contrast, liberals sought to eliminate work requirements and to supplement the incomes of low-wage workers who were already participating in the labor market but who remained poor. The second issue, which was also a continuation of the prior year's debates, was fiscal relief for state and local governments. Because Nixon had linked welfare reform to his broader "new federalism" package, especially to revenue-sharing programs that distributed federal money to the states, governors and mayors continued to lobby in favor of Nixon's program because they viewed it as a major source of fiscal relief.

The revised FAP (designated below as FAP II when contrasted with the original legislation) that became part of H.R. 1 was significantly different from the GAI program contained in H.R. 16311.[6] It was simultaneously more liberal and more conservative than the previous bill. Many of the changes were a response to the criticisms levied at the previous legislation and an attempt by the administration to preempt similar criticisms in the 92nd Congress. One of the main changes involved work, more specifically, the institutional differentiation between three groups of beneficiaries based on their work status. In FAP II, the program caseload was divided into three categories and benefits for each were administered by different government agencies: (1) programs for the aged, blind, and disabled were administered by the Social Security Administration at HEW; (2) programs for families with no employable members were to be administered by a new agency within HEW; and (3) programs for families with one or more employable members would be administered by the Department of Labor. These new administrative distinctions—particularly between families with employable members and those with unemployable members—reflected and reinforced the categorical distinctions between types of poor people that had become so central in the debates over the original FAP. Moving administration for employable recipients to the Department of Labor, in particular, was intended to carry symbolic overtones emphasizing the centrality of work in programs serving these individuals.[7] Notably, however, these three groups were still included in the same overall legislative program and would still receive the same form of benefits.

There were other changes as well. The new legislation replaced food stamps with cash benefits and increased the income floor from $1,600 to $2,400 for a family of four, which roughly equaled the benefit levels for a four-member family under the old plan when income and food stamps were combined. This integration avoided the "notch" effects that had sparked so much controversy in the Finance Committee and also meant further consolidation of antipoverty programs. FAP II also contained a marginal tax rate of 67 percent on earned income, which roughly equaled the tax rate of FAP I when it was combined with food stamps. Work requirements were more strict: FAP II required that recipients working full-time sign up for job training programs to increase their skills; mothers were exempted from work requirements only if they had children under the age of three (as opposed to under six years old under the earlier plan). "Suitable employment" language was also dropped and guidelines for the types of work that could be refused without losing benefits were tightened.

Under FAP II, the fiscal relief for states was even greater. The new legislation omitted previous provisions that required states to supplement federal payments above the established floor. With its higher floor, the bill completely wiped out welfare expenses in twenty-two states and it saved the other states substantial amounts of money. These changes made the new legislation an even stronger alternative to the revenue-sharing legislation that was simultaneously working itself through Congress. Congressman Wilbur Mills strongly opposed revenue-sharing legislation on technical and political grounds, so he favored making the fiscal relief aspects of welfare reform as strong as possible. Furthermore, the administration of FAP II was completely federal, since it abolished all the existing federal-state public assistance programs, such as AFDC and old-age assistance.

The FAP II, in short, was a more radical break with the past than Nixon's first reform proposal had been. It offered more features that liberals and conservatives alike could call their own, but simultaneously offered more that they could oppose. The new changes it contained also raised the cost of the legislation to $6 billion over the estimated costs of FAP I. These costs concerned some members of Congress, yet conservative legislation proposed as an alternative to Nixon's program carried even higher price tags, suggesting that cost alone was not an overwhelming obstacle to the FAP.

THE HOUSE OF REPRESENTATIVES

The Ways and Means Committee

The Ways and Means Committee in the House of Representatives did not hold public hearings on the revised FAP as it had in 1970. Instead it debated welfare reform from January through May in closed-door executive sessions that mainly included members of the Ways and Means Committee and administration officials. Throughout this process, Chairman Mills tried to address all the weaknesses of the previous legislation. When his committee eventually reported out the bill, he considered the new FAP to be *his* legislation, rather than the Nixon administration's.[8]

Despite Mills's proprietary feelings toward the bill, the White House continued its own dialogue with members of Congress and interest groups over the course of these months, and it brought the concerns expressed by these groups to the Ways and Means Committee. Most of these concerns continued to pertain to the work-related and fiscal relief elements of the bill. Clifford Hansen, a conservative Democrat from Wyoming, wrote Nixon a five-page letter enumerating his criticisms of the bill, all of which were rooted in the rehabilitation paradigm of welfare reform. Some of the criticisms were pitched broadly: he considered the main problem in the nation to be welfare dependency, yet the administration's proposal would still increase the welfare rolls by thirteen million people. Other criticisms were more narrowly focused on the details of the bill, for instance, problems with the "suitable employment" definition and the declaration of need system. Each of these problems, in his consideration, reduced the program's likelihood of moving recipients from welfare to work.[9] State officials expressed different concerns. Richard Ogilvie, governor of Illinois, asked that the new benefits in the bill be effective in January 1972 rather than January 1973. The governor felt that this early effective date was not only necessary for the fiscal situation of his state and those similar to it, but that it would hurt both his and the president's reelection campaigns if the fiscal relief came after the 1972 elections.[10] A team of welfare experts in the administration and the House crafted the new legislation with these concerns in mind, and in May 1971 the Ways and Means Committee

once again overwhelmingly approved the FAP by a vote of 22–3. In his announcement of the vote, Nixon reminded the public of the symbolic designa-
tion of the bill as his top domestic priority, and emphasized the legislation's
work and revenue-sharing aspects.[11]

The work theme appeared to play well to the conservative sentiments of
blue-collar workers Nixon was trying to court. Two weeks before the Ways and
Means Committee approved the legislation in H.R. 1, Nixon received one of
many letters from the general public expressing approval of his welfare reform
plan. The letter included a petition from workers at the Pontiac Motor Division in Pontiac, Michigan, that stated the following:

> We strongly support your efforts to bring about Welfare Reform. We believe
> the welfare programs should be for those who really need it, and not for
> those *men* and *women* who are able to work at something. They too should
> help share the tax burden of this nation. This is a *non-partisan* petition.[12]

The accompanying letter informed Nixon that the most hotly discussed subject during the lunch breaks at the factory was the "deadwood" condition of
the nation's welfare system, and that the workers approved "emphatically of
your plan for able-bodied men and women to work or starve. We know that
we will always have the poor with us, but feel that the majority of them could
be self-supporting if they wanted."[13]

It appeared that the administration's conservative framing of the issue,
which was aimed to appeal to working-class voters, was effective. Nevertheless,
some of Nixon's advisors felt that Nixon's electoral chances might suffer because of his emphasis on welfare reform relative to other issues. The day after
the Ways and Means vote, H. R. Haldeman, Nixon's chief of staff, wrote a
memo to Ehrlichman about the administration's domestic priorities: "We
should quit emphasizing or expanding all the programs for the poor and con-
centrate on programs directed to middle income people—suburbanites, old
people, etc.—where we can gain some productive votes." Since the administration could do little at this point to reverse the direction of the FAP, it further
escalated its rhetoric. By the middle of the summer, based on a directive from
the White House, all members of the administration were told to refer to the
FAP as a "workfare" program.[14]

The South and Competing Regional Interests

Part of the administration's strategy was its continuing effort to sell the South
on the benefits of the FAP. Southern senators had been a major obstacle in
the Senate in the first round of welfare reform debates. In addition, only three
of twelve southern governors and only three major southern newspapers had
supported Nixon's plan. There was also a near complete absence of popular

support for the bill in the region, even though over 50 percent of the poor who would benefit from the plan lived in the southern states. In response, the administration worked to highlight the work and fiscal relief aspects of the FAP. The White House prepared a background paper to be circulated to southerners that emphasized the bill's benefits to the region. According to the memo, a total of $522 million in direct fiscal relief would accrue to the southern states under the legislation. Nixon's program would additionally bring millions of new dollars into the region through increasing the purchasing power of low-income groups. This in turn would benefit southern industry and thus open up employment opportunities for welfare recipients who complied with work requirements and participated in job training programs. The crux of this southern strategy, as a report from the administration indicated, was to convince southern politicians that the FAP really would be effective at getting people from the welfare rolls into gainful employment.[15]

The administration's southern strategy pointed to the importance of regionalism in the politics of the GAI debates, and these regional differences influenced the policy stances of both blacks and whites. A coalition of black politicians in South Carolina wrote to the Congressional Black Caucus explaining how the passage of H.R. 1 would tremendously benefit the southern states, in particular the states' poor black communities. In South Carolina alone, the level of annual benefits available to families receiving welfare would double— from $1,236 to $2,400—and eligibility would be extended to an additional 265,000 parents and children. The poor in other states would benefit even more. Arkansas, Alabama, and Mississippi currently gave families of four annual payments of $1,212, $972, and $720, respectively. These levels would be raised to the federal minimum of $2,400 in each state. Taken together, 3.6 million poor parents and children would become newly eligible for payments under H.R. 1.[16] Despite these indisputable gains for blacks in the South, eleven of the twelve African American members of the House would oppose the FAP in 1971. They appeared to be voting their constituencies, since ten of the twelve members were from northern urban districts and the remaining two were from urban districts in Oakland, California, and St. Louis, Missouri. Current AFDC recipients in these urban areas would not benefit as much as would those in the rural South.

Some liberals in the South made similar arguments to those made by the black politicians from South Carolina. A professor at Vanderbilt University, Lester Salamon, wrote an article in the *New Republic* urging liberals to support the FAP, despite its flaws, if only for its potential impact on democracy in the rural South.[17] He argued that the Voting Rights Act of 1965 and other legislative advances had only partially delivered democracy to southern blacks. Voter turnout was still low and black political gains, to the extent they existed, were fragile. While federal legislation had eliminated *political* barriers to voting and other forms of political participation, the *economic* barriers were still daunting. Studies showed that blacks' likelihood of voting depended not on the amount of their income but on its source. Blacks who depended on white employers, white creditors, or the local welfare system were much less likely to vote or otherwise engage in political action for fear of economic recrimination. This was an explicit strategy among southern whites for maintaining black subordination. Salamon quoted a white county attorney in Mississippi: "Those fellers from the Justice Department thought they were so smart when they gave the vote to these illiterate darkies. What those smart fellers didn't realize is that we can still get these darkies in a whole lot of subtle ways."[18] Seen in this light, the FAP promised to change the power structure in the South by providing blacks with higher income benefits, thereby granting them greater economic independence, and by turning more welfare administration duties over to the Treasury Department or other federal agencies. Welfare payment administered federally, not locally, would be treated impartially, without regard for a recipient's political activities. Salamon concluded, "Liberals and moderates who dismiss the Family Assistance Plan because it fails to do enough for the poor of the urban North run the proverbial risk of throwing out the baby with the bath."[19]

The NWRO had gone to considerable lengths both to criticize Nixon's plan as racist and to highlight how it would affect welfare recipients in the North. The most publicly visible of these efforts, which occurred in 1970 after the first House vote, was the two-day hearing convened in the Senate by Eugene McCarthy. NWRO activism continued throughout the early part of 1971. During the spring of that year, the NWRO launched a public relations offensive—using rallies, pamphlets, and word of mouth—against H.R. 1, saying it would curtail existing benefits and threaten recipients' welfare rights. Chants at one rally at the Capitol included "Kill FAP instead of me!" and song lyrics sung included the lines that the FAP

> [Is] coming to destroy us,
> Every mother's son.
> F-A-P is what they call it,
> And you'd better understand
> The letters stand for Family Annihilation Plan.[20]

As the NWRO's opposition to the FAP grew more vociferous, commentators contended that it swayed liberal groups in the urban North, not solely liberals in the black community, because of their feelings of "white liberal guilt."[21] George Wiley, the director of the NWRO, repeatedly attacked H.R. 1 as "racist," and many liberal groups, who were suspicious of Nixon's motivations anyway, seemed to be persuaded by these claims. Groups such as the National Council of Churches, Americans for Democratic Action, Common Cause, and child development and social work associations withdrew their support from the revised FAP, even though it provided relief for more poor families at higher benefit levels than the previous version had.

Legislative alternatives to the FAP soon followed. The twelve black members of the House—along with nine white liberals from urban areas—introduced an NWRO bill, "The Adequate Income Act of 1971," in April. The bill would guarantee a family of four annual payments of $6,500 without a work requirement and it expanded benefit eligibility to include fully one half of the American population. The bill represented an escalation of NWRO demands over the previous years from $4,400 for a family of four in 1968 to $5,500 in 1969 and then again to the existing level of $6,500 in 1971. Most mainstream economists felt that a guaranteed income at such levels would bring spirals of inflation and lead to economic disaster.[22]

In late June 1971, the full House of Representatives passed H.R. 1 by a vote of 288–132. The more significant vote for assessing support for the FAP came on a motion to strike FAP from the larger bill; this motion was defeated by a vote of 234–187. This suggests that 32 fewer members of the House supported Nixon's welfare reform plan than had supported it in the previous year. Opposition came from both liberals and conservatives. Liberals argued that the benefit levels were too low; conservatives opposed the principle of an income floor embodied in the legislation. In the House debate, Representative Gerald Ford defended the legislation against conservatives' complaints, arguing that it was the existing system that provided "a guaranteed annual income for idleness. Under this [FAP] program, you'd have a guaranteed annual income for work, and I think the latter is preferable."[23] Clearly there remained substantial disagreement over the basic question of what constituted a "guaranteed income."

THE SENATE AND THE 1972 PRESIDENTIAL CAMPAIGN

Laissez-faire vs. Rehabilitation

As Nixon's plan moved to the Senate agenda, a familiar batch of challenges presented itself to the administration. These involved the work-related and fiscal relief elements of the legislation. Under pressure from legislators, HEW and the Department of Labor (DOL) explored the possibilities of implementing either "work relief" or "public employment" programs. Work relief (also considered "workfare") programs were those that required welfare recipients to work for their benefits, usually consisting of jobs provided by a government agency; public employment programs were government-subsidized jobs in the private market that often involved a training component. The recently appointed secretary of labor, James Hodgson, recognized the considerable public appeal of work relief, or workfare, programs, yet he forcefully resisted them.

Like his predecessor, George Shultz, Hodgson embraced the laissez-faire vision of welfare reform and preferred programs that operated according to market principles, in contrast to the more coercive elements of workfare programs that many members of Congress and the public favored. Hodgson emphasized that the administration valued the role of free market mechanisms in the labor market and argued that work relief programs interfered with these mechanisms by muddling work incentives for workers, providing costless labor for employers, producing an immediate and substantial manpower surplus, and failing to follow the principle of equal pay for equal work. For these reasons, he opposed work relief programs and favorably considered public employment with subsidized wages in addition to the administration's FAP legislation, even though the path to reform would be longer and less direct by following this route.[24]

As the administration began substantive dialogue with the members of the Senate Finance Committee, and in particular with its chairman, Russell Long, issues relating to work continued to recur. Officials at HEW optimistically reported that Long would "have a more open mind this year on the [FAP] provisions"; however, there were signs that the going would not be easy.[25] Though John Williams, one of the original FAP's biggest nemeses, had retired at the end of 1970, the Finance Committee retained him as a consultant on the legislation. The committee had also directed HEW to replicate the same set of "Williams tables" that had been the basis for criticisms of the "notch effects" in the administration's previous proposal.[26]

The committee's concerns about the work issue were fourfold. The first issue was the persistent question of whether it was desirable to extend welfare benefits to the working poor. Second, as anticipated by the administration, the committee wanted detailed assurance that the DOL would be able to effectively implement the bill's provision to put all "employable" recipients into some type of job or training program. A third, and related, concern was the strength of the work incentives. The committee pressed for tougher work requirements that would be sufficient to move recipients from welfare to work. Fourth was the adequacy of child-care services for welfare recipients. Child-care provisions needed to be extensive enough so that mothers of young children would still be able to participate in job and training programs.[27] These four concerns would soon enough be reflected in alternative legislation proposed by Senator Long and supported by other members of the Finance Committee.

Fiscal Relief, State Waivers, and "California-Style" Reform

Operating along a somewhat separate track from work issues were those that revolved around fiscal relief. This issue so dominated the debates during the middle of 1971 that Alvin Schorr, a former deputy secretary at HEW under

Johnson and a family allowance supporter, felt compelled to write an article in *The Nation* criticizing the narrow range of debate over Nixon's plan: "Welfare programs are presumably intended to assist the poor, but federal welfare is being debated as if its sole purpose were to relieve the financial problems of states and localities. . . . In the argument that is now widely being made, federal welfare is seen as an alternative to the President's revenue sharing plan."[28] The high levels of interest in the fiscal dimension of welfare reform were being driven largely by high-profile governors and especially by coverage devoted to Governor Reagan's views on welfare reform.[29]

Days before the House approved H.R. 1, Reagan circulated a memo to all the California members of the House saying that he supported any effort to strike the FAP from the bill. He argued that the effects of the FAP were not yet open to examination because there were too many options and discretionary powers contained in the bill. Given this state of uncertainty, Reagan contended, the fiscal stakes for California were too great to let the FAP become law. According to his calculations, Californians contributed over 10 percent of the costs of any federal program and the passage of H.R. 1 would consequently cost them over $500 million. Yet the savings that would accrue to Californians directly from the legislation in the form of fiscal relief would be substantially less than that.[30] The administration was aware of Reagan's concerns. Nixon wanted to try to rally Reagan's support for his program.[31] Consequently, high-level officials within the administration were in negotiation with Reagan throughout the summer.

Soon after Reagan announced his opposition to the FAP, the work-related and fiscal relief components of the legislation converged in requests from California and New York for waivers from H.R. 1 in order to implement welfare "demonstration" programs with strong work components in their states. The two demonstration programs were quite different from one another and the administration found itself trying to balance these differences and their implications for the upcoming Senate vote. The tensions the White House experienced reflected larger tensions within the Republican Party itself, since Reagan embodied a resurgent conservatism within the party, while Nelson Rockefeller, governor of New York, represented its more liberal northern wing.

According to Nixon's secretary at HEW, Elliot Richardson, New York's proposed plan was compatible with the overall philosophy and programmatic details of the FAP, while the California program was meant to be an alternative to it. Both would save the states substantial sums of money. The plan in New York would be limited to testing in only three social service districts. It provided additional incentives for "personal responsibility," contained a work relief program, modified some of the earned income tax formulae in the FAP, and contained a modest work program for children between the ages of fifteen and eighteen. Richardson supported the waiver for New York. He only cautioned that the administration would have to prepare itself for similar requests for waivers from other states, such as Illinois, New Jersey, and Pennsylvania, since "the internal political pressures on these states for fiscal relief are very high."[32]

In contrast, California's proposed demonstration project was more wide-ranging and, according to Richardson, considerably at odds with the welfare reform philosophy embodied in the FAP. California's program would apply to all the existing AFDC recipients in the state. The plan provided lower benefits and contained more stringent work requirements and harsher penalties for recipients who refused to participate—for instance, denying aid to an entire family, as opposed to just the portion of family benefits allocated to the employable member. As Richardson described it,

> The California proposal is a significant challenge to the basic design of H.R. 1, which relies on the work incentives of the free market. California does not believe that these incentives are worth their public cost, or that a person should always be better off by working than by not working. They feel that if a family has a working member, it does not need public assistance. . . . Thus, rather than a fundamental reform of the present work-incentive system, as in H.R. 1, this California proposal is simply a *fiscal retrenchment*, a return to the concept that welfare is a program to support the most needy and that's all.[33]

Thus the California plan represented a distillation of the rehabilitation paradigm for welfare reform in contrast to the administration's more laissez-faire approach, and it represented a fiscal retrenchment in contrast to the administration's additional fiscal commitment.

As Richardson stressed to Nixon, the importance of the decision of whether to grant the state waivers went beyond the immediate issue at hand. Due to the public prominence of the governors, the "emotional overtones" of the welfare reform, the relationship between the Senate liberals and the conservatives in the Finance Committee, and the reactions of interest groups, he warned the president that the decision to grant a waiver to California could affect the wider course of H.R. 1 legislation.[34] By early August 1971, there was still a standoff: the administration had not made concessions to Reagan on the California proposal nor had Reagan adopted a more moderate stance with his own plan.[35]

Nixon Undercuts the Fiscal Relief Dimension

On August 15, Nixon made an announcement that undercut the fiscal relief rationale for supporting H.R. 1. Nixon recommended a year's delay in the effective start date of his welfare plan as part of a tax-cutting and job-stimulation package to boost the economy. This meant a delay in fiscal relief. Such a delay helped address Nixon's federal budget problems but it forestalled hopes for additional welfare funds for states until the middle of 1973 at the earliest. This effectively wiped out support for the FAP among governors, who, by this point, were among the plan's few solid sources of support.[36]

The announcement had negative consequences for the FAP in both short-term and long-term ways. When Senator Long heard that Nixon was delaying the effective date of the welfare reform plan, he immediately set aside the bill for the higher-priority legislation contained in Nixon's economic package, promising to return to the welfare issue early in 1972.[37] When the governors heard about the delay, their fiscal anxieties were only further heightened. The governor of Illinois, Richard Ogilvie, asked Governors Reagan and Rockefeller to join him in drafting an "emergency welfare bill" that the administration would introduce and enact in the current year. Welfare, he said, "is the number one social problem in America; and it is the number one financial problem for the States."[38] Other governors turned against the bill altogether. In a letter to the White House the following month, the governor of Washington withdrew his support for the FAP, citing fiscal concerns, even though he said he had actively supported the plan over the two previous years.[39]

In the longer term, the president's revenue-sharing bill became viewed as a substitute for the fiscal relief the governors had hoped for in the welfare reform package. Congressman Mills had been an ardent opponent of Nixon's revenue-sharing proposal, which Nixon had announced in the same speech on domestic policy that contained the FAP proposal. But in 1972 Mills entered the presidential race and this changed his politics. Influential governors and mayors were able to pressure him into capitulating on the revenue-sharing issue. In April 1972, the House passed a revenue-sharing package worth $5.3 billion in its first year. This alternative source of direct, no-strings-attached fiscal relief siphoned off the little surefire support the FAP had in its last round of legislative battles in that year.[40]

Economic Citizenship vs. Rehabilitation

During the same period, competing welfare reform alternatives further diluted support for the FAP. Members of the Senate Finance Committee developed two such alternative plans. The first was a more liberal plan proposed by Senator Abraham Ribicoff; the second was a more conservative plan introduced somewhat later by Senator Long. Ribicoff had been a proponent of amending the FAP in a more liberal direction since the debates over the first FAP proposal during the spring of 1970. In December of that year, he tried to attach his amendments to H.R. 16311 once it was on the Senate floor, but his attempt was thwarted by Senator Long and other conservatives. In the summer of 1971, Ribicoff developed a new proposal for amending Nixon's plan. The proposal was universal in its coverage, including single people and childless couples in addition to the families included under the FAP. It increased payments for a family of four from $2,400 to $2,800 and pegged welfare benefits to inflation rates; proposed to phase in annual increases in benefit levels until they reached the poverty level; included measures to allow for regional variation on payments; and included substantially more money for child-care and job training programs. Administration officials projected that Ribicoff's amendments would cost $3.4 billion more than Nixon's proposal in H.R. 1 and expand the number of people on the welfare rolls from twenty-five million covered under Nixon's plan to thirty-two million under the Ribicoff proposal. Despite the increased costs and further expansion of the welfare rolls, officials within the administration advised the White House to take Ribicoff's proposal seriously, in part because he had been one of the strongest supporters of the principles embodied in the FAP, and in part because his proposal opened up new options for further reforming the existing system. The only area in which they advised standing firm was raising the $2,400 payment level for a family of four.[41]

Pressure to liberalize the FAP provisions contained in H.R. 1 continued into the fall. In early October, thirty-two members of the House of Representatives signed a letter submitted to Nixon that was highly critical of his legislation. The letter argued that the delayed effective date he had announced two months previously belied his repeated statements that welfare was his number one domestic priority. The letter went on to criticize particular elements of the FAP—including the inadequacy of benefits and coverage, the demeaning elements of increased recipient monitoring, and the workfare component in which recipients would work for less than the minimum wage.[42] Later that month, Ribicoff formally introduced his measure as an amendment to H.R. 1. The measure was co-sponsored by eighteen senators and endorsed by a variety of interest groups—civic, labor, and religious.[43] Coalitions of local political leaders, such as the U.S. Conference of Mayors, the National Association of Counties, and the National League of Cities, also endorsed the bill as a means of seeking fiscal relief they knew would not be forthcoming in the Nixon proposal. The details of the bill were even more liberal than those Ribicoff had previously proposed, including an income guarantee of $3,000 for a family of four and cash assistance to all families whose household income was below $5,720. (In contrast, the Nixon plan's benefit cutoff level for the equivalent family was $4,140.) Liberal criticism of H.R. 1 had been increasing ever since the bill's announcement. The Ribicoff proposal gave Nixon's liberal critics an alternative and they migrated in their support accordingly.

In his State of the Union address in January 1972, Nixon once again affirmed that welfare reform was a top domestic priority and criticized Congress for delaying progress on the issue. On the same day, the Senate Finance Committee began hearings on H.R. 1 and made it clear that they planned to drop

Nixon's FAP proposal from the legislation. The hearings were stacked to favor the conservatives. Administration officials were not called in to answer questions about the legislation, as they had been before. Instead, the Finance Committee called in witnesses from the U.S. Chamber of Commerce and the conservative Liberty Lobby to testify against Nixon's plan. In his budget message to Congress a few days later, Nixon defended his proposal, saying it was "infinitely better than the wasteful, demeaning program that now calls itself welfare," and that it was time to "start the replacement of welfare with 'workfare.' "[44]

The NWRO continued to oppose all the welfare reform proposals, including Ribicoff's, except its own, which Senator McGovern had sponsored on behalf of the organization. In March, the organization conducted a protest march and rally at the Washington Monument. The rally was called the "Children's March for Survival" and the leaders distributed posters for children to carry that depicted Nixon, Mills, Ribicoff, and Long as "the D.C. Four Against the Poor."[45] Few, if any, other groups could have conceivably lumped such different men, particularly Ribicoff, and their respective welfare proposals under the same "antipoor" rubric. The fact that the NWRO did so suggested the deep, racially tinged anger they felt toward the government establishment, and their continued call for an income guarantee of $6,500 for a family of four—more than twice the level of the next most liberal alternative—illustrated their uncompromising demands for change.

A month later, the Senate Finance Committee voted 10–4 to delete the FAP from H.R. 1 without a single Republican supporting Nixon's plan. The committee instead opted to replace it with a more expensive but work-oriented program sponsored by Senator Long. Long had recently developed a working relationship with one of Reagan's welfare advisors from California, Robert Carleson, who brought "California-style" ideas about welfare reform to Washington. Long's plan reflected this new influence.[46] It proposed cutting the number of people on the existing AFDC rolls by 40 percent and replacing those lost benefits with a "workfare" program in which private-sector jobs would be subsidized by federal funds and the government would be the employer of last resort. Under the plan, all mothers except those with children under the age of six would be expected to work for their welfare benefits. Families would lose all their benefits if eligible family members did not comply with the work requirement. Long defended the plan, saying it was necessary to get rid of "welfare chiselers." Long's description of welfare fraud and abuse among the shiftless poor was a recurring theme in his criticism of Nixon's plan, even though there was little aside from anecdote to back up his claims.[47] Because conservative welfare reform strategies such as Long's required so much administration and monitoring of recipients, officials estimated that his workfare plan would cost between $3 and $9 billion dollars *more* than the Nixon proposal.[48] This substantial increase was part of recurring evidence that cost constraints, per se, were not a limiting factor on Nixon's proposals.

Ribicoff denounced Long's plan as "slavefare, not workfare or welfare" and said that it was "barbaric" to "imagine a civilized society penalizing innocent babies for the wrong-doing of a parent." Richardson, the secretary at HEW, called it "a step backward into the leaf-raking schemes of the 1930s." Both Ribicoff and the administration expected a fight in the Senate in which they would introduce a more liberal plan on the Senate floor later in the summer.[49]

The contrast between the plans proposed by Ribicoff and Long represented a direct clash between the economic citizenship and rehabilitation paradigms of welfare reform. Ribicoff's plan was universal and eligibility was based on need alone. It did not distinguish between categories of recipients. According to a former Ribicoff staff member, Ribicoff was concerned with "the problem of income poverty, which included all persons, employable or unemployable, working or not working, with incomes below the poverty level. He now believed direct cash assistance was the most effective and probably most efficient way for the federal government to assist the poor."[50] Long, on the other hand, distrusted the scruples of most welfare recipients and believed that, with the exception of mothers with very young children, the able-bodied poor needed to be rehabilitated through training and exposure to the disciplines of the labor market. After the committee voted to approve his plan, Long said, "[I]f they're able to work, we're going to put them to work, and that's that."[51]

Yet contemporaneous research suggested that, Long's beliefs notwithstanding, if the poor were capable of working, they would either already be working or looking for employment, unless they were mothers raising young children. This is what evidence from the HEW analyses and the OEO's experiments indicated and it was also the main finding of a well-publicized academic book, published during the same year, titled *Do the Poor Want to Work?*[52] The author, Leonard Goodwin, found that there were no significant differences in life goals or work ethic between the poor and the non-poor, regardless of whether they were black or white, male or female. On that basis the study concluded that the work requirements contained in proposals like Long's might be not only unnecessary but counterproductive. Negative work experiences, which were more likely to occur under a work requirements regime, were likely to harm the work ethic. The study's conclusions called into question both the work requirements proposed by Long and the insistence on higher benefits called for by liberals: "Excessive concern that a relatively low level of guaranteed income—around the poverty level—would cause people to drop out of the work force reflects a misunderstanding of the life and work orientations of the poor. They are no more likely to settle for this meager income and cease working than are middle class people."[53] This was a clear rebuke of the rehabilitationist approach to welfare reform, which held as its premise that the poor did not share mainstream values regarding work. Instead Goodwin argued that the poor sometimes relied on welfare benefits because they lacked, especially if they were black, adequate employment opportunities.

Located somewhere on the ideological spectrum between Long's workfare legislation and Ribicoff's more liberal proposal was Nixon's own plan. In June, the administration assessed whether it would be able to construct a compromise with Ribicoff on a mutually satisfactory welfare reform proposal. Cabinet secretaries Richardson and Hodgson both implored Nixon do so. Others did as well. A joint report prepared by HEW, DOL, the Office of Management and Budget, and the Domestic Council staff outlined three options for the president: standing firm with the FAP; compromising with Senator Long; or compromising with Senator Ribicoff. The report recommended compromising with Ribicoff as the only way to get passage of a bill and stated that a compromise could be found that would satisfy both parties. The report also listed the liabilities of such a strategy, namely that the administration "will be open to increased criticism from the Chamber of Commerce and conservatives, particularly Republican members of the Senate Finance Committee, whose votes we will need on other issues."[54]

On June 22 Nixon announced at a news conference on domestic affairs that he had decided to remain in his "middle position" on the administration's FAP proposal as passed by the House. He would compromise with neither Ribicoff nor Long. Embracing rehabilitationist rhetoric, however, Nixon stated that his own position was the "right position" and that the country needed to move in the direction of getting people off the welfare rolls.[55] He highlighted this goal for welfare reform despite the fact that his plan was projected to increase the number of people receiving government benefits by many millions.

The 1972 Presidential Race: Rhetoric versus Reality

Nixon's decision not to compromise was contrary to the advice of his welfare experts within the administration, but it may have had more to do with his political strategizing for the upcoming presidential elections of 1972. Both Ribicoff and Long were Democrats, one quite liberal, the other quite conservative. Compromising with either of them held political hazards in an election year.[56] Moreover, welfare reform itself appeared to be a hazard. Earlier in June, Ehrlichman had submitted to Nixon a strategy memo for the presidential race titled "Selling Our Line on Domestic Issues." In the memo, Ehrlichman outlined eleven domestic priorities Nixon should focus on in the coming months. Welfare was not on the list, despite the fact that the president had called it his top domestic priority six months earlier.[57]

Nixon also had to position his plan against that of George McGovern, the South Dakota senator who would soon be nominated as the Democratic presidential candidate. McGovern had been actively involved in food stamp legislation in the 1960s, had proposed a welfare reform program of his own soon after Nixon introduced his, and in 1970 had announced a children's allowance called the Human Security Plan, though these latter two initiatives received little public attention. In 1971, he introduced the NWRO's welfare reform bill in the Senate. Then, in January 1972, he made a widely publicized proposal to guarantee every person in America, regardless of income, $1,000 in the form of what he called a "demogrant." This type of universal program provided government assistance to all Americans and thus completely ignored existing normative distinctions drawn between categories of beneficiaries.

As the presidential campaign heated up, McGovern's demogrant proposal came under heavy attack. High-level officials within the Nixon administration levied detailed criticisms against the bill on both political and economic grounds. They also claimed that the McGovern plan was a left-leaning, elitist proposal embraced by "certain academic economists."[58] McGovern was indeed being advised by academic economists, many of whom had signed the 1968 petition calling for a GAI proposal—among them were James Tobin, John Kenneth Galbraith, and Lester Thurow. These advisors disputed that McGovern's plan was a radical one by tracing the roots of the idea back to Milton Friedman's search for ways of expanding individual liberty and economic choice. Some of these advisors, such as Joseph Pechman at the Brookings Institution, went further to compare the demogrant favorably to Nixon's H.R. 1 plan.[59]

In response to the backlash the demogrant proposal generated, McGovern not only backtracked on his proposal but almost completely reversed himself by proposing a new *categorical* plan and by emphasizing the importance of work. In a well-publicized speech to security analysts on Wall Street in late August, he announced the outlines of "a system of national income insurance" predicated on work and public service jobs: "The best incentive is a job opening. The best answer to welfare is work. And that is my answer."[60] McGovern's new plan actually comprised three separate programs: an expanded Social Security system for the aged and infirm; a guaranteed jobs program for those who were able to work; and a more generous income maintenance program for those others who could not work—mainly dependent mothers with children, supported at a level of $4,000 for a family of four.[61]

In comparison to Nixon's plan, McGovern's new proposal was more liberal in some ways, but more conservative in others. Most notably, it was different from his previous welfare proposals—both the children's allowance and the demogrant plan—because it introduced a categorical system rather than one that provided universal benefits without distinctions between categories of recipients. This was a concession to the prevailing national mood. Making distinctions according to categories of worthiness was advisable for electoral candidates from both parties, regardless of their political constituencies. The plan did not expand welfare eligibility beyond the existing AFDC rolls, nor did it give income supplements to the working poor. However, it did provide considerably higher benefits to single mothers with young children (such as the members of the NWRO) and it did not contain work requirements.

Despite McGovern's change in welfare reform tactics, he was sharply criticized by Nixon and the Republican Party. However, the rhetoric was clearer than the reality. Taking aim at the Democrats, the Republican platform stated that the party would "flatly oppose programs or policies which embrace the principle of a government-guaranteed income." On the campaign trail, Nixon claimed the country faced a choice "between the 'work ethic' that built the nation's character and the new 'welfare ethic' that could cause the American character to weaken." Journalists covering the campaign described such rhetoric as "calculated to appeal to millions of largely white and increasingly prosperous blue-collar workers who seem divided on Mr. McGovern's candidacy and whose divisions the President obviously hopes to exploit for his own political profit."[62] Journalists themselves adopted Nixon's rhetorical distinction between the "work ethic" and "welfare ethic" in their general coverage of the debates over welfare reform.[63] Unnoted in the press was the fact that it was Nixon's proposal that would expand the provision of benefits to thirteen million additional people, while McGovern's new plan would maintain the existing number of people on the rolls. Moreover it was Nixon's plan that proposed blurring the boundaries between "welfare" and "work," while McGovern's plan maintained the existing categorical distinctions. Yet Nixon's rhetoric once again won the day.

In October 1972, one month before the presidential election, the prospects of a GAI program died for the remainder of the Nixon administration. Earlier in the summer, the Finance Committee had deleted the FAP from H.R. 1, so on October 4, Ribicoff offered his liberalized version of the FAP as an amendment to the larger legislation.[64] Long motioned to kill the Ribicoff amendment and the motion carried by a vote of 52–34. On October 15, a House-Senate conference committee followed the Senate's lead in keeping the FAP out of the broader legislation, and two days later Congress passed H.R. 1 without a guaranteed income program, but with elements of Long's work-oriented provisions.

THE POLICY LEGACY: REINFORCING CATEGORICAL DISTINCTIONS

Following the failure of Nixon's FAP, two closely related pieces of social policy legislation passed into law. These policies—SSI and EITC—partially attained some of the goals of GAI proposals. So the contrast between their success and the FAP's failure can shed further light on the obstacles that proved insurmountable to the Nixon legislation. In particular, the passage of both the SSI and EITC legislation revealed that maintaining the symbolic and programmatic separation between categories of poor people was at the heart of the opposition to the FAP, and that legislation able to attain some antipoverty goals while also retaining this separation was substantially easier for conservatives to accept. Moreover, the passage of SSI and the EITC illustrates the process through which categories of deservingness became further institutionalized in the structure of government programs. The existence of these new programs raised additional barriers to subsequent GAI legislation considered by the Carter administration.

Supplemental Security Income

The SSI program provided a guaranteed annual income for the aged, blind, and disabled. Amid the emotion-laden, ideological controversies over Nixon's FAP, the development and eventual passage of SSI legislation went virtually unchallenged, despite the fact that it was the first federally recognized minimum income guarantee for any category of persons.[65] The FAP had originally aimed to consolidate and integrate a number of existing state-run "adult" public assistance programs, but to still leave the management of these programs up to the states.[66] Much in following with the broader philosophy of the FAP, however, Nixon asked Congress to require that states provide benefits for individuals in these programs at a federally prescribed minimum income level. When the Ways and Means Committee revised the FAP as part of the H.R. 1 legislation in the spring of 1971, it also revised the programs for needy adults by creating a fully federal income guarantee program for the aged, blind, and disabled who were poor. These government benefits were not based on work, nor did they require payment into the Social Security payroll tax fund. Moreover, SSI payments were a supplement to regular Social Security checks, for which over 70 percent of SSI recipients were eligible, and could function as wage supplements because SSI recipients were allowed to add a considerable portion of earnings to their SSI benefits.

The SSI legislation created a programmatic separation between the groups included under its provision and those who were not. The elderly, blind, and disabled were viewed as worthy of governmental support without oversight or requirements. Other categories of unemployed poor people, however, were not defined as worthy and, to the extent they received governmental support, the growing consensus was that such benefits should be stigmatizing. Nixon inadvertently made this clear on the campaign trail in 1972 when he stated in a speech, "And while we're talking about welfare, let us quit treating our senior citizens in this country like welfare recipients."[67] By implication, other types of recipients deserved the stigma of "welfare." This sentiment was shared by members of the Senate Finance Committee and other members of the Nixon administration. In the closing months of debate over H.R. 1, they changed the name of Title II of the legislation from "Assistance for the Aged, Blind, and Disabled" to "Supplemental Security Income" explicitly to ensure that the program would not be called "welfare."[68]

The Earned Income Tax Credit

A similar process of programmatic differentiation occurred with income supplements for the working poor. Throughout the debate over the FAP, conservatives had argued that these types of supplements were the most troublesome element of Nixon's proposal. Sentiments against including the working poor in the legislation were widely shared and nowhere were they propounded more strongly than by members of the Finance Committee. Yet three years later, in 1975, Congress passed legislation for the EITC—legislation that originated in the Finance Committee and gave income supplements to the working poor by reducing their tax burden and often providing a tax refund.

Senator Long developed the EITC, which grew out of the work-oriented legislation he had proposed as an alternative to Nixon's welfare reforms in 1972. The plan was essentially a negative income tax scheme that provided benefits only for those people in the workforce, thereby distinguishing the working poor from the "welfare" poor and ostensibly preserving the work ethic. In the words of a leading scholar of the EITC, "Long had essentially jettisoned FAP's guaranteed income [for the unemployed] but kept the plan's work incentives and benefits for the working poor. Long's work bonus, typically viewed as the earliest version of the EITC, actually owed much in spirit and structure to Nixon's family assistance supplement."[69] Indeed, the only substantial opposition the EITC received before its passage in 1975 was from conservative members of the House who misunderstood it as a full-fledged NIT plan. One member, for instance, opposed the plan by saying it used "the Social Security system as an excuse for paying a guaranteed income out of the Treasury."[70] Although the legislation added considerable costs to existing antipoverty expenditures (it cost $1.4 billion in 1977), the legislation passed by a bipartisan majority vote of 57–21 in the Senate.

This ease of passage belied the rhetoric coming from the Finance Committee, the U.S. Chamber of Commerce, and conservatives in the administration that income supplements to the working poor would harm work incentives and damage the free market economy. This type of income supplement was precisely what the EITC provided. Its uncontentious passage revealed two related things. First, it revealed that the opposition to income supplements to the working poor in the Nixon plan was not based on the *economic* threat of giving such benefits to the working poor. Indeed, income supplements worked to the advantage of employers because it dampened pressure for wage increases. Instead it was based on the *moral* threat of giving stigmatizing benefits labeled as "welfare" to employed workers and on the fears that such benefits raised.[71] The earliest opposition to income benefits to the working poor within the Nixon administration, articulated by Arthur Burns and Anderson, had been laden with moral language. The evidence suggests that this was not simply rhetoric cloaking economic interests. Nixon's advisors had had no contact with business elites at that point, nor did they have any reason to dissemble with Nixon. Moral concerns *were* economic concerns. Especially because the working poor had never received direct income supplements before, the moral threat posed by the FAP's "welfare" benefits to the working poor was perceived as a *real* threat. Second, the passage of the EITC revealed the impossibility of achieving two conservative goals—providing morally acceptable income supplements to the working poor and stigmatizing and meager benefits to the "welfare" poor—within the same program. By the conservatives' logic, the reason that benefits for the "welfare" poor needed to be demeaning, as comments made throughout the debate over GAI had made clear, was that they believed that the "welfare" poor did not share mainstream work values and therefore needed shame and the spur of poverty to push them into greater participation in the labor market. To be sure, economic considerations were a core concern, but these considerations were mediated by conservatives' views of the poor themselves.

Guaranteed Income Plans during the Ford Administration

Over this same period, GAI plans briefly resurfaced during the Ford administration, once again advanced by experts within the government.[72] At least within federal policymaking circles, even those dominated by Republicans, GAI plans had not been discredited. Two NIT proposals were introduced in 1974, one by Caspar Weinberger, secretary of HEW under Gerald Ford, and the other by a joint congressional committee headed by Representative Martha Griffiths. Weinberger was a late convert to support for GAI plans and he grew to favor them for the libertarian reasons first espoused by Milton Friedman. His plan in many ways went further than Nixon's had, because it included childless couples and single individuals as well as families. Despite the fact that Ford had voted for the FAP twice as a member of Congress, he rejected Weinberger's plan in favor of more incremental goals. Griffiths' plan received brief consideration by Congress in 1976, but it ultimately stalled. Proponents of GAI proposals, who were largely located in the offices at HEW, would have to wait until the Carter administration for their next realistic chance at reform.

Conclusion

Though another presidential administration would soon consider its own GAI proposal, by the mid-1970s the boundaries between categories of the poor had been programmatically reinforced through SSI and the EITC. This posed considerable challenges to any future GAI proposal because such a plan would have to deconstruct these new programs and combat concerns about stigma and benefit levels raised by their new "deserving" constituencies. The existence of these new programs also stripped away the strongest rationale for a unified, comprehensive income strategy, since these new programs did actually improve social provision for significant sectors of the poor population. The absolute need for welfare reform was therefore not as great. Yet the SSI and EITC reforms left the programs for the most vulnerable poor untouched. This programmatic isolation of the "welfare" poor within the AFDC program was intentional. The challenge posed by Nixon's proposal, a program that dissolved existing symbolic and programmatic categories, had inadvertently led to the reinforcement of the boundaries it sought to dismantle.

Many of the political dynamics set into motion during the first round of debates over the FAP continued during the deliberation over Nixon's newer legislation. Despite the fact that the revised FAP differentiated between categories of poor people through its administrative structure, the plan still threatened conservatives because it provided benefits to the poor based on their economic need and not their work capacity. Thus in the Senate Finance Committee, where the FAP ultimately died, concerns about issues such as entitlements and work requirements presented the biggest obstacle to the legislation. Conservatives on the committee wanted "workfare" legislation instead. The salience of the distinction between the deserving and undeserving poor was also reflected in the alternative proposals developed by members of the Senate Finance Committee. Ribicoff's plan firmly embraced the economic citizenship paradigm of welfare reform. It was a universal, noncategorical program that provided benefits based on economic need alone. Yet the moral legitimacy this type of plan extended to the poor became increasingly untenable over the course of debate over the FAP, particularly in the Finance Committee.

Guaranteed annual income programs were linked to other policy domains as well. Perhaps the most significant was fiscal policy. Nixon's welfare proposal originally packaged welfare reform together with fiscal relief measures for state governments, partly as a cost-saving measure and partly as a component of his "new federalism" initiatives to devolve federal power to more local administrative units. As a result, one of the most influential blocks of supporters for the FAP comprised governors and big-city mayors. However, when Nixon decoupled welfare reform from fiscal relief through the passage of separate revenue-sharing legislation, he undercut this important basis of support. Guaranteed income plans had also been associated with urban policy. The social unrest of the late 1960s had propelled the issue of poverty to the top of the legislative agenda and the civil rights movement constituted a highly visible pressure group. With the waning of social unrest and the fracturing of the civil rights movement, grassroots pressure to deal with poverty, especially poverty resulting from male unemployment, subsided.

Given the waning associations between GAI plans and these other policy goals, it may seem surprising that the Carter administration advanced its own GAI proposal. Yet as continuing consideration of GAI plans during the Ford years suggests, the idea still retained its credibility as an effective antipoverty measure among policy experts. While Carter favored GAI plans for this reason, he also favored them for reasons that Friedman first advanced: their promise for administrative reform.

CHAPTER SIX

Carter and the Program for Better Jobs and Income

Guaranteed annual income plans received renewed attention with the election of Jimmy Carter in 1976. In keeping with his popular campaign promise to bring comprehensive reform to the beleaguered welfare system, Carter's new administration formulated a proposal based on a modified negative income tax scheme. During the formulation process, Carter's secretary at HEW, Joseph Califano, consulted a wide variety of groups and discovered firsthand the multiple meanings that reform entailed. According to a close follower of the proceedings, "the first thing Califano learned . . . was that welfare reform means very different things to different people."[1] When Califano announced the Carter plan, he quipped that welfare reform had become the "Middle East of domestic politics."[2] The comment was prescient. The challenge of overhauling the welfare system with a GAI plan ultimately proved to be too daunting for the administration. By 1979, few traces of the negative income tax proposal remained. Instead, administration officials struggled to defend a more modest, incremental bill from narrow concerns in Congress about welfare costs and the work ethic. Ronald Reagan's subsequent election in 1980 brought to the forefront of domestic politics new welfare reform ideas that had arisen in direct opposition to GAI policies and that signaled the eclipse of GAI plans from national policymaking. This chapter examines the debate over Carter's proposal.

As during the Johnson and Nixon years, government experts were the prime movers in putting GAI plans on the welfare reform agenda. Yet if welfare reform had come to mean a great variety of things by the late 1970s, as Califano discovered early on, GAI plans themselves had come to mean fewer. Proponents associated them with a narrower range of social problems than they had during the 1960s. For policymakers at HEW, who still adhered to the economic citizenship paradigm, GAI plans meant social provision based on need alone. They successfully placed a negative income tax proposal at the center of the administration's welfare reform debate, though a variety of factors diluted it substantially in the months leading up to the president's welfare announcement. Guaranteed income plans attracted Carter and some of his advisors for a different reason. The plans promised to rationalize and consolidate an unwieldy welfare system that was the target of increasing allegations of waste, fraud, and abuse. Fiscal management and comprehensive overhaul were Carter's highest welfare reform priorities, and GAI plans seemed, at least initially, to fit the bill.

Notably absent from the welfare reform debates within the administration was the laissez-faire paradigm, which had been a vital source of bipartisan support for GAI policy during the Nixon administration. Because the administration was Democratic, there were few representatives of this libertarian view in its domestic policy agencies. There were no laissez-faire supporters among Republicans either. The laissez-faire approach emphasized extending more freedom of choice to the poor, but this strand of conservatism had been overtaken by "California-style" conservatism that impugned the morality of the able-bodied poor. Carter's GAI plan also lacked advocates rooted in the family stability paradigm. This perspective would resurface following Carter's announcement of his plan, though in ways that undercut support for a GAI plan rather than strengthening it.

In comparison to the FAP, Carter's Program for Better Jobs and Income (PBJI) faced both familiar and new obstacles, many of which were associated with the fact that Carter's plan, by design, consolidated a number of existing antipoverty programs. As during the Nixon years, erasing the distinctions between different categories of poor people by placing them in the same program exposed it to the risk of symbolic pollution. Yet there were three significant differences from the Nixon years. First, government experts had learned lessons from the FAP's failure. As scholars who study "social learning" among experts would anticipate, both supporters and sympathetic critics of GAI plans understood the risk of symbolic pollution in the wake of the FAP's failure and evaluated Carter's plan on this basis.[3] Among some policy experts, this led to efforts to repackage the program in culturally resonant ways. For others, it led to "second-order" policy changes that still identified labor market conditions as a source of poverty, but that proposed new solutions, such as public jobs legislation, that they hoped would be deemed more plausible.[4] In either case, government experts were a key conduit through which cultural categories of worth exerted influence on policy development. Second, as a "policy feedback" argument would suggest, the recent SSI and EITC programs proved to be new obstacles to reform.[5] They created new "deserving" constituencies who did not want to be placed in a broader program that included AFDC recipients. The plans also created technical problems for program consolidation. And the EITC program in particular proved to be a resource that policymakers could use both to hide welfare costs and to provide income supplements to the working poor without the stigma of "welfare." Third, within broader public discourse, journalists and others employed the distinction between the "welfare rolls" and "payrolls" that Nixon had strategically advanced. This rhetorical trope treated the relationship between work and welfare as mutually exclusive categories while negative income plans treated the relationship as a continuum.

While the FAP had developed during a period of heightened concern about urban disruption and racial unrest, Carter's proposal emerged amid growing concern about the American family and increasing attention to changes in female labor force participation. These concerns shaped the prospects of Carter's plan. Worries about family life held implications for the interpretation of the results from the government's NIT experiments, which concluded during the Carter years. In addition, critics of Carter's program also questioned why poor women should be paid by the government to stay home with their children while middle-class women worked at increasingly high rates. In the late 1960s, a prominent concern among conservatives had been family stability and keeping mothers at home with their children. By the late 1970s, the reverse was often true, particularly among the most influential conservatives in Congress.

Carter's legislation did not proceed very far legislatively once he announced it, so far fewer stakeholders involved themselves in lobbying on the proposals. Carter also explicitly distanced himself from traditional Democratic constituencies, so they played a lesser role than they might have otherwise. Organized labor was an influential lobby in Washington, but its representatives provided only tepid support for the Carter plan because of disagreements over the jobs component of the legislation. Civil rights groups were weaker than they had been in the 1960s and Carter was particularly unresponsive to them. Women's groups, on the other hand, were more active because of the galvanizing effects of the women's movement in the early 1970s. The NWRO was defunct because its leader, George Wiley, had died in an accident in 1973. State representatives and local leaders were still among the most dependable source of support for GAI plans because their welfare expenses continued to mount despite the passage of fiscal relief legislation earlier in the decade. Yet Carter's pledge to balance the budget and limit social spending virtually ensured that the support from this group would be limited.

The social context of the mid-1970s provided a new set of conditions within which the debates over GAI policy took place. Perhaps foremost, the nation faced an economic crisis. Inflation rates hit a high of 11 percent in 1974 and unemployment rates peaked above 8 percent in 1975. Many liberals felt that this called for an employment-based antipoverty strategy as opposed to a GAI plan. The new "welfare crisis" was the alleged runaway fraud and abuse in social programs—not only in public assistance but also in other areas such as Medicaid, Medicare, and education programs. These allegations of fraud fed a growing dissatisfaction with government programs of all kinds. Critics complained that costs were increasing while levels of government performance dropped. Riding the crest of antigovernment sentiments was a taxpayer backlash that would soon manifest itself as the "tax revolt" of 1978, a movement fueled in part by opposition to the very type of GAI policy that the Carter administration would consider.

Developing the Carter Plan

Carter's Policy Priority: Comprehensive Reform

Jimmy Carter learned of the inadequacies of the existing welfare system as governor of Georgia, and he was the only southern governor to support Nixon's FAP in 1970. On the campaign trail in 1976, he found that welfare reform was a popular issue. Most people were dissatisfied with the existing system for one reason or another, so he drew welcome applause when he promised to "clean up the welfare mess," no matter who his audience was: Manhattan liberals, Detroit's African Americans, construction workers in the South, or Midwestern farmers. Among these different audiences, however, the actual meaning of welfare reform differed. It could mean higher benefits, lower costs, stronger work requirements, increased fiscal relief, less stigma, simplified administration, or ending fraud and abuse. When Carter himself defined what he meant by welfare reform, his most consistent themes were comprehensive overhaul, fraud reduction, and vague references to a plan that would be "pro-work" and "pro-family."[6]

Carter's vision of welfare reform was shaped by his overall governing style, which was often described as managerial or technocratic. He viewed himself as a "trustee" of the nation and he sought long-term goals, such as national security, inflation reduction, and a balanced budget.[7] This fiscal conservatism was at odds with the shorter-term goals sought by many Democratic constituent groups, including civil rights groups and advocates for the poor. Carter hoped that fundamental reforms of government processes could restore the country's faith in government after it had been shaken by Vietnam and Watergate. This emphasis on governmental restructuring had deep roots. As governor of Georgia, one of Carter's greatest successes was the reform of the state bureaucracy, and as president he hoped to bring about the same kind of changes at the national level. "Comprehensive change" became a buzzword, and Carter portrayed such fundamental change—wiping the slate clean—as the only way to ensure that politics did not fall prey to destructive, parochial interests.[8]

These presidential imperatives shaped the entirety of domestic social programming, from urban policy to health care to welfare, and they often subordinated substantive goals to procedural or managerial reforms. Process ruled over substance. The president's advisors inside government recognized as much. On the issue of welfare reform, they often suggested to Carter that they needed more guidance on the substantive goals of welfare reform, aside from fraud reduction and simplified administration. To experts outside the government, the almost exclusive attention to procedural reform was even more glaring. According to one external consultant to the White House, the administration was missing the big picture; it was letting technical issues dominate discussions "without even having achieved basic conceptual agreement on the framework of welfare reform, the target population to be served, and the government's capacity to deliver a program."[9]

Despite the value Carter placed on reforming the welfare system, he was never very deeply involved in the policy formulation process, nor did his critics (and sometimes even his supporters) feel that he really understood the welfare system, its politics, and the measures it would take to change it. In a note to Califano early on in the development process, Carter suggested that over the course of the following months he would be willing to attend "several hours" of deliberation once the plan was "beginning to firm up and you need me."[10] As the development process continued, Carter's advisors worried that Carter really did not understand all that he needed to know about welfare reform, and that he had devoted only a fraction of the attention to it that he had devoted to other issues, such as energy policy, that engaged him more deeply.[11]

Califano and the Experts at HEW

The bulk of the task of reforming the system fell to Califano and his staff at HEW. Califano had been President Johnson's assistant for domestic affairs and had a basic understanding of the welfare proposals and policies of that era. During the Carter transition period, before Califano knew he would be secretary of HEW, Carter informally asked him how long it would take to formulate a new welfare reform proposal. Califano offhandedly responded that it could be accomplished by May 1. Carter subsequently appointed Califano as secretary and without further consultation publicly stated that he would be announcing his new welfare plan on May 1. Califano reportedly took up the task with the enthusiasm of a liberal anxious to be back in power. At one of the first meetings with his staff, he declared, "We've got to pick up where we were in 1968. We've lost a lot of time."[12]

But time had not stood still since the late 1960s. Public assistance programs had evolved, costs had increased, and fraud and abuse were the targets of public opprobrium. Comprehensive reform now involved consolidating SSI and the EITC, neither of which had existed during the fight over the FAP. The food stamps program, which worked like a non-cash negative income tax, had been expanded. The number of people who were poor was about 12 percent of the population, a level similar to the poverty rate in the late 1960s, but the poverty threshold had increased substantially because of inflation, from $3,553 for a family of four in 1968 to $5,500 for the same family in 1975. Over the same period, the unemployment rate had jumped from roughly 3 to 8 percent. The rate of increase in the number of people receiving AFDC had largely leveled off since 1972, but the composition of the poor had changed. Most important, the proportion of female-headed households among all poor households had increased by 14 points—from 33 percent in

1965 to 47 percent in 1975. Blacks and Hispanics were three times as likely to be poor as comparable whites.[13]

In late January 1977, Califano held a press conference during which he publicly announced that HEW was working to fulfill Carter's campaign promise of welfare reform. He enumerated the many longstanding criticisms of the existing system—its inefficiency, disincentives for work and family stability, heavy fiscal burden for states, and the insensitive treatment of those who could not work or should not be expected to. Though the list was similar to the criticisms routinely invoked during the Nixon era, the rhetorical tenor of the statement did not impugn welfare recipients' character to nearly the same extent as Nixon had. The most significant departure from the Nixon era—significant because of its relative newness—was reference to the costs of fraud and abuse within the system. "The American taxpayer," Califano admitted, "is impatient with the inability of our government to remove from the welfare rolls those persons improperly on them."[14]

The policy development process under Carter was also different from the development of the FAP. In the same statement, Califano emphasized that the White House would be in constant consultation with members of Congress, state and local officials, and interest groups during the formulation process: "The executive branch of the Federal Government, acting alone, cannot and should not attempt to devise a program that must receive wide acceptance if it is going to succeed."[15] This wide consultation process was specifically mandated by Carter. Over the following weeks, Califano and his staff met with over 350 individuals and groups, formed and met with formal advisory committees, and held public hearings.[16] This was in marked contrast to Nixon-era policy development, which took place almost exclusively within the administration itself. In theory, it was hoped that this greater openness would lead to greater public acceptance of the resultant welfare plan. In practice, it exposed the administration to a web of fundamentally conflicting interests. Carter was reluctant, or unable, to provide a clear direction for reform, and he had not designated a White House office or staff coordinator—such as Moynihan and the Urban Affairs Council under Nixon—to fulfill this role either.

As a result, initial formulation largely took place within HEW. Califano appointed Henry Aaron, a well-regarded economist and welfare expert, as head of HEW's systems analysis office. Aaron had written a number of books on welfare and social policy, including *Why Is Welfare So Hard to Reform?*[17] The book described the fundamental tension of welfare reform as consisting of the unavoidable trade-offs between work incentives, benefit levels, and program costs. Aaron argued that it was impossible to improve one without hurting at least one of the other two. This set of trade-offs became known by welfare experts as the "tough triangle." Because welfare reform consisted of tough choices between multiple public goods—the value of work, cost-effective government programs, and adequate income security—Aaron was not sanguine about the prospects of comprehensive change.

However, Aaron the incrementalist was a minority voice at HEW. Most analysts favored comprehensive reform through the negative income tax. Many of them had worked on NIT plans during the previous Republican administration. Under Gerald Ford, HEW officials had developed a short-lived NIT program called the Income Supplement Program. Califano and Aaron recruited almost the entire development staff of this plan to work for the Carter administration. After several years of relative inactivity since the Weinberger plan had been abandoned, the analysts were reportedly eager to work on welfare reform again.[18]

One of the new evaluative criteria that emerged from the systems analysis office at HEW was the notion of "target efficiency," which evaluated income transfer programs based on the percent of total transfers to the target populations. Social Security, for instance, was not a target-efficient poverty reduction strategy because its benefits went to a high percentage of people who were not poor. Means-tested programs were more target efficient than social insurance programs, but politically they were much more vulnerable. Analysts realized there was a trade-off. However, given the comprehensive nature of change that Carter and Califano wanted to bring about, target-efficient programs were crucial, especially in keeping costs as low as possible. Programs based solely on need were target efficient, but distinguishing between different types of needy people (e.g., the aged, women with young children, employable fathers) was even more so because different populations had different needs. Therefore the drive for target efficiency worked against rationales for NIT programs. This created conflicting goals within HEW and lent itself to other reform strategies, such as the categorical programs being developed outside HEW.[19]

The Push for Categorical Differentiation

Because of Carter's desire to provide jobs for the unemployed, he directed Califano to work closely with the Department of Labor (DOL) to integrate a jobs program into the welfare legislation. People at DOL had opposed NIT programs under the Ford administration, and they did not favor them during the Carter administration either. Arnold Packer was the assistant secretary of policy, evaluation, and research at DOL—Henry Aaron's counterpart—and he favored a two-track "jobs/cash" program that would categorize households based on their employability. For those in which a member was expected to work, the government would provide a job; households without an employable member would receive cash assistance. The job component was based on public service jobs at a relatively high wage. DOL's program would provide coverage for all low-income families, childless couples, and individuals; therefore, coverage was universal.[20]

Though professional interests partially explained the reasons why experts at DOL preferred a program that emphasized the provision of jobs, the planners also had a well-developed ideological and political rationale for favoring their approach over an NIT. Packer said the NIT plan was based on "bloodless analysis by economists" that did not recognize the moral necessity of society to provide jobs for people who wanted to work. Moreover, he argued,

> with an economist, cash is cash—you don't care where you get it. But people do care where they get it. If recipients are assisted by taking a job . . . they feel different about the income than if it comes in the form of a check from the government. . . . There [is] a tendency among economists not to deal with those issues, to get lost in a lot of economics, numbers, efficiency, and well, a lot of bullshit as far as I'm concerned.[21]

Packer's description of policy development at HEW typified the animosity that existed between the two departments throughout the Carter administration as they repeatedly clashed over the welfare issue. His characterization also revealed an understanding of the "social meaning" of money, in which income from different sources holds different meanings for the recipient.[22]

There was a third approach that contrasted with both the HEW and DOL plans (though more similar to DOL's), and that was Tom Joe's "triple-track" approach, which essentially added a program for the working poor to DOL's two-track plan. Joe was an outside consultant on welfare policy who participated in working group meetings. He was also a personal friend of Carter's and had advised him during his 1976 presidential campaign. As a candidate, Carter sometimes referred to Joe's three categories of recipients as groups who needed their own particular government programs.[23]

In Joe's three-tiered approach, the "welfare track" was intended to be a truly residual program for recipients who were not expected to work; it would have a federally financed national minimum at a decent standard of living. The "manpower track" was for those who could be reasonably expected to work; it would integrate and expand existing work-based programs, such as those falling under the provisions of the Comprehensive Employment and Training Act, and create a full employment policy that would provide public service jobs where necessary. The "working poor" track would provide income supplements for low-income workers through the expansion and liberalization of the EITC; this would ensure that no one was better off on welfare than they could be working, which was another of Carter's frequent campaign promises.[24]

During the Nixon administration, Joe had been a central player at HEW in advancing the FAP over the incremental Nathan plan. Therefore his changing view of welfare reform over the intervening eight years is instructive, since it illustrates a type of "second-order" policy change. Joe had originally favored the FAP because of his economic citizenship perspective that blamed poverty largely on the labor market's lack of sufficient jobs at adequate wages. Under

Carter, this labor market critique was stronger than ever. He complained to the White House staff that "full employment" had been defined downward from 97 to 92 percent and that government calculations understated actual unemployment by anywhere from 50 to 100 percent.[25] But he now favored a categorical jobs approach over a GAI plan for programmatic and political reasons. Programmatically, his approach was geared toward the different needs of the poor population—including "the desire to be a productive member of society"—rather than relying purely on economic incentives for its functioning as a consolidated NIT would. He felt that "although a single system does respond to objectives of simplicity and equity, the work incentives provision [of an NIT] has in the past created serious technical and philosophical hang-ups which are best solved by a multi-system approach."[26]

These "philosophical hang-ups" were the root of the political rationale for the triple-track approach.

> While some strategically argue that if welfare becomes more inclusive (i.e., subsumed employable but unemployed adults and the working poor) it will become more acceptable to the public, I do not believe this to be the case. In my opinion, welfare will remain unpopular as long as we try to subsume other problems (i.e., unemployment) under the welfare umbrella . . . successful welfare reform must result in smaller caseloads of people who cannot be expected to work.[27]

The contrast drawn by Joe between his categorical approach and the consolidated approach sought by NIT supporters recapitulated the debate during the Nixon era over the meanings of the welfare rolls. The essence of the question was this: If formerly separate groups were treated equally within the same program, which population would "contaminate" the other with its status? Advocates of GAI plans believed that if all the poor were treated according to the same criteria, including the aged, the disabled, and the working poor, then the stigma of welfare would diminish. By this rationale, the dominant status of the program would be determined by the presence of the working poor or those not expected to work. Opponents of the consolidated approach, such as Senators Russell Long and Carl Curtis on the Finance Committee, believed that the influence would run the other way—the working poor would be stigmatized because they received "welfare" benefits. Joe tried to split the difference. He sought many of the objectives of the NIT proponents but categorized recipients similarly to the way in which Long did. Joe felt that if "welfare" programs were targeted solely at those whom society deemed were not expected to work, then "welfare" would lose its stigma. Other subpopulations of the poor—those who worked and those who did not but were expected to—would be in categorically different programs, that is, not "welfare" programs. In Joe's scheme it was those who were expected to work but did not that were the contaminating group, and his plan isolated them in the manpower track.

Competing Welfare Reform Options and Carter's Emphasis on Costs

Throughout February and March, Califano's staff continued their consultation with a diverse set of parties interested in welfare reform, and experts at HEW and DOL worked on their alternative proposals. In preparation for the first presidential meeting on welfare reform at the end of March, Califano's staff prepared a briefing book containing five interrelated papers and submitted it to Carter. In his cover letter, Califano could barely hide his frustration with Carter's lack of involvement up to this point. He asked the president five questions, without the answers to which, he said, his staff could not proceed with development any further: Which existing programs should be included in welfare reform? What level of income should be established for the national standard? Should intact families be covered in addition to single-parent families? Should mothers with children be encouraged or required to work? Was the government prepared to guarantee government jobs to "employable" populations?[28]

The briefing book included a paper on "leading welfare reform options," and the document was notable for its number and diversity of policy alternatives. Nine fully distinct options were described. Perhaps never before had such a wide array of welfare reform options been considered simultaneously. They ranged from reforms based on the AFDC structure of the 1930s, social service and guaranteed income approaches from the 1960s, and guaranteed jobs programs developed in the 1970s to the "workfare" and block grant plans that came to characterize welfare reform in the 1980s. Califano's staff had presented a full spectrum of options, yet without a strong sense of the main goals of reform. This lack of clear goals helps explain a list of policy options containing so many competing or antithetical objectives.[29]

In the welfare meeting on March 25, Carter did in fact express a few strong preferences, though they were procedural and not substantive: He wanted comprehensive reform and he wanted it at no additional cost beyond existing expenditures. Califano first reviewed the failings of the existing system by illustrating them with dramatic examples: for instance, a woman would lose $3,000 in benefits under the Wisconsin system if she moved from a part-time to a full-time job. This was a clear case of a system containing disincentives to work. After hearing many such examples, the president said that "when the people really understand this, I'm sure they will do something about it." In a follow-up exchange, Carter asked Califano, "If you had to start from scratch, is this the kind of system you would create?" Califano responded negatively and Carter continued: "In that case I want you to take all the money that is now being spent on welfare programs and redesign the whole system using the same amount of money. Then show what you can do, adding new money in $1 billion increments."[30] This preference for comprehensive reform reduced the number of policy options discussed in the briefing book to less than a handful, with the competing contenders consisting of HEW's negative income tax plan, DOL's two-track plan, and Joe's triple-track plan.

In asking Califano to hold the costs of welfare reform constant, Carter used one of his favorite managerial techniques: zero-cost planning. The process called for questioning the premises and assumptions built into existing systems and trying to improve them without increasing costs. It was one of Carter's many austerity tools. Yet it was also unavoidably a political decision about welfare policy. According to the "tough triangle" Aaron had outlined, welfare reform consisted of tensions between work incentives, welfare benefits, and program costs. Of these three variables, Nixon had emphasized work and it appeared that Carter would emphasize costs. Under both presidents, benefit levels for the poor suffered in the balance.

What Aaron had not factored into his three-part equation was fiscal relief, but ever since the late 1960s, welfare reform had been viewed by state and local officials as a central vehicle for obtaining federal funds. In the wake of the meeting with Carter, Califano scrambled for ways to get additional money reassigned to the welfare package so he would have more money to use when he figured his zero-cost base. He contacted the energy secretary to see if he had any "extra" energy funds to divert to welfare, under the rubric of money for low-income recipients to pay for energy costs. Money for the states and money for higher benefits, Califano said, were his two chief concerns. As welfare formulation continued through the spring and summer, fiscal relief and benefit levels would repeatedly be pitted against each other in a zero-sum contest for funds. Because state and local officials were much more influential than the poor, money for fiscal relief usually survived longer than money for higher benefits. Yet throughout the process, Carter pressed for reductions in funding for both.[31]

Califano prepared to brief the president on the three plans in a second meeting on April 11. Stuart Eizenstat, the president's chief domestic advisor and the head of the Domestic Policy Staff (DPS), prepared Carter for what to expect from the meeting. He told him that Califano would outline the pros and cons of the three programs at zero-cost, but then push for additional funding. He explained that the reason for additional funding was that while some groups would be better off under each proposal, others would be worse off. Therefore Califano would not recommend any of the plans without funding increases. Eizenstat and his staff agreed with Califano on the political importance of more funds.[32]

Carter did not. At the meeting, he railed at Califano: "Are you telling me that there is no way to improve the present system except by spending billions of dollars? In that case, to hell with it! We're wasting our time." When Califano explained about some recipients being worse off, and the additional need for fiscal relief, Carter challenged him: "I don't buy the assumption that once you set a benefit level you have to bring everybody up to it. I'm offended and I think the American people are offended that people can choose not to work and get more than people who are working."[33] Further, Carter doubted whether fiscal relief for the states was a necessary part of welfare reform. For the remainder of the meeting, Califano, the president, and the staff focused on issues related to costs rather than debating the substantive differences among the three plans.[34]

Program Consolidation and the Stigma of "Welfare"

To aim the welfare debate in a more substantive direction, Califano followed up the meeting by circulating a memo to the president, the White House staff, and cabinet members that enumerated ten "principles to guide our welfare reform initiative." Califano's first and most expensive principle was program consolidation: "Simplify administration and introduce efficient systems management by consolidating in one cash assistance programs: SSI, AFDC, food stamps, 'Section 8' housing, earned income tax credit, extended unemployment benefits." The other nine principles dealt primarily with the long-standing rationales for reform: improving work incentives, maintaining incentives for family stability, federal minimum benefits, and more job training.[35]

The high priority that Califano placed on program consolidation sheds light on why he continued to press for an NIT scheme. HEW staff supported the NIT largely because they believed in the equity of treating people solely on the basis on need, regardless of the reasons why they were poor. The NIT did this by collapsing the existing programmatic distinctions between groups of people. It also showed trust in the poor by providing them with cash benefits, whereas other programs provided vouchers or in-kind benefits. Califano may have shared these sentiments, but the value of the NIT for him lay in large part in its promise for consolidation. This, after all, had been one of the NIT's attractions for Milton Friedman. Carter wanted comprehensive change, he put pressure on Califano to design a comprehensive bill, and the NIT offered such a program. Program consolidation and streamlining also promised to address the allegations of fraud that plagued a number of HEW's most publicly visible programs.[36]

Califano's statement of welfare reform principles elicited strong reactions from the White House staff, in part because Califano was goading the president and his staff to make substantive decisions about the direction of the planning process. Eizenstat's two main advisors on the DPS both expressed further concerns about Califano's emphasis on consolidation. These concerns revolved around the issue of stigma, and more specifically the fear that the moral stigma associated with AFDC would contaminate recipients of other programs if they were all consolidated into one comprehensive program.

> You should be aware that folding into the "welfare system" the earned income tax credit, extended unemployment benefits, "Section 8 housing,"

and attaching CETA jobs will appear to be an expansion of the welfare system and will label as "welfare recipients" people who are not now so perceived.[37]

Another staffer made a similar point, saying that the "stigma" issue had not been directly addressed by HEW planners: "To the extent that a consolidated assistance program brings additional people within a 'welfare package', stigma may be increased."[38]

In a summary memo to the president, the White House staff gleaned Carter's sentiments on welfare reform as expressed in public speeches over the preceding years and, paraphrasing his words, enumerated a number of "principles" that they argued reflected "healthy national consensus" on welfare. Some of these sentiments were at odds with Califano's principles, including two on program consolidation.

> The working poor who labor every day, but by reason of life circumstances do not earn enough to adequately support their families, should be assisted in a manner that does not label them as "welfare recipients."

> The stigma of "welfare" should be reduced by reserving the term for those who are not expected to be employed outside the home and keeping that group to the minimum number possible.[39]

Carter wanted differentiation between categories of the poor. This was a vision of comprehensive reform based not on HEW's or even DOL's welfare plan, but on Joe's triple-track approach to welfare reform, and it created a problem. With less than three weeks remaining before Carter was scheduled to publicly announce his welfare plan, HEW officials could not agree with DOL planners on a compromise, and Joe (and possibly Carter) were in favor of yet a third choice. All the parties involved were frustrated and a number of key issues remained undecided, such as how heavily reform should depend on public jobs creation, the form in which to give benefits to those who worked, whether to cash out the food stamps program, and how to administer the overall program. Carter asked the chair of his Council of Economic Advisors, Charles Schultze, to mediate a compromise between HEW and DOL, but Schultze was unable to reconcile their differences.[40]

Carter Announces His Policy Principles

As a result, instead of laying out plans for comprehensive overhaul on May 2, Carter announced twelve "principles" of welfare reform only. In his introductory remarks, he said that the existing system "should be scrapped and a totally new system implemented."[41] Then he moved on to his principles for welfare reform. The first was: "No higher initial cost than the present system." Califano, who was present with Carter for the press briefing to follow, was disappointed that Carter made zero-cost constraints his first priority. The president was virtually alone on this decision and he stood by it firmly. The rest of the principles were based on items Califano, Secretary of Labor Ray Marshall, and others had discussed in the past, and they were in fact similar to those Carter had stated in January. The *Los Angeles Times* said that Carter's principles "sounded about as controversial as the Boy Scout oath."[42]

But in fact they were controversial. To experts at HEW, Carter's announcement sounded like Joe's triple-track plan, rather than the NIT-based system they were working on. Principles 2, 7, and 8 sounded to their ears like the three components of Joe's plan—respectively, the manpower, working poor, and welfare components.

2. Under this system every family with children and a member able to work should have access to a job.
7. Earned income tax credit should be continued to help the working poor.
8. A decent income should be provided also for those who cannot work or earn adequate income, with federal benefits consolidated into a simple cash payment, varying in amount only to accommodate differences in costs of living from one area to another.[43]

The welfare component did consolidate a number of cash-based systems for administrative simplification, but there were still sharp programmatic distinctions between recipients in each tier. In the press conference following the president's statement, only one reporter caught the implication of what Carter seemed to be saying. He asked Califano whether the plan for a universal system had been jettisoned. Califano equivocated. The experts at HEW were despondent. According to one, "A lot of people said [Joe's] triple-track had won out! We all went out and got drunk."[44]

Califano and Marshall ran the press conference that took place after Carter's announcement. Califano began by illustrating the complexity and waste in the existing system. He described the situation in California where the written rules and regulations for state welfare administration stood over six feet in height if stacked together. He also showed the press corps a roll of paper that represented the seven feet of forms that welfare recipients had to fill out to receive benefits. "It is this kind of unbelievable morass," Califano said, "that we have leveled on the American taxpayer and the American people."[45] By repeatedly making statements such as these, Califano and other members of the administration unwittingly provided fuel for the growing anti-welfare backlash in the country. Another reporter asked Califano how the administration planned to get mothers "off the AFDC rolls and onto the work rolls." This juxtaposition between the welfare rolls and the work rolls recurred repeatedly throughout the debates over Carter's plan, and it perfectly replicated Nixon's rhetoric in the debates over the FAP.

The Carter administration's welfare planning developed in explicit contrast with welfare reform strategies that emerged from California. References to California came up repeatedly during the press conference, in reference not only to the paperwork involved in their system but to the state's former welfare commissioner, Robert Carleson, who was the central architect of the welfare retrenchment and workfare programs that Governor Reagan initiated during the Nixon era. The "California-style" welfare reform strategy had now taken a more prominent place in the national arena, not only because California was the state that spent most on welfare payments but because Reagan had taken the national stage in the 1976 presidential campaign. Carleson had also become a welfare consultant to Senator Long. In the press conference, Califano referred to Carleson as his "shadow cabinet member" and indeed reporters contrasted the administration's plans with those developed in California.[46] These opposing strategies would become even more salient in the following year in the wake of the "tax revolt" of 1978.

The Carter Plan and Its Critics

Is It a Negative Income Tax Plan?

In the two weeks following Carter's statement, HEW and DOL staff members, under the direction of Aaron and Packer, had a series of meetings in which they worked through their many differences, and on May 13 they negotiated a preliminary compromise. In a memo to Carter, Califano characterized the compromise plan as a two-tiered system. The "income supplement tier" applied to recipients from whom work was not required. The basic benefit level for a family of four on this tier was $4,700, roughly three-quarters of the poverty level. The "work supplement tier" applied to those expected to work. It was based on a jobs program that paid near the minimum wage with work supplements for a family of four up to $2,600. If the employable member of a household refused to work, their benefits would be cut, but those for their children would remain intact. The cash part of the program would include a consolidation of SSI, AFDC, and food stamps.[47] A remaining issue was the "flip-up/ flip-down" debate. It involved which of the two tiers would be the default tier for recipients. Depending on the resolution, the plan would either be similar to an NIT plan (specifically an NIT with a work test) or be a public jobs program with an income component for those not expected to work. In either system, the result would be similar for recipients; but for administrative and political reasons, especially concerning how Congress perceived the plan symbolically, the distinction was crucial.[48]

Joe harshly criticized the compromise plan. Understanding it to be the HEW version, he said it was a "thinly veiled" NIT proposal—albeit with two tiers—and that it would increase welfare caseloads. Joe contended that the "flip-down" design was illogical because there would be little incentive for people to work; the plan provided no fiscal relief for states; the SSI benefits would have to be lowered, which was politically hazardous; and the plan did not take full advantage of the existing EITC program. His main criticism, however, was that the program did not rely enough on jobs programs, and that the plan thus simply continued the flawed philosophy of existing welfare programs.

> The provision once again leaves the manpower system off the hook with the welfare system left assuming the costs and caseload. In that respect, it mirrors the current welfare system in which failures of WIN and manpower programs revert to the welfare system. . . . In summary, the cash assistance provisions of the proposal are structured as they have been because it is assumed that the manpower system will fail to provide jobs in significant numbers. This perpetuates the existence of the manpower system as adjunct and not an indispensable part of total reform.[49]

Joe's focus on jobs and manpower programs was rooted in the economic citizenship paradigm that located the sources of poverty in the labor market and wage structure. Yet in contrast to his earlier support for NIT legislation during the Nixon years, his new solution was based on employment programs and not income transfers.

Government Experts Seek to Circumvent "Welfare" Stigma

The HEW-DOL compromise plan received further criticism from Carter's White House staff, who reprised earlier criticisms of the cash-consolidation approach. They said that there was much to commend in the plan: national minimum standards, coverage of children of unemployed fathers, equity for children of the working poor, coverage of singles and childless couples, a commitment to public jobs, and the administrative efficiency of a unified system. However, a consolidated system such as an NIT had substantial political drawbacks; namely, that "combined with the work incentives provisions, it has the consequence of vastly enlarging the size of the group being subsidized under the welfare program label." An alternative, they suggested, had to do with expanding the use of the EITC.

> Although the earned income tax credit is retained [in the compromise proposal], that plan makes no suggestion for using it in an expanded way. One hope was that such a mechanism would enable many of the working poor to be assisted *without labeling them as welfare recipients*, or requiring that they undergo a means test.[50]

In a follow-up memo, one of the staff members made the point even more sharply. The administration was being criticized because the compromise plan would lower benefits for certain groups. However, he said, it seems to me like the issue of expanded eligibility is more of a problem. It seems to me we should do everything we can to project our plan as drawing a tight line around the residual welfare group and explain them as people who *ought not* to be required to work.[51]

These comments concerned stigma and moral pollution. The prospect outlined here reprised Joe's earlier argument that if "welfare" programs were designated as only for those whom society agreed were not required to work—for example, the aged, blind, disabled, and mothers of young children—the "welfare" label would lose its stigma. Likewise, expanding the EITC to include the working poor would avoid the "welfare" label. The staff admitted that a strong argument against drawing such distinctions was administrative, since this type of differentiation would require HEW, DOL, and the Treasury Department each to administer benefits to different categories of people. "This argument," they contended, "has merit but might turn out to be a small price to pay for a plan that is more acceptable to Congress, less divisive and less stigmatizing."[52]

Reactions to the Plan

The prospects for the plan in Congress were ambiguous. Eizenstat informed Carter that "Senator Long will be conciliatory, Senator Moynihan is generally supportive, but Representative Al Ullman [chair of the Ways and Means Committee] is inclined to attack our proposal as a 'negative income tax' and 'a rerun of the FAP.' "[53] Eizenstat expressed hope that Ullman would see that the Carter plan was different from the FAP, because it provided employment opportunities and had stronger work incentives but did not rely on a "bureaucratic work requirement."[54] However, the signals from Moynihan and Long were mixed at best. As a newly elected senator for New York, Moynihan was concerned foremost with fiscal relief for his state, yet the Carter plan provided little, and it was not clear whether Carter would even leave the existing amount of relief in his final legislation. In congressional testimony soon after Carter's May 2 announcement, Long said that he was pleased with the direction of the plan because, unlike Ullman, he believed that it did not go down the path of Nixon's FAP but instead placed a much greater emphasis on work: "If you can put people to work, you should not have them sitting there doing nothing." Ironically, Moynihan, who had been the main proponent of Nixon's plan, which Long had blocked, concurred. He told Califano, "This effort, which has eluded three administrations, is now triumphantly yours to resolve, to create the right program, and the first word in that program is work, and the second is jobs."[55] Moynihan's emphasis on work and jobs is further indication of how much the terms of debate had shifted since the Nixon years.

On May 19, the administration firmed up the plan's details and on May 25 Califano announced the compromise plan in a press statement. He outlined the elements of the two tiers and made passing reference to the fact that the EITC would be retained at its existing levels. Califano repeatedly emphasized that the plan was tentative and that the administration would proceed with a state-by-state evaluation of the plan's impact over the next month. Final legislation would be drafted in July. Responses in the media were generally favorable, emphasizing the work components of the legislation. However, some liberals argued that a plan that did not increase welfare spending could not possibly improve the situation of the poor.[56]

Over the summer criticisms from interest groups mounted, especially those regarding the effects of Carter's zero-cost constraint on benefit levels for the poor and the lack of sufficient fiscal relief for states and cites. In early July, a group of twenty-eight organizations—including labor, religious, and civil rights groups—wrote an open letter to Carter that deplored his unwillingness to spend more money on assistance to the poor, especially in light of spending in other policy areas, such as transportation, health, energy, and farm programs, which they noted were not subject to such constraints. "Why should one program," the letter asked, "which is most crucial to the welfare of the poorest and most disadvantaged among us be singled out for an arbitrary ceiling based on current expenditures?"[57] Later in the month, Mayor Abraham Beame of New York, along with seventy-five other business, labor, and community leaders, launched a campaign to pressure the president to keep his campaign promise of fiscal relief for local governments through welfare reform. The campaign aimed to gather one million signatures to present to the president. Beame encouraged other cities to follow suit. One of Carter's aides advised the president to be more generous with assistance to New York City. The aide argued that the additional money the city was requesting in financial aid was a small price to pay for the political benefits of support in New York. He further informed Carter that critics in New York were depicting him as "a shrewd and uncaring manager who, because of your Southern background, doesn't understand and/or care about the cities generally and New York City particularly."[58]

In contrast to the Nixon years, there was little explicit discussion of race among policy experts during the development of Carter's plan. The plan emerged during an interregnum bracketed by concerns about urban unrest and black militancy in the 1960s and concerns about the "underclass" (which was code for black inner-city poverty) in the 1980s.[59] Yet welfare reform had clear racial dimensions that interest groups tried to bring to the administration's attention. In keeping with the themes raised by the open letter to Carter earlier in the month, the National Urban League raised their criticisms in the broader context of Carter's emphasis on the balanced budget. The Urban League's director, Vernon Jordan, said that Carter had neglected the needs of the urban poor: "Black people and poor people resent the stress on balanced budgets instead of balanced lives. We resent unfulfilled promises of jobs . . .

and the continued acceptance of high unemployment." The AP story that covered these complaints said that this was the harshest criticism of Carter's policies from a major black organization to date.[60]

A women's task force on welfare reform also contacted Carter to outline their concerns about the gendered dimension of his plans for reform. They emphasized that welfare reform was of special concern to women because so many welfare recipients were female heads of families. They hoped that in Carter's press statement or his address to Congress he would stress

> the fact that women who choose to stay home and raise their children are not lazy, shiftless people who do not want to work. . . . Most want jobs outside the home to supplement family income, but if jobs are not available and you want to encourage more parental attention to children, these women should be given a new respect and dignity. Furthermore . . . if you stressed that single parent households are complete family units it would help remove the stigma that currently exists.[61]

In the margin next to the sentence about women who stay home not being lazy, Carter wrote, "I agree." He further informed Califano and Marshall about the women's concerns about jobs, training, and child care.[62]

The larger question the letter raised was whether women with child-care responsibilities should be considered part of the "deserving" category in the structure of American social provision. It appeared that Carter believed they should be. Yet as the debates over the plan progressed, it became clear that Carter and influential members of Congress viewed this issue differently, and the key question became the age a mother's youngest child must be in order to exempt her from the plan's work requirement.

Veering Away from the NIT, Expanding the EITC

Toward the end of July, the final push on the plan took place. The working consensus was that the plan would be a universal cash-based system with an integrated manpower component. Yet a number of highly significant details remained to be resolved before the next presidential briefing on July 28. Two that affected how much the plan would resemble an NIT were the flip-up/flip-down dispute and the expansion of the EITC. Califano and his staff at HEW decided to acquiesce to DOL on the tier-placement issue. Starting households out in the job tier would toughen the look of the proposal and hopefully win them much needed support among conservatives on the House and Senate committees.[63] With this decision, the plan moved away from HEW's original NIT plan, though the difference was as symbolic as it was substantive.

The other issue that HEW and DOL were trying to agree on was expansion of the EITC. DOL had long favored expansion and had solicited papers from welfare experts on how to assist the needy more fully through the tax system. HEW had been flatly against this approach, but experts there were becoming convinced that expanding the EITC would improve the functioning of work incentives. Califano, who was still mainly concerned about costs, increasingly liked the idea because it allowed him to shift some of the costs of the welfare reform package to the tax reform package that the administration was working on simultaneously. As Carter's domestic policy staff at the White House considered this option, they agreed: "The advantage of giving the working poor the *status* of being helped through a non-welfare system is enormous, both from the point of view of the poor individual and in terms of Congressional consideration."[64]

As the formal presidential briefing approached, the policy experts decided to expand the EITC, adding a third "track" to the plan. They did so for a number interrelated reasons having to do with political strategy, costs, administration, and symbolism. First, the EITC was popular in Congress because it assisted people who worked, so it was likely to improve the political chances of the plan. Moreover, if the administration did not include EITC expansion in their legislation, Senator Long was likely to expand it anyway, and Carter would lose credit for the issue. Second, Califano could reduce his costs, and therefore stay closer to zero-cost projections, by shifting the fiscal burden of this antipoverty measure from welfare expenditures to revenue reductions in the tax bill. Third, the programmatic benefit was that by distinguishing among those eligible for the EITC, the plan would lower the benefit reduction rate for the working poor. Fourth, expanding the number of working poor in the EITC program, rather than folding them into the new program, reduced the number of people who appeared to receive "welfare" by 17 percent instead of increasing the number by one quarter as the May 19 plan had. Fifth, using the EITC decreased the stigmatization of recipients. According to an official at DOL,

> On a theoretical level there may be no reason to distinguish transfer payments paid by the IRS from those paid by HEW. On a practical level there are important reasons for doing so. Congressional leaders, reflecting the opinions of most of the public, dislike the idea of expanding the number of those receiving welfare-like benefits, particularly if recipients come to constitute a major portion of the local population in certain areas. Low income persons resist the inconvenience and stigma imposed upon them by participation in direct means-tested programs with burdensome requirements for income and assets reporting. This is particularly true of the working poor, relatively few of whom have elected to participate in such programs as food stamps.[65]

Thus, according to the experts' analysis, using the EITC rather than "welfare" benefits, wherever possible, aligned with the preferences of congressional leaders, the general public, and the working poor themselves.

Internal Debate on Unresolved Issues

In preparation for the presidential briefing, Califano submitted a sixty-two-page document, dubbed the "monster memo" by the administration, that outlined the details of the new plan. In his cover letter, Califano said that the current proposal was a modified version of the May 19 proposal, and that the paper proposed further modifications subject to the president's approval. The proposal was divided into two sections, one describing the cash assistance program, the other describing the jobs program.[66] The cash program included the following details:

- a single cash assistance grant that replaced the federal share of SSI, AFDC, and food stamps;
- an income support tier for those not required to work; the basic benefit for a family of four was $4,200 with a marginal tax rate of 50 percent on earned income;
- an earned income supplement tier for those required to work; the basic benefit for a family of four was $2,300. To create a strong incentive to work, the first $3,800 of earnings were disregarded; the remaining earned income was taxed at a 50 percent rate;
- a recommendation that the age of youngest child be set at fourteen for the income support tier; therefore a single parent with a child younger than fourteen would not be expected to work;
- an eight-week waiting period for the earned income supplement tier, after which time a household not provided with a training slot or job could "flip-up" to the income support tier;
- an expansion of the EITC that extended tax credits up to the entry point in the positive tax system (as opposed to a gradual reduction in credits far before the entry point under current law).[67]

The jobs program aimed to ensure employment for the principal earner in families with children. DOL would assume the responsibility of placing job seekers in private and public sector jobs, providing training for those who needed it, and creating subsidized jobs for those who could not find employment in the private or regular public sector job market. The administration estimated that it could create between 1.1 and 1.4 million jobs using the structure of local job administration under the existing CETA program.[68]

Carter's advisors had three days to read the plan and provide comments to him before the briefing on July 28, and the complexity and scope of the proposal gave them many potential facets to highlight in their commentary. The tone of these comments ranged from favorable commendations from Charles Schultze to stinging criticisms levied by Tom Joe and members of the DPS.

Substantively, most of the comments dealt with a handful of issues: benefit levels for the poor, fiscal relief, expansion of the EITC, and work requirements for mothers. Discussions of benefit levels and fiscal relief were related because the program pitted them against one another. A number of Carter's advisors said that he would have to make a decision as to which was more important to him. With the zero-cost constraint, he could not provide both high benefit levels and considerable fiscal savings for state and local government. Some claimed that the plan was stingy toward the poor by pointing out that Nixon's FAP was more generous than Carter's plan, both because its benefit levels, adjusted for inflation, were higher overall and because it guaranteed that no one would be worse off than they had been under the AFDC system. Joe suggested that Carter find sources of fiscal relief other than the welfare system.[69]

The expansion of the EITC had not been part of the original May 19 plan, so incorporating it into the new version required presidential approval. Califano listed this as the highest priority decision that the president had to make in the July 28 meeting. He further stated that there was "near unanimity within the administration that the political viability of welfare reform turns on the inclusion of this enlarged EITC proposal." The unanimity, however, only pertained to the basic expansion of the EITC, not the details of the matter. Schultze complained to the president that the EITC expansion was too generous. Joe, like some of the members of the DPS, preferred a true triple-track approach that would take far more advantage of the EITC. The Califano plan, Joe contended, was simply a modified NIT proposal that would increase the welfare rolls to include 39.5 million people under the new benefits regime.[70]

The final topic of broad significance was work requirements for mothers, and the specific question was the age cutoff for children above which mothers would be expected to work. There was near unanimity among those in the administration that the age should be fourteen. Ideologically, the planners felt that mothers should have the opportunity to raise their children until their teenage years. Moreover, there were strong programmatic reasons for their stance. If the cutoff age was lowered, HEW would have to expand child-care facilities considerably and DOL would need to provide more public service jobs. Both of these efforts would raise the price of reform. Carter himself worried that Senator Long would never settle for the cutoff age being so high, and Eizenstat and the DPS suggested this possibility as well, though they too favored the higher age.[71]

At the July 28 presidential briefing, Carter was generally enthusiastic about the plan, though he had more concerns about the cash component than the jobs component, which pleased him overall. Schultze convinced Carter to accept the EITC expansion by arguing that the president was getting both additional welfare reform and tax reform through a single policy instrument. Carter was further concerned that the benefit level of $4,200 was too high, particularly for the southern states, even though Califano had already reduced the level from the $4,700 proposed in May. After some debate, Califano was able to convince him not to cut the benefit levels further because SSI and food stamp recipients, who would be folded into the consolidated welfare plan, would also have their benefits cut. Though a strong proponent of this consolidation, Califano worried that SSI recipients would protest being included in the same program as former AFDC recipients because of the stigma associated with it. Carter suggested using "attractive semantical phrases" to get around this issue.[72]

Costs were the other major issue discussed. A representative from the Office of Management and Budget reiterated their concerns about the high cost of the program but was overruled by everyone else at the meeting. In fact, Carter surprised his advisors on the matter. With reservations, he signaled that he might be willing to increase costs to get around the apparent trade-off between fiscal relief and benefit levels. He then resorted to budgetary gimmickry to improve the program within the initial "zero-cost" promise. He decided to allocate the $3 billion cost of the expanded EITC to the tax reform bill rather than treat it as an addition to welfare reform. Then he increased the baseline zero-cost figure that HEW could use by crediting as welfare expenditures money spent on a number of programs, including expenditures within Unemployment Insurance, Social Security, and CETA programs. Pleased with his budgetary shell game, Carter smiled to the participants and said, "There no longer seems to be a no-cost proposal."[73]

Concerns in Congress: Work, Family, and Fraud

Carter asked his advisors to discuss the plan with Senator Long and Representative Ullman in the days leading up to his announcement. They were the chairs of the Senate Finance Committee and House Ways and Means Committee, respectively, and would therefore play a central role in the politics of Carter's plan. Long had a number of concerns that he enumerated in a memo to Carter on August 3. Robert Carleson was an advisor to Long on welfare reform by this time, and it is unclear whether he had input on this particular memo, but the themes raised by Long were quite similar to those raised in attacks on welfare programs in California under Carleson's tenure a few years earlier. Carter read the memo and responded in a note to Eizenstat: "We must be prepared to answer these questions."[74]

All of the "flaws" that Long identified in the Carter plan were based on Long's explicit premise that the goal of welfare reform was to reduce the number of people receiving welfare. He described this as a widespread view in which the "taxpaying public" would only support welfare reform if it meant "*less* money to pay recipients for doing *nothing* and more money in the form of wages and wage supplements to low-income persons who work."[75] He objected to Carter's proposal to require mothers to work only if their children were over the age of fourteen. This policy, Long argued, would only apply to 10 percent of the women currently receiving welfare, and it ignored recent changes in labor market participation. He cited figures that in 1975, nearly 55 percent of mothers without preschool-aged children worked. Why, he asked, should working-class mothers work while mothers on welfare were allowed to stay home?[76]

These concerns about women working resonated with Ullman's major concern, which was the fact that welfare benefits were based largely on family size. Ullman had strongly opposed this feature of the Nixon plan and likewise opposed it in Carter's plan. Califano wrote that Ullman believed that this payment structure encouraged poor people to have more children. Ullman stated additional reservations: he opposed any type of consolidated program; he agreed with Long that women with children over the age of six should work; he did not like paying cash to individuals who were employed; and, in contrast to Long, he did not like the government creating "makework jobs where people just sit at courthouse desks."[77]

Long expressed further concerns, too. One was fraud and abuse in the welfare system. He argued that the country's approach to welfare had extended "an invitation to defraud the Government," a situation in which recipients failed to report earnings, falsified information, and broke up families to receive more benefits. A second was the nature of Carter's program itself, which he considered to be a GAI program. He argued that this type of program, as opposed to a true work-oriented program, did not encourage initiative to work in the private sector. A third concern was perhaps the most far-reaching, namely that the philosophies of the existing welfare system and Carter's plan exacerbated the very problems that they intended to solve, such as problems of dependency and family stability. This final argument, implicit in some earlier critiques of GAI programs, came to be the one used most forcefully against all types of welfare programs in the coming years.[78]

Despite Carter's sentiments that mothers receiving welfare who stayed home were not lazy, the president acquiesced to Long's desire to require mothers to work when their children were at a much younger age. Eizenstat had warned the president that the age cutoff was an important symbolic issue to women's groups and other liberals. However, the day after Eizenstat's meeting with Long on a number of these issues, Carter signed off on a recommendation from the DPS to require part-time work from mothers with children between the ages of six and thirteen. Though this added to the costs of the program, it made the plan more palatable to conservatives like Long. The administration had less success in finding common ground with Ullman, who, as Califano put it, "was still burned by the FAP fight, and has no stomach for welfare reform."[79]

The administration was also trying to address the concerns about fraud in the welfare system. Califano had known from the beginning of his tenure as HEW secretary that allegations of fraud would be a major obstacle to achieving welfare reform because people were increasingly skeptical of both the administrative capacity of government and the moral integrity of recipients. To combat arguments that recipients themselves were maliciously defrauding the government, HEW released reports showing that most of the errors in the allocation of benefits were due to mistakes on the part of social workers and governmental systems and not recipients' malfeasance. However, press accounts of fraudulence continued to mount. One concerned public official wrote a letter to the administration at the end of July saying that "hardly a week passes when the American public is not bombarded with media opinion about increasing welfare fraud and other forms of welfare abuse." Califano hoped one of the attractions of Carter's consolidated program would be its promise to decrease fraud by simplifying the system.[80]

The Program for Better Jobs and Income

Welfare reform under the Nixon administration had been inextricably linked to the urban crises of the 1960s. In contrast, Carter chose to make his August 6 welfare announcement in a televised broadcast from an agricultural experimentation station in Plains, Georgia. He christened the plan the Program for Better Jobs and Income (PBJI), a name of his own design, and the opening words of his statement pronounced his agenda for comprehensive reform.

> As I pledged during my campaign for the Presidency, I am asking the Congress to abolish our existing welfare system and replace it with a job-oriented program for those able to work and a simplified, uniform, equitable cash assistance program for those in need who are unable to work by virtue of disability, age or family circumstance. The Program for Better Jobs and Income I am proposing will transform the manner in which the Federal government deals with the income needs of the poor, and begin to break the welfare cycle.[81]

Descriptively, the plan sounded like a triple-track program. Carter distinguished among the three populations the program would serve, just as he had on the campaign trail. Rhetorically, his reference to the "welfare cycle," which documents suggest he rarely mentioned in private communication, set the tone early for his repeated emphasis on work and self-reliance. In comparing this aspect of his speech to Nixon's own welfare announcement, there was scant difference except for Carter's greater insistence that people in poverty wanted to work. There was little that could have been perceived as either overweening liberalism or a sense of social injustice.

Carter also emphasized administrative simplification and fraud, and thereby played to the sentiments of taxpayers who had lost patience with the system.

The few providers and recipients guilty of fraud and abuse in our welfare programs not only rob the taxpayers but cheat the vast majority of honest recipients. One of the most significant benefits of consolidation of existing cash assistance programs is the opportunity to apply sophisticated management techniques to improve their operations. . . . No longer will people easily claim benefits in more than one jurisdiction.[82]

The details of the plan were those that had been decided within the administration in the weeks prior to the announcement. The only difference from the May plans that he drew attention to was the cost. Carter said that after consultation with state and local leaders, he had decided to add more money to the original zero-cost proposal. His plan would cost $2.8 billion more than the existing system. More than $2 billion of this, Carter indicated, would go to fiscal relief for the states.[83]

The Public Reaction

Initial reaction to Carter's announcement was favorable, though short-lived, most likely because of the way he had portrayed the plan. HEW reported that editorial support was overwhelming: 140 out of the 150 newspapers it had surveyed supported the PBJI, and the support was nationwide. A Harris poll taken shortly after the president's statement showed that 70 percent supported the plan, and large majorities favored specific provisions. Among the plan's critics, most objected to the increased costs of reform rather than to the philosophy of the PBJI.[84]

The favorable public response to Carter's program was generated by frustration with the existing system and most likely a misreading of the PBJI based on Carter's rhetoric. Attitudes toward the poor in the mid-1970s were not beneficent. Studies conducted at the time showed that the working class and urban dwellers—populations that would have benefited from the EITC expansion and fiscal relief—held deep antipathies toward the poor, whom they felt did not truly want to work.[85] These sentiments were further exacerbated by racial antagonisms that had worsened throughout the decade. Welfare reform was a nexus where attitudes toward work and race had merged. In the words of one white working-class respondent in a study of political attitudes, "Who's feeling sorry for me? The colored have gotten enough. Let them do for themselves like we do."[86] Many such individuals could have supported the plan out of self-interest because they themselves were likely to benefit. But their support was not sustained. Sentiments turned against the plan once opponents began to rail against its expansion of "welfare" and increasing cost estimates.

Even after eight years of debating the merits of GAI plans, there was still not a consensus on what constituted a "guaranteed income" policy, and experts disagreed on whether the PBJI was one or not. Experts within HEW and DOL said that the PBJI was really an incremental policy, even though the administration was trying to sell it as comprehensive reform. One expert noted this with apparent dismay, considering the unpopularity of comprehensive reform schemes. Another HEW insider remarked on the irony of the administration's policy development process, which ended up "recreating the very categorization [we] said [we] didn't want." HEW experts equated comprehensive reform with a consolidated, noncategorical program and they had not gotten one. Opponents of the scheme, however, referred to the plan as a comprehensive GAI. Senator Curtis, a member of the Finance Committee who had strongly opposed the FAP, called the plan a "warmed-over version of what HEW policy planners have been pushing for a decade, a guaranteed annual income."[87] Similarly, Tom Joe, a proponent of the triple-track scheme, had repeatedly referred to the Carter plan as a thinly veiled NIT. Despite these divergent perceptions of the plan, one thing that seemed apparent was that any program that contained the AFDC population was considered a "welfare" program, no matter who else it contained or what its benefits structure. As the implications of the plan became clearer, most participants in the debates considered the plan an expansion of "welfare."

A Limited Response among Interest Groups

Compared to the FAP, the PBJI was never the target of serious lobbying. This was the case for a number of reasons. Carter overloaded the congressional agenda during his first year in office with a number of sweeping legislative proposals. He indicated that other domestic policy initiatives, such as energy and tax reform programs, held higher priority than welfare reform. The PBJI also never got as far legislatively as the FAP—it never emerged from the House Ways and Means Committee—therefore, interest groups were not as focused on the bill. State and local officials, who constituted one of the strongest lobbies for welfare reform, had been thoroughly consulted during the development process, so their stances on the plan were already well known. And the NWRO, which had played an active role in previous welfare legislation, had been rendered defunct after the death of George Wiley in 1973.

The lack of active lobbying did not mean that interest groups did not take positions on the PBJI. Notably, most interest group attention focused on the jobs provision of the bill rather than the cash program. Civil rights groups were generally dismayed by Carter's lack of attention to their concerns, even though he received 94 percent of the black vote in 1976. (In comparison to the previous president, they said he was no better than "a second-hand Ford.") The National Urban League guardedly recognized Carter's plan as "a signal" that he was taking the interests of blacks to heart. Despite their disappointment that he was not pressing for full employment, Vernon Jordan said the Urban League would urge Congress to support and improve the plan. Six months later, however, the league was more critical, chastising the president for reasons that precisely mirrored the economic citizenship paradigm: "The plan should be revised so as to treat all people in need alike, avoiding the present format which divides recipients into different categories each with its own benefit scales and conditions."[88]

Women's groups, such as the National Women's Political Caucus, supported the cash-consolidation provision because they argued that "poor people will benefit more when they receive CASH ASSISTANCE, rather than being forced to comply for the services they need by filling out many personal, inhumane forms and also being forced to stand in line to receive such services—and then to top it off—to being treated like beggars by those who provide the public services." Still, they complained that the jobs provision did not provide enough job training and opportunities, and that the wage levels were not adequate. The most divisive issue among women, according to a statement circulated to Carter's staff, was whether women with young children should be expected to work. Some women felt that it was important for mothers to stay at home with their children and that this should be considered work. Others felt that this would restrict women's employment opportunities once their children grew up because they would not have valuable skills or training. This was particularly true for minority women. Given this internal conflict, the statement called for a welfare reform strategy that allowed for maximum "self-determination" for single-parent family heads, giving them the option to work for adequate wages or to stay at home.[89]

The influence of business and labor organizations was the mirror image of the situation during the Nixon years. Business leaders did not participate in welfare policy development, nor did business organizations, such as the U.S. Chamber of Commerce or the National Association of Manufacturers, lobby on the bill. Oddly, one of the few contacts between the administration and a business group was based on a Chamber of Commerce report that made a libertarian case for the NIT along very similar lines to Milton Friedman's thinking fifteen years earlier.[90] Organized labor had the most active involvement and influence of all the civic groups. The AFL-CIO and AFSCME worried that the large-scale creation of public service jobs at near the minimum wage would undermine local labor markets. They also criticized the plan for setting the benefit levels too low. Labor would come to have the most direct influence through lobbying a House subcommittee, the Corman committee, which was established to seek compromise on an early version of the bill before it reached the House Ways and Means Committee.[91]

Confronting Legislative Complexities

In September, James Corman introduced the PBJI in the House and Moynihan introduced it in the Senate. Both chambers of Congress held hearings. Califano and Ray Marshall testified separately on the two components of the plan, a situation that illustrated the lack of integration between the cash and job elements of the program. Much of the attention to the plan at the hearings emphasized costs rather than ideology. There were mounting sentiments that the program would cost considerably more than Carter had suggested in his announcement. Some said $14 billion, Ullman estimated $18 billion, and weeks earlier Long had stated at a press conference that costs might increase "up to $60 billion or even $120 billion." Corman asked the Congressional Budget Office to estimate the costs of the plan. Their preliminary cost estimates were reported in late November. Corman, a supporter of the plan, was dismayed to learn that the budget office estimated costs of $14 billion, five times the amount Carter had estimated.[92]

The PBJI was more legislatively complicated than the FAP because it aimed to consolidate a number of programs under the jurisdiction of various committees—public assistance in the Ways and Means Committee, food stamps in the Agriculture Committee, and the jobs program in the Education and Labor Committee. These three deliberative bodies had to agree on the substance of the plan before it could go to the House floor. Corman, a liberal Democrat, chaired a special Welfare Reform Subcommittee charged with shaping the bill so it would proceed successfully through these separate committees. Corman's subcommittee was more liberal than its three parent committees and the House on the whole. Its membership included powerful representatives from states with large welfare populations, many of which had sizable organized labor constituencies. Most of them wanted welfare reform, though there was little consensus on what shape it should take. Many worried about the complexity of Carter's program, whether it would be administrable, and whether the government could provide enough jobs. Some expressed concerns that an incremental program might be better. Liberals favored increasing the wages for public service jobs from the minimum wage to prevailing wages (as did the countercyclical CETA public service employment program). Some opposed cashing out food stamps. Corman, in particular, was concerned about Carter's commitment to a tough fight for welfare reform. In preparation for a meeting with the committee, Califano coached the president to emphasize his commitment to the plan; the importance of comprehensive reform; the necessity of full consolidation (including food stamps) to maintain the integrity and rationale of the program; and the fiscal impossibility of paying prevailing wages for jobs.[93]

Corman's concerns about Carter's commitment to his own welfare legislation turned out to be prescient. A week before the president's meeting with the committee, Eizenstat circulated a memo in the White Hose on 1978 legislative priorities. He described a number of committees in Congress, including Ways and Means, Finance, and Education and Labor, as being overloaded. Therefore, he called for the "establishment of clear priorities and serious consideration of postponing major initiatives." Of the five highest priority items, welfare was not on the list. In his marginal notes, Carter agreed. Eizenstat placed welfare reform in the second tier of priorities, but argued that the White House could only push for passage in the House, which, if attained, should be considered a success, since the congressional timetable made it unlikely that the Senate could take up the bill before the 95th Congress ended. Carter jotted a question mark by this entry on welfare reform. Weeks later, Carter appeared to back away from his commitment to welfare reform in an interview in the *New York Times*.[94] In the following month, January 1978, Carter did not mention welfare in his State of the Union address.

Despite the apparent lack of full support, Corman's committee continued their deliberation in January and on February 8 approved a liberalized version of the PBJI. (A much more conservative bill by Ullman was narrowly defeated in the process.) Once the bill was approved by the Corman subcommittee, it had to be approved by the three parent committees before moving to the floor of the House. The chairs of two of these committees—Ullman in Ways and Means and Thomas Foley in Agriculture—opposed the bill. Ullman had longstanding feelings of antipathy toward the bill, largely because he opposed the concept of guaranteed annual income. He thought welfare reform should decrease welfare spending and he did not like programs that based benefit levels on family size. Foley opposed cashing out food stamps because SSI beneficiaries did not want to be included in the same program as AFDC recipients. Organized labor feared that the jobs component would replace other jobs programs in the administration's economic package.

THE FALL OF GUARANTEED ANNUAL INCOME

The outlook for a plan that contained any type of GAI component worsened. Carter met with Long, Moynihan, Ullman, and Corman on March 10. Ullman said his priorities were first the energy program and then tax reform. Long said he favored expansion of the EITC but suggested running only pilot programs for everything else. Corman expressed irreconcilable differences with Ullman. Between the congressmen, there seemed to be no resolution. By the end of March, the administration was signaling that it would accept an incremental, compromise bill. Comprehensive reform, at least for 1978, was dead.[95] Through the spring and summer, a consensus of sorts on a less costly, incremental reform package emerged among some senators seeking a compromise bill. Califano and Carter both reluctantly indicated that they would pursue scaled-back versions of welfare reform. (Califano informed the president that there was "no chance to pass a more ambitious package.") As discussions of a compromise began, Califano noted an emerging consensus on welfare reform: national minimum standards, work requirements, basic benefit levels at roughly 65 percent of the poverty line for those not expected to work, the extension of benefits to two-parent families (AFDC-UP), expansion of the EITC, provision of public service jobs to make work requirements more meaningful, and fiscal relief for states and cities. Variation in emphasis, degree, and costs produced many of the differences between the competing, incremental proposals. Elements that were not included in the negotiations on the compromise bill were cash consolidation, provision of benefits without job or training requirements, large-scale job provision, and extension of benefits to single people and childless couples. Notably, the compromise plan tried to retain some form of minimum income guarantee, but it also sharply differentiated among categories of poor people.[96]

Two sets of events further affected the fate of welfare reform in 1978. The first damaged the prospects for any type of welfare reform proposal that increased welfare spending. The second undermined a key rationale for GAI proposals.

The Tax Revolt

The passage in California of Proposition 13—a measure to significantly cut property taxes—was the signal event in the growing national tax revolt of the late 1970s. The tax revolt began in postwar southern California, originally as a series of protests against the extraordinary growth of property taxes. By the late 1960s it had become a more sweeping antistatist movement with social welfare provision as one of its principal targets. Reagan's governorship stoked antiwelfare sentiments by making arguments about wastefulness and inefficiency in the AFDC program, and by castigating the morality of the poor—especially their putative laziness and lack of virtue and self-discipline—in ways that resonated with the increasing social conservatism of the region. By the early 1970s, Reagan and his advisor Robert Carleson had considerable popular sentiment behind them as they countered Nixon's FAP with more conservative programs aimed at reducing welfare costs and welfare rolls.[97]

Nationally, tax protests appeared sporadically in other regions, such as Massachusetts, but it was the rising prices and unemployment rates of the 1970s, coupled with the decade's increasing dissatisfaction with government, that made the ground fertile for a national movement for tax cuts that entailed a reduction in government expenditures. Americans had grown accustomed to the many services provided by the government, but welfare programs were a prime target for cuts because of increasingly negative depictions of the poor and the fraud and inefficiency associated with the social welfare bureaucracy.[98]

Proposition 13 passed by a 2–1 margin on June 6. Local polls indicated that supporters' first choice of areas in which to cut government spending was welfare policy. (In contrast, they wanted to retain existing spending on schools, the police and fire departments, and other local services.) Commentators interpreted the revolt as a middle-class rebellion against taxation for programs intended to redistribute income to the poor; some analysts further argued that the backlash was motivated by symbolic racism. Within a month, the tax revolt had become national news and a favorite subject of pollsters and magazine covers, and soon thereafter many states voluntarily cut their taxes as a preemptive measure. A CBS/*New York Times* poll found that support for measures like Proposition 13 was, if anything, stronger outside California, and that there was substantial concern over wasteful, inefficient government. A sizable minority of respondents—31 percent—agreed that "almost all welfare services paid for by the government could be eliminated."[99]

The day after the vote on Proposition 13, the chairman of the Agriculture Committee told Califano "to bury that damn welfare bill. With this vote in California, [the House] will destroy it on the floor and the President will suffer a humiliating defeat."[100] Supporters of a compromise bill still pressed onward, even though the *New York Times* quoted congressional leaders later in the month who said that welfare was dead for the year. In June, Senators Moynihan, Alan Cranston, and Long proposed a "no frills" bill to compete with the administration's compromise bill. The main aim of this bill was to provide $2.5 billion in fiscal relief through block grants to the states. Considering the fact that Moynihan and Cranston were from New York and California, respectively—the states with the two highest welfare expenditures—onlookers were surprised only by the naked self-interest underlying the proposal. The administration fought the bill and it was never voted out of committee.[101] The "no frills" bill portended continuing pressure to provide the states with extra money coupled with conservatives' persistent emphasis on work. Later in the year, a White House aide solicited Senator Ted Kennedy's active involvement as a liberal anchor in the Senate in order "to keep Congress from dragging welfare reform into the hell of fiscal relief and slave labor."[102]

The NIT Experiments and the Politics of the Family

If the tax revolt meant one blow against GAI proposals, the dominant interpretation of the long-awaited results of the OEO's negative income tax experiments brought the coup de grâce. Analyses of the data had been slowly proceeding for some time but occurred largely out of the public eye. Senator Moynihan held hearings in November 1978 to bring the findings to a broader audience. With his background in social science, he had long been a proponent of the experiments, which he considered one of the largest social scientific endeavors ever undertaken. Altogether, OEO and HEW had conducted four different NIT experiments in seven locations with over 8,500 people in the total sample population. The hearings emphasized the results from the Seattle and Denver income maintenance experiments (known as SIME/DIME), which began in 1970. These studies were considered by the experts to be the most scientifically rigorous.[103]

Since the first OEO experiment began in New Jersey in 1968, the main objective of the government's experimental program had been to assess the effects of the NIT on work effort. Would receipt of NIT benefits reduce a person's work effort and, if so, by how much?[104] The results from the SIME/DIME experiments, as most people expected, showed that receiving NIT payments influenced people's work behavior, yet in some cases not by much. The work reduction for employed men, the main target group of interest for the government, was 5–10 percent. This was considerably less than most people expected, but it was consistent with previous experimental results. Some evidence suggested that the extra income for household heads meant that recipients had more time to look for satisfying work at higher wages or to undertake additional schooling, so even the work reduction could be viewed positively. Work effort for married mothers decreased by 20–25 percent and for single mothers about 10–15 percent. These work reductions, analysts assumed, probably meant that women were reducing their work hours to spend more time at home with their families. There was no evidence from the experiments that receiving GAI benefits would lead wage earners to defect from the labor market altogether. All in all, there was little support for the view that welfare would become "a way of life" under a GAI plan as many conservatives had worried. In the words of the chief data analyst of the Denver experiments, "The 'laziness' contention is just not supported by our findings. There is not anywhere near the mass defection the prophets of doom predicted."[105]

Yet even before Moynihan's hearings, the result that gained the most coverage in the media was the SIME/DIME experiments' findings on marital dissolution.[106] Rates of marital breakup among participants receiving NIT payments were about 60 percent higher than rates among the control group. Though there was some question about the validity of the findings, including the fact that the pattern of marital breakup had not been found in other NIT experiments, most experts did not strongly contest the results.[107] They did, however, call into question the interpretation and implications. Was family dissolution necessarily negative? Some commentators did not think so. One prominent interpretation of the results discussed the probability of an "independence effect": Given that each family member could have an independent source of income under the experimental NIT program, women in particular were less dependent on their husbands for economic security and therefore had increasing freedom to leave unsatisfactory relationships.[108] The implication of this, however, was ambiguous and its determination rested largely on one's perspective. As the *New Republic* put it, "Even though it should not be governmental policy to encourage marital separations, there is not a particular advantage in keeping couples together only out of poverty." Or as Tom Joe, one of Carter's welfare advisors, asked more bluntly, "What will you do—starve people to make them stay together?"[109]

For Moynihan, however, the results were completely damning. At the hearings he exclaimed, "We were wrong about guaranteed income! Seemingly it is calamitous. It increases family dissolution by 70 percent, decreases work, etc. Such is now the state of science, and it seems to me we are honor-bound to abide by it at the moment." Moynihan's critics were skeptical of his true motivations for turning his back on GAI policies, since after becoming a New York senator he had so clearly pursued welfare reform as a source of fiscal relief, and Carter's PBJI program contained little. Yet what these critics overlooked was Moynihan's longstanding view of GAI plans as a strategy to bolster family stability, which since the mid-1960s he had believed was the cornerstone of reducing poverty and rebuilding inner-city communities. For instance, his congressional testimony on welfare reform in 1977, given considerably before his hearings on the NIT experiments, demonstrated the priority he placed on programs that would keep families intact. Based on his position as a New York senator, fiscal concerns must have certainly played a role in his views of Carter's plan. Yet for Moynihan, perhaps for more than any other participant in the debate, if GAI policies did not improve family life, which for him meant bolstering marital stability, they were not worth pursuing.[110]

Thus by the late 1970s, critics painted GAI plans as threatening both the work ethic, which conservatives had long claimed, and threatening what feminist scholars call the "family ethic," which is based on traditional views of marriage and the gendered division of labor.[111] If interpretations of the "independence effect" were correct, then GAI plans had the potential to extend to poor women a greater capacity to exert independence by leaving the labor market or unsatisfactory marriages by choice rather than out of necessity.[112] Yet this ran at odds not only with Moynihan's view of welfare reform but with society's increasing concerns during the mid-1970s about the rise of single-parent families, out-of-wedlock births, and teen pregnancy.[113] Indeed, only two years later, the administration sponsored the White House Conference on the Family, which was a response to precisely these mounting concerns.[114] Neither the Carter White House nor prevailing social norms were in favor of granting women the type of independence that GAI plans seemed to promise, which meant that poor women remained fundamentally "undeserving" of basic income security.

"Abandoning the Idea of Guaranteed Income"

An item in the National Review on the experiments emphasized their high costs and their effects on marital stability and work. It concluded sarcastically, "The [SIME/DIME] study cost $112 million. For another hundred million they might have discovered that if you pay people for not working, they'll not work." The New Republic, a supporter of GAI programs, reluctantly pronounced that the congressional hearings were "a funeral for welfare reform." Martin Anderson, one of the FAP's principal opponents in the Nixon administration, argued in a lengthy *New York Times* op-ed piece that it was finally time to give up on the idea of guaranteed income. His piece captured the spirit of the times as seen by many people. Anderson enumerated the past decade's attempts at reform through GAI strategies and asserted that "radical welfare reform is an impossible dream." This recent history, he argued, held lessons.

> It means abandoning the idea of guaranteed income. And it means devising ways to achieve the public's number one priority in welfare reform—the elimination from the welfare rolls of those who can care for themselves. Americans have a generous, benevolent attitude toward those who are truly needy, but they never have understood why they should work to support those who are capable of supporting themselves.[115]

This emphasis on work was confirmed in late 1978 when an expansion of the EITC was signed into law virtually without controversy. The expansion demonstrated that the public was not completely against increased government spending on the poor. What was more important was that the recipients were deemed worthy of government support and that the program increased the incentive to work. Because EITC recipients were by definition part of the labor market, because the expansion "made work pay," and because recipients received benefits in tax credits, not cash (like government "welfare" checks), the EITC expansion passed with relatively little trouble. This was a virtual repeat of the sequence that took place under Nixon: a GAI plan produced great controversy and failed; the EITC expanded easily in its aftermath.[116]

In 1979, the Carter administration took on welfare reform again, this time with a scaled-down version of the compromise bill that Califano had been working on. The less expensive $5.7 billion plan set national minimum standards, covered intact families, cashed out food stamps for SSI recipients, increased the EITC, and provided a modest number of jobs. It also completely separated the cash and jobs components of the legislation. The plan lacked both presidential and congressional enthusiasm, and it failed for a number of reasons, including preelection year politicking, inflation, recession, and late-year foreign crises.[117]

Even before Reagan's election, the year 1980 boded poorly for welfare policy expansion. A number of antiwelfare intellectuals working in newly established conservative think tanks came to increasing national prominence. Moynihan held hearings on welfare reform, and his list of witnesses in February included George Gilder and Martin Anderson. Gilder, in the following year, would publish his book *Wealth and Poverty*, which became known as "the bible" of the Reagan administration's efforts to scale back the welfare state. Anderson, Gilder, and a third antiwelfare intellectual, Charles Murray, would prominently use the results of the negative income tax experiments—all in exaggerated ways—as ammunition in their broader attacks on public assistance programs.[118]

CONCLUSION

Guaranteed annual income plans emerged within the Carter administration in ways similar to those in which Nixon's FAP emerged. Neither president planned to propose a GAI plan upon taking office, but government experts within both administrations succeeded in placing GAI plans on the presidential agenda. Carter's experts at HEW, like those under Nixon, advanced GAI plans in light of the economic citizenship paradigm. They favored the plans because GAI programs promised to alleviate monetary poverty through the equal treatment of all the poor based on their economic need alone. Yet Carter and Califano initially supported GAI plans primarily as a tool for systemic reform. The plans looked like a way to deliver on Carter's campaign promise of comprehensive reform and for Califano to reduce the levels of fraud and abuse that plagued both social welfare programs and others administered by his agency. A number of factors, including Carter's own reluctance, led to the plan's dilution until it lost the essential character of a GAI program.

Categories of worth continued to pose a substantial challenge to a GAI plan. The overall program was viewed as a "welfare" program and the stigma associated with AFDC contaminated the entire population of recipients. During the Nixon years, one result of this contamination had been concern that a GAI plan would damage economic productivity by placing the working poor in a state of dependency. These concerns did not arise much within the Carter administration, both because business interests were not well represented in deliberations and because the EITC now existed. But concerns about stigmatizing "deserving" recipients of government benefits were still pervasive. Concerns about costs were the other obstacle directly linked to the polluting effects of dissolving existing categorical distinctions. As long as the PBJI was defined as a "welfare" proposal, its costs increases, though relatively small, were untenable in a political climate that was increasingly hostile to government spending on the "welfare" poor. Expansion of the EITC in 1978 showed that increasing spending on the "right" kind of antipoverty program was not impossible, even in the tough fiscal climate of the late 1970s.

The institutional and symbolic legacy of the FAP's failure also affected attitudes toward GAI plans within the Carter administration. In the face of the arguments lodged against Nixon's plan, many liberals, such as Tom Joe, felt that a guaranteed jobs program would be able to garner stronger public and congressional support. This second-order policy change siphoned off much of the potential support for GAI plans. Two programmatic issues also undercut

GAI plans. First, the existence of the EITC created an alternative policy resource that government experts could use to provide income supplements to the working poor without the stigma of "welfare." Debates within the Carter administration repeatedly showed that support for the EITC's expansion drew support away from a consolidated GAI plan that included the working poor. Second, the increasing emphasis on "target efficiency" by experts recommended a categorical plan rather than a universal one. Targeting benefits to different categories of recipients based on their particular needs (and, not coincidentally, moral statuses) was more cost-effective than programs that did not draw these distinctions. Thus Carter's decision to prioritize cost containment over other considerations was, intentionally or not, a decision against GAI programs.

In laying the groundwork for comprehensive reform, Carter, Califano, and other administration officials repeatedly criticized the existing welfare system, particularly in relation to its putative disincentives for work, the rising governmental expenditures on social welfare, and fraud and abuse within the system. They hoped that dissatisfaction with the existing system could be channeled in support for their comprehensive reform strategies. Instead, these criticisms generated ammunition for "California-style" reforms of a completely different type under Ronald Reagan.

CHAPTER SEVEN

Lost Opportunities, Consequences, and Lessons

Ronald Reagan's presidency marked the eclipse of GAI proposals on the national agenda. In their place, the Reagan administration initiated policy reforms that centered on cutbacks to existing antipoverty programs. The AFDC program was especially hard hit. The "new consensus" on welfare reform that emerged during this period culminated in President Bill Clinton's 1996 welfare reform legislation, which terminated government-sponsored welfare entitlements. When seen in this light, the failure of GAI proposals stands out as a lost opportunity to ensure basic economic security for America's poor. Instead, the debate over these ultimately ill-fated proposals sowed the seeds of welfare retrenchment in ways that are not obvious, since GAI plans themselves left little trace on social policy. Because inadequate economic security for the nation's poor is still a pressing problem, scholars, activists, and a few policymakers have expressed renewed interest in GAI-style proposals in the years since the 1996 welfare reform legislation. This chapter examines the lost opportunity that the failure of GAI plans represents, shows how the debate they generated contributed to the rise of conservative welfare retrenchment in the 1980s, and highlights a few lessons to be learned from the failure of GAI plans that could prove useful for future consideration of similar plans.

A Lost Opportunity

Despite the fact that Nixon's plan came so close to passage in the early 1970s, the failure of GAI plans is treated in retrospective accounts as though it were inevitable. According to this reasoning, the proposals ran contrary to the traditional American approach to social policy in general and contrary to broader trends toward conservatism during the 1970s in particular. Could the passage of the Family Assistance Plan in the early 1970s have countered, or at least mitigated, the conservative direction of subsequent policy development?

Although the answer to this question must of course remain speculative, I believe that it could have for two reasons. Nixon's program would have removed the easiest target of attacks on the welfare state because there would no longer have been a public assistance program that served solely the undeserving poor. Many of the antipoverty programs launched during the 1960s and early 1970s—including Medicare, Medicare, Head Start, SSI, and the

EITC—have succeeded in alleviating poverty and its symptoms. Despite this success, there has been a remarkable amount of disillusionment with the existing welfare system, so much so that its defenders have had to repeatedly highlight the many successes of government antipoverty programs in books with names such as *America's Misunderstood Welfare State*, *What Government Can Do*, and *America's Hidden Success*.[1] One strategy many conservatives have used for sowing seeds of discontent with government programs is to make the AFDC program, usually referred to simply as "welfare," a synecdoche for a broad array of welfare state programs and often for "big government" itself. If a GAI proposal had passed, this political lightning rod would no longer exist. In its place would be a GAI program that includes more white, more male, and more employed recipients living in both one- and two-parent families. Though certainly not impervious to criticism, a GAI program would be inoculated from the harshest types of moral and race-based criticisms that have been directed at AFDC and have generated much of the popular animus toward government social programs.

A related point is that a GAI program would be harder to retrench. As scholars of policy feedback processes have argued, new policies create new politics. Paul Pierson spells out some of these mechanisms quite clearly.[2] New policies create new constituencies with vested interests in protecting the programs that serve them. In the case of a GAI program, many of these recipients would have been well situated to protect the program because they were part of the "deserving" population. Programs that served these constituents were spared the worst of the cutbacks that other programs for the "undeserving" received during the 1980s and 1990s. The EITC program, for instance, expanded while AFDC was eventually dismantled. One big factor in explaining this is that elected officials are motivated by blame avoidance, so they mainly seek to scale back unpopular policies. Moreover, people respond more negatively to the loss of the status quo than to foregone potential gains. Pierson argues that the logic for advocates of retrenchment is straightforward: redistributive transfers from program beneficiaries to taxpayers are usually a losing proposition. Thus while it is probable that the Reagan years might have seen some cutbacks to a GAI program, most likely in regard to reducing benefits and tightening eligibility requirements, the scope of cutbacks would almost certainly have been less than those suffered by AFDC because the political influence of the deserving populations in such a GAI program could have protected the most vulnerable of the poor.

Would the passage of Nixon's plan have indicated that America's dominant policy principles had suddenly changed after more than two hundred years? Not necessarily. Social policies do not simply reflect American principles; they reflect America's *competing* principles. There is not a unitary social order in the United States, but a number of different institutional and ideological patterns that exist in uneasy relation to one another.[3] Americans value individualism, hard work, and the entrepreneurial spirit, but they also value community, equality, and compassion. Each of these values is embedded in a variety of social policies, labor market institutions, and business practices. Policy conflicts are often the result of two competing principles coming into tension with one another. The Civil Rights Act of 1964, for instance, formally prescribed a *color-blind* approach to hiring practices in order to mitigate employment discrimination against blacks. Yet over the next decade, the government also established a number of *race-conscious* hiring practices—namely, affirmative action policies—that prescribed taking race explicitly into account. Each of these policy prescriptions can be seen as consonant with American values: race-blind policies reflect the importance placed on judging people by their individual merits, and affirmative action policies reflect the value placed on fair treatment for historically disadvantaged groups. The country's contentious debate over racial policy has been rooted in this fundamental tension ever since.[4]

It is not difficult to imagine a similar dynamic in antipoverty policy. The passage of Nixon's plan would have embedded in social policy the values of basic economic security and positive freedom for American families. These principles are resonant with the American experience. However, conservatives would surely have countered the plan by highlighting their own set of competing principles, especially the "paternalist" emphasis placed on hard work, discipline, and social obligation. One near certainty is that, had the FAP passed, conservatives would have fought for strengthening work requirements, though this would contradict the very notion of an "income guarantee." The result would have been continued contention over the direction of welfare reform. But the passage of Nixon's plan would have created a powerful institutional resource for the poor that drew elements of American social policy into alignment with values such as equality, security, and freedom. The truly revolutionary aspect of the plan was its programmatic structure—the fact that it was noncategorical—not the rhetorical rationale on which it was sold to the public.

THE ROOTS OF WELFARE RETRENCHMENT

In the absence of the implementation of a successful GAI plan in the 1970s, the Reagan administration initiated policy cutbacks directed overwhelmingly at the poor.[5] The rationale for these spending cuts was to manage the federal budget. Yet even though social programs for the middle class, such as Social Security, Medicare, and unemployment insurance, made up a much greater percentage of social spending, the administration focused its cutbacks on more politically vulnerable programs such as AFDC. Prominent in Reagan's retrenchment strategy was strengthening work requirements and tightening eligibility requirements so that only the "truly needy" were included in the AFDC program. Some saw Reagan's approach as a sudden reversal in the nation's commitment to the poor, and many liberals were caught off-guard by the speed with which the administration launched its attack on the welfare state. However, the foundation for this retrenchment effort had been established in the longstanding battles over GAI policy. Years before, as the Nixon administration formulated its GAI strategy to deal with the alleged "welfare mess," Reagan and his advisors had devised their own alternative reform strategy in California. As one commentator observed about the early Reagan years, "The administration moved so quickly on welfare because it had over a decade of preparation. It hit the beach running, but running on a course set a decade before."[6]

The Reagan-era attack on the welfare state is more commonly seen as a response to Johnson's War on Poverty initiatives of the 1960s rather than as a product of the debate over GAI proposals. But this perception results from the fact that the debates over GAI plans have virtually disappeared from the nation's collective memory. Johnson's antipoverty initiatives were liberal, not radical. They largely kept within mainstream New Deal values. They emphasized work and opportunity; they were based on providing social services and in-kind benefits to the poor; and they reflected views toward welfare reform long held by social workers.[7] They were not the foil for the mounting conservative attacks on the welfare state. The main target of these attacks was GAI policy: the income-based strategy formulated by OEO and HEW economists that provided economic security to the poor based solely on their economic need.

In short, the debates over GAI policy left a substantial policy legacy, even though GAI legislation itself never passed into law. Though scholars have recognized the influence that the creation of new policies exerts on subsequent policy formation through policy feedbacks, the debate over GAI policy exemplifies a case in which the development of an ultimately failed policy idea held significant consequences as well. This influence can be seen in five areas.

First, the debates over GAI policy established the terms of debate for the welfare backlash that began in the 1970s. Though the country's welfare system had received criticism prior to the mid-1960s, it was the creation of the OEO as part of Johnson's War on Poverty initiatives that established an agency specifically charged with evaluating existing antipoverty efforts and developing potential alternatives. As part of their advocacy for GAI plans, government welfare experts enumerated many criticisms of the AFDC system, among which were the system's inefficiency and inadequacy; its incentives for laziness, family breakup, and interstate migration; and the fiscal burdens it imposed on state and local governments. These criticisms became the warrant for GAI proposals. As the decade drew to a close, public officials, business leaders, social activists, and others repeatedly invoked these criticisms in support of replacing existing programs with a GAI plan. By the time Nixon took office, these critiques were well established and there was virtual unanimity across the political spectrum that something needed to be done about the "welfare mess."

Insurgent conservatives took this welfare-critical discourse virtually whole cloth and turned against it against the welfare system at large. The criticisms diffused widely across the conservative landscape and were taken up by "California-style" reformers such as Reagan and Robert Carleson. In contrasting Nixon's FAP with Reagan's reform strategy in California, Edward Berkowitz captured this dynamic well: "[I]n response to the same welfare crisis, the two leaders reached different conclusions and set the tone for the debate over welfare that stretched through the 1970s."[8] Yet the "welfare mess" was not an objective problem. It was constructed as one. There was little clear evidence that the incentives in the existing AFDC system generated the type of behavioral problems that concerned critics. Nor were rising caseloads necessarily a problem if the growing number of recipients were eligible and deserving. But President Carter invoked some of these same criticisms in his own effort to bring about comprehensive reforms. Once GAI proposals lost their potential as a viable policy alternative during his administration, California-style reform was the leading contender to become the next paradigm because it purported to address the same problems. As Carleson told Reagan's budget director in the early 1980s in regard to his new welfare reform plan, "Here's something that's already been approved. All you have to do is plug it in. It's like a cassette."[9]

Second, the formulation of GAI proposals gave rise to a mode of expert analysis that antiwelfare critics effectively turned against the welfare system. From the Progressive Era through the early 1960s, antipoverty policy was primarily the jurisdiction of social workers who drew from sociology, anthropology, and psychology in developing their policy ideas. After the development of Johnson's War on Poverty initiatives, antipoverty strategies expanded to include community action plans and GAI proposals, and within the policy community there was considerable competition between social workers who favored the family allowance, local organizers who favored community action strategies, and economists who favored negative income tax approaches. By the time Nixon took office, support for the negative income tax predominated and the transformation in poverty knowledge and professional jurisdiction that occurred over the course of the decade was largely complete. In the words of one commentator, "social workers gave way to community organizers, and these, after a hectic few years, gave way to economists."[10]

Thus the eventual triumph of an NIT proposal within the Nixon administration marked the culmination of economists' rising influence within the policy community. Their upward trajectory was part and parcel with changes in poverty analysis that involved the redefinition of poverty in absolute terms (based on earned income) and the growing reliance on quantitative data and advanced statistical analysis in determining the characteristics of needy populations. Importantly, this shift to econometric thinking entailed changes in conceptualizing poverty and its solutions.[11] It shifted the unit of analysis from the poor community to the poor individual, thereby directing attention away from the influence of the labor market and other social factors that shed light on systemic sources of poverty. In addition, econometric analysis was premised on the assumption that the poor would respond in rational, economically self-interested ways to incentives in the welfare system. This approach assumed that the poor possessed considerable knowledge of welfare program details, weighed their options in terms of clear costs and benefits, and discounted other factors in decision making, such as the importance of dignity, family, and community.

During the Reagan administration, this individualistic, incentive-based approach to poverty analysis was turned against the welfare state with considerable effect. The most notable example was Charles Murray's 1984 book *Losing Ground*.[12] (An earlier example is Martin Anderson's book *Welfare*.)[13] The thesis of Murray's book was that government social policies designed to ameliorate poverty actually exacerbated the problem. In other words, government efforts to combat poverty had perverse effects. This "perversity" thesis was not new. Conservatives have argued that antipoverty policy exacerbates poverty since the creation of the poor laws in nineteenth-century England.[14] Where Murray innovated was in his mode of argument. He employed the same assumptions and "neutral" tools of policy analysis that liberal GAI plan supporters in the OEO had developed in the 1960s. Using the hypothetical example of a low-income couple—Harold and Phyllis—who are expecting a baby, Murray argued that the incentives contained in the welfare system discouraged them from forming a family and seeking gainful employment. Notably, he specified that neither Harold nor Phyllis was "of a special lower-class culture," meaning they were not socialized into the culture of poverty. Nor, according to Murray, did either one have a "propensity for 'serial monogamy.' " In other words, they had upright moral standards. Instead, Murray outlined the decision they faced: get married and seek employment or receive welfare benefits. Using cost-benefit analysis, Murray argued that "from an economic point of view, getting married is dumb." The couple would "take the economically logical step." They would have their baby, live together out of wedlock, and drift in and out of the labor market.[15] Murray concluded the hypothetical example by contending that this scenario of rational choice among alternatives accounted for the crisis of dependency that beset the country. After the publication of his book, welfare experts enumerated a long series of flaws in Murray's analysis, but the damage had been done in the public mind.[16] This damage was premised on the notion that the poor behaved like rational actors motivated by the incentives in the welfare system. This was the intellectual framework established by the liberal economists who advocated GAI plans.

Third, the rise of GAI plans as a vehicle for extending welfare rights provided the foil for the growing critique of the "entitlement" mentality. This critique crystallized into the "new consensus" on welfare reform that dominated debates over reform after the mid-1980s. Changes in the AFDC program during the Kennedy and Johnson years liberalized social provision by expanding eligibility and social services, but critics on the left complained that eligibility was still too restrictive and social services were stigmatizing. The demand by these critics for the "right to welfare" soon became associated with the GAI proposals advanced by government welfare experts. After Nixon announced his proposal, some of the harshest criticisms levied against the FAP came from conservatives who stridently opposed the notion of welfare entitlements.

This opposition served as the basis for a paradigm shift in social provision that later become known as the "new paternalism." One of the leaders of this movement is Lawrence Mead. His 1986 book, *Beyond Entitlement*, consolidated this new philosophy for welfare reform and the book's title telegraphed that it was a direct response to the entitlement mentality ascribed to GAI policies. Mead in fact argued that the defeat of GAI plans "was the womb from which a new kind of welfare policy emerged."[17] This new approach criticized liberal reforms not because they expanded the scope of government, as other conservatives had previously charged, but because they were too permissive. For too long, Mead contended, reformers had been devoted to extending individual rights to the poor without also requiring that they fulfill basic social obligations. Above all this meant the obligation to work. According to Mead, this history of permissiveness led to declining levels of "functioning" among the poor, by which he meant their capacity to learn, work, and take responsibility for a family.

This approach was a striking contrast to the libertarian strand of conservatism that strongly influenced the debate over GAI plans during the 1960s and early 1970s. Both Milton Friedman and many conservatives within the Nixon administration had favored GAI plans because they promised to streamline the government bureaucracy and increase the individual freedom of the poor to do as they chose. These conservatives opposed coercion and surveillance. Oversight by social workers and in-kind benefits (as opposed to cash) would largely be abandoned. In marked contrast, the paternalist strand of conservatism emphasized authority and social order. The vehicle through which this transformation of conservative thought occurred was the fight over GAI proposals. As Mead retrospectively observed, the debate over guaranteed income "had shifted the center of social controversy from freedom to functioning, and from the size of government to its nature."[18]

Fourth, the debates over GAI policy reinforced the distinctions between categories of the poor in both program design and public discourse, and thus facilitated the Reagan administration's cutbacks to programs that served the "undeserving" population. As discussed in previous chapters, the creation of the SSI and EITC programs intentionally reinforced the distinctions between these groups and provided substantial political protection for the deserving poor. The debates over GAI proposals also strengthened the symbolic distinctions between poor people that they had sought to dissolve. The public language used during contestation over the proposals drew contrasts between the "work ethic" and the "welfare ethic," and between the "welfare rolls" and the "payrolls." This type of language conveyed the message that being employed and receiving government benefits were mutually exclusive categories, and this dichotomy buttressed the invidious distinction between the deserving and undeserving poor. Notably, the structure of the EITC recognized what many GAI supporters had long known—namely, that full-time employment in the low-wage labor market *did not* provide enough income to keep many families out of poverty. So on its face, the very existence of the program contradicted the sharp distinction between welfare and work. Yet since the EITC was not labeled as a "welfare" plan, and because it received little public attention or scrutiny, it did not dislodge the sharp distinction between work and welfare.

Fifth, the broadest outcome of the debate over GAI proposals was the naturalization of the labor market as the only legitimate source of economic security.[19] Seeing the market in this way depended on thinking of the poor as somehow outside the social mainstream, viewing the labor market as capable of providing enough jobs at decent wage levels to lift Americans out of poverty, downplaying the effects of systemic factors that could account for poverty, and viewing unbuffered exposure to the market as a condition of full citizenship. This was a causal story in which either liberal policy interventions or the poor themselves were to blame for poverty. In 1981, George Gilder wrote a highly influential book titled *Wealth and Poverty* that contained all the elements in this causal story.[20] Critics rightly noted that it propounded a "theology of capitalism."[21] What the debates over GAI policy had helped reaffirm, albeit inadvertently for the plans' supporters, was the counterpart to Gilder's narrative—a "theodicy of capitalism" that provided an explanation for continuing poverty within an affluent capitalist society.

The strands of this theodicy could be seen most clearly in depictions of the poor and their relationship to the labor market. As governor of California, Reagan had premised his welfare reforms on the belief that the existing welfare rolls needed to be "purified."[22] This was a clear example of stigmatizing the unemployed poor as undeserving of public assistance, a view reinforced by Gilder, Mead, and other conservative commentators. All made sweeping associations between poverty and the "choice" not to work, and Mead proclaimed that the poor suffered because they had "difficulty coping." (Mead further derided "sociological arguments" that the poor were not responsible for their problems though he offered no evidence to the contrary.)[23] What was perhaps more striking in this conservative poverty discourse was the invisible role played by the market. Nathan Glazer unreflectively summed up the Reagan-era orthodoxy well when he argued that the conservative approaches to welfare reform taken in the 1980s, unlike the liberal ones from prior decades, resisted "social engineering."[24] Yet these conservative approaches were overwhelmingly motivated by the drive to discipline the poor through unregulated exposure to the labor market. To believe that this was not "social engineering," one could only believe that the labor market was an entirely natural phenomenon that operated outside the realm of human power relations and that neither depended on nor warranted intervention of any kind. This view, of course, was precisely what many advocates of GAI proposals had fought against, but by the mid-1980s it seemed the struggle had only fortified their opponents.

A Future for Guaranteed Income Plans in the United States?

Though guaranteed income plans disappeared from the national agenda during the 1980s, scholars and activists have recently expressed renewed interest in them. In his bid to "end welfare as we know it," President Clinton's 1996 welfare reform bill dismantled the AFDC program altogether and replaced it with a temporary assistance program. In response, some liberals and progressives have sought out new strategies to combat poverty, hopeful that the absence of an income-based entitlement program for the poor of any kind could be turned into a political opportunity for a renewed commitment to fighting poverty. Contemporary economic trends and poverty rates convincingly show that income maintenance policies of some type are still warranted. In light of this recent reconsideration of GAI proposals, this section discusses the contemporary state of poverty in the United States, highlights the similarities and differences between current GAI proposals and those proposed in the 1960s and 1970s, and outlines a few insights that can be drawn from past debates over GAI proposals.

When compared to debates over GAI policy during the 1960s and 1970s, one striking aspect of contemporary discussions is what has not changed. Though people support GAI plans for a number of reasons, many advocates still point to persistent poverty, changing labor market conditions, and the inadequacy of existing antipoverty measures as among the plans' most important rationales. About 12 percent of Americans, or about 34 million people, live in poverty. For a family of four, this means that their household income is less than $18,400 a year. Rates of poverty in the United States *before* taking into consideration receipt of government benefits are actually among the lowest in the industrialized world. However, once government transfers are factored in, the United States has the highest rate of poverty compared to other industrial countries. This means that the high rate of poverty in the United States is a policy failing, not a failing in the behavior of poor individuals.

The poverty rate is this high because the U.S. government devotes a smaller percentage of its GDP to social welfare programs than any other industrialized nation except Japan.[25]

In light of this circumstance, and in the wake of the 1996 welfare reform bill, guaranteed income plans have once again captured the interest of academics and activists. This interest has been fed by the discussions of "basic income" plans that emerged in Western Europe during the 1980s.[26] One of the leaders of this movement is the political theorist Philippe Van Parijs. Over the course of the 1990s, he elaborated a philosophical rational for a "universal basic income" that is paid by the government to all adult members of a society, an idea similar to the Basic Economic Security plan advanced by Robert Theobald in the 1960s.[27] Members of a second school of thought have advanced revamped negative income tax plans, similar to those considered during the 1960s and 1970s, as a potential policy alternative.[28] A third type of proposal, "stakeholder grants" as proposed by Anne Alstott and Bruce Ackerman, would provide a one-time lump sum payment (the authors propose $80,000) to all citizens once they reach adulthood in order to ensure basic equal opportunity for all.[29] While some proponents of GAI plans discuss them in isolation from other types of social provision, others envision the possibility of GAI plans working in conjunction with other types of social policy extensions, including in the areas of tax reform, public jobs, housing policy reform, universal health care, and expanded child-care provision.[30]

Based on its affinities with the EITC, the NIT may stand the best chance of any type of GAI proposal. As proponents of this type of plan have argued, the most plausible political strategy would involve expanding the EITC downward into the ranks of part-time workers and then the unemployed poor until it approximated a basic income plan. This would be an NIT that includes all Americans, not just those in the paid labor force, and the strategy would take advantage of the NIT-based structure that already exists in the EITC. Proponents of this idea argue that since the NIT-based structure is already in the "gene pool" of U.S. social policy, broadening the eligibility standards could be programmatically easier than introducing a completely different type of policy design.

In light of the debates over GAI plans a generation ago, what types of lessons can be drawn that might inform the prospects for them in the future? Perhaps the most important insight from the debate over the Nixon plan is that liberals and progressives were not adequately attuned to the cultural dimension of welfare reform politics and thus they did not fully grasp the potential value of the plan. Instead, their criticisms focused almost entirely on the FAP's benefit levels and work requirements, which they deemed inadequate and stigmatizing, respectively. Had they been more attuned to the moral distinction between the deserving and undeserving poor and the obstacle it poses to income security for the able-bodied poor, they would have seen the value of a proposal that, through its program design, would blur this distinction and thus render it less salient. In contrast, conservatives were more attuned to the significance of the structure of Nixon's plan and its potential to reconfigure dominant understandings of both deservingness and social provision more broadly. Seen with the benefit of hindsight, it appears that any proposal that blurs the distinction between the deserving and undeserving poor is likely to benefit the most vulnerable of the poor in the long run because it folds them into antipoverty programs with more meritorious recipients. Advocates for the able-bodied poor should have a strong bias in favor of any GAI plan that does this, even if it comes from a libertarian-conservative provenance.

Though some current GAI proposals come from conservatives—for instance, Charles Murray's recent proposal titled "The Plan"—most of them come from the liberal end of the political spectrum.[31] Another obstacle to passing GAI plans during the 1970s was division among liberals and progressives on the specifications of GAI plans. Especially salient divisions were based on race, region, and the different agendas of movement activists and policy experts. NWRO constituents distrusted Nixon and the conservatives in Congress, and felt entitled to benefit levels that would have tripled the benefit level in the FAP. Some key northern politicians ended up opposing Nixon's plan due to the potential dilemma posed by not supporting the welfare rights movement. Another tension was based on the sectional divide. Southern liberals, both black and white, repeatedly drew attention to how the FAP would benefit the poor in the South, yet northern liberals had their own agenda for reform and evidenced little concern for their counterparts in the South. Finally, throughout the debate over GAI plans during the 1960s and 1970s, there was little dialogue between movement activists and government experts. One thing, however, that seems clear from prior debates is that it takes both "insider" and "outsider" groups to get GAI plans firmly on the governmental agenda.

Even among sympathizers, one of the most consistent concerns that GAI plans raise is their apparent challenge to the principle of reciprocity. Critics charge that GAI benefits enable recipients to reap the benefits of citizenship without contributing to the common good. This concern reflects the priority placed on social obligation articulated by Mead and centers on worries about work. One way to address this concern is to broach a broader discussion of the definition of socially valuable "work." This is a longstanding issue among feminist scholars, who propose that caregiving be reconceptualized more clearly as "work," and among advocates of the idea of "participation income," which would provide benefits to people for positive contributions to the collective good.[32] More broadly, concerns about reciprocity suggest that GAI advocates downplay the prominent argument that GAI benefits are desirable because they enhance "real freedom."[33] The American dream notwithstanding, enhancing freedom is one of the greatest political liabilities of GAI proposals. There is a fundamental tension between the increased liberty that GAI benefits grant poor recipients and the societal trust upon which benefits are based. The libertarian rationale for GAI plans in the 1960s, based on liberty and efficiency, ran up against the paternalistic principles found in a different strand of conservativism. If the American public is to be convinced that "real freedom" is a desirable goal for reforming American social provision, they also need to be convinced that recipients of basic income payments will generally act responsibly with the freedom accorded them. Some proponents of GAI plans may hesitate to downplay the real freedom rationale because it seems to concede the normative "paternalist" point. But pervasive distrust of the poor is a political reality in the United States that is impossible to ignore, especially when poverty is so inextricably interwoven with racial stereotypes about laziness and gender- and race-based concerns about sexual mores.[34]

If GAI plans were ever to gain a place on the national agenda, one crucial aspect of strategizing for advocates is finding and maintaining a voice in public discourse, particularly through media coverage. Press accounts in the mid-1960s framed GAI policies in a variety of ways, many of which favored the plans. Yet once Nixon and Carter announced their proposals, the range of discourse on the plans constricted substantially and many ways of potentially framing GAI plans were marginalized. Supporters were able to get their preferred frames in periodicals and alternative media, but not in mainstream coverage. So advocates need to be creative in sustaining media coverage of their preferred frames. Protest and disruption are likely to generate press coverage, but they are also likely to feed public concerns about reciprocity and social order. Spokespeople who come across as moderate in temperament (not necessarily in politics) need to engage in "credibility struggles" in public forums, which, if successful, would result in being viewed as legitimate voices in antipoverty policy.[35] Civic leaders, social service providers, members of the clergy, and advocates for the homeless are likely to fit this description. In contrast, while the main goals for some GAI advocates may be a radical rethinking of the link between income and work, or a renewed attention to unconditional economic rights, the past suggests that this is not a convincing public relations strategy.

One of the fascinating things about the scholarly debate over recent GAI proposals is that the debates can take place at all, since so much depends on the actual details of the plans, especially details concerning the guaranteed minimum income level, the target population, and the basic design itself. Yet clearly there are strong sentiments toward GAI proposals on all sides of the debates, even in the absence of such details, because the proposals are rich in symbolism. They connote certain things to their supporters and opponents alike: social democratic principles, a threat to the work ethic, the recognition of care work, reducing government bureaucracy, the promise of enhanced autonomy for women, and so forth. These debates over GAI plans, in short, mirror some of the same dynamics as debates over GAI policy generated in the 1960s, and this means that the ways in which current basic income proposals come to be defined in public will carry substantial consequences for their political fate. Proponents may want to keep the justifications for proposals as multifaceted as possible in order to garner the widest support.

But just as important, if the past is any guide, liberal GAI proponents need to be focused and pragmatic. Advocates should consistently reiterate the fact that most of the problems addressed by GAI plans are located within the labor market, the changing global economy, and patterns of privilege in society, not within the perverse design of existing antipoverty policies or the values held by the poor themselves. Historically, conservative opponents of GAI plans have proven adept at linking their legislative solutions to the problems identified by GAI supporters. Therefore, the problem identification phase of any debate over GAI plans is crucial in shaping the outcome of the struggle. Yet Nixon's plan—one that promised to benefit the poor due to its innovative structure—almost passed, and not because Nixon drew attention to structural sources of poverty. (Indeed, GAI plans have never been presented to the American public mainly as a vehicle to reduce poverty. They have always served other presidential goals.) Nixon's plan almost passed not because he challenged prevailing cultural understandings but because his administration strategically capitalized on them. Though his rhetoric was a cynical appeal to prevailing stereotypes of the poor, it almost resulted in landmark legislation that would have changed the face of U.S. social provision.

CHAPTER EIGHT

Culture and Welfare Policy Development

In examining the rise and fall of guaranteed income proposals, I have presented an account that emphasizes the influence of cultural categories of worth and their interaction with stakeholder interests and institutional configurations in shaping welfare policy development. As many studies have documented, the distinction between the deserving and undeserving poor is an enduring aspect of American political culture.[1] Yet for various reasons, the dominant approaches to explaining social policy development downplay the influence of cultural factors in favor of other influences. As a result, they exhibit little recognition that policymaking takes place within moral and symbolic orders that channel the development of government programs. In contrast, this study invokes a cultural point of reference. It highlights three mechanisms through which cultural categories of worth affected the rise and fall of GAI proposals—through their constitutive contribution to collective schemas, their usage by actors as cultural resources in private deliberation and public discourse, and their institutionalization in social programs that reinforced the symbolic and programmatic boundaries between categories of poor people. These mechanisms—which identify schematic, discursive, and institutional influence, respectively—can be seen more generally as conduits through which elements of culture can influence policy development.

This concluding chapter situates the book's analytic orientation within the broader scholarship on the welfare state. It outlines and then addresses some reasons for the neglect of cultural arguments within much of the mainstream literature on the state and social policy. It then discusses analytic issues raised by the contention that cultural categories of worth are central to welfare state development in the United States. In conclusion, the chapter outlines ways in which to amend and extend existing class- and institution-based approaches to social policy development by showing how they can be integrated with a more culturally informed approach.

CULTURE, SOCIAL POLICY, AND THE STATE

Political sociology as an intellectual field has been relatively slow to embrace the "cultural turn" that reoriented a number of academic disciplines and areas of inquiry beginning in the 1970s.[2] This has been especially true for scholarship on the state, which remains one of the central foci in the field. While studies in other areas—such as social movements, civic participation, and nationalism—have incorporated cultural elements into their explanatory accounts, research on state formation and state policy still largely perpetuates a view of states as producing culture but not being influenced by it. Instead, the state and its internal dynamics are typically conceptualized as a domain in which noncultural factors, such objective interests, material resources, and universal rationality, predominate.

A few strands of theorizing have begun to challenge this view, two of which are often mentioned as part of this cultural turn and a third of which has been less remarked upon. French poststructuralism, particularly the seminal works of Michel Foucault, drew analysts' attention to the interconnections between power and knowledge and to the constitutive role of discourse and categories in social relations.[3] Feminist scholarship appropriated many of these poststructualist insights and extended them to examinations of the construction of gendered selves, citizens, and needs. This expanded the boundaries of political sociology by reconceptualizing many scholars' working assumptions, analytic frameworks, and outcomes of interest.[4] Finally, the key concepts developed by organizational theorists of the "neoinstitutionalist" school have been increasingly incorporated into studies of policymaking. Particularly central to these analyses have been concepts such as policy paradigms, legitimacy concerns, logics of action, and the socially constructed nature of interests and rationality.[5]

Despite the ascendancy of these modes of scholarship, their insights have yet to be extensively integrated into the mainstream of political sociology. Recent characterizations of cultural work as a "new wave" or as a "challenger" to existing perspectives make this continuing outsider status evident.[6] A few factors help account for this state of affairs. Cultural approaches have been equated with "interpretive" and postmodern theoretical perspectives in which causal analysis and the production of generalizable knowledge is not the end goal.[7] Since macrolevel political sociology is heavily informed by comparative-historical epistemology and methodology, in which causal analysis is the overarching objective, cultural perspectives construed as either ideographic or antipositivist have been easy to discount. Though it is certainly true that some cultural accounts do not share these analytic goals, others clearly do.[8] Thus equating cultural analysis exclusively with thick description and postmodern analysis is based on a partial reading of culturally oriented work.

In addition, scholars have equated cultural accounts with the "national values" perspective. As discussed in the introduction of the book, this approach has been criticized, among other reasons, for its assumption of cultural homogeneity and lack of specificity in regard to causal mechanisms. These criticisms have considerable merit when applied to scholarship from a generation ago. Strong claims about the impact of national values on policymaking would be plausible if there were a one-to-one correspondence between an abstract value, such as equality, and policy design. But there is not. As the struggle over GAI proposals illustrates, people subscribing to different normative commitments—such as libertarians and social democrats—coalesced behind similar proposals and, conversely, people holding similar values supported different proposals. Yet more recent culturally oriented work places little causal emphasis on abstract values; the elements of culture given emphasis are typically more cognitive and symbolic than normative.[9] Moreover, this more recent work takes factors into consideration that the "national values" perspective overlooked—factors such as power asymmetry and cultural diversity—and devotes greater attention to both specifying the elements of culture that matter and tracing out the mechanisms through which they do so.

Finally, many scholars still view culture as more or less epiphenomenal, an especially strong tendency among analysts influenced by Marxian views of political economy. Though reflection theories of the relationship between the material conditions and symbolic-expressive dimension of society have been convincingly critiqued on analytic and empirical grounds, the contention that culture is epiphenomenal raises one of a few analytic questions about categories of worth that I address in the following section.[10]

CATEGORIES OF WORTH: ANALYTICAL ISSUES

Culture, Ideology, Hegemony

The cultural distinction between deserving and undeserving poor emerged concurrently with the spread of wage labor in nineteenth-century America.[11] Those who were deemed employable, yet did not work, were defined as undeserving of poor relief. The simultaneous spread of the wage labor market along with categories of worth raises an important question about their function. If these categories are so closely intertwined with capitalist labor markets, does not a neo-Marxist interpretation of their role in society seem compelling? Since there are a number of ways to conceptualize culture within a Marxian framework, this question can be addressed by discussing the relationship of categories of worth with both ideology and hegemony.[12]

There is no single adequate definition of ideology. However, a definition that approximates many scholars' working definition is that ideology signifies ideas and beliefs used by a dominant class to promote and legitimate its interests.[13] This definition draws the crucial connection between culture and the exercise of power explicit in most definitions of ideology, but does not, as some other definitions do, prejudge ideology as necessarily distorting. In addition, it fits Theda Skocpol's definition of ideology as she expressed it in a well-known debate over the role of culture in historical analysis and which has subsequently become a common point of reference within political sociology.[14]

There are two interrelated reasons why conceptualizing categories of worth as a dimension of ideology does not fit the debates over GAI proposals. First, the practice of distinguishing between the deserving and undeserving poor was pervasive. People of all ideological stripes, from all regions of the country, and from all professional backgrounds invoked this distinction. It was not only invoked by groups whose direct interests, however defined, it served; supporters of GAI plans regularly distinguished between the deserving and undeserving poor. Second, this distinction was not solely invoked instrumentally, as a means of advancing or legitimating group interests. It was a widely shared schema that actors routinely invoked without apparent strategizing. As policy discourse among government experts illustrated, it was oftentimes even invoked when it worked at cross-purposes with policy goals. So the argument that categories of worth were influential only when they were instrumentally invoked as a resource by interested actors finds little support. To be sure, the ability to convincingly label some of the poor as "undeserving" proved a valuable rhetorical device for opponents of GAI plans. The fact that categories of worth *can* be a resource, and the fact that categories of worth are functional for many business owners, clearly should not be overlooked. But to reduce the influence of these categories *only* to instrumental claims for legitimacy purposes misapprehends the pervasive and constitutive nature of this distinction.

Another way of viewing cultural categories through a neo-Marxist lens would be to define them as an element of capitalist hegemony. Antonio Gramsci developed the notion of hegemony to explain how the capitalist class continued to win the active consent of subordinate classes.[15] Hegemony, in his view, meant the "ideological predominance of bourgeois values and norms over the subordinate classes . . . in which one concept of reality is diffused through society . . . informing with its spirit all taste, morality, customs," and so forth.[16] Thus in contrast to the notion of ideology, hegemonic culture is tacit, pervasive, and multifaceted, though it still serves the interests of the dominant class. This Gramscian interpretation appears in many ways to be consistent with the account presented in the book, since the influence of cultural categories of worth did not rely solely on their strategic deployment by interested actors.

Equating categories of worth with hegemonic culture in this manner is plausible only if one begins with the major assumption of Marxian analysis, namely that economic interests are the only "real" interests, and then proceeds to find a set of singular "real" interests within the capitalist class while finding "false" interests in the remainder of the populace. But people have a number of competing identities and value commitments, and their interests are often unclear, mixed, or mutually incompatible. Moreover, imputing a set of singular hegemonic interests to society at large suffers from the same flaws as those identified in the "national values" perspective, except that "capitalist" values supplant "national" ones. Despite these caveats, it is in fact the case that categories of worth have been a dominant element of American culture, though their dominance is neither uncontested nor inevitable. Moderate business leaders, among many other collective actors, explicitly challenged categories of worth in their support of GAI plans and, in doing so, proposed alternative schemas through which to understand poverty, the labor market, and the poor themselves. Against this opposition, however, the continuing moral classification of the poor held a privileged position due in part to opposition from a powerful set of actors and to the historical legacy of prior institutional arrangements and interpretive understandings based on this classification scheme. Though not inevitable, the very diffuseness of categories of worth—interwoven as they are into shared perceptions, resonant language and symbolism, and the design of government programs—made the distinction between the deserving and undeserving poor difficult to overcome.

Race, Gender, and Categories of Worth

As episodes throughout the debates over GAI proposals illustrate, categories of worth, based on assessments of a person's work ethic and work capacity, overlapped with racial stereotypes and prescribed gender roles. When this type of overlap exists, it makes the markers that distinguish the poor as "the other" literally more visible, since race- and gender-based categories are rooted in ascriptive characteristics. Yet categories based on work, race, and gender are both analytically and substantively distinct, so it is important both to acknowledge the differences between them and to show their mutual entanglement in the structure of American social policy.

Patterns of work and poor relief in nineteenth-century America illustrate that the able-bodied poor have long been stigmatized and subjected to being defined as "the undeserving other," even in the absence of distinctions based on race or gender.[17] The roots of this distinction can be located in the Malthusian view of poverty that became the basis of the English poor laws in the early 1800s.[18] A number of studies also show that the populations accorded "deserving" and "undeserving" status in American social policy shifted considerably over the twentieth century and that no social marker (race, gender, occupation, age, and so forth) consistently demarcated the two categories. So race- and gender-based distinctions are neither a necessary condition nor a permanent axis of differentiation for categories of worth. This is a key distinction because the primary threat posed by GAI plans was to prevailing understandings of deservingness based on work. Having said that, however, recent scholarship makes an incontrovertible case that racial stereotypes and prescribed gender roles have been reproduced through the structure of the welfare state in ways that deeply entangle them with work-based categories.

As Michael Brown and Robert Lieberman both contend, race-neutral social policies really do not exist, a circumstance that can be traced back to the structure of the Social Security Act of 1935 and its policy legacies.[19] Yet it was during the 1960s that "welfare" became racially coded outside the South and stereotypes about shiftless behavior and laziness among blacks reinforced and exacerbated concerns about the work ethic that defined the boundaries of worthiness.[20] This entanglement was especially central to debates over GAI proposals, in contrast to previous debates over AFDC, since male unemployment among minorities was among the top concerns of policymakers in the late 1960s. As Nixon developed his plan, opponents within the administration tried to turn the president against the GAI idea by highlighting the racially motivated animus toward the welfare system expressed by working-class whites. Though these efforts did not dissuade Nixon from advancing his GAI plan, they did influence the language and symbolism he used to try to sell it to the American public. Nixon's rhetoric consolidated the association between race and worthiness even further. By the Carter era, antiwelfare sentiment, which many observers interpreted as an expression of symbolic racism, was a driving factor in a tax revolt predicated on the view that the poor were undeserving of public assistance.[21]

Feminist scholars of the welfare state have contended that social policy regulates not only labor market behavior but also other types of social behavior, such as sexual, marital, and child-rearing practices. This entails gender-differentiated definitions of worthiness in which men are held accountable to the work ethic while women are held primarily accountable to the "family ethic."[22] These gendered definitions of worthiness were apparent during the debates between proponents of the family allowance and NIT plans during the mid-1960s and in aspects of the congressional deliberation over Nixon's plan. Feminist scholarship has also shifted the locus of analysis within studies of welfare policy from labor market decommodification to women's autonomy, which can be defined as "the freedom to make choices about reproduction, family, and work and the resources to act on those choices."[23] These issues were particularly salient during the Carter era, when debates related to women's labor force participation and personal autonomy came to the fore. Congressional conservatives objected to early versions of Carter's proposal because it exempted mothers from the labor force if they had children as old as fourteen and seemed to contain incentives for increased childbearing. In the alternative formulation developed by the plans' opponents, benefits would not be based on family size, and even mothers with children in elementary school would not be deemed deserving of government benefits. Though feminists themselves expressed some ambivalence on the relative merits of work and "welfare," most argued that government policy should allow women to decide what was best for themselves and their families. The results from the NIT experiments raised these issues once again. The government's analyses showed considerably higher rates of marital breakup among families receiving GAI payments. Though commentators noted that these results were consistent with the view that GAI benefits increased women's autonomy, policymakers objected to programs that granted women greater autonomy if it led to these consequences.

The successful implementation of a GAI policy would have gone a long way toward untying the complicated knot that binds worthiness based on work, race, and gender together in the design of the welfare state. The major reason that the proposals faltered was that they brought into the same program categories of the poor who had been previously treated as undeserving and mixed them with deserving populations. The structure of GAI programs treated the unemployed and working poor, blacks and whites, men and women, and single- and two-parent families all equally on the basis of need alone. Thus the plans threatened dominant understandings of labor market dynamics and gender ideology, and undermined sources of white working-class identity. Among this complex mix of challenges to the status quo, concerns about employment and the labor market were foremost among policymakers and in media accounts. Yet racial stereotypes permeated concerns about work and social spending, and fears of family structure deterioration and uncontrolled fertility preoccupied key players at crucial junctures during the debate.

The Paradox of Categories of Worth: Constitutive Yet Malleable

When seen in historical perspective, there is an apparent paradox at the center of cultural categories of worth and their influence. Scholars have long noted that categories constitute the very nature of social reality, and more recent writings by policy scholars, feminist scholars, and others show that official governmental categories are especially consequential. They define the nature and meaning of things such as occupations, identity groups, and needs.[24] In the case of the poor in particular, we have seen that they have been distinguished according to moral evaluations for generations. So it seems that these categories are an enduring feature of our political culture that have meaningful consequences both for the poor and for public perceptions of the poor. Yet, on the other hand, as the history of twentieth-century social policy reveals, the populations deemed "deserving" and "undeserving" have shifted considerably over time. So how can a categorical scheme whose boundaries shift in this way play an explanatory role in policy development? Put differently, how can boundaries that are so seemingly malleable be influential?

The distinction between the deserving and undeserving poor is part of a class of binary distinctions that contribute to what scholars have called the "discourse of American civil society." This discourse provides a ready arsenal of language and symbolism with which to distinguish between normatively desirable and undesirable characteristics of citizenship, including the difference between "dependent" and "autonomous" citizens.[25] Yet as research on social categories has illustrated, the influence and longevity of these types of distinctions often hinge on their flexibility.[26] People can invest categorical distinctions with meaning even while the contents of the categories remain contested or even ambiguous. They do so because people invest meaning, and often have stakes, in the very existence of a boundary itself, such as the boundary between science and non-science or the boundary between normal and deviant sexuality. In the case of classifying the poor, it is therefore important to distinguish between deservingness as a boundary marker and the varying populations to whom the labels "deserving" and "undeserving" have been applied. These populations have shifted based on changes in popular sentiments, demographic trends, and the nature of work, yet the boundary marker between categories of the poor has endured.

Importantly, rather than shifting the boundaries of deservingness even further, GAI proposals threatened to do away with the boundary marker altogether. The foremost implication was that all citizens would be deserving of economic security as a matter of right. It was this threat—the eradication of unworthiness as an official category—that so fundamentally threatened the conservative worldview rooted in notions of rehabilitating the poor. This explains the source of Arthur Burns's deep concern when Nixon incautiously stated in a public speech that the main benefit of his plan was that it did not place recipients in categories. As Burns conveyed to one of Nixon's advisors, this was the "classic definition" of a guaranteed income, a prospect that Burns and others found intolerable. The ultimate consequence of this debate mirrored a pattern found in prior episodes of reform, one in which concerns about public provision (or "relief") becoming an entitlement subsequently resulted in renewed efforts to categorize the poor and move the able-bodied poor off the welfare rolls.[27] As it was in the past, so it was again during the 1970s. Neither key policymakers nor the public was ready for a society in which all were deemed officially deserving of economic security.

INTEGRATING CULTURAL CATEGORIES WITH EXISTING PERSPECTIVES

The perspective I have outlined so far is part of a broader scholarly movement that emphasizes the importance of cultural elements in shaping policy development. The goal of much of this work is not to supplant existing perspectives but to bring greater "theoretical hybridization" to studies of social policy in the hope of broadening their explanatory power.[28] The analysis presented in this book suggests that integrating these types of cultural influences into the current synthesis of class- and institution-based accounts entails four points of reorientation.[29]

Culture and Cognition

Most broadly, cultural categories of worth enabled and constrained strategies of policy development by shaping perceptions. This cognitive influence is independent from group resources and the programmatic constraints of institutional arrangements, though it often interacts with these factors. This influence was most apparent when categories of worth were under threat of being dissolved, such as in Burns's argument that Nixon's initial proposal (the FSS), which transgressed these categories, was actually two proposals—"FSS-Welfare" and "FSS-Working Poor." Both supporters and opponents of Nixon's plan within the administration viewed the proposal in this light. In other words, they all sorted its beneficiaries into a binary scheme based on shared constructs in American culture. The disagreement between administration officials was not based on their *cognitive* perception of the situation but on the *normative* implications of Burns's observation: whether it was desirable to blur the distinction between the deserving and undeserving poor or to reinforce it. Had these policymakers (and later the general public) instead viewed the relationship between welfare and work as a *continuum,* as the structure of NIT plans implied, the content and political fate of GAI proposals would almost certainly have been much different.

The mutually exclusive nature of categories of worth, coupled with the status differences between the various categories of the poor, resulted in symbolic pollution. The fact that Nixon's proposal and other GAI programs were considered "welfare" proposals, even though the majority of benefits went to populations aside from AFDC recipients, provides the strongest prima facie evidence for the pollution that resulted from blurring existing symbolic boundaries. The stigma associated with AFDC benefits threatened to contaminate the social status of other "deserving" beneficiaries contained in the same program. This symbolic pollution helps account for the lack of support for GAI plans among members of the working class, who did not consider themselves to be "welfare" recipients. It held other implications as well. For instance, because the FAP was viewed as a "welfare" proposal, it became immediately susceptible to criticisms that it would further exacerbate the problems posed by increasing welfare costs and caseloads, and fuel the mounting welfare backlash.

Culture and Interests

Second, cultural perceptions channeled preference formation and the direction of influence among important groups of actors. Recognizing this interaction between collective understandings and stakeholder influence helps illuminate puzzles that remain unexplained by the application of existing approaches. For instance, new information about poverty and new norms of justice emerged in the early 1960s that challenged existing categories of worthiness and the policies based on them. It was the weakening of these normative categories that made noncategorical GAI policies attractive to many supporters within and outside government. Johnson's War on Poverty initiatives then greatly expanded the administrative capacity of government experts, which enabled them to act on their innovative policy ideas. Amid the many competing policy proposals, the ideological and technical attractions of overriding existing programmatic categories made GAI plans a frontrunner. The welfare rights movement embraced the idea and their multivocal calls for "welfare rights," coupled with the uncoordinated urban unrest that swept the country from 1964 to 1968, moved welfare reform up the nation's agenda by the end of the decade. Only by incorporating the weakening of the normative distinction between deserving and undeserving poor with increased state capacity and pressure from collective action do the reasons for the rise of GAI proposals, as compared to competing policy alternatives, become clearer.

Along similar lines, perceptions of the poor mediated how actors viewed the FAP's impact on labor market dynamics and accordingly shaped their policy preferences. Integrating these perceptions with a more conventional analysis of business influence helps explain both the split between various business coalitions on the FAP and the reasons why business conservatives opposed benefits to the working poor within a GAI program but favored them in the context of the EITC. Prominent business coalitions and many corporate leaders favored GAI plans. This support was central to Nixon's decision to proceed with such a nontraditional proposal. As policy papers and reports demonstrated, these groups were convinced that the categorical distinctions in existing policy were socially and programmatically harmful, and that a GAI plan could actually advance their interests by strengthening work incentives and socializing the costs of low-wage labor.[30] These business groups viewed the poor as structurally disadvantaged in the economy, not as lacking mainstream values. Therefore they supported programs that contained work incentives but that also treated all the poor in the same way within the same program. Business moderates perceived little threat in the Nixon plan.

On the other hand, conservatives such as Burns, Martin Anderson, and the leaders of the U.S. Chamber of Commerce vociferously opposed Nixon's plan. Their main rationale for opposing the plan, which they reiterated repeatedly, was that the FAP would threaten the work ethic of the working poor. The program's payments would strip the working poor of their drive and motivation by rendering them dependent on government. In doing so, the FAP would jeopardize the nation's economic productivity. Yet the easy passage of the EITC a few years later cast a different light on these concerns. It revealed that these claims were not based on the *economic* threat of the FAP's income subsidies to the working poor, since the EITC provided income subsidies to this group as well. Instead, the opposition was based on the *cultural* threat of stigmatizing the working poor with benefits defined as "welfare" payments in Nixon's plan and the perceived effects this might have on the labor market. As contemporaneous observers themselves noted, payments that connoted "welfare" raised concerns about dependency; payments defined as income supplements did not. Thus for both supporters and opponents of the FAP within the business community, policy positions were mediated by the meaning they attributed to dissolving the boundaries between the deserving and undeserving poor and its subsequent effects on their material interests. The broader point is that cultural arguments should not be *opposed* to interest-based explanations. Cultural perceptions *mediated* the calculation of business interests.[31]

Other scholars have offered a different account of business opposition, one in which self-evident economic interests proved to be the main stumbling block to Nixon's plan. John Myles and Paul Pierson argue that business owners in the South opposed the FAP because of their concerns about work defection from low-wage jobs and upward pressure on wages, and that these concerns served as the basis for the opposition from the U.S. Chamber of Commerce.[32] Though it is true that southern business owners did oppose the FAP for these reasons, these concerns were not self-evident, nor were they the main source of opposition from conservatives. As a contrast to the views of policymakers within the Nixon administration shows, the moral threat posed by GAI plans loomed large during debates within the administration over Nixon's plan, and concerns about workplace defection in the South were predicated on cultural preconceptions about the work behavior of the poor, preconceptions that were not shared by the administration's poverty experts.

During the debate over Nixon's nascent GAI plan in 1969, both Burns and Anderson repeatedly articulated concerns about how the behavior of the working poor would be affected by Nixon's plan. Throughout the summer, the inclusion of the working poor continued to be one of the most contentious issues among administration officials. Central to understanding the basis of this opposition is the fact that up to this point, the working poor had never received income supplements from the government. Because it was a new and untested idea, it created uncertainty and provoked emotions because it seemed to many people to threaten the functioning of the labor market, especially when the benefits were construed as "welfare" benefits. The basic question was this: What would happen when *even people who worked* received welfare? This was a driving concern, one that was simultaneously moral and economic. Neither Burns nor Anderson nor others raised concerns about upward wage pressures—most likely because the NIT plans were seen as a substitute for the minimum wage—nor did they express concerns about the political economy in the South. In fact, as the archival evidence makes clear, Nixon's advisors believed that the FAP would be a boon to the South. Similarly, the correspondence from the U.S. Chamber of Commerce during the spring of

1970 failed to mention these concerns. Instead, just as Nixon's advisors had, the leaders of the chamber emphasized the threat of paying income supplements to the working poor under the FAP. These sentiments, both within the administration and as expressed by the chamber, illuminate the worldviews of the political participants at the time and suggest that concerns about the southern political economy were not the foremost reasons for opposing the plan during this period.

In the South, the views were different. Southern conservatives did in fact oppose the FAP because of their concerns about the unemployed poor continuing to opt out of employment. But these concerns were based on the view that the poor did not share in the mainstream values of work and self-advancement. As administration officials and moderate business leaders repeatedly emphasized, the incentives structure of the FAP made it more financially attractive to work than to remain on "welfare." It was true that a southerner's income, if unemployed, would be higher under the FAP than under AFDC or general relief. But working would still pay more than staying on relief. Moreover, businesses would carry little of the burden of these higher incomes because the government would supplement low wages through income subsidies. For these reasons, Nixon's poverty experts expressed little concern about mass unemployment, because they believed the poor were willing to work. However, this view was not widely shared. Particularly in the South, where opinions about the poor were so intertwined with racial stereotypes, many business owners and politicians saw poor blacks as freeloaders and calculated the potential impact of the FAP on this basis.

Culture and Institutions

Third, the multifaceted relationship between institutional arrangements and cultural understandings requires disentangling. Institutional arrangements advantage some schemas and discourses over others. Skocpol argues as much in her critique of "national values" approaches to welfare state development.[33] But since neither she nor most other institutional welfare state scholars develop this point theoretically, institutional effects and cultural effects are frequently conflated. For instance, sectionalism and the structure of congressional committees are often cited as institutional barriers to federal policy expansion.[34] And indeed, in the case of GAI politics, Senator Russell Long, a southern Democrat, opposed the FAP from his influential position as chair of the Senate Finance Committee and advanced the EITC for similar reasons to those of conservative business leaders—to keep benefits for different categories of poor people separate. However, existing approaches often conflate the influence of institutional design, such as the congressional committee system, with the cultural dispositions of incumbents in structurally powerful (and historically contingent) positions. Although American institutions may grant more institutional leverage to some groups than others, the precise mechanisms at work in limiting policy expansion are often based on the worldviews of those in power.

The longitudinal relationship between institutional and cultural patterns also requires disentangling in regard to both mechanisms and causation. Policy feedback approaches argue that preexisting policy design shapes future development by distributing material resources, creating incentives, and shaping interpretive meanings.[35] A variety of studies have lent credence to the explanatory value of this perspective, and the findings in this study regarding the influence of the EITC on policy development during the Carter era further bolster the argument. Yet the influence of the interpretive dimension of policy feedback arguments has been underemphasized in empirical work. The debates over GAI policy indicate that the absence of existing income maintenance programs for the working poor constrained supporters' ability to effectively frame GAI policies analogically. There were few *symbolic* resources from which they could draw to make their case for extending social provision to low-income workers. Therefore, benefits for this group, especially when included in a "welfare" reform package, sounded radical. In contrast, advocates of similar policies in Canada were able to garner support for GAI policies because there was a "natural bridge" between GAI proposals and other preexisting policies that shared a similar program structure, such as an income transfer program for working families.[36] Notably, the logic of policy feedback arguments takes preexisting program design as a given and then examines its effects on interpretive meanings. However, the relationship between culture and institutions should be treated explicitly as a dialectical process in which cultural understandings also shape new institutional arrangements.[37] The creation of the SSI and EITC legislation in the early 1970s illustrates this other phase in the dialectic when categories of worth were threatened and then reinforced through the structure of new social programs.

Public Discourse and Public Opinion

Fourth, existing studies underplay two additional factors that proved to be of consequence in the debates over GAI policy: public discourse and popular sentiments. The debates over GAI policy show that presidential administrations hold considerable power to shape the public understanding of social policy through public pronouncements and that this presidential discourse has considerable political consequences. Nixon was especially effective in rhetorically reinforcing the symbolic boundaries between the poor that his program effectively blurred. Though his advisors presented him with bolder and more innovative framing strategies, Nixon's use of a more resonant policy framing played to his electoral advantage while leaving the dominant understandings of poverty and the aims of welfare reform intact. One consequence was that the working class never exhibited wide recognition that the FAP was in their material interest. Sustained attention to this type of public discourse and its links to policymaking has been virtually absent from the welfare state literature, despite the fact that some scholars have noted the essential role of presidential discourse in creating collective justifications for new policy reforms.[38]

The analysis also reveals that public sentiments were instrumental in shaping the content and rhetorical framing of GAI proposals during their development in both the Nixon and Carter administrations. Nixon's policy advisors perceived that the public distinguished between the "welfare" poor and the working poor and then shaped the design and symbolism of the FAP accordingly. Carter administration officials recognized this obstacle and, despite their sympathies toward a unified GAI proposal, ultimately designed a plan that fit the cultural distinctions held by the public. Greater attention to the impact of popular sentiments on program design and fate provides one way to "bring the public back in" to analyses of social policy development that have largely neglected the potential importance of public opinion.[39]

CONCLUSION

The demise of guaranteed income plans as a strategy to reform the American welfare system marks a lost opportunity to improve the economic security of the nation's poor. But theoretical lessons can still be learned from this failed attempt at reform. These lessons can not only improve our scholarly accounts of the U.S. welfare state but, more indirectly, may inform a fuller understanding of the persistent obstacles to social policies that improve the lives of the "welfare" poor.

Because GAI plans so directly challenged the tacit cultural perceptions on which the existing welfare system was based, the structuring role these perceptions play in policy development was more visible than usual. To acknowledge that elements of culture play a role in shaping welfare reform does not by any means suggest that other factors, such as group resources, do not matter. But in the same way that historical institutionalists have argued that aspects of the American policymaking process bias the trajectory of reform in particular directions, so too do cultural structures like the enduring distinction between the deserving and undeserving poor. For instance, given the expense of the program, a number of commentators have expressed surprise at the EITC's ease of passage in the mid-1970s and its subsequent growth in the following years. Yet the creation and growth of this program is far less puzzling when one recognizes that it not only conforms to categories of worth but reinforces them.

Recognizing the influence of culture is important because academic understandings of policymaking can influence the ways in which social policies are formulated, justified, and critiqued.[40] The risk then is that underemphasizing the role of culture analytically may lead to underemphasizing its impact politically. This seems to be a risk that liberals are more prone to run than conservatives, as highlighted by the recent debate within the Democratic Party over the merits of devoting more attention to the language used by politicians to align policy positions with core American values.[41]

In the case of guaranteed income proposals, it is striking that one of the few social scientists to discuss the cultural obstacles confronted by the Nixon and Carter proposals in any sustained way was Lawrence Mead, a conservative political scientist and a leader of the "paternalist" approach to welfare reform that emphasizes rehabilitating the poor through the design of the welfare system's behavioral incentives and eligibility requirements.[42] Mead has observed that "the main political difficulty for FAP and PBJI was that they provided essentially the same income benefits to all families whether or not they had employable members," and it is clear from his analysis that the main reasons this posed a problem for GAI plans were concerns about work and deservingness.[43] Of course, liberals by and large deemed these concerns to be illegitimate. But as Mead suggests, they did little to directly counter them during the debates over GAI plans. Instead the most prominent voices from the left, when heard at all, emphasized rights and entitlements, which only exacerbated existing concerns about work. Mead picked up on the cultural obstacles confronted by GAI plans in part because they ran counter to his rehabilitationist worldview. But just as important, his analytic orientation to social policy development takes the causal impact of ideas and culture seriously.

Unfortunately, it seems that two types of cultural arguments frequently get conflated: those that contend that cultural factors influence policy development and those that use cultural arguments as an excuse for government inaction when it comes to fighting poverty. The latter, of course, make up "culture of poverty" arguments. They hold that generous government programs to assist the poor are ineffective, or even counterproductive, because poverty stems from the moral failings of the poor, not from the conditions in which the poor often find themselves. Countless studies over the past forty years have generated evidence that cast doubt on this formulation. But it endures nevertheless and continues to limit the possibilities for providing adequate economic security for many of the nation's poor, just as it did during the struggle over guaranteed income policies. For scholarly studies of policy development in the United States, acknowledging the power of this argument to shape policy outcomes is a crucial step, and perhaps one that will reverberate in the continuing political battle to fight poverty.

Notes

1. President's Commission on Income Maintenance Programs, *Poverty Amidst Plenty: The American Paradox* (Washington, DC: GPO, 1969), pp. 23–24.

2. Quoted in Milton Friedman, "Negative Income Tax—I," *Newsweek*, September 16, 1968; see also Paul A. Samuelson, "Negative Income Tax," *Newsweek*, June 10, 1968, p. 76.

3. Moller et al. (2003). For an extensive analysis of pre- and post-transfer poverty rates in advanced industrial countries, see Goodin et al. (1999).

4. Myles and Pierson (1997).

5. Amenta, Bonastia, and Caren (2001) and Burstein (1991) discuss the insights to be gained from studying failed policy proposals.

6. Katz (2001, p. 61).

7. On these contemporary problems, see Aronowitz (2005), Iceland (2003), Rank (2005), and Shipler (2004).

8. The most high-profile proposals are the "stakeholder grants" proposed by Alstott and Ackerman (1999) and Murray's (2006) plan for an annual $10,000 stipend to all Americans over the age of twenty-one.

9. Of the few books written about GAI policy in America, all were written contemporaneously to legislative episodes. On Nixon's proposal, see Bowler (1974), Burke and Burke (1974), and Moynihan (1973); on Carter's proposal, see Lynn and Whitman (1981). Only Leman's account (1980) examines both the Nixon and Carter proposals, but it mainly compares how guaranteed income policies developed differently in the United States and Canada.

10. There was a wide variety of plans that fell under the rubric of "guaranteed annual income" programs during this time period. The differences between them are important for understanding the politics of these proposals, but for ease of exposition I will refer to them generally as "guaranteed annual income" proposals until their differences become relevant.

11. For overviews of these approaches, see Amenta (1998), Amenta, Bonastia, and Caren (2001), and Manza (2000).

12. Most of the government documents examined in the book are located in the Nixon presidential archives in College Park, Maryland, and the Carter presidential archives in Atlanta, Georgia. I examined media coverage in the *New York Times* and twenty-six national periodicals.

13. Campbell (2002).

14. On the role the media plays in creating "common knowledge," see Neuman, Just, and Crigler (1992).

15. Esping-Andersen (1990).

16. Amenta (1998).

17. Piven and Cloward (1977) make the seminal statement of this argument. Other scholars, such as Jenkins and Brents (1989), Quadagno (1992), and Amenta, Caren, and Olasky (2005), have subsequently elaborated on the social movements (or "mass turmoil") argument by integrating other factors into their explanatory models.

18. Hicks and Swank (1983).

19. Berkowitz and McQuaid (1980); Domhoff (1990); Quadagno (1984). Deriving any general statement from the literature on the role of business is challenging because claims concerning capitalists' interests, policy preferences, degree of influence, and mode of influence are each highly contested (see Amenta, Bonastia, and Caren [2001]; Hacker and Pierson [2002]; Manza [2000]; Reese [2005]). However, the conventional assumption within the literature (an assumption built into what Swenson [2002] calls the "equivalency premise") is that capitalists, in contrast to working-class movements, oppose most social policy expansion.

20. E.g., Quadagno (1984).

21. Heclo (1974); Orloff and Skocpol (1984); Skocpol (1985a).

22. On the relationship between state capacity and ideational innovation, see Rueschmeyer and Skocpol (1996).

23. Huber, Ragin, and Stephens (1993); Korpi (1989).

24. See Orloff (1993) for an example of an account that blends its focus on state actors and institutions with attention to subjective understandings and ideology in this manner.

25. Skocpol and Ikenberry (1983); Skocpol (1992); Weir, Orloff, and Skocpol (1988).

26. Amenta, Bonastia, and Caren (2001).

27. E.g., Steinmo and Watts (1995).

28. Pierson (1993); Skocpol (1992); Weir, Orloff, and Skocpol (1988).

29. An important exception to this neglect of interpretive feedback processes is Pedriana and Stryker's (1997) discussion of equal opportunity law as a symbolic resource.

30. Myles and Pierson (1997).

31. See Orloff (1993) and Skocpol (1992) for discussion of the studies associated with the "national values" perspective. For examples of the dominant conceptions of culture that informed national values approaches, see Almond and Verba (1963) and Parsons and Shils (1951). A more recent version of the national values argument can be found in Lipset (1996).

32. Rimlinger (1971).

33. Weir, Orloff, and Skocpol (1988); Orloff (1993); Skocpol (1992).

34. Skocpol (1992, p. 22).

35. For two collections that discuss the impact of the cultural turn on the study of political processes, see Steinmetz (1999) and Adams, Clemens, and Orloff (2005a). See especially Orloff (2005) on social policy.

36. E.g., Weir (1992) and Clemens (1997). For an overview, see Hall and Taylor (1996) on sociological institutionalism.

37. On the centrality of policy meanings to policymaking, see Skrentny (2002).

38. For reviews of the role of ideas in policymaking, see Béland (2005), Campbell (1998, 2002), and Goldstein and Keohane (1993).

39. Sewell (1992). Though my thinking about mutual constitution draws directly from Sewell, my terminology is different from his because it uses a more common meaning of "structure."

40. The more analytic point here concerns the relative autonomy of culture. See Alexander and Seidman (1990).

41. McAdam (1982).

42. Sewell (1999).

43. Swidler (2001).

44. Clemens and Cook (1999); Fligstein (2001). The chapters collected in Steinmetz (1999) illustrate the utility of seeing the constitutive role of culture in political processes in the ways discussed in this paragraph.

45. On the impact of policy feedback on ideas, see Hall (1989), Pierson (1993), Rueschmeyer and Skocpol (1996), and Steinmo, Thelen, and Longstreth (1992).

46. Skrentny (2002).

47. Pedriana and Styker (1997).

48. Goldstein and Keohane (1993).

49. Jepperson and Swidler (1994, p. 362).

50. Handler and Hasenfeld (1991); Katz (1986, 1989); Mohr (1994).

51. Katz (1989); Piven and Cloward (1993 [1971]).

52. Handler and Hasenfeld (1991) make a consonant point. More generally, there are many parallel cases in which ideas that were once related to the influence of particular groups diffuse to become constitutive elements of a society's culture. Weber's (1930) Protestant ethic thesis is a canonical example. (On the diffusion of this ethic in contemporary America, see McCloskey and Zaller [1984].) Similarly, the influence of distinctions based on race and gender cannot simply be ascribed to instrumental claims-making on the part of the actors whose direct interests (however defined) those claims advance. These distinctions are rooted in institutional practices and embedded in the broader culture in myriad ways. For this reason, Orloff (1993) urges distinguishing between the influence of ideology and culture in studies of policymaking. For a more general discussion of this distinction, see Wuthnow (1987).

53. Gordon (1994); Teles (1996).

54. For this reason, the civil rights movement's nonviolent direct action during the Eisenhower and Kennedy years is an important backdrop for the rise of GAI programs. However, through the early 1960s, the movement's main impact on emerging GAI proposals had more to do with consciousness-raising than it did with the threat of social turmoil, which is the type of influence ascribed to it by social movement perspectives on policymaking.

55. Block and Manza (1997); O'Connor (2001).

56. Douglas (1966) argues that the social categories that differentiate one group from another form the basis of status hierarchies in society. The boundaries between groups are often reinforced by pollution beliefs that maintain the integrity of group boundaries and form the basis of rules of exclusion. One of the main mechanisms through which symbolic pollution takes place is the allocation of stigma and the avoidance of spoiled identities (Goffman 1963). One example from nineteenth-century American racial classification is the "one-drop rule," in which people of mixed-race ancestry were defined as black (F. Davis 1991). This kept the "white" category racially and morally pure.

57. The argument that follows is elaborated in more theoretical detail in Steensland (2006).

58. Schneider and Ingram (1993).

59. Quadagno (1990) also discusses the role of race and gender in the political debate over Nixon's Family Assistance Plan. However, the mechanisms she emphasizes are somewhat different, mainly concerning labor market position and discrimination rather than perceptions of deservingness.

60. Gilens (1999); Kellstedt (2003). For ethnographic evidence of the connection between welfare and race that emerged during the period, see Halle (1984) and Rieder (1985). For accounts of social policymaking that focus on the influence of race, see Brown (1999), Lieberman (1998), Neubeck and Cazenave (2001), and Quadagno (1994).

61. Despite the racialization of welfare politics during this period, it is important to avoid reducing the influence of cultural categories of worth to racial stereotyping. Katz (1986), among others, discusses the long history of cultural categories of worth in American society through the colonial era. Similarly, though she does not explicitly theorize their importance, Skocpol (1992, p. 149) observes that the "institutional and cultural oppositions between morally 'deserving' and the less deserving run like fault lines through the entire history of American social provision." Though race has become a powerful marker of deservingness, concerns about work were more fundamental to the debates over GAI proposals because the proposals threatened to reconfigure the very basis of antipoverty policy.

62. Abramovitz (1988); Gordon (1994); Mettler (1998); Orloff (1999).

63. Though not all the categorical language in the debates over GAI plans was used strategically, cultural categories of worth were clearly a powerful cultural resource (Swidler 1986) for both supporters and opponents of the plans.

64. See Wright (2004) on this point in the contemporary context.

65. To take the given fate of GAI policy as inevitable would be to mistakenly begin the analysis from the policy's failure and then retrospectively search back to its causes, rather than to search forward from the beginning for different reasons why alternative outcomes did not come to pass. Tilly (1975) makes this analytical point about the importance of "prospective" analysis in his examination of the development of nation-states in Western Europe. Looking at the evolution of meanings as a process of selection and institutionalization draws from Wuthnow (1989).

66. Teles (1996).

67. Hall (1993).

68. On the distinction between paradigms and programs, see Campbell (1998).

69. Stone (1989).

70. Hall (1993).

71. This process of actors linking existing solutions to new problems fits what organizational theorists call "garbage-can" models of decision making (Cohen, March, and Olsen 1972). Kingdon's (1984) classic work on agenda setting applies this idea to the policymaking process, and Hacker (1996) uses this approach to study the rise of President Clinton's national health care proposal.

72. Though Nixon's plan contained a work requirement, there was widespread doubt among conservatives that it could ever be strongly enforced. This is why the

label "guaranteed income" proved to be so divisive, because it signaled the extent to which the benefits would be considered entitlements.

73. Luker (1996).

74. For a discussion of the data and methods used in these media analyses, see Steensland (2002). A methodological appendix is also available from the author on request.

75. Entman (1993, p. 52); also see Gamson and Modigliani (1989).

76. The literature on policy framing has grown substantially in recent years. For an experimental study that shows framing effects on how people think about antipoverty policy, see Iyengar (1990). For a more general argument about the role of elite framing in shaping citizens' policy preferences, see Zaller (1992). Callaghan and Schnell (2005) provide a recent overview of this literature within political science.

CHAPTER ONE
THE RISE OF GUARANTEED ANNUAL INCOME

1. Handler and Hasenfeld (1991); Katz (1986).

2. Katz (1986).

3. Skocpol (1992).

4. On race, see Brown (1999) and Lieberman (1998); on gender, see Abramovitz (1988), Gordon (1994), and Mettler (1998); on local labor markets, particularly in the South, see Alston and Ferrie (1999).

5. Gordon (1994).

6. For the changing evaluative connotation of "welfare" during this period, see Katz and Thomas (1998).

7. Reese (2005); Teles (1996).

8. On the development of the idea in England, see Van Trier (2002). On some analogous proposals in the United States, see Gordon (1994).

9. Moynihan (1973, p. 50).

10. Stigler (1946).

11. Ibid., p. 362.

12. Ibid., p. 365.

13. Cohen (2003).

14. Galbraith (1984 [1958]). For a discussion of the broader intellectual climate of the 1950s, see Jamison and Eyerman (1994) and Pells (1985).

15. Galbraith (1984 [1958], p. 224).

16. In these later editions, Galbraith wrote that a negative income tax provided a more immediate solution than did unemployment insurance, but he did not think such an idea was politically feasible when he first published the book in 1958 (Galbraith 1984 [1958], p. 228n4).

17. Sugrue (1996, ch. 5).

18. Harrington (1962, p. 12).

19. Arendt (1958).

20. See Theobald (1963, p. 17) on the origins of the term "cybernation."

21. Theobald (1961, p. 108).

22. O'Connor (2001, p. 183).

23. Theobald offered few specifics concerning how the benefits under his plan would be delivered, saying "the full economic implications of any particular level of BES [Basic Economic Security] entitlements would probably have to be worked through" (1963, p. 193).

24. President's Commission on Income Maintenance Programs (1969, p. 119).

25. Friedman (1962, p. 191).

26. Ibid., p. 194.

27. Ibid., p. 33.

28. Berlin (1969).

29. Branch (1988); Sitkoff (1981).

30. For an overview of this debate, see Brown (1999) and Quadagno (1994).

31. Skrentny (2002).

32. Existing examinations of the emergence of GAI policy grant little influence to the civil rights movement. See Burke and Burke (1974), Moynihan (1973), O'Connor (2001), Patterson (1994), and Steiner (1971). Though direct evidence is in short supply, the indirect evidence is suggestive. There can be little doubt that the domestic policy atmosphere of the early 1960s was influenced by the civil rights movement's consciousness-raising activities.

33. Brown (1999).

34. Ibid.

35. Katz (1986); Patterson (1994).

36. For a historical overview of this northern migration, see Lemann (1991). More generally, the belief that blacks migrated in search of higher benefits has found little support. A report by the Urban Institute published in 1970 countered many of the existing perceptions about interstate migration but also found that data of any type on the matter were scant (Wertheimer 1970). It is also possible, as Moynihan (1973) suggests, that although pure economic incentives for migration, however small, did exist in the welfare structure, their impact on mounting welfare expenditure in places like New York and Chicago was overblown by city and state officials looking for fiscal relief from the federal government.

37. On Newburgh and its public significance, see Berkowitz (1991, pp. 103–6), Patterson (1994, pp. 107–8), and Sundquist (1968, pp. 127–28). On the history of state-level variation in AFDC payments, see Peterson and Rom (1990, ch. 4).

38. Quoted in Patterson (1994, p. 108).

39. Matusow (1984); Sundquist (1968). The focus on Harrington's book in some accounts neglects the broader factors that contributed to the Kennedy administration's receptivity to Harrington's argument, such as civil rights protests and economists' increasing awareness of structural unemployment.

40. Harrington (1962, p. 3).

41. Ibid., p. 12.

42. Ibid., pp. 71, 63.

43. Ibid., p. 162.

44. Ibid., p. 16.

45. See, for instance, Banfield (1970) and Ryan (1971).

46. Dwight Macdonald, "Our Invisible Poor," New Yorker, January 19, 1963, pp. 82–132.

47. Brauer (1982).

48. The committee also included Gunner Myrdal, Robert Heilbroner, Irving Howe, Bayard Rustin, and twenty-five others.

49. A publicly accessible version of the committee's report (hereafter cited as Triple Revolution) is available at http://www.pa.msu.edu/people/mulhall/mist/Triple.html (accessed June 2002). The quote appears on page 3 of this version.

50. Ibid., p. 9.

51. Ibid., p. 10.

52. Ibid., p. 14.

53. The press coverage of the report is located in the Wilbur Hugh Ferry Papers collection (MC046), Mudd Manuscript Library, Princeton University.

54. Quoted in Steiner (1971, p. 9).

55. On views of poverty within the Kennedy administration, see Bernstein (1991); Katz (1986); Matusow (1984); Patterson (1994); and Sundquist (1968).

56. Aaron (1978, pp. 17, 23).

57. Bernstein (1991); Brown (1999).

58. Block and Manza (1997, p. 480) describe a similar transition from an "employment paradigm" that characterized the 1940s to a "transfer paradigm" ascendant in the 1960s.

59. O'Connor (2001, pp. 146–51) provides an excellent account of this transition to targeted, income maintenance approaches within the Kennedy administration.

60. Brauer (1982); Patterson (1994, p. 135).

61. Patterson (1994, p. 186).

62. Quoted in Sundquist (1968, p. 137).

63. For overviews of Johnson's War on Poverty, see Davies (1996), Katz (1986), Patterson (1994), and Sundquist (1968).

64. "National Anti-Poverty Plan," Office of Economic Opportunity, October 20, 1965, p. 2 (emphasis in original).

65. These factors are distilled from accounts of the development of the OEO written by two of its former directors of research and planning within the OEO, Joseph Kershaw (1970) and Robert Levine (1970).

66. On the development of systems analysis, see Kershaw (1970), Levine (1970), and Rivlin (1971).

67. Quoted in Schlesinger (1965, p. 592). See Bell (1960) for a contemporaneous account of this sentiment and Glazer (1988) for a retrospective one.

68. Rivlin (1971).

69. For a detailed examination of these shifting definitions of poverty within the policy community during the 1960s, see O'Connor (2001, chs. 6–7).

70. Burke and Burke (1974, p. 20); Levine (1970, p. 60).

71. "National Anti-Poverty Plan," p. 2 (emphasis in original).

72. Levine (1970, p. 60).

73. The differences between the two approaches were only briefly outlined in the actual policy documents. This paragraph and the following two are based on more detailed accounts of the two income maintenance alternatives in Kershaw (1970), Levine (1970), Moynihan (1973), and Schorr (1966).

74. This debate was an example of the broader debate over the relative merits of universal policies as opposed to targeted ones. See Skocpol (1995).

75. See Burke and Burke (1974) and Levine (1970) for more extensive discussion of the reasons for the differences between the 1965 and 1966 reports.

CHAPTER TWO
GUARANTEED ANNUAL INCOME GOES PUBLIC

1. "Now, a Tax Plan That Pays People," *U.S. News and World Report*, February 14, 1966, p. 63.

2. Bowen and Magnum (1966, p. 26).

3. See M. Davis (1993), Kornbluh (2000, chs. 4–7), Melnick (1994), and Piven and Cloward (1977, ch. 5).

4. Davis (1993).

5. Kornbluh (2000).

6. Melnick (1994, p. 295).

7. M. Davis (1993); Melnick (1994).

8. Reich (1964, p. 733).

9. Ibid., p. 785.

10. Richard A. Cloward and Frances Fox Piven, "A Strategy to End Poverty," *The Nation*, May 2, 1966.

11. For their own account of these events, see Piven and Cloward (1993 [1971], 1977).

12. Along these lines, Kertzer (1988) discusses how ambiguous language and symbolism can actually play a more powerful role in collective action than well-defined symbolism.

13. Cloward and Piven, "A Strategy to End Poverty," p. 511.

14. For a biographical and historical account of Wiley and the NWRO, see Kotz and Kotz (1977).

15. M. Davis (1993, p. 45). The details of the desired system were left unspecified.

16. M. Davis (1993).

17. Otto Eckstein and Robert Harris, *Program Analysis: Income and Benefit Programs* (Washington, DC: Office of the Assistant Secretary for Program Evaluation, Department of Health, Education, and Welfare, 1966).

18. Burke and Burke (1974, p. 16).

19. Rivlin (1971).

20. Levine (1970, p. 78). For a succinct overview of the analytic perspectives and research design of these experiments, see Rivlin (1971, pp. 94–102).

21. Rivlin (1971).

22. Lemann (1991). For a detailed examination of the relationship between welfare policy and migration, see Peterson and Rom (1990).

23. Rivlin (1971, p. 18).

24. Patterson (1994, p. 174).

25. Levine (1970, p. 201).

26. On the lack of data available to the policy community in the 1960s, see Aaron (1978), Burke and Burke (1974), Moynihan (1973), and Steiner (1971).

27. Kelman (1981) and Rhoads (1985) discuss economists' behavioral assumptions and broader professional worldview.

28. For contemporaneous discussion and comparison of the family allowance and the NIT, see Kershaw (1970, pp. 106–27) and Schorr (1966, pp. 129–65).

29. Burke and Burke (1974); Moynihan (1973).

30. Steiner (1971, p. 98).

31. Both Moynihan (1973, pp. 124–26) and Rivlin (1971) suggest this line of reasoning for why economists favored the NIT.

32. Levine (1970).

33. Kershaw (1970, pp. 146–47); Rivlin (1971).

34. For a fuller exploration of this point, see Aaron (1978).

35. Bernstein (1996); Kershaw (1970); Levine (1970, ch. 6).

36. Office of Policy Planning and Research, *The Negro Family: The Case for National Action* (Washington, DC: United States Department of Labor, 1965).

37. Ibid., p. 29.

38. Kershaw (1970); Moynihan (1973).

39. On the immediate political fallout of the Moynihan Report, see Rainwater and Yancey (1967). On the report's longer-term effects on policymaking, see Glazer (1988) and Wilson (1987).

40. "T.R.B. from Washington," *New Republic*, December 12, 1966, p. 4.

41. U.S. Chamber of Commerce, "Proceedings of the National Symposium on Guaranteed Income," December 9, 1966 (Washington, DC: U.S. Chamber of Commerce), p. 1.

42. Ibid., p. 3.

43. Ibid., p. 6.

44. Ibid., p. 10.

45. Ibid.

46. Ibid., p. 13.

47. Ibid.

48. Ibid., p. 17.

49. "Report from the Steering Committee of the Arden House Conference on Public Welfare," Albany, New York, ca. 1968, p. 1.

50. For further discussion of the Arden House conference and report, see Moynihan (1973).

51. "Arden House Conference," p. 13.

52. Patterson (1996, p. 663). On black violence during this period and the government response, see Button (1978).

53. Quoted in Matusow (1984, p. 365).

54. Quoted in ibid., p. 397.

55. Kerner Commission, *Report of the National Advisory Commission on Civil Disorders. United States: Kerner Commission* (Washington, DC: GPO, 1968), p. 1.

56. Ibid., pp. 457–67.

57. Katz (1989, p. 104) also discusses some of these reasons for business support of the NIT.

58. "Economists Urge Assured Income," *New York Times*, May 28, 1968, p. 1.

59. Ibid.

60. Steiner (1971, p. 96) suggests that the meaning of "guaranteed income" was deliberately left vague so that supporters of both family allowances and the NIT could sign the statement. Tobin argued in favor of the NIT (and sometimes against a family allowance) in a number of publications during the mid-1960s, including *Daedalus*, *Public Interest*, and the *New Republic*.

61. Matusow (1984, p. 214); Patterson (1996, pp. 648–52).

62. Davies (1996); Edsall and Edsall (1991); Matusow (1984).

63. Bernstein (1996, p. 360); Kershaw (1970); Schwartz (1983); Patterson (1994, p. 164).

64. Edsall and Edsall (1991, p. 64); Matusow (1984, p. 215).

65. Patterson (1994).

66. Davies (1996, p. 183); Kornbluh (2000).

67. Burke and Burke (1974); Moynihan (1973).

68. Davies (1996, pp. 203–10).

69. Button (1978) reports that officials at the OEO had the most "radical" agenda of any of the policy agencies in Washington.

70. For discussions of these different elements of GAI's politics during the Johnson administration, see Burke and Burke (1974), Davies (1996), Katz (1989), Levine (1970), Moynihan (1973), and Patterson (1994).

71. Mann (1996). Another Democratic presidential contender, Eugene McCarthy, came closer to an outright endorsement of guaranteed income. See "Economists Urge Assured Income," p. 22.

72. Kornbluh (2000, p. 126).

73. Quoted in Hoff (1994, p. 116).

74. See Matusow (1984, ch. 14) on the presidential campaign.

75. Hoff (1994); Moynihan (1973).

76. See Davies (1996, p. 217) on Nixon's interest in the argument of the book.

77. Paul A. Samuelson, "Negative Income Tax," *Newsweek*, June 10, 1968, p. 76.

78. "How 'Negative Income Tax' Works—Who Would Get What?" *U.S. News and World Report*, May 27, 1968; "Needed: Guaranteed Income?" *Newsweek*, July 1, 1968, p. 16; "T.R.B. from Washington," *New Republic*, April 27, 1968, p. 2.

79. Robert Theobald, "The Goal of Full Unemployment," *New Republic*, March 11, 1967, p. 15.

80. Tom Wicker, "Should the Poor Get Richer?—I," *New York Times*, December 18, 1966, p. E3; Wicker, "Should the Poor Get Richer?—II," *New York Times*, December 20, 1966, p. 43; Wicker, "Should the Poor Get Richer?—III," *New York Times*, December 22, 1966, p. 32.

81. E.g., "'Unions' for People on Relief," *U.S. News and World Report*, October 30, 1967, p. 36.

82. James Tobin, "Do We Want Children's Allowances?" *New Republic*, November 25, 1967; Leon Keyserling, "Guaranteed Annual Incomes," *New Republic*, March 18, 1967.

83. Henry Hazlitt, "The Coming Crisis in Welfare," *National Review*, May 18, 1967, p. 416.

84. "After 30 Years—Relief a Failure?" *U.S. News and World Report*, July 7, 1967, p. 44.

85. "Needed: Guaranteed Income?" *Newsweek*, July 1, 1968, p. 16.

86. Milton Friedman, "Negative Income Tax—I," *Newsweek*, September 16, 1968, p. 86.

CHAPTER THREE
THE ORIGINS AND TRANSFORMATION OF THE NIXON PLAN

1. Amenta (1998, pp. 31–34).

2. Elements of these perspectives were of course apparent in debates over GAI policy prior to 1969. However, I deal with them in this chapter, instead of the previous ones, because the process of intense and detailed deliberation within the administration forced policymakers to elaborate their working assumptions with greater explicitness.

3. Bowler (1974, p. 65); Moynihan (1973, p. 71).

4. On revenue sharing and its eventual relationship to Nixon's "new federalism" initiatives, see Conlan (1988).

5. Task Force on Public Welfare, "Programs to Assist the Poor: Report to President-Elect Richard M. Nixon," December 1968, folder Public Welfare, 1969–70, Box 3, White House Central Files (hereafter WHCF): EX FG 221–11, Nixon Project Materials (hereafter NPM).

6. This account of Finch's response to the Nathan report is taken from Burke and Burke (1974).

7. Hoff (1994, p. 117); Moynihan (1973, p. 73).

8. See, for instance, the correspondence between the White House and the U.S. Chamber of Commerce in folder 2/11/69–3/11/69, Box 4, WHCF: EX FG 6–12, NPM; and memo, Dwight Chapin to Spiro Agnew, February 27, 1969, folder Mar.–Apr. 10, Box 1, WHCF: LG, NPM.

9. Memo, Daniel Patrick Moynihan, "Toward a National Urban Policy," February 3, 1969, p. 9, folder Begin–2/23/69, Box 1, WHCF: FG 6–12, NPM.

10. On Moynihan's biography, see Hodgson (2000).

11. Memo, Moynihan to Nixon, January 9, 1969, p. 2, folder Jan.–Feb. 1969, Box 1, WHCF: LG, NPM.

12. Moynihan, "Toward a National Urban Policy," p. 4.

13. Burke and Burke (1974, p. 45).

14. Memo, Moynihan to Nixon, January 31, 1969, folder Begin–3/12/69, Box 1, WHCF: EX WE, NPM.

15. Burke and Burke (1974, p. 51).

16. O'Connor (2001).

17. The facts of the following account of the subcommittee task force rely on Burke and Burke (1974), since the nature of events left little documentary evidence. Vincent Burke, a Washington bureau reporter for the *Los Angeles Times*, interviewed the principals in the development of Nixon's Family Assistance Plan for his book on the subject.

18. Quoted in Burke and Burke (1974, p. 53).

19. Quoted in ibid., p. 52.

20. Bowler (1974, p. 65).

21. Quoted in Burke and Burke (1974, p. 60).

22. Moynihan to Nixon, January 31, 1969; memo, Moynihan to Paul McCracken, February 8, 1969, folder Begin–3/13/69, Box 1, WHCF: EX WE, NPM; memo, Moynihan to Nixon, March 1, 1969, folder 2/25/69–3/18/69, Box 1, WHCF: FG 6–12, NPM. See O'Connor (2001, pp. 205–8) for a critique of Moynihan's analysis of this correlation (though as he made it in his report on the black family). One element of this critique is that welfare and employment rates had not recently become "unglued" because they were never as closely related as Moynihan suggested.

23. Two of these four reasons did not actually *explain* the increase. Reasons 2 and 4 merely described the characteristics of welfare recipients.

24. Moynihan to Nixon, March 1, 1969, p. 4.

25. Ibid.

26. Memo, Moynihan to Nixon, March 13, 1969, folder 2/25/69–3/18/69, Box 1, WHCF: FG 6–12, NPM.

27. Though this was the widespread perception, it was in fact untrue. In 1969, 44 percent of AFDC recipients were African American (Gilens 1999, p. 106).

28. Arch Booth to Nixon, January 7, 1969, folder 2/11/69–3/11/69, Box 4, WHCF: EX FG 6–12, NPM.

29. Memo, Alexander Butterfield to John Ehrlichman and Herbert Klein, March 27, 1969, folder 3/19/69–4/14/69, Box 1, WHCF: FG 6–12, NPM.

30. Memo, Burns to Nixon, April 1, 1969, folder 3/31/69–4/30/69, Box 1, WHCF: EX WE, NPM.

31. Quoted in Burke and Burke (1974, p. 66).

32. Cover letter from Moynihan to Nixon included in a report titled "Domestic Proposals," April 1, 1969, folder CF WE 10–5, Box 69, White House Staff Files (hereafter WHSF): [CF]: WE, NPM.

33. "Report of the Committee on Welfare of the Council for Urban Affairs," April 4, 1969, p. 5, folder CF WE 10–5, Box 69, WHSF: [CF]: WE, NPM.

34. Ibid.

35. Burke and Burke (1974, p. 67).

36. Memo, Alexander Butterfield to Ehrlichman, April 14, 1969, folder Welfare Proposals (1 of 2), Box 40, WHSF: Ehrlichman, NPM.

37. Martin Anderson, "A Short History of a 'Family Security System,'" April 14, 1969, folder Welfare Proposals (2 of 2), Box 40, WHSF: Ehrlichman, NPM.

38. Ibid.

39. For a competing account of the Speenhamland episode and its effects, see Block and Somers (2003).

40. Memo, Moynihan to Nixon, April 22, 1969, memo, McCracken to Nixon, April 24, 1969, and Shultz to Nixon, May 7, 1969, all in folder Welfare Proposals (2 of 2), Box 40, WHSF: Ehrlichman, NPM.

41. Memo, Shultz to Nixon, May 7, 1969, p. 2.

42. Memo, Burns to Nixon, April 21, 1969, folder Welfare Proposals (2 of 2), Box 40, WHSF: Ehrlichman, NPM.

43. Ibid., p. 6.

44. Ibid., p. 7.

45. Ibid., pp. 13, 14, 15.

46. Ibid., p. 25.

47. Moynihan to Nixon, March 13, 1969, p. 6.

48. Memo, Laird to Nixon, May 7, 1969, p. 1, folder Welfare Proposals (1 of 2), Box 40, WHSF: Ehrlichman, NPM.

49. Memo, Mayo to Nixon, April 28, 1969, folder Welfare Proposals (2 of 2), Box 40, WHSF: Ehrlichman, NPM; memo, Agnew to Ehrlichman, April 24, 1969, p. 3, folder Welfare Book, [FSS 1969], (1 of 2), Box 38, WHSF: Ehrlichman, NPM; memo, Kennedy to Nixon, April 28, 1969, folder Welfare Proposals (1 of 2), Box 40, WHSF: Ehrlichman, NPM.

50. Memo, Finch to Nixon, April 30, 1969, folder Welfare Proposals (2 of 2), Box 40, WHSF: Ehrlichman, NPM.

51. Ibid., p. 11.

52. Ibid.

53. "Questions and Answers on the Family Security System," n.d., attachment in memo, Finch to Ehrlichman, May 27, 1969, folder Welfare Book [Reports and Speeches], Box 38, WHSF: Ehrlichman, NPM.

54. Ibid., p. 3.

55. Ibid., p. 2.

56. Memo, McCracken to Nixon, April 25, 1969, p. 1, folder Welfare Proposals (1 of 2), Box 40, WHSF: Ehrlichman, NPM.

57. Memo, McCracken to Nixon, May 7, 1969, folder Welfare Proposals (1 of 2), Box 40, WHSF: Ehrlichman, NPM.

58. "Technical Evaluation of Income Maintenance Proposals," May 9, 1969, folder Welfare Proposals (1 of 2), Box 40, WHSF: Ehrlichman, NPM.

59. Memo, Stans to Nixon, May 7, 1969, memo, Charls Walker to Nixon, May 7, 1969, and memo, Melvin Laird to Nixon, May 7, 1969, all in folder Welfare Proposals (1 of 2), Box 40, WHSF: Ehrlichman, NPM.

60. Laird to Nixon, May 7, 1969, p. 1.

61. Finch to Nixon, April 30, 1969, p. 9.

62. By this point the USS had dropped out of the comparative analyses without comment, and Moynihan (1973) and Burke and Burke (1974) do not mention the plan at all.

63. Memo, McCracken to Nixon, May 24, 1969, folder Welfare Book [Reports and Speeches], Box 38, WHSF: Ehrlichman, NPM.

64. Memo, Burns to Nixon, June 6, 1969, folder WE-10, FSS, Begin–7/17/69, Box 60, WHCF: WE, NPM.

65. Memo, Moynihan to Nixon, June 6, 1969, p. 3, folder WE-10, FSS, Begin–7/17/69, Box 60, WHCF: WE, NPM.

66. Memo, Rumsfeld to Nixon, May 29, 1969, folder 5/1/69–7/31/69, Box 1, WHCF: EX WE, NPM.

67. Memo, Burns to Nixon, May 26, 1969, folder Welfare Book, Attitudes toward Welfare, Box 39, WHSF: Ehrlichman, NPM. The essence of the growing backlash is captured well in Lukas (1985) and Rieder (1985).

68. Quoted in Burns to Nixon, May 26, 1969, p. 2.

69. Ibid., p. 4.

70. Quoted in memo, Alexander Butterfield to Ehrlichman, June 2, 1969, folder Welfare Book, Attitudes toward Welfare, Box 39, WHSF: Ehrlichman, NPM.

71. Memo, John Whitaker to Dwight Chapin, April 25, 1969, Box 1, WHCF: EX FG 6–12, NPM.

72. Memo, Burns to Nixon, April 28, 1969, folder WE 10–5, FSS, Begin–7/17/69, Box 60, WHCF: WE, NPM.

73. Finch to Nixon, April 30, 1969.

74. Memo, Stephen Bull to Agnew et al., June 11, 1969, p. 3, folder 5/1/69–7/31/69, Box 1, WHCF: WE, NPM (emphasis in original).

75. Ibid., p. 2.

76. William J. Casey to Nixon, June 10, 1969, folder WE 10–5, FSS, Begin–7/17/69, Box 60, WHCF: WE, NPM.

77. Ibid.

78. Memo, Burns to Nixon, June 23, 1969, p. 2, folder WE 10–5, FSS, Begin–7/17/69, Box 60, WHCF: WE, NPM.

79. Ibid.

80. Bull to Agnew et al., June 11, 1969, p. 3.

81. Memo, Shultz to Nixon, June 10, 1969, folder Welfare Book, Report and Speeches (2 of 2), Box 38, WHSF: Ehrlichman, NPM.

82. Ibid., p. 1.

83. Shultz's examples have a striking similarity to the hypothetical examples, also based on economic maximizing, that critiques of the welfare state in the 1980s used in an attempt to cut back public assistance programs (see, for instance, Murray [1984], ch. 12). Though the implications they drew were different, the mode of analysis was almost identical.

84. Memo, Burns to Nixon, July 12, 1969, p. 4, Welfare Book, [FSS 1969], (1 of 2), Box 38, WHSF: Ehrlichman, NPM; memo, Edward L. Morgan to Ehrlichman, July 13, 1969, p. 2, Welfare Book, Reports and Speeches, Box 38, WHSF: Ehrlichman, NPM.

85. Memo, John R. Price to Moynihan, June 18, 1969, folder 6/13/69–6/30/69, Box 2, WHCF: EX FG 6–12, NPM.

86. Memo, Moynihan to Nixon, June 26, 1969, folder WE 10–5, FSS, Begin–7/17/69, Box 60, WHCF: WE, NPM.

87. Ibid.; Alfred C. Neal to Nixon, June 30, 1969, telegram, Harold E. Gray to Nixon, July 2, 1969, memo, Moynihan to Nixon, July 9, 1969, and Philip M. Klutznick to Nixon, July 14, 1969, all in folder WE 10–5, FSS, Begin–7/17/69, Box 60, WHCF: WE, NPM; and National Association of Manufacturers, "Incentives and the Welfare Programs," folder Family Assistance Plan, Box 63, WHSF: Colson, NPM.

88. Lindsay to Nixon, May 7, 1969, folder 5/1/69–7/31/69, Box 1, WHCF: EX WE, NPM.

89. Memo, Ehrlichman to Edward L. Morgan, July 10, 1969, folder Welfare Book, [FSS 1969], (1 of 2), Box 38, WHSF: Ehrlichman, NPM.

90. Memo, Burns to Nixon, July 12, 1969, folder Welfare Book, [FSS 1969], (1 of 2), Box 38, WHSF: Ehrlichman, NPM.

91. Burns stated, "The basic goal of a sound welfare reform program should be to help the individual become independent and self-sufficient. The current system has failed miserably in this respect. It has encouraged idleness instead of work. It has put the accent on relief, instead of rehabilitation. . . . The best way of ending dependency and rehabilitating people is through employment." Memo, Burns to

Nixon, July 14, 1969, p. 5, folder Welfare Book, [FSS 1969], (1 of 2), Box 38, WHSF: Ehrlichman, NPM.

92. Ibid., p. 11.

93. Morgan to Ehrlichman, July 13, 1969.

94. Memo, McCracken to Nixon, July 23, 1969, folder Welfare Book, [FSS 1969], (2 of 2), Box 38, WHSF: Ehrlichman, NPM.

95. Department of Health, Education, and Welfare, "Comments on Dr. Burns' Memorandum of July 12," July 14, 1969, folder Welfare Book, [FSS 1969], (1 of 2), Box 38, WHSF: Ehrlichman, NPM.

96. Ibid., p. 3 (emphasis in original).

97. Ibid., p. 10.

98. Report, James Lyday, July 28, 1969, attached in memo, Rumsfeld to Ehrlichman, July 29, 1969, folder 5/1/69–7/31/1969, Box 1, WHCF: WE, NPM. Lyday said that he did not evaluate the Burns plan because, since the plan left the AFDC program intact, it was impossible to estimate its costs and coverage, which were largely under the discretion of state officials.

99. Memo, Moynihan to Nixon, July 8, 1969, folder WE 10–5, FSS, Begin–7/17/69, Box 60, WHCF: WE, NPM.

100. Ibid.; memo, Butterfield to Moynihan, July 14, 1969, folder WE 10–5, FSS, Begin–7/17/69, Box 60, WHCF: WE, NPM.

101. Memo, Safire to Ehrlichman, July 15, 1969, folder Welfare Book, Name of Program, Box 39, WHSF: Ehrlichman, NPM.

102. Memo, Safire to Ehrlichman, July 18, 1969, p. 1, folder Welfare Book, Name of Program, Box 39, WHSF: Ehrlichman, NPM.

103. Memo, Burns to Nixon, July 21, 1969, p. 2, folder Welfare Book, Name of Program, Box 39, WHSF: Ehrlichman, NPM.

104. Memo, Jim Keogh to Nixon, August 6, 1969, folder Welfare Book, Reports and Speeches (2 of 2), Box 38, WHSF: Ehrlichman, NPM.

105. Memo, Agnew to Nixon, August 4, 1969, p. 1, folder Welfare Book, [FSS 1969], (2 of 2), Box 38, WHSF: Ehrlichman, NPM.

106. Ibid., p. 3.

107. Memo, Burns to Nixon, July 31, 1969, p. 1, folder Welfare Book, [FSS 1969], (2 of 2), Box 38, WHSF: Ehrlichman, NPM.

108. Memo, Burns to Nixon, August 4, 1969, p. 2, folder Welfare Book, [FSS 1969], (2 of 2), Box 38, WHSF: Ehrlichman, NPM.

109. Rockefeller to Nixon, July 14, 1969, folder WE 10–5, 7/18/69–9/30/69, Box 61, WHCF: WE, NPM.

110. Memo, Burns to Nixon, July 19, 1969, memo, Moynihan to Nixon, July 21, 1969, and memo, John R. Price to Moynihan, July 29, 1969, all in folder WE 10–5, 7/18/69–9/30/69, Box 61, WHCF: WE, NPM.

111. Handwritten notes, John Ehrlichman, n.d., folder Welfare Book, Congressional Briefings, Box 39, WHSF: Ehrlichman, NPM.

112. Memo, Alexander Butterfield to All Cabinet Members, August 7, 1969, folder Welfare Book, Congressional Briefing, Box 39, WHSF: Ehrlichman, NPM. See also Burke and Burke (1974, pp. 101–7).

113. Butterfield to All Cabinet Members, August 7, 1969, p. 8.

114. Handwritten notes, John Ehrlichman, n.d., folder Welfare Book, Domestic Speech, Box 39, WHSF: Ehrlichman, NPM.

115. "Transcript of Nixon's Address to Nation Outlining Proposals for Welfare Reform," *New York Times*, August 8, 1969, p. 10. The quotes in the remainder of the section are all taken from the same page of the article.

116. Quoted in Moynihan (1973, p. 270).

CHAPTER FOUR
NIXON'S FAMILY ASSISTANCE PLAN STALLS

1. Burke and Burke (1974, p. 130).

2. This was not inevitable; it was context specific. For a comparison, see Myles and Pierson's (1997) discussion of the development of GAI policies in Canada during the same era, which did not connote "welfare" reform.

3. Ehrlichman (1982, p. 264). On Nixon's concern with control over media depiction of his administration and its programs, see Hoff (1994) and McGinniss (1988).

4. Memo, Bryce Harlow to Staff Secretary, August 11, 1969, folder 8/1/69–9/30/69, Box 1, WHCF: WE, NPM.

5. Telegram, Herbert Klein to Martin Hayden et al., August 9, 1969, folder 8/1/69–9/30/69, Box 1, WHCF: WE, NPM; memo, Klein to Edward L. Morgan, August 9, 1969, folder Welfare Book, Congressional Briefing, Box 39, WHSF: Ehrlichman, NPM; memo, Margita White to Ken Cole, August 22, 1969, folder 8/1/69–9/30/69, Box 1, WHCF: WE, NPM; John Price, "Record of Action for the Sixteenth Meeting, Council for Urban Affairs," August 25, 1969, 8/1/69–9/39/69, Box 2, WHCF: EX FG 6–12, NPM.

6. Memo, Art Klebanoff to Moynihan, September 5, 1969, folder WE 10–5, 7/18/69–9/30/69, Box 61, WHCF: WE, NPM.

7. "Editorial/Column Analysis, President's Welfare Proposals," August 20, 1969, attachment in memo, Ken Cole to Arthur Burns et al., September 22, 1969, folder Welfare Book, Reports and Speeches, Box 38, WHSF: Ehrlichman, NPM.

8. Memo, Tod Hullin to Ehrlichman, August 12, 1969, folder Welfare Book, Reaction 1969, Box 39, WHSF: Ehrlichman, NPM. Letters to the White House are not, of course, a nationally representative sample of public sentiments. But they do reveal the grounds on which letter writers base their policy preferences. Moreover, in the absence of widespread public opinion data during this period, constituents' letters, along with news articles and editorials, were the primary way in which presidential administrations gauged public opinion (Lee 2002).

9. Memo, Noble M. Melencamp to John Brown, September 11, 1969, folder WE 10–5, 7/18/69–9/30/69, Box 61, WHCF: WE, NPM.

10. Moynihan (1973, p. 268). Data on public attitudes toward GAI proposals were sparse prior to 1969, so it is difficult to gauge the effect of Nixon's rhetoric in public attitudes. However, the limited data suggest that his framing strategies were influential because prior to his announcement there was relatively weak support for GAI proposals. A Gallup poll from 1968 showed that only 36 percent of respondents favored a GAI proposal while 78 percent supported a plan that provided guaranteed jobs at the same level of income (Moynihan 1973, p. 245). Another study described the public

as "hugely opposed," based on a May 1968 Gallup poll that showed that even low-income respondents favored GAI proposals at levels under 50 percent (Wildavsky and Cavala 1970, p. 349).

11. Memo, Ehrlichman to Nixon, August 12, 1969, folder WE 10–5, 7/18/69–9/30/69, Box 61, WHCF: WE, NPM.

12. For studies that discuss the role of the South in the New Deal, see, for instance, Alston and Ferrie (1999), Amenta (1998), and Quadagno (1994). On the influence of the South in Congress, see Rae (1994).

13. "Memo to State Chairmen and Members of the National Committee of the Southern States," August 11, 1969, folder Welfare Book, Reaction 1969, Box 39, WHSF: Ehrlichman, NPM.

14. On Nixon's southern strategy, see Frymer and Skrentny (1998), Rieder (1989), and Shulman (2001, pp. 35–42).

15. Memo, Harry Dent to Ehrlichman, August 11, 1969, folder Welfare Book, Reaction 1969, Box 39, WHSF: Ehrlichman, NPM.

16. Alston and Ferrie (1999); Lieberman (1998).

17. Reese (2005).

18. Richard Armstrong, "The Looming Money Revolution Down South," *Fortune*, June 1970. Officials within the White House, including Nixon, Ehrlichman, and Moynihan, were aware of the article. See memo, Ehrlichman to Nixon, July 7, 1969, folder WE 10–5, 7/1/70–12/70, Box 61, WHCF: WE, NPM.

19. Armstrong, "Looming Money Revolution," p. 68.

20. Ibid.

21. Myles and Pierson (1997).

22. Armstrong, "Looming Money Revolution," p. 152.

23. Ibid.

24. Neubeck and Cazenave (2001); Reese (2005).

25. Neubeck and Cazenave (2001, p. 99).

26. Quadagno (1994, p. 131).

27. Ibid., pp. 128–29.

28. Armstrong, "Looming Money Revolution," p. 68.

29. Ibid.

30. Ehrlichman (1982, p. 228).

31. Moynihan (1973, p. 263).

32. Telegram, Young to Moynihan, August 8, 1969, folder Welfare Book, Reaction 1969, Box 39, WHSF: Ehrlichman, NPM.

33. For instance, Moynihan briefed many leaders within the black community on the FAP in the days leading up to Nixon's announcement. See memo, Stephen Hess to Staff Secretary, August 9, 1969, folder WE 10–5, 7/18/69–9/30/69, Box 61, WHCF: WE, NPM.

34. Memo, Ken Cole to Moynihan and Ehrlichman, September 9, 1969, memo, Moynihan to Cole, September 17, 1969, and its attachment, Bob Distefano, "Poverty Warriors Rap Nixon Policies," *Oakland Tribune*, September 13, 1969, p. 3E, all in folder Welfare Book, Notes and Memos, 1969–1970, Box 39, WHSF: Ehrlichman, NPM.

35. This account of the trajectory of the NWRO's views of the FAP draws from Kornbluh (2000).

36. Quoted in Kornbluh (2000, p. 169).

37. Nixon's close advisors provide considerable evidence from their private conversations with him of Nixon's prejudiced racial views (Ehrlichman 1982; Haldeman 1994), and his "southern strategy" was widely recorded in the press.

38. Kornbluh (2000).

39. Matusow (1998).

40. The trajectory of the chamber's political activity during these months is drawn from the discussion in Moynihan (1973, ch. 4) and from the following: on the chamber's early disinterest in the FAP relative to other issues, see memo, Ehrlichman to Nixon, November 25, 1969, folder 11/1/69–12/9/69, Box 3, WHCF: EX FG 6–12, NPM; for the chamber's increased interest by the following February, see memo, Don Webster to Lamar Alexander, February 19, 1970, folder Family Assistance Plan, Box 63, WHSF: Colson, NPM; and memo, Webster to Edward L. Morgan, February 20, 1970, folder WE 10–5, 2/12/70–2/28/70, Box 61, WHCF: WE, NPM.

41. On the chamber's opinion polling, see memo, Webster to Morgan, March 11, 1970, folder 3/1/70–3/31/70, Box 61, WHCF: WE, NPM; on their public relations strategy, see memo, Webster to Morgan, April 3, 1970, folder WE 10–5, 4/1/70–6/30/70, Box 61, WHCF: WE, NPM.

42. Letter and attachment, Charles Harbaugh to Webster, March 13, 1970, folder Family Assistance Plan, Box 63, WHSF: Colson, NPM; Arch N. Booth to Nixon, April 3, 1970, folder WE 10–5, 4/1/70–6/30/70, Box 61, WHCF: WE, NPM.

43. "Special Report on Welfare," attachment in Harbaugh to Webster, March 13, 1970, p. 3.

44. Booth to Nixon, April 3, 1970, pp. 1–3. Moynihan (1973, p. 289) notes the same reason for opposition—the inclusion of the working poor—from the Chamber of Commerce in House Ways and Means Committee testimony.

45. This recognition of uncertainty was widely noted. The CED made a similar point in its research report *supporting* GAI proposals during the same month. See "Improving the Public Welfare System," April 1970, Research and Policy Committee of the Committee for Economic Development, folder 4/1/70–4/21/70, Box 2, WHCF: EX WE, NPM.

46. Press release, Office of the White House Press Secretary, February 18, 1970, p. 2, folder Family Assistance Plan, Box 63, WHSF: Colson, NPM.

47. Memo, Webster to Morgan, March 20, 1970, folder 3/1/70–3/31/70, Box 61, WHCF: WE, NPM.

48. The discussion of NAM draws from National Association of Manufacturers, "Incentives and the Welfare Programs," n.d., folder Family Assistance Plan, Box 63, WHSF: Colson, NPM; and memo, Morgan to Webster, March 3, 1970, and memo, Morgan to Webster, March 5, 1970, both in folder 3/1/70–3/31/70, Box 61, WHCF: WE, NPM.

49. Moynihan (1973, p. 288). For an account of the origins of the CED, see Schriftgiesser (1967).

50. "Improving the Public Welfare System."

51. Ibid., p. 9. On the press coverage of the CED report, see Moynihan (1973, p. 288).

52. Press release, National Federation of Independent Business, Inc., March 17, 1970, p. 1, folder 3/1/70–3/31/70, Box 61, WHCF: WE, NPM.

53. Report, National Federation of Independent Business, Inc., n.d., pp. 2–3, attached in memo, Webster to Morgan, April 13, 1969, folder 4/1/70–6/30/70, Box 61, WHCF: WE, NPM. The federation mailed the report to each member of Congress.

54. Burch (1973).

55. Barton (1985).

56. Moynihan (1973, p. 289).

57. Martin (1995).

58. Moynihan (1973, p. 278).

59. Quoted in Moynihan (1973, p. 281).

60. Webster to Morgan, March 20, 1970.

61. Burke and Burke (1974, p. 138ff.); Klein (2003); Moynihan (1973, p. 274).

62. Moynihan to Cole, September 17, 1969.

63. According to Matusow (1998, p. 3), "Nixon courted no businessman, or even all of them put together, as assiduously as he courted [Meany]."

64. These sentiments were expressed by Meany in a conversation with Charles Colson; see memo, Colson to Haldeman, October 7, 1970, folder Family Assistance Plan, Box 63, WHSF: Colson, NPM.

65. Memo, Webster to Morgan, March 25, 1970, p. 2, folder WE 10–5, 3/1/70–3/31/70, Box 61, WHCF: WE, NPM.

66. "Welfare Reform Fact Sheet," August 8, 1969, pp. 7–8, folder Welfare Book, President's Proposals for Welfare Reform, Box 38, WHSF: Ehrlichman, NPM.

67. On the concerns of the big-city mayors, see memo, Ehrlichman to Nixon, November 3, 1969, folder WE 10–4 10/1/69–2/11/70, Box 61, WHSF: WE, NPM; for the endorsement from the National Association of Counties, see Webster to Morgan, March 25, 1970.

68. Quoted in Ehrlichman to Nixon, November 3, 1969.

69. Memo, Webster to Morgan, March 3, 1970, folder WE 10–5, 3/1/70–3/31/70, Box 61, WHCF: WE, NPM.

70. On the response to the FAP from these civic groups, see Burke and Burke (1974, ch. 7) and Moynihan (1973, ch. 4). The quote from the American Jewish Committee's lobbyist appears in Moynihan (1973, p. 300). On the notoriety of the quote, see John Price to Hyman Bookbinder, November 24, 1969, folder WE 10–5, 10/1/69–2/11/70, Box 61, WHCF: WE, NPM.

71. Ehrlichman (1982); Hoff (1994); Moynihan (1973).

72. Memo, Harlow to Ehrlichman, July 28, 1969, folder 5/1/69–7/31/69, Box 1, WHCF: EX WE, NPM; memo and attachment, Kay to Susan, n.d., WE 10–5, 7/18/69–9/30/69, Box 61, WHCF: WE, NPM.

73. "Welfare Reform Fact Sheet."

74. Moynihan (1973, p. 352).

75. Bowler (1974, p. 124); Moynihan (1973).

76. Memo, Moynihan to Ehrlichman, August 19, 1969, folder Welfare Book, Reports and Speeches (2 of 2), Box 38, WHSF: Ehrlichman, NPM; memo, Moynihan to Nixon, September 26, 1969, folder WE 10–5, 7/18/69–9/30/69, Box 61, WHCF: WE, NPM; Heineman quoted in memo, Moynihan to Nixon, November 12, 1969, folder WE 10–5, 10/1/69–2/11/70, Box 61, WHCF: WE, NPM.

77. This paragraph and the following one draw on Moynihan's account (1973, pp. 402–17).

78. Moynihan (1973, p. 404).

79. On Mills's political influence, see Zelizer (1998).

80. Memo, John Price to Moynihan, November 6, 1969, memo, Moynihan to Nixon, November 14, 1969, both in folder WE 10–5, 10/1/69–2/11/70, Box 61, WHSF: WE, NPM.

81. Memo, Moynihan to Mayo, January 15, 1969, folder Welfare Book, Family Assistance 1970, Box 38, WHSF: Ehrlichman, NPM; memo, John Price to Staff Secretary, January 26, 1970, folder WE 10–5, 10/1/69–2/11/70, Box 61, WHSF: WE, NPM.

82. See Ehrlichman (1982, p. 207) and Burke and Burke (1974) on Nixon's domestic priorities. For just one of dozens of documents outlining the detailed legislative strategy undertaken by the administration and its allies, see memo, Morgan to Ehrlichman, January 13, 1970, folder WE 10–5, 10/1/69–2/11/70, Box 61, WHSF: WE, NPM.

83. Morgan to Ehrlichman, January 13, 1970.

84. Memo, Harlow to Staff Secretary, January 26, 1970, folder WE 10–5, 10/1/69–2/11/70, Box 61, WHSF: WE, NPM.

85. Webster to Morgan, February 20, 1970, p. 2.

86. Press conference transcript, Office of the White House Press Secretary, February 18, 1970, folder Family Assistance Plan, Box 63, WHSF: Colson, NPM. Rumsfeld quoted on p. 2.

87. Memo, Webster to Morgan, February 27, 1970, folder WE 10–5, 2/12/70–2/28/70, Box 61, WHCF: WE, NPM.

88. According to my media analysis, the fiscal management frame made up about 24 percent of the framing discourse while work frames made up 19 percent.

89. Memo, Moynihan to Nixon, January 20, 1970, p. 1, folder Welfare Book, Notes and Memos, 1969–1970, Box 39, WHSF: Ehrlichman, NPM.

90. Quoted in memo, Burns to Ehrlichman, December 4, 1969, folder Welfare Book, Reports and Speeches, Box 38, WHSF: Ehrlichman, NPM.

91. Ibid.

92. Memo, Ehrlichman to Burns, December 5, 1969, folder Welfare Book, Reports and Speeches, Box 38, WHSF: Ehrlichman, NPM.

93. Memo, Moynihan to Nixon, January 31, 1970, p. 1, folder Welfare Book, Notes and Memos, 1969–1970, Box 39, WHSF: Ehrlichman, NPM.

94. United Press International, "Mills Staff Report Critical of Nixon Welfare Reform," New York Times, January 25, 1970, p. 1.

95. Webster to Morgan, February 20, 1970; memo, HEW to Nixon, February 27, 1970, folder WE 10–5, 2/12/70–2/28/70, Box 61, WHCF: WE, NPM.

96. Moynihan (1973, ch. 6).

97. On Reagan's reversal, see memo, Webster to Morgan, March 9, 1970, folder WE 10–5, 3/1/70–3/31/70, Box 61, WHCF: WE, NPM. The other activities are discussed elsewhere in the chapter, and memos on them are found in folders WE 10–5, 3/1/70–3/31/70 and WE 10–5, 4/1/70–6/30/70, Box 61, WHCF: WE, NPM.

98. "Deeper and Deeper Still," National Review, March 24, 1970, p. 293. This article was also circulated within the White House by the Nixon staff; see memo and attachments, Webster to Morgan, March 26, 1970, folder WE 10–5, 3/1/70–3/31/70, Box 61, WHCF: WE, NPM.

99. The following discussion of the House floor debates draws on Moynihan (1973, pp. 428–38).

100. Quoted in Moynihan (1973, p. 433).

101. Moynihan (1973, pp. 430–38).

102. Warren Weaver, "Welfare: Not Going According to the Script," *New York Times*, May 10, 1970, sec. IV, p. 4; Burke and Burke (1974, p. 157).

103. Caro (2002); Rae (1994).

104. Burke and Burke (1974, p. 153).

105. On Long and Williams, see memo, Webster to Morgan, March 13, 1970, and memo, Webster to Morgan, March 19, 1970, both in folder WE 10–5, 3/1/70–3/31/70, Box 61, WHCF: WE, NPM. On Ribicoff and his amendments, see memo, Moynihan to Bill Timmons, April 28, 1970, folder Welfare Book, Miscellaneous, Box 39, WHSF: Ehrlichman, NPM; and Moynihan (1973, p. 453).

106. Moynihan to Timmons, April 28, 1970.

107. The following account of these preliminary hearings draws on Burke and Burke (1974, pp. 152–57); Moynihan (1973, ch. 7); "Nixon Welfare Plan Attacked in Senate by Both Liberals and Conservatives," *New York Times*, April 30, 1970, p. 22; and William Weaver, "Senators Block Welfare Reform and Ask for Revisions," *New York Times*, May 2, 1970, p. 1.

108. Quoted in Burke and Burke (1974, p. 157).

109. Memo, Moynihan to Nixon, May 11, 1970, folder WE 10–5, 4/1/70–6/30/70, Box 61, WHCF: WE, NPM.

110. Memo, Webster to Moynihan, July 15, 1970, and memo, Morgan to Ehrlichman, July 16, 1970, both in folder WE 10–5, 7/1/70–12/70, Box 61, WHCF: WE, NPM.

111. Memo, Moynihan to Nixon, July 10, 1970, folder WE 10–5, 7/1/70–12/70, Box 61, WHCF: WE, NPM.

112. Finch's entire tenure at HEW had been embattled and he collapsed from mental strain in June. Nixon reassigned him to work in the White House. This paragraph and the following are based on Burke and Burke's (1974, pp. 157–58) account of the Senate hearings.

113. Quoted in Burke and Burke (1974, p. 158).

114. Webster to Morgan, March 11, 1970; memo, Moynihan to Nixon, July 21, 1970, folder WE 10–5, 7/1/70–12/70, Box 61, WHCF: WE, NPM; Long quoted in memo, Moynihan to Nixon, August 6, 1970, folder WE 10–5, 7/1/70–12/70, Box 61, WHCF: WE, NPM.

115. Memo, Elliot Richardson to Nixon, August 8, 1970, folder WE 10–5, 7/1/70–12/70, Box 61, WHCF: WE, NPM.

116. Memo, John G. Veneman to Nixon, September 2, 1970, folder WE 10–5, 7/1/70–12/70, Box 61, WHCF: WE, NPM.

117. Ibid.; memo, Moynihan and Bill Timmons to Nixon, September 4, 1970, folder WE 10–5, 7/1/70–12/70, Box 61, WHCF: WE, NPM.

118. Memo, Moynihan to Nixon, June 4, 1970, folder CF FG 23 (HEW) 1969–1970, Box 20, WHSF: WHCF: [CF], NPM.

119. Memo, Charles Colson to H. R. Haldeman, October 7, 1970, folder Family Assistance Plan, Box 63, WHSF: Colson, NPM.

120. "Welfare Reform: The Family Assistance Act," Department of Health, Education, and Welfare, November 1970, p. B3, folder Welfare Book, Family Assistance, 1970, Box 38, WHSF: Ehrlichman, NPM.

121. Memo, Howard Cohen and Robert Patricelli to Richardson, October 12, 1970, folder WE 10–5, 7/1/70–12/70, Box 61, WHCF: WE, NPM. The members they expected support from were Republican senators Wallace Bennett, Jack Miller, and Clifford Hansen and Democratic senators Russell Long, Clinton Anderson, Abraham Ribicoff, Fred Harris, Eugene McCarthy, and J. William Fulbright.

122. This account of the NWRO hearings draws from Burke and Burke (1974, pp. 161–65) and Davies (1996, ch. 9).

123. Quoted in Burke and Burke (1974, p. 162).

124. Burke and Burke (1974, p. 162); see also Piven and Cloward (1977, pp. 345–46).

125. Davies (1996, p. 229).

126. Burke and Burke (1974, p. 165).

CHAPTER FIVE
DEFEAT AND ITS POLICY LEGACY

1. "Transcript of President's State of the Union Message to Joint Session of Congress," *New York Times*, January 23, 1971, p. 12.

2. For instance, see Lukas's (1985) book, *Common Ground*, for a journalistic account of the politics of school desegregation set within the broader context of racial and urban politics in the 1960s and 1970s. For a more analytical discussion, see Edsall and Edsall (1991).

3. Martin Gilens contends that welfare came to be viewed as a "black" program in part because the national media overrepresented African Americans as welfare recipients in their pictorial images that accompanied news stories about welfare and poverty. This overrepresentation hit its apex in 1972, when approximately 75 percent of pictures that accompanied news stories about poverty contained images of blacks, while in reality only 30 percent of the poor were African American (Gilens 1999, p. 114).

4. On the economic climate at the time, see Matusow (1998).

5. Memo, Anderson to Nixon, January 21, 1971, folder WE 10–5, Family Security Plans, 1/1/71–12/72, Box 62, WHCF: WE, NPM. By this point, Arthur Burns, another arch opponent, had been appointed chair of the Federal Reserve Board.

6. For accounts of the differences between the two bills, see Bowler (1974, ch. 5), Burke and Burke (1974, ch. 8), and Handler (1972, ch. 6).

7. Memo, Richard Nathan to Shultz and Ehrlichman, June 14, 1971, folder WE 6/1/71–6/30/71, Box 8, WHCF: WE, NPM.

8. Bowler (1974, ch. 6); Burke and Burke (1974, p. 166).

9. Hansen to Nixon, February 10, 1971, folder WE 10–5, Family Security Plans, 1/1/71–12/72, Box 62, WHCF: WE, NPM.

10. Memo, Bill Timmons to Shultz and Ehrlichman, March 25, 1971, folder WE 10–5, Family Security Plans, 1/1/71–12/72, Box 62, WHCF: WE, NPM.

11. "Draft Statement for the President on H.R. 1," folder WE 5/16/71–5/31/71, Box 8, WHCF: WE, NPM.

12. Letter and attachment, Mrs. Warren A. Kline to Nixon, April 22, 1971, p. 1 of attachment (emphasis in original), folder WE 5/16/71–5/31/71, Box 8, WHCF: WE, NPM.

13. Ibid., p. 1 (of letter).

14. Memo, Haldeman to Ehrlichman, May 18, 1971, folder WE 5/16/71–5/31/71, Box 8, WHCF: WE, NPM; memo, Tod Hullin to Staff Secretary, July 14, 1971, folder WE 10–5, Family Security Plans, 1/1/71–12/72, Box 62, WHCF: WE, NPM.

15. "Welfare Reform—H.R. 1," attachment in memo, Arthur Kimball to Tod Hullin, May 21, 1971, folder WE 5/16/71–5/31/71, Box 8, WHCF: WE, NPM.

16. Burke and Burke (1974, pp. 131, 171–72).

17. Lester M. Salamon, "Family Assistance: The Stakes in the Rural South," *New Republic*, February 20, 1971.

18. Ibid., p. 17.

19. Ibid., p. 18.

20. Chant and song lyrics quoted in Burke and Burke (1974, p. 173). The NWRO's efforts are also described in Kornbluh (2000) and Kotz and Kotz (1977).

21. Burke and Burke (1974, ch. 8); Moynihan (1973, ch. 4).

22. See Burke and Burke (1974, p. 174) and Moynihan (1973, p. 445) on the NWRO legislation and its projected effects on the economy.

23. Warren Weaver, Jr., "House Approves Welfare Reform by 288–132 Vote," *New York Times*, June 23, 1971, p. 1.

24. Memo, Hodgson to Elliot Richardson, n.d., folder WE 7/1/71–7/31/71, Box 8, WHCF: WE, NPM.

25. Memo, Richard Nathan to Ehrlichman, July 20, 1971, p. 2, folder WE 7/1/71–7/31/71, Box 8, WHCF: WE, NPM.

26. Ibid.

27. In an eventual concession to conservatives, Nixon ended up vetoing a national child-care bill in 1971 that would have expanded national day care provision well into the middle class (Morgan 2001; Quadagno 1994). His veto kept child-care provision restricted to the existing welfare population.

28. Alvin Schorr, "The Case for Federal Welfare," *Nation*, May 3, 1971, p. 555.

29. E.g., "Welfare: America's No. 1 Problem—An Interview with California's Ronald Reagan," *U.S. News and World Report*, March 1, 1971, p. 36.

30. Memo, Ronald Reagan to All California Members of Congress, June 18, 1971, folder WE 6/1/71–6/30/71, Box 8, WHCF: WE, NPM.

31. Memo, Ehrlichman to Richardson, June 25, 1971, folder WE 6/1/71–6/30/71, Box 8, WHCF: WE, NPM.

32. Memo, Richardson to Nixon, June 30, 1971, p. 9, folder WE 7/1/71–7/31/71, Box 8, WHCF: WE, NPM.

33. Ibid., p. 8 (emphasis added).

34. Ibid., p. 6.

35. Memo, Ken Cole to the President's File, August 2, 1971, folder 8/1/71–8/10/71, Box 8, WHCF: WE, NPM.

36. Burke and Burke (1974, p. 179); memo, Ehrlichman to Nixon, n.d., folder 8/25/71–8/31/71, Box 8, WHCF: WE, NPM.

37. Burke and Burke (1974, p. 180).

38. Ogilvie to Reagan, August 25, 1971, p. 1, folder 8/25/71–8/31/71, Box 8, WHCF: WE, NPM. A senator from Illinois also went on record on the issue, saying that although he supported the FAP in principle, the poor people of his state could not wait until 1973 for help (Burke and Burke 1974, p. 181).

39. Daniel Evans to Ehrlichman, September 3, 1971, folder 9/1/71–9/10/71, Box 8, WHCF: WE, NPM.

40. Burke and Burke (1974).

41. Memo, Richard Nathan to Director and Deputy Director, July 14, 1971, and memo, Nathan to Ehrlichman, July 20, 1971, both in folder WE 7/1/71–7/31/71, Box 8, WHCF: WE, NPM.

42. Bella Abzug et al. to Nixon, October 4, 1971, folder 11/20/71–11/31/71, Box 9, WHCF: WE, NPM.

43. The interest groups included such influential ones as the League of Women Voters, Common Cause, Americans for Democratic Action, the AFL-CIO, the United Auto Workers, AFSCME, the National Association of Social Workers, the American Jewish Committee, and the National Conference of Catholic Charities (Burke and Burke 1974, p. 180).

44. "An Examination of the Written Message," New York Times, January 21, 1972, p. 5; Marjorie Hunter, "Curb Is Planned in Welfare Bill," New York Times, July 21, 1972, p. 20; "Excerpts from President Nixon's Budget Message as Presented to Congress," New York Times, January 25, 1972, p. 17.

45. Burke and Burke (1974, p. 183).

46. Berkowitz (1984, p. 31). On how Reagan's welfare reform ideas aligned with his broader pro-business political strategy in California, see McGirr (2001).

47. On Long's criticisms, for instance, see " 'Fraud and Bad Management': A Senator Reports on Welfare," U.S. News and World Report, April 3, 1972; and "Payrolls, Not Relief Rolls—Latest Welfare Proposal," U.S. News and World Report, May 15, 1972.

48. Marjorie Hunter, "Senate Unit Puts 'Must Work' Plan into Relief Bill," New York Times, April 29, 1972, p. 1.

49. Quoted in Marjorie Hunter, "Ribicoff Decries Long's Relief Bill," New York Times, April 28, 1972, p. 24; Richardson quoted in ibid.

50. Bowler (1974, p. 131). Bowler was a former American Political Science Association Congressional Fellow in Ribicoff's office in 1970–71.

51. Quoted in Hunter, "Senate Unit Puts 'Must Work' Plan into Relief Bill," p. 13.

52. Goodwin (1972). The book was reviewed in the New Republic, among other places.

53. Ibid., p. 117.

54. Quoted in Burke and Burke (1974, p. 185).

55. "Transcript of the President's New Conference Emphasizing Domestic Matters," New York Times, June 23, 1972, p. 14.

56. For instance, as Lynn and Whitman (1981, p. 30) point out, a compromise with Ribicoff, who was an advisor to McGovern's presidential campaign, might have threatened a closer association with McGovern's "extravagant" view of welfare reform, even though both candidates were supporting versions of a GAI policy.

57. Memo, Ehrlichman to Nixon, June 1, 1972, WE 10–5, Family Security Plans, 1/1/71–12/72, Box 62, WHCF: WE, NPM. This lack of enthusiasm for the welfare issue was apparent to the press as well. In the June 22 news conference on domestic affairs, reporters' first question about welfare to Nixon was, "Mr. President, how badly do you want a welfare bill to pass Congress?" See "Transcript of the President's New Conference Emphasizing Domestic Matters."

58. Quoted in Edwin L. Dale, Jr., "McGovern Income Plan Ridiculed by a Nixon Aide," *New York Times*, June 18, 1972, p. 1. For an example of continuing criticism through the summer, see James T. Wooten, "G.O.P. Study Sees a Big Deficit in McGovern Fiscal Proposal," *New York Times*, August 17, 1972, p. 24.

59. Robert Reinhold, "Scholars Starting to Advise McGovern," *New York Times*, June 18, 1972, p. 28; Leonard Silk, "McGovern Tax Proposal," *New York Times*, June 29, 1972, p. 28.

60. Quoted in "Excerpts from Senator McGovern's Address Explaining His Economic Program," *New York Times*, August 30, 1972, p. 22.

61. For a more detailed discussion of factors that may have contributed to McGovern's policy reversal, see Davies (1996, ch. 9) and Lynn and Whitman (1981, ch. 2).

62. Quotes from the Republican platform appear in "Excerpts from Platform Approved by G.O.P. Resolutions Panel for the Convention," *New York Times*, August 22, 1972, p. 35; a related article on the platform contained its rejection of a GAI policy in the lead paragraph: John Herbers, "Platform Appeals to the Right But Adds Liberal Stands," *New York Times*, August 21, 1972, p. 21. Nixon is quoted in Robert Semple, Jr., "President Scores 'Welfare Ethic,' " *New York Times*, September 4, 1972, p. 1.

63. E.g., Steven V. Roberts, "Welfare: Explosive Issues for '72," *New York Times*, September 10, 1972, sec. 4, p. 6.

64. Ribicoff's final amendments were more moderate than those he had proposed earlier; for instance, his benefit level for a family of four under the October 4 amendments was $2,600, only $200 higher than Nixon's FAP. Noting the similarities between the two bills, Ribicoff interpreted Nixon's continuing refusal to endorse his plan as a sign that Nixon preferred to have a campaign issue rather than welfare reform. For members of Congress, the defeat of the amendments was viewed as a defeat of the Nixon plan as well. See Marjorie Hunter, "Senate Rejects a Welfare Plan," *New York Times*, October 4, 1972, p. 24.

65. See Quadagno (1988, ch. 6) and Burke and Burke (1974, ch. 9) on the development of SSI legislation.

66. There were three major state-run categorical programs for adults: Old Age Assistance, Aid to the Blind, and Aid to the Partially and Totally Disabled.

67. "Transcript of Nixon's Acceptance Address and Excerpts from Agnew's Speech," *New York Times*, August 24, 1972, p. 47.

68. Burke and Burke (1974, p. 197).

69. Howard (1999, p. 67). This account of the development of the EITC relies on Howard's analysis.

70. Quoted in Howard (1999, p. 69).

71. For this reason, a Nixon administration official had, in the immediate wake of the FAP's defeat, recommended that future legislation refer to benefits for the working poor as "income supplements" and not "welfare." See Richard Nathan, "What Went

Wrong with FAP: Should We Give Up?" (paper presented to the National Conference on Social Welfare, May 28, 1973, Atlantic City, NJ), folder WE 10–5, Family Security Plans, 1/1/73–[7/74], Box 62, WHCF: WE, NPM.

72. See Leman (1980, pp. 90–94).

CHAPTER SIX
CARTER AND THE PROGRAM FOR BETTER JOBS AND INCOME

1. Nick Kotz, "The Politics of Welfare Reform," *New Republic*, May 14, 1977, p. 18.

2. Press conference transcript, Office of the White House Press Secretary, May 2, 1977, p. 17, folder Welfare Reform, Box 25, WHCF: Martha Mitchell, Jimmy Carter Library (hereafter JCL).

3. On social learning, see Heclo (1974) and Hall (1993).

4. On "second-order" policy change, see Hall (1993). On employment policy developing during this era, see Weir (1992).

5. Pierson (1993).

6. Kotz, "Politics of Welfare Reform"; Califano (1981, ch. 8); and Lynn and Whitman (1981, ch. 3). For an example of Carter's campaign literature, see his letter to Mayor Abraham Beame of New York: Carter to Beame, May 25, 1976, folder 5/77, Box 318, Domestic Policy Staff (hereafter DPS): Eizenstat, JCL.

7. On the "trusteeship" presidency, see Jones (1988). Other accounts of Carter's presidential style and its influence on domestic policy decisions include Califano (1981), Shulman (2001), and the chapters collected in Fink and Graham (1998).

8. On Carter's rationale for comprehensive reform, see Shulman (2001) and Sugrue (1998).

9. Fink and Graham (1998). The quote appears in memo, Tom Joe to Stu Eizenstat, May 11, 1977, p. 1, folder 5/77, Box 317, DPS: Eizenstat, JCL.

10. Handwritten note on memo, Jack Watson to Carter, February 9, 1977, folder WE 10 Ex: 1/20/77–4/30/77, Box WE 13, WHCF: WE, JCL.

11. Memo, Hamilton Jordan to Carter, n.d., folder Welfare Reform, Box 37, WHCF: Jordan, JCL.

12. Kotz, "Politics of Welfare Reform"; Califano (1981, ch. 8). Califano is quoted in Lynn and Whitman (1981, p. 36).

13. Lynn and Whitman (1981, p. 32) discuss the rate of increase in AFDC enrollments. The other descriptive data are taken from Current Population Survey (CPS) data, as reported in a HEW briefing book located in memo, Califano to Carter, March 23, 1977, folder 3/23/77, Box 13, Staff Secretary, JCL. Trends in the unemployment and poverty rates were found in Paper #4, pp. 5–8; poverty threshold data in Paper #4, pp. 2–6; longitudinal data on household head, sex, and race in Paper #4, pp. 5–12.

14. Press release, "Statement by Joseph A. Califano, Jr.," January 26, 1977, p. 3, folder 1/1/77, Box 317, DPS: Eizenstat, JCL.

15. Ibid., p. 2.

16. Handwritten note, Carter to Califano, February 3, 1977, folder 2/77, Box 317, DPS: Eizenstat, JCL; memo, Califano to Carter, February 5, 1977, folder WE 10 Ex: 1/20/77–4/30/77, Box WE 13, WHCF: WE, JCL.

17. Aaron (1973).

18. Lynn and Whitman (1981, p. 49).

19. For an extended discussion of target efficiency, see Papers #1 and #4 in the welfare briefing book, Califano to Carter, March 23, 1977.

20. Califano to Carter, March 23, 1977; see Paper #1, p. 10. The DOL proposal was significantly different in a number of ways from "workfare" programs, such as those Senator Long preferred, which restricted coverage to families with children and provided only low-wage, low-skill jobs in order to encourage movement into the private sector.

21. Quoted in Lynn and Whitman (1981, p. 51).

22. On the social meaning of money, especially in regard to public assistance, see V. Zelizer (1994, ch. 4.).

23. See Carter to Beame, May 25, 1976.

24. Tom Joe, "Designing a Three-Tiered Approach to Welfare Reform," January 12, 1977, folder 1/21/77, Box 4, Staff Secretary, JCL.

25. Tom Joe, "Double Social Utility: The Needy Serving Others in Need through a Job Creation Strategy," March 1977, folder 4/77, Box 317, DPS: Eizenstat, JCL. Burke and Burke (1974) and Lynn and Whitman (1981) both discuss Joe's policy objectives.

26. Joe, "Designing a Three-Tiered Approach to Welfare Reform," pp. 2–3.

27. Ibid., p. 2.

28. Califano to Carter, March 23, 1977, p. 1.

29. Ibid.; see especially Papers #1 and #5.

30. Carter quotes are taken from Kotz, "The Politics of Welfare Reform," pp. 18, 19.

31. Memo, Califano to James Schlesinger, March 31, 1977, folder 4/77, Box 19, WHCF: Schlesinger, JCL.

32. Memo, Eizenstat and Frank Raines to Carter, April 8, 1977, folder 4/77, Box 317, DPS: Eizenstat, JCL.

33. Carter quote in Kotz, "The Politics of Welfare Reform," p. 19.

34. Ibid.

35. Memo, Califano to Carter, April 11, 1977, folder WE 10 Ex: 1/20/77–4/30/77, Box WE 13, WHCF: WE, JCL.

36. Califano to Carter, March 23, 1977; see also Califano (1981) and memo, Califano to Carter, October 20, 1977, folder 8/77, Box 318, DPS: Eizenstat, JCL.

37. Memo, Jim Parham to Jack Watson, April 15, 1977, p. 1, folder 4/22/77 [1], Box 20, Staff Secretary, JCL.

38. See also memo, Frank Raines to Eizenstat, April 15, 1977, folder 4/77, Box 317, DPS: Eizenstat, JCL.

39. Memo, Jack Watson and Jim Parham to Carter, April 15, 1977, p. 2, folder WE 10 Ex: 1/20/77–4/30/77, Box WE 13, WHCF: WE, JCL.

40. Memo, Eizenstat et al. to Carter, April 26, 1977, folder 4/77, Box 317, DPS: Eizenstat, JCL; memo, Jack Watson and Jim Parham to Carter, April 26, 1977, folder WE 10 Ex: 1/20/77–4/30/77, Box WE 13, WHCF: WE, JCL. On Schultze's involvement, see Lynn and Whitman (1981, ch. 5).

41. "Statement by the President," Office of the White House Secretary, May 2, 1977, p. 1, folder 5/77 [2], Box 318, DPS: Eizenstat, JCL. The lead paragraph of

the *New York Times'* coverage emphasized comprehensive overhaul as well: David E. Rosenbaum, "Carter Would Scrap Welfare Programs for a New System," *New York Times*, May 3, 1977, p. 1.

42. Quoted in Lynn and Whitman (1981, p. 137). Califano notes his own reaction to Carter's statement in Califano (1981, pp. 341–42).

43. "Statement by the President," p. 1.

44. The reporter, Nick Kotz, had been a close follower of welfare reform since the Nixon administration, and he and his wife had just completed a biography of George Wiley and the NWRO. His question appears in the transcript of the press conference: "Question and Answer Session," Office of the White House Press Secretary, May 2, 1977, p. 11, folder Welfare Reform, Box 25, WHCF: Martha Mitchell, JCL. The reaction from the HEW expert is quoted in Lynn and Whitman (1981, p. 138).

45. "Question and Answer Session," p. 7.

46. Ibid., p. 16.

47. Memo, Califano to Carter, May 19, 1977, folder 5/77 [1], Box 317, DPS: Eizenstat, JCL.

48. See Lynn and Whitman (1981, pp. 146–56) for a discussion of this debate.

49. Memo, Joe to Eizenstat, May 18, 1977, p. 3, folder 5/77 [1], Box 317, DPS: Eizenstat, JCL.

50. Memo, Jack Watson and Jim Parham to Carter, May 23, 1977, p. 1, folder 5/77 [2], Box 318, DPS: Eizenstat, JCL (emphasis in original).

51. Memo, Jim Parham to Aaron and Packer, June 6, 1977, p. 1, folder WE 10 Ex: 6/1/77–7/31/77, Box WE 13, WHCF: WE, JCL (emphasis in original).

52. Watson and Parham to Carter, May 23, 1977, p. 2.

53. Memo, Eizenstat to Carter, May 25, 1977, folder 5/77 [2], Box 318, DPS: Eizenstat, JCL.

54. Ibid.

55. Long and Moynihan both quoted in Lynn and Whitman (1981, p. 143).

56. Press release, "Statement of Secretary Joseph A. Califano, Jr. on Welfare Reform," Department of Health, Education, and Welfare, May 25, 1977, folder 5/77 [2], Box 318, DPS: Eizenstat, JCL; David E. Rosenbaum, "President Stresses Welfare Limit Despite Warning," *New York Times*, May 27, 1977, p. A11.

57. Quoted in David E. Rosenbaum, "28 Groups Protest Welfare Fund Curb," *New York Times*, July 6, 1977, p. 15.

58. Quote in memo, Vernon Jordan to Carter, July 30, 1977, folder 8/77 [2], Box 41, Staff Secretary, JCL; memo, Bruce Kirschenbaum to Eizenstat, July 26, 1977, folder 7/77 [3], Box 318, DPS: Eizenstat, JCL.

59. On the underclass, see Katz (1989, ch. 5) and O'Connor (2001, ch. 10).

60. AP story attached in memo, Eizenstat and Robert Malson to Carter, July 27, 1977, folder National [1/77–12/78], Box Urban League, WHCF: Names Files, JCL.

61. Margaret Costanza to Carter, July 29, 1977, folder 7/30/77, Box 41, Staff Secretary, JCL.

62. Ibid.

63. Lynn and Whitman (1981, pp. 176–77).

64. Memo, Jim Parham to Carter, July 6, 1977, folder WE 10 Ex: 6/1/77–7/31/77, Box WE 13, WHCF: WE, JCL; memo, William Spring to Bert Carp, July 13, 1977, p. 4, folder 7/77, Box 18, DPS: Eizenstat, JCL (emphasis in original).

65. Memo, Packer to White House Staff, July 15, 1997, p. 2, folder 7/77, Box 318, DPS: Eizenstat, JCL. All five of these reasons can be located in this memo and in Spring to Carp, July 13, 1977; they are also discussed in Lynn and Whitman (1981).

66. Memo, Califano to Carter, July 25, 1977, folder 7/25/77, Box 40, Staff Secretary, JCL.

67. Ibid., pp. 4–20.

68. Ibid., pp. 21–32.

69. Memo, Eizenstat et al. to Carter, July 25, 1977, folder 8/77, Box 319, DPS; Eizenstat, JCL; memo, Joe to Eizenstat, July 27, 1977, folder 7/77, Box 318, DPS: Eizenstat, JCL; memo, Eizenstat to Carter, July 27, 1977, folder 7/28/77 [2], Box 41, Staff Secretary, JCL; memo, Jim Parham to Carter, July 27, 1977, folder WE 13 Ex: 6/1/77–7/31/77, Box WE 13, WHCF: WE, JCL.

70. Joe to Eizenstat, July 27, 1977; Califano to Carter, July 25, 1977; Parham to Carter, July 27, 1977; memo, Charlie Schultze to Carter, July 27, 1977, folder 8/77, Box 319, DPS: Eizenstat, JCL.

71. Eizenstat et al. to Carter, July 27, 1977, folder 8/77, Box 319, DPS: Eizenstat, JCL. Carter did not generally make extensive notes on the margins of his advisors' memos to him. However, in the two places in this memo where the White House staff recommended that the cutoff age for children be fourteen, Carter wrote "Long won't buy" and "Long will never buy this."

72. This account of the July 28 meeting draws on Califano (1981, pp. 348–49) and Lynn and Whitman (1981, pp. 215–16). Carter is quoted in Califano (1981, p. 348).

73. Quoted in Califano (1981, p. 349).

74. Memo, Long to Carter, August 3, 1977, folder 8/77, Box 319, DPS: Eizenstat, JCL. Carter's handwritten message to Eizenstat appears on the front sheet of Long's memo.

75. Ibid., p. 1 (emphasis in original).

76. Ibid., p. 3. Long's numbers may have been exaggerated for political effect, but not drastically. By the late 1970s, almost 50 percent of all women participated in the workforce (Patterson [1998, p. 122]).

77. Quoted in memo, Califano to Carter, August 1, 1977, p. 2, folder 8/77, Box 319, DPS: Eizenstat, JCL; memo, Eizenstat to Carter, August 1, 1977, folder 8/77, Box 319, DPS: Eizenstat, JCL.

78. Califano to Carter, August 1, 1977.

79. Memo, Eizenstat et al. to Carter, August 2, 1977, p. 2, and memo, Eizenstat and Frank Raines to Carter, August 2, 1977, both in folder 8/77, Box 319, DPS: Eizenstat, JCL. Califano quoted in Califano to Carter, August 1, 1977.

80. On Califano and Carter's overall concerns about fraud, see Califano (1981, ch. 8), Lynn and Whitman (1981), and handwritten note, Carter to Califano, March 15, 1977, folder 3/77, Box 317, DPS: Eizenstat. The HEW report and findings are cited in Rosenbaum, "28 Groups Protest Welfare Fund Curb." The quote on media depictions of fraud is contained in Raul Jimenez to Carter, April 27, 1977, folder WE 10 Gen: 7/1/77–12/31/77, Box WE 13, WHCF: WE, JCL.

81. Statement transcript, August 6, 1977, p. 1, folder 8/1/77–12/31/77, Box WE 13, WHCF: WE, JCL.

82. Ibid., p. 16.

83. Statement transcript, August 6, 1977.

84. The initial response to the plan is discussed in Califano (1981, p. 354) and Lynn and Whitman (1981, pp. 228–31).

85. Halle (1984); Rieder (1985). Both authors conducted their studies in the late 1970s in the New York/New Jersey area. For an example of letters to the White House expressing the same sentiments, see, for instance, Ruby J. Cravins to Carter, March 23, 1977, WE 10 Gen: 1/20/77–4/30/77, Box WE 13, WHCF: WE, JCL. For survey responses from the same time period on GAI policy and other economic issues, see Hochschild (1981).

86. Rieder (1985, p. 101).

87. Both these quotes are found in Lynn and Whitman (1981, p. 229).

88. Sitkoff (1981, p. 225); United Press International, "Urban League Chief Hails Two 'Signals' by Carter," *New York Times*, August 22, 1977, p. 21; quote appears in National Urban League press release, January 17, 1978, folder National [1/77–12/78], Box Urban League, WHCF: Names Files, JCL.

89. Statement, Lupe Anguiano to Ruth J. Abram et al., December 9, 1977, attachment in Frank Raines to Anguiano, February 8, 1978, folder WE 10 Gen: 1/1/78–12/31/78, Box WE 13, WHCF: WE, JCL.

90. U.S. Chamber of Commerce, "High Employment and Income Maintenance Policy," attachment in Cabell Brand to Frank Raines, November 15, 1977, folder 11/1/77–12/31/77, Box LA 2, WHCF: Labor-Management, JCL.

91. Labor concerns cited in Lynn and Whitman (1981, pp. 193, 231).

92. Lynn and Whitman (1981, pp. 231–35; Long quoted on p. 232).

93. Memo, Califano to Carter, November 30, 1977, folder 12/1/77, Box 61, Staff Secretary, JCL; see also memo, Eizenstat and Frank Raines to Carter, November 8, 1977, memo, Califano to Carter, November 8, 1977, and memo, Eizenstat and Raines to Carter, November 30, 1977, all in folder 8/77, Box 318, DPS: Eizenstat, JCL.

94. Memo, Eizenstat and Bert Carp to Walter Mondale, November 23, 1977, folder 11/28/77 [2], Box 61, Staff Secretary, JCL; Califano (1981, p. 256). On Carter's diminishing commitment to welfare reform, see Lynn and Whitman (1981, p. 238), and David Rosenbaum, "Outlook Is Gloomy on Welfare Changes," *New York Times*, December 11, 1977, p. 1.

95. Memo, Eizenstat and Frank Moore to Carter, March 9, 1978, folder 10/1/77–6/30/78, Box Long, WHCF: Names Files, JCL; Califano (1981, pp. 360–61); Lynn and Whitman (1981, pp. 238–40).

96. Califano (1981, pp. 361–62); Lynn and Whitman (1981, pp. 240–49); Califano quote in memo, Califano to Carter, May 23, 1978, p. 3, 5/23/78 [1], Box 87, Staff Secretary, JCL.

97. On the California tax revolt, see Lo (1990), McGirr (2001), and Sears and Citrin (1982). Gilder (1981, pp. 119–22) also discusses Reagan's welfare rhetoric and aims.

98. Shulman (2001, ch. 8) discusses the increasingly national scope of the tax revolt.

99. Rabushka and Ryan (1982, pp. 36–39); Shulman (2001, pp. 211–12). Survey question and results quoted from Rabushka and Ryan (1982, p. 38). Claims about symbolic racism partially motivating the tax revolt are made by Sears and Citrin (1982).

100. Quoted in Califano (1981, p. 362).

101. Lynn and Whitman (1981, pp. 244–46); "Briefing Paper on Moynihan/Cranston/Long Bill," attachment in memo, Ben Heineman, Jr., to Eizenstat, July 12, 1978,

folder 8/77, Box 318, DPS: Eizenstat, JCL; Associated Press, "Welfare Bill Reported Dead for This Year," *New York Times*, June 23, 1978, p. 12.

102. Christopher Edley to Jay Urwitz, November 1, 1978, folder WE 10 Ex: 1/1/ 78–12/31/78, Box WE 13, WHCF: WE, JCL.

103. There have been over two hundred scholarly articles written about the NIT experiments (see Widerquist [2005] for a extensive bibliography). The edited volumes by Munnell (1986), Pechman and Timpane (1975), and Robins et al. (1980) provide good summaries of the key findings.

104. Notably, the government analysts who ran the program never established what level of work disincentives would be considered unacceptable (Widerquist [2005, p. 55]).

105. Quoted in Melinda Beck, "Welfare: A Surprising Test," *Newsweek*, November 27, 1978, p. 34.

106. E.g., Associated Press, "Experiment Finds Cash Grants Tend to Split Welfare Families," *New York Times*, May 21, 1978, p. 50.

107. Subsequently, the findings regarding family dissolution did produce a good deal of controversy among academics. See, for instance, the exchange between Cain and Wissoker (1990) and Hannan and Tuma (1990).

108. On discussion of the "independence effect" in the popular press, see, for instance, Beck, "Welfare: A Surprising Test"; "Some Negative Evidence about the Negative Income Tax," *Fortune*, December 4, 1978, p. 145; and Andrew Cherlin, "No Long Delay Needed," *New Republic*, December 17, 1978, p. 14.

109. "Poor Laws," *New Republic*, December 2, 1978, p. 8; Joe is quoted in Lynn and Whitman (1981, p. 248).

110. Quoted in Lynn and Whitman (1981, p. 248). On Moynihan's September 30, 1977, congressional testimony before the Special House Subcommittee on Welfare Reform, see the attachment to memo, Moynihan to Carter, September 30, 1977, folder 8/77, Box 318, DPS: Eizenstat, JCL.

111. On the family ethic, see Abramovitz (1988).

112. Orloff (2005) and others refer to this potential for greater women's independence as "defamilization" as a counterpart to the more familiar notion of decommodification in the labor market.

113. On these concerns, see Luker (1996).

114. Shulman (2001, pp. 185–89).

115. "Welfare Reform, Family Breakups," *National Review*, December 12, 1978, p. 1526; "Poor Laws," p. 8; Martin Anderson, "Welfare Reform on 'the Same Old Rocks,'" *New York Times*, November 27, 1978, p. 19.

116. Howard (1999).

117. Memo, Eizenstat et al. to Carter, May 15, 1979, folder 5/21/79 [3], Box 132, Staff Secretary, JCL; Califano (1981, p. 364).

118. Memo, Michael Barth to Florence Prioleau, February 1, 1980, folder Welfare Reform [CF O/A 732] [1], Box 317, DPS: Eizenstat, JCL. In reference to Anderson's portrayal of the NIT experiments' findings, Barth said, "He has misused these data in a major way in the past." And indeed, Anderson's *New York Times* op-ed piece exaggerated the numbers reported in all the other publications by manyfold. For these authors' discussions of the NIT experiments and welfare programs more generally, see Ander-

son (1978), Gilder (1981), and Murray (1984). On the influence of Gilder's book in the Reagan administration, see Katz (1989, ch. 4).

CHAPTER SEVEN
LOST OPPORTUNITIES, CONSEQUENCES, AND LESSONS

1. Marmor, Mashaw, and Harvey (1990); Page and Simmons (2000); Schwartz (1983).

2. Pierson (1996); also see Weir, Orloff, and Skocpol (1988).

3. E.g., Huntington (1981) and McCloskey and Zaller (1984).

4. On the competing values inherent in debates over racial policy, see Lieberman (2002) and Skrentny (1996).

5. On the early Reagan-era welfare reform initiatives, see Berkowitz (1984), Block et al. (1987), Joe (1984), and Patterson (1994).

6. Berkowitz (1984, p. 34).

7. See Davies (1996) on the programmatic and philosophical differences between the War on Poverty and guaranteed income approaches.

8. Berkowitz (1984, p. 30).

9. Quoted in Berkowitz (1984, p. 34).

10. Glazer (1988, p. 22). For a more detailed account of this trajectory, see O'Connor (2001).

11. O'Connor (2001) documents this transformation in poverty knowledge and its implications for policymaking. For discussions of these assumptions and the ways they shaped policy evaluations by practitioners at the time, see Kershaw (1970), Levine (1970), and Rivlin (1971). Each was a poverty expert within the government in the 1960s.

12. Murray (1984). See Katz (1989) on the influence of Murray's book within the Reagan administration and the broader policy community.

13. Anderson (1978).

14. Somers and Block (2005).

15. Murray (1984, pp. 160–61).

16. See Katz (1989) for an account of the response to Murray's book.

17. Mead (1986, p. 104). On the paternalistic perspective in social policy, see Mead (1997).

18. Mead (1986, p. 111). For a similar perspective, see Berkowitz (1984), who argues that the conservative welfare backlash was largely based on the threat to the work ethic seen in the Nixon plan.

19. For a fuller discussion of naturalization in debates over social policy, see Stone (1989).

20. Gilder (1981). On the book's influence, see Katz (1989, pp. 143–47).

21. E.g., Winston Davis, "The Gospel According to Gilder," *Christianity and Crisis*, February 1, 1982.

22. Berkowitz (1984, p. 31).

23. Mead (1986, p. 7).

24. Glazer (1988, p. 42).

25. Rank (2005, pp. 23, 31, 60–61).

26. For an early discussion, see the articles collected in *Theory and Society* 15, no. 5 (1986).

27. Van Parijs (1992, 2001).

28. Block and Manza (1997); Myles and Quadagno (2000).

29. See Alstott and Ackerman (1999). The grant would be financed by a 2 percent annual wealth tax and would emphasize that Americans have the responsibility of providing equal opportunity for all.

30. For discussion of GAI plans as part of a larger policy reform, see, for instance, Aronowitz (2005) and Page and Simmons (2000).

31. Murray (2006).

32. For feminist arguments along these lines, see Alstott (2001) and Pateman (2004); on participation income, see Atkinson (1996).

33. Van Parijs (1995).

34. Gilens (1999); Reese (2005).

35. See Epstein (1996) on "credibility struggles" over AIDS and scientific knowledge for a useful comparison. For the importance of gaining "standing" in the media and how it affects public discourse, see Ferree et al. (2002).

CHAPTER EIGHT
CULTURE AND WELFARE POLICY DEVELOPMENT

1. For evidence from interviews, see Halle (1984), Hochschild (1981), and Lamont (2000); from public opinion research, see Cook and Barrett (1992) and McCloskey and Zaller (1984); and from the analyses of organizational practices, see Mohr (1994). For historical examinations, see Handler and Hasenfeld (1991) and Katz (1986, 1989).

2. Adams, Clemens, and Orloff (2005a); Jasper (2005); Steinmetz (1999).

3. E.g., Foucault (1972, 1980). On poststructuralism within cultural sociology, see Wuthnow (1987).

4. Fraser's (1989) work is exemplary here and it informs more empirical work on social policy by scholars such as Gordon (1994), Mettler (1998), and O'Connor, Orloff, and Shaver (1999).

5. E.g., Clemens (1997); Dobbin (1994); Skrentny (1996); and Soysal (1994). For a review of this "sociological institutionalism" within studies of politics, see Hall and Taylor (1996), and for a collection of the seminal writings on neoinstitutionalism, see Powell and DiMaggio (1991).

6. Adams, Clemens, and Orloff (2005b); Hicks, Janoski, and Schwartz (2005).

7. Hicks, Janoski, and Schwartz (2005); Mahoney and Rueschmeyer (2003).

8. For examples of causal cultural arguments based on an explicitly comparative design, see Biernacki (1995), Dobbin (1994), and Skrentny (2002).

9. Even recent work that does place a greater emphasis on collective values has a more nuanced view of the impact of popular preferences on social policy and the interconnection among collective sentiments, institutional arrangements, and path dependency than does previous scholarship of this nature (e.g., Brooks and Manza [2006]).

10. For instance, for an extended critique of "reflection theories" as applied to three world-historical social transformations, see Wuthnow (1989).

11. Katz (1986).

12. See Carnoy (1984) and Eagleton (1991) on the variety of neo-Marxist approaches to understanding the relationship among capitalist interests, the state, and culture. Bergeson's (1993) discussion of "semiotic Marxism" provides an overview of Marxian work that is more heavily indebted to poststructuralism and literary theory, especially as represented by Laclau and Mouffe (1985).

13. This paraphrases one of the six definitions of ideology offered by Eagleton (1991, p. 29).

14. See Skocpol's (1985b) rejoinder to Sewell (1985) in their exchange over the role of culture and ideology in the French Revolution.

15. Gramsci (1971).

16. Carnoy (1984, p. 66); also see Eagleton (1991, pp. 112–20).

17. Katz (1986); Rodgers (1974).

18. Somers and Block (2005).

19. Brown (1999); Lieberman (1998).

20. On the racialization of welfare during the 1960s and whites' beliefs about blacks being lazy, see Gilens (1999) and Kellstedt (2003). On the racial dimension of welfare reform during the 1960s more broadly, see Quadagno (1994) and Neubeck and Cazenave (2001).

21. Sears and Citrin (1982) present evidence for the symbolic racism latent in the tax revolt. Also see Edsall and Edsall (1991, pp. 129–31).

22. Abramovitz (1988).

23. O'Connor, Orloff, and Shaver (1999, p. 35).

24. See Zerubavel (1991) and Lamont and Molnar (2002) on the constitutive nature of social categories, and Fraser (1989) and Starr (1992) on official categories and their influence.

25. Alexander and Smith (1993).

26. Gieryn (1983).

27. Katz (1986, p. 60).

28. Orloff (2005).

29. This synthesis can be seen, for instance, both in Amenta's (1998) historical work on U.S. social policy and in cross-national work by Huber, Ragin, and Stephens (1993) and Hicks and Misra (1993).

30. The first NIT proposal was in fact presented by a conservative economist as an alternative to minimum wage legislation (Stigler 1946).

31. This point is similar to Weir's claim that economic interests are heavily mediated by ideas and that analysts should thus seek not to identify economic interests per se but to discern why "some definitions of interests win out over others" (Weir 1992, p. 17).

32. Myles and Pierson (1997).

33. Skocpol (1992).

34. E.g., Amenta (1998) and Weir, Orloff, and Skocpol (1988).

35. Pierson (1993).

36. In their policy feedback discussion of the U.S. and Canadian cases, Myles and Pierson (1997) emphasize the "material" influence of policy legacies in contrast to the "symbolic" influence discussed here.

37. Goldstein and Keohane (1993).

38. See Amenta (1998, pp. 270–71) and Skocpol (1988).

39. Burstein (1998); Jacobs (1992).

40. Reich (1988).

41. Matt Bai, "The Framing Wars," *New York Times Sunday Magazine*, July 17, 2005, p. 38.

42. See Mead (1997).

43. Mead (1986, p. 111).

References

Aaron, Henry J. 1973. *Why Is Welfare So Hard to Reform?* Washington, DC: Brookings Institution.

―――. 1978. *Politics and the Professors: The Great Society in Perspective.* Washington, DC: Brookings Institution.

Abramovitz, Mimi. 1988. *Regulating the Lives of Women: Social Welfare Policy from Colonial Times to the Present.* Boston: South End Press.

Adams, Julia, Elisabeth S. Clemens, and Ann Orloff, eds. 2005a. *Remaking Modernity: Politics, History, and Sociology.* Durham: Duke University Press.

Adams, Julia, Elisabeth S. Clemens, and Ann Shola Orloff. 2005b. "Introduction: Social Theory, Modernity, and the Three Waves of Historical Sociology." Pp. 1–72 in *Remaking Modernity: Politics, History, and Sociology,* ed. Julia Adams, Elisabeth S. Clemens, and Ann Shola Orloff. Durham: Duke University Press.

Alexander, Jeffrey C. 1992. "Citizen and Enemy as Symbolic Classification: On the Polarizing Discourse of Civil Society." Pp. 289–308 in *Cultivating Differences: Symbolic Boundaries and the Making in Inequality,* ed. Michèle Lamont and Marcel Fournier. Chicago: University of Chicago Press.

Alexander, Jeffrey C., and Steven Seidman, eds. 1990. *Culture and Society: Contemporary Debates.* New York: Cambridge University Press.

Alexander, Jeffrey C., and Philip Smith. 1993. "The Discourse of American Civil Society: A New Proposal for Cultural Studies." *Theory and Society* 22:151–207.

Almond, Gabriel A., and Sidney Verba. 1963. *The Civil Culture: Political Attitudes and Democracy in Five Nations.* Princeton: Princeton University Press.

Alston, Lee J., and Joseph P. Ferrie. 1999. *Southern Paternalism and the American Welfare State.* New York: Cambridge University Press.

Alstott, Anne L. 2001. "Good for Women." Pp. 75–79 in *What's Wrong with a Free Lunch?* ed. Philippe Van Parijs. Boston: Beacon Press.

Alstott, Anne, and Bruce A. Ackerman. 1999. *The Stakeholder Society.* New Haven: Yale University Press.

Amenta, Edwin. 1998. *Bold Relief: Institutional Politics and the Origins of Modern American Social Policy.* Princeton: Princeton University Press.

Amenta, Edwin, Chris Bonastia, and Neal Caren. 2001. "U.S. Social Policy in Comparative and Historical Perspective." *Annual Review of Sociology* 27:213–34.

Amenta, Edwin, Neal Caren, and Sheera Joy Olasky. 2005. "Age for Leisure? Political Mediation and the Impact of the Pension Movement on U.S. Old-Age Policy." *American Sociological Review* 70:516–38.

Anderson, Martin. 1978. *Welfare: The Political Economy of Welfare Reform in the United States.* Stanford, CA: Hoover Institution.

Arendt, Hannah. 1958. *The Human Condition.* Chicago: University of Chicago Press.

Aronowitz, Stanley. 2005. *Just Around the Corner: The Paradox of the Jobless Recovery.* Philadelphia: Temple University Press.

Atkinson, A. B. 1996. "The Case for Participation Income." *Political Quarterly* 67: 67–70.

Banfield, Edward C. 1970. *The Unheavenly City: The Nature and Future of Our Urban Crisis*. Boston: Little, Brown.

Barton, Alan. 1985. "Determinants of Economic Attitudes on the American Business Elite." *American Journal of Sociology* 91:54–87.

Béland, Daniel. 2005. "Ideas and Social Policy: An Institutionalist Perspective." *Social Policy and Administration* 39:1–18.

Bell, Daniel. 1960. *The End of Ideology: On the Exhaustion of Political Ideas in the 1950s*. Glencoe, IL: Free Press.

Bergeson, Albert. 1993. "The Rise of Semiotic Marxism." *Sociological Perspectives* 36:1–22.

Berkowitz, Edward D. 1984. "Changing the Meaning of Welfare Reform." Pp. 23–42 in *Maintaining the Safety Net: Income Redistribution Programs in the Reagan Administration*, ed. John C. Weicher. Washington, DC: American Enterprise Institute.

———. 1991. *America's Welfare State: From Roosevelt to Reagan*. Baltimore: Johns Hopkins University Press.

Berkowitz, Edward D., and Kim McQuaid. 1980. *Creating the Welfare State: The Political Economy of Twentieth-Century Reform*. New York: Praeger.

Berlin, Isaiah. 1969. "Two Concepts of Liberty." Pp. 118–72 in *Four Essays on Liberty*, ed. Isaiah Berlin. New York: Oxford University Press.

Bernstein, Irving. 1991. *Promises Kept: John F. Kennedy's New Frontier*. New York: Oxford University Press.

———. 1996. *Guns or Butter: The Presidency of Lyndon Johnson*. New York: Oxford University Press.

Biernacki, Richard. 1995. *The Fabrication of Labor: Germany and Britain, 1640–1914*. Berkeley: University of California Press.

Block, Fred, Richard A. Cloward, Barbara Ehrenreich, and Frances Fox Piven. 1987. *The Mean Season: The Attack on the Welfare State*. New York: Pantheon.

Block, Fred, and Jeff Manza. 1997. "Could We End Poverty in a Postindustrial Society? The Case for a Progressive Negative Income Tax." *Politics and Society* 25:473–511.

Block, Fred, and Margaret R. Somers. 2003. "In the Shadow of Speenhamland: Social Policy and the Old Poor Law." *Politics and Society* 31:283–323.

Bowen, Howard R., and Garth L. Mangum, eds. 1966. *Automation and Economic Progress*. Englewood Cliffs, NJ: Prentice-Hall.

Bowler, Kenneth M. 1974. *The Nixon Guaranteed Income Proposal: Substance and Process in Policy Change*. Cambridge, MA: Ballinger.

Branch, Taylor. 1988. *Parting the Waters: America during the King Years, 1954–1963*. New York: Simon and Schuster.

Brauer, Carl M. 1982. "Kennedy, Johnson, and the War on Poverty." *Journal of American History* 69:98–119.

Brooks, Clem, and Jeff Manza. 2006. "Social Policy Responsiveness in Developed Democracies." *American Sociological Review* 71:474–94.

Brown, Michael K. 1999. *Race, Money, and the American Welfare State*. Ithaca, NY: Cornell University Press.

Burch, Phil. 1973. "The NAM as an Interest Group." *Politics and Society* 4:97–130.

Burke, Vincent J., and Vee Burke. 1974. *Nixon's Good Deed: Welfare Reform*. New York: Columbia University Press.

Burstein, Paul. 1991. "Policy Domains: Organization, Culture, and Policy Outcomes." *Annual Review of Sociology* 17:327–50.

———. 1998. "Bringing the Public Back In: Should Sociologists Consider the Impact of Public Opinion on Public Policy?" *Social Forces* 77:27–62.

Button, James. 1978. *Black Violence: Political Impact of the 1960s*. Princeton: Princeton University Press.

Cain, Glen G., and Douglas A. Wissoker. 1990. "A Reanalysis of Marital Stability in the Seattle-Denver Income-Maintenance Experiment." *American Journal of Sociology* 95:1235–69.

Califano, Joseph A., Jr. 1981. *Governing America: An Insider's Report from the White House and Cabinet*. New York: Simon and Schuster.

Callaghan, Karen, and Frauke Schnell, eds. 2005. *Framing American Politics*. Pittsburgh: University of Pittsburgh Press.

Campbell, John L. 1998. "Institutional Analysis and the Role of Ideas in Political Economy." *Theory and Society* 27:377–409.

———. 2002. "Ideas, Politics, and Public Policy." *Annual Review of Sociology* 28:21–38.

Carnoy, Martin. 1984. *State and Political Theory*. Princeton: Princeton University Press.

Caro, Robert A. 2002. *Master of the Senate: The Years of Lyndon Johnson*. New York: Knopf.

Clemens, Elisabeth. 1997. *The People's Lobby: Organizational Innovation and the Rise of Interest Group Politics in the United States*. Chicago: University of Chicago Press.

Clemens, Elisabeth S., and James M. Cook. 1999. "Politics and Institutionalism: Explaining Durability and Change." *Annual Review of Sociology* 25:441–66.

Cohen, Lizabeth. 2003. *A Consumers' Republic: The Politics of Mass Consumption in Postwar America*. New York: Knopf.

Cohen, Michael, James March, and Johan Olsen. 1972. "A Garbage Can Model of Organizational Choice." *Administrative Science Quarterly* 17:1–25.

Conlan, Timothy. 1988. *New Federalism: Intergovernmental Reform from Nixon to Reagan*. Washington, DC: Brookings Institution.

Cook, Fay Lomax, and Edith J. Barrett. 1992. *Support for the American Welfare State: The Views of Congress and the Public*. New York: Columbia University Press.

Davies, Gareth. 1996. *From Opportunity to Entitlement: The Transformation and Decline of Great Society Liberalism*. Lawrence: University of Kansas Press.

Davis, F. James. 1991. *Who Is Black? One Nation's Definition*. University Park: Pennsylvania State University Press.

Davis, Martha F. 1993. *Brutal Need: Lawyers and the Welfare Rights Movement, 1960–1973*. New Haven: Yale University Press.

Dobbin, Frank. 1994. *Forging Industrial Policy: The United States, Britain, and France in the Railway Age*. New York: Cambridge University Press.

Domhoff, G. William. 1990. *The Power Elite and the State: How Policy Is Made in America*. New York: Aldine de Gruyter.

Douglas, Mary. 1966. *Purity and Danger: An Analysis of the Concepts of Pollution and Taboo*. New York: Routledge.

Eagleton, Terry. 1991. *Ideology: An Introduction.* New York: Verso.

Edsall, Thomas Byrne, and Mary Edsall. 1991. *Chain Reaction: The Impact of Race, Rights, and Taxes on American Politics.* New York: W. W. Norton.

Ehrlichman, John. 1982. *Witness to Power: The Nixon Years.* New York: Simon and Schuster.

Entman, Robert M. 1993. "Framing: Toward Clarification of a Fractured Paradigm." *Journal of Communication* 43:51–58.

Epstein, Steven. 1996. *Impure Science: AIDS, Activism, and the Politics of Knowledge.* Berkeley: University of California Press.

Esping-Andersen, Gøsta. 1990. *The Three Worlds of Welfare Capitalism.* Princeton: Princeton University Press.

Ferree, Myra Marx, William A. Gamson, Jurgen Gerhards, and Dieter Rucht. 2002. *Shaping Abortion Discourse: Democracy and the Public Sphere in Germany and the United States.* New York: Cambridge University Press.

Fink, Gary M., and Hugh Davis Graham, eds. 1998. *The Carter Presidency: Policy Choices in the Post–New Deal Era.* Lawrence: University Press of Kansas.

Fligstein, Neil. 2001. "Social Skill and the Theory of Fields." *Sociological Theory* 19:105–25.

Foucault, Michel. 1972. *The Archaeology of Knowledge.* New York: Pantheon.

———. 1980. *Power/Knowledge: Selected Interviews and Other Writings, 1972–1977.* New York: Pantheon.

Fraser, Nancy. 1989. *Unruly Practices: Power, Discourse, and Gender in Contemporary Social Theory.* Minneapolis: University of Minnesota Press.

Friedman, Milton. 1962. *Capitalism and Freedom.* Chicago: University of Chicago Press.

Frymer, Paul, and John D. Skrentny. 1998. "Coalition-Building and the Politics of Electoral Capture during the Nixon Administration: African Americans, Labor, Latinos." *Studies in American Political Development* 12:131–61.

Galbraith, John Kenneth. 1984 [1958]. *The Affluent Society.* 4th ed. Boston: Houghton Mifflin.

Gamson, William A., and Andre Modigliani. 1989. "Media Discourse and Public Opinion on Nuclear Power: A Constructionist Approach." *American Journal of Sociology* 95:1–37.

Gieryn, Thomas F. 1983. "Boundary-Work and the Demarcation of Science from Non-Science: Strains and Interests in Professional Ideologies of Scientists." *American Sociological Review* 48:781–95.

Gilder, George. 1981. *Wealth and Poverty.* New York: Basic Books.

Gilens, Martin. 1999. *Why Americans Hate Welfare: Race, Media, and the Politics of Antipoverty Policy.* Chicago: University of Chicago Press.

Glazer, Nathan. 1988. *The Limits of Social Policy.* Cambridge, MA: Harvard University Press.

Goffman, Erving. 1963. *Stigma: Notes on the Management of Spoiled Identity.* Englewood Cliffs, NJ: Prentice Hall.

Goldstein, Judith, and Robert O. Keohane. 1993. "Ideas and Foreign Policy: An Analytical Framework." Pp. 3–30 in *Ideas and Foreign Policy: Beliefs, Institutions, and Political Change,* ed. Judith Goldstein and Robert O. Keohane. Ithaca, NY: Cornell University Press.

Goodin, Robert E., Bruce Headey, Ruud Muffels, and Henk-Jan Dirven. 1999. *The Real Worlds of Welfare Capitalism*. New York: Cambridge University Press.

Goodwin, Leonard. 1972. *Do the Poor Want to Work? A Social Psychological Study of Work Orientations*. Washington, DC: Brookings Institution.

Gordon, Linda. 1994. *Pitied But Not Entitled: Single Mothers and the History of Welfare, 1890–1935*. Cambridge, MA: Harvard University Press.

Gramsci, Antonio. 1971. *Selections from the Prison Notebooks*. New York: International Publishers.

Hacker, Jacob. 1996. *The Road to Nowhere: The Genesis of President Clinton's Plan for Health Security*. Princeton: Princeton University Press.

Hacker, Jacob, and Paul Pierson. 2002. "Business Power and Social Policy: Employers and the Formation of the American Welfare State." *Politics and Society* 30:277–325.

Haldeman, H. R. 1994. *The Haldeman Diaries: Inside the Nixon White House*. New York: G. P. Putnam's.

Hall, Peter. 1993. "Policy Paradigms, Social Learning, and the State: The Case of Economic Policy Making in Britain." *Comparative Politics* 25:275–96.

Hall, Peter, and Rosemary Taylor. 1996. "Political Science and the Three Institutionalisms." *Political Studies* 44:936–57.

Hall, Peter A., ed. 1989. *The Political Power of Economic Ideas: Keynesianism across Nations*. Princeton: Princeton University Press.

Halle, David. 1984. *America's Working Man: Work, Home, and Politics among Blue-Collar Property Owners*. Chicago: University of Chicago Press.

Handler, Joel F. 1972. *Reforming the Poor: Welfare Policy, Federalism, and Morality*. New York: Basic Books.

Handler, Joel F., and Yeheskel Hasenfeld. 1991. *The Moral Construction of Poverty: Welfare Reform in America*. Newbury Park, CA: Sage Publications.

Hannan, Michael T., and Nancy Brandon Tuma. 1990. "A Reassessment of the Effect of Income Maintenance on Marital Dissolution in the Seattle-Denver Experiment." *American Journal of Sociology* 95:1270–98.

Harrington, Michael. 1962. *The Other America: Poverty in the United States*. New York: Macmillan.

Heclo, Hugh. 1974. *Modern Social Politics in Britain and Sweden*. New Haven: Yale University Press.

Hicks, Alexander, and Joya Misra. 1993. "Political Resources and the Growth of Welfare in Affluent Capitalist Democracies, 1960–1982." *American Journal of Sociology* 99:668–710.

Hicks, Alexander, and Duane H. Swank. 1983. "Civil Disorder, Relief Mobilization, and AFDC Caseloads: A Reexamination of the Piven and Cloward Thesis." *American Journal of Political Science* 27:695–716.

Hicks, Alexander M., Thomas Janoski, and Mildred A. Schwartz. 2005. "Political Sociology in the New Millennium." Pp. 1–30 in *The Handbook of Political Sociology: States, Civil Societies, and Globalization*, ed. Thomas Janoski, Robert Alford, Alexander M. Hicks, and Mildred A. Schwartz. New York: Cambridge University Press.

Hochschild, Jennifer. 1981. *What's Fair? American's Attitudes toward Distributive Justice*. Cambridge, MA: Harvard University Press.

Hodgson, Godfrey. 2000. *The Gentleman from New York: Daniel Patrick Moynihan— A Biography*. New York: Houghton Mifflin.

Hoff, Joan. 1994. *Nixon Reconsidered*. New York: Basic Books.

Howard, Christopher. 1999. *The Hidden Welfare State: Tax Expenditures and Social Policy in the United States*. Princeton: Princeton University Press.

Huber, Evelyne, Charles Ragin, and John D. Stephens. 1993. "Social Democracy, Christian Democracy, Constitutional Structure, and the Welfare State." *American Journal of Sociology* 99:711–49.

Huntington, Samuel P. 1981. *American Politics: The Promise of Disharmony*. Cambridge, MA: Harvard University Press.

Iceland, John. 2003. *Poverty in America: A Handbook*. Berkeley: University of California Press.

Iyengar, Shanto. 1990. "Framing Responsibility for Political Issues: The Case of Poverty." *Political Behavior* 12:19–40.

Jacobs, Lawrence R. 1992. "Institutions and Culture: Health Policy and Public Opinion in the U.S. and Britain." *World Politics* 44:179–209.

Jamison, Andrew, and Ron Eyerman. 1994. *Seeds of the Sixties*. Berkeley: University of California Press.

Jasper, James M. 2005. "Culture, Knowledge, Politics." Pp. 115–34 in *The Handbook of Political Sociology: States, Civil Societies, and Globalization*, ed. Thomas Janoski, Robert Alford, Alexander M. Hicks, and Mildred A. Schwartz. New York: Cambridge University Press.

Jenkins, J. Craig, and Barbara G. Brents. 1989. "Social Protest, Hegemonic Competition, and Social Reform: A Political Struggle Interpretation of the Origins of the American Welfare State." *American Sociological Review* 54:891–909.

Jepperson, Ronald L., and Ann Swidler. 1994. "What Properties of Culture Should We Measure?" *Poetics* 22:359–71.

Joe, Tom. 1984. "Shredding an Already Tattered Safety Net." Pp. 189–202 in *Maintaining the Safety Net*, ed. John C. Weicher. Washington, DC: American Enterprise Institute.

Jones, Charles O. 1988. *The Trusteeship Presidency: Jimmy Carter and the United States Congress*. Baton Rouge: Louisiana State University Press.

Katz, Michael B. 1986. *In the Shadow of the Poorhouse: A Social History of Welfare in America*. New York: Basic Books.

———. 1989. *The Undeserving Poor: From the War on Poverty to the War on Welfare*. New York: Pantheon Books.

———. 2001. *The Price of Citizenship: Redefining the American Welfare State*. New York: Metropolitan Books.

Katz, Michael B., and Lorrin R. Thomas. 1998. "The Invention of 'Welfare' in America." *Journal of Policy History* 10:399–418.

Kellstedt, Paul M. 2003. *The Mass Media and the Dynamics of American Racial Attitudes*. New York: Cambridge University Press.

Kelman, Steven. 1981. *What Price Incentives: Economists and the Environment*. Boston: Auburn House.

Kershaw, Joseph A. 1970. *Government Against Poverty*. Washington, DC: Brookings Institution.

Kertzer, David I. 1988. *Ritual, Politics, and Power*. New Haven: Yale University Press.

Kingdon, John W. 1984. *Agendas, Alternatives, and Public Policies*. Boston: Little, Brown.

Klein, Jennifer. 2003. *For All These Rights: Business, Labor, and the Shaping of America's Public-Private Welfare State*. Princeton: Princeton University Press.

Kornbluh, Felicia. 2000. "A Right to Welfare? Poor Women, Professionals, and Poverty Programs, 1935–1975." Ph.D. diss., Princeton University.

Korpi, Walter. 1989. "Power, Politics, and State Autonomy in the Development of Social Citizenship: Social Rights during Sickness in Eighteen OECD Countries since 1930." *American Journal of Sociology* 54:309–28.

Kotz, Nick, and Mary Lynn Kotz. 1977. *Passion for Equality: George Wiley and the Movement*. New York: W. W. Norton.

Laclau, Ernesto, and Chantal Mouffe. 1985. *Hegemony and Socialist Strategy: Toward a Radical Democratic Politics*. London: Verso.

Lamont, Michèle. 2000. *The Dignity of Working Men: Morality and the Boundaries of Race, Class, and Immigration*. New York and Cambridge, MA: Harvard University Press and Russell Sage Foundation.

Lamont, Michèle, and Virag Molnar. 2002. "The Study of Boundaries in the Social Sciences." *Annual Review of Sociology* 28:167–95.

Lee, Taeku. 2002. *Mobilizing Public Opinion: Black Insurgency and Racial Attitudes in the Civil Rights Era*. Chicago: University of Chicago Press.

Leman, Christopher. 1980. *The Collapse of Welfare Reform: Political Institutions, Policy, and the Poor in Canada and the United States*. Cambridge, MA: MIT Press.

Lemann, Nicholas. 1991. *The Promised Land: The Great Black Migration and How It Changed America*. New York: Knopf.

Levine, Robert A. 1970. *The Poor, Ye Need Not Have with You: Lessons from the War on Poverty*. Cambridge, MA: MIT Press.

Lieberman, Robert C. 1998. *Shifting the Color Line: Race and the American Welfare State*. Cambridge, MA: Harvard University Press.

———. 2002. "Ideas, Institutions, and Political Order: Explaining Political Change." *American Political Science Review* 96:697–711.

Lipset, Seymour Martin. 1996. *American Exceptionalism: A Double-Edged Sword*. New York: W. W. Norton.

Lo, Clarence Y. H. 1990. *Small Property Versus Big Government: Social Origins of the Property Tax Revolt*. Berkeley: University of California Press.

Lukas, J. Anthony. 1985. *Common Ground: A Turbulent Decade in the Lives of Three American Families*. New York: Knopf.

Luker, Kristen. 1996. *Dubious Conceptions: The Politics of Teenage Pregnancy*. Cambridge, MA: Harvard University Press.

Lynn, Lawrence E., Jr., and David DeF. Whitman. 1981. *The President as Policy Maker: Jimmy Carter and Welfare Reform*. Philadelphia: Temple University Press.

Mahoney, James, and Dietrich Rueschmeyer. 2003. "Comparative Historical Analysis: Achievement and Agendas." Pp. 3–38 in *Comparative Historical Analysis in the Social Sciences*, ed. James Mahoney and Dietrich Rueschmeyer. New York: Cambridge University Press.

Mann, Robert. 1996. *The Walls of Jericho: Lyndon Johnson, Hubert Humphrey, Richard Russell and the Struggle for Civil Rights*. New York: Harcourt Brace.

Manza, Jeff. 2000. "Political Sociological Models of the U.S. New Deal." *Annual Review of Sociology* 26:297–322.

Marmor, Theodore R., Jerry L. Mashaw, and Phillip L. Harvey. 1990. *America's Misunderstood Welfare State: Persistent Myths, Enduring Realities*. New York: Basic Books.

Martin, Cathie Jo. 1995. "Nature or Nurture? Sources of Firm Preference for National Health Reform." *American Political Science Review* 89:898–913.

Matusow, Allen J. 1984. *The Unraveling of America: A History of Liberalism in the 1960s*. New York: Harper and Row.

———. 1998. *Nixon's Economy: Booms, Busts, Dollars, and Votes*. Lawrence: University Press of Kansas.

McAdam, Doug. 1982. *Political Process and the Development of Black Insurgency, 1930–1970*. Chicago: University of Chicago Press.

McCloskey, Herbert, and John Zaller. 1984. *The American Ethos: Public Attitudes toward Capitalism and Democracy*. Cambridge, MA: Harvard University Press.

McGinniss, Joe. 1988. *The Selling of the President*. New York: Penguin.

McGirr, Lisa. 2001. *Suburban Warriors: The Origins of the New American Right*. Princeton: Princeton University Press.

Mead, Lawrence. 1986. *Beyond Entitlement: The Social Obligations of Citizenship*. New York: Free Press.

Mead, Lawrence M., ed. 1997. *The New Paternalism: Supervisory Approaches to Poverty*. Washington, DC: Brookings Institution.

Melnick, R. Shep. 1994. *Between the Lines: Interpreting Welfare Rights*. Washington, DC: Brookings Institution.

Mettler, Suzanne. 1998. *Dividing Citizens: Gender and Federalism in New Deal Public Policy*. Ithaca, NY: Cornell University Press.

Mohr, John W. 1994. "Soldiers, Mothers, Tramps, and Others: Discourse Roles in the 1907 New York City Charity Directory." *Poetics* 22:327–57.

Moller, Stephanie, Evelyn Huber, John D. Stephens, David Bradley, and Francois Nielson. 2003. "Determinants of Relative Poverty in Advanced Capitalist Democracies." *American Sociological Review* 68:22–51.

Morgan, Kimberly. 2001. "A Child of the Sixties: The Great Society, the New Right, and the Politics of Federal Child Care." *Journal of Policy History* 13:215–50.

Moynihan, Daniel P. 1973. *The Politics of a Guaranteed Income: The Nixon Administration and the Family Assistance Plan*. New York: Vintage Books.

Munnell, Alicia H., ed. 1986. *Lessons from the Income Maintenance Experiments*. Boston: Federal Reserve Bank of Boston.

Murray, Charles. 1984. *Losing Ground: American Social Policy, 1950–1980*. 2nd ed. New York: Basic Books.

———. 2006. *In Our Hands: A Plan to Replace the Welfare State*. Washington, DC: AEI Press.

Myles, John, and Paul Pierson. 1997. "Friedman's Revenge: The Reform of 'Liberal' Welfare States in Canada and the United States." *Politics and Society* 25:443–72.

Myles, John, and Jill Quadagno. 2000. "Envisioning a Third Way: The Welfare State in the Twenty-first Century." *Contemporary Sociology* 29:156–67.

Neubeck, Kenneth J., and Noel A. Cazenave. 2001. *Welfare Racism: Playing the Race Card against America's Poor*. New York: Routledge.

Neuman, Russell W., Marion R. Just, and Ann N. Crigler. 1992. *Common Knowledge: News and the Construction of Political Meaning*. Chicago: University of Chicago Press.

O'Connor, Alice. 2001. *Poverty Knowledge: Social Science, Social Policy, and the Poor in Twentieth-Century U.S. History*. Princeton: Princeton University Press.

O'Connor, Julia S., Ann Shola Orloff, and Sheila Shaver. 1999. *States, Markets, Families: Gender, Liberalism and Social Policy in Australia, Canada, Great Britain and the United States*. New York: Cambridge University Press.

Orloff, Ann, and Theda Skocpol. 1984. "Why Not Equal Protection? Explaining the Politics of Public Social Spending in Britain, 1900–1911, and the United States, 1880s–1920." *American Sociological Review* 49:726–50.

Orloff, Ann Shola. 1993. *The Politics of Pensions: A Comparative Analysis of Britain, Canada, and the United States, 1880–1940*. Madison: University of Wisconsin Press.

———. 1999. "Motherhood, Work, and Welfare in the United States, Britain, Canada, and Australia." Pp. 321–54 in *State/Culture: State-Formation after the Cultural Turn*, ed. George Steinmetz. Ithaca, NY: Cornell University Press.

———. 2005. "Social Provision and Regulation: Theories of States, Social Policies, and Modernity." Pp. 190–224 in *Remaking Modernity: Politics, History, and Sociology*, ed. Julia Adams, Elisabeth S. Clemens, and Ann Shola Orloff. Durham: Duke University Press.

Page, Benjamin I., and James R. Simmons. 2000. *What Government Can Do: Dealing with Poverty and Inequality*. Chicago: University of Chicago Press.

Parsons, Talcott, and Edward A. Shils, eds. 1951. *Toward a General Theory of Action: Theoretical Foundations for the Social Sciences*. New York: Harper Torchbooks.

Pateman, Carole. 2004. "Democratizing Citizenship: Some Advantages of Basic Income." *Politics and Society* 32:89–105.

Patterson, James T. 1994. *America's Struggle against Poverty, 1900–1994*. Cambridge, MA: Harvard University Press.

———. 1996. *Great Expectations: The United States, 1945–1974*. New York: Oxford University Press.

———. 1998. "Jimmy Carter and Welfare Reform." Pp. 117–57 in *The Carter Presidency: Policy Choices in the Post–New Deal Era*, ed. Gary M. Fink and Hugh Davis Graham. Lawrence: University Press of Kansas.

Pechman, Joseph A., and Michael T. Timpane, eds. 1975. *Work Incentives and Income Guarantees: The New Jersey Negative Income Tax Experiment*. Washington, DC: Brookings Institution.

Pedriana, Nicholas, and Robin Stryker. 1997. "Political Culture Wars 1960s Style: Equal Employment Opportunity–Affirmative Action Law and the Philadelphia Plan." *American Journal of Sociology* 103:633–91.

Pells, Richard. 1985. *The Liberal Mind in a Conservative Age: American Intellectuals in the 1940s and 1950s*. New York: Harper and Row.

Peterson, Paul E., and Mark C. Rom. 1990. *Welfare Magnets: A New Case for a National Standard*. Washington, DC: Brookings Institution.

Pierson, Paul. 1993. "When Effect Becomes Cause: Policy Feedback and Political Change." *World Politics* 45:595–628.

———. 1996. "The New Politics of the Welfare State." *World Politics* 48:143–79.

Piven, Frances Fox, and Richard A. Cloward. 1977. *Poor People's Movements: Why They Succeed, How They Fail*. New York: Vintage Books.

———. 1993 [1971]. *Regulating the Poor: The Functions of Public Welfare*. New York: Vintage.

Powell, Walter W., and Paul D. DiMaggio, eds. 1991. *The New Institutionalism in Organizational Analysis*. Chicago: University of Chicago Press.

Quadagno, Jill. 1984. "Welfare Capitalism and the Social Security Act of 1935." *American Sociological Review* 49:632–47.

———. 1988. *The Transformation of Old Age Security: Class and Politics in the American Welfare State*. Chicago: University of Chicago.

———. 1990. "Race, Class, and Gender in the U.S. Welfare State: Nixon's Failed Family Assistance Plan." *American Sociological Review* 55:11–28.

———. 1992. "Social Movements and State Transformation: Labor Unions and Racial Conflict in the War on Poverty." *American Sociological Review* 57:616–34.

———. 1994. *The Color of Welfare: How Racism Undermined the War on Poverty*. New York: Oxford University Press.

Rabushka, Alvin, and Pauline Ryan. 1982. *The Tax Revolt*. Stanford, CA: Hoover Institution.

Rae, Nicol C. 1994. *Southern Democrats*. New York: Oxford University Press.

Rainwater, Lee, and William L. Yancey. 1967. *The Moynihan Report and the Politics of Controversy*. Cambridge, MA: MIT Press.

Rank, Mark Robert. 2005. *One Nation, Underprivileged*. New York: Oxford University Press.

Reese, Ellen. 2005. *Backlash against Welfare Mothers: Past and Present*. Berkeley: University of California Press.

Reich, Charles. 1964. "The New Property." *Yale Law Journal* 73:733–87.

Reich, Robert B., ed. 1988. *The Power of Public Ideas*. Cambridge, MA: Harvard University Press.

Rhoads, Steven. 1985. *The Economist's View of the World*. New York: Cambridge University Press.

Rieder, Jonathan. 1985. *Canarsie: The Jews and Italians of Brooklyn against Liberalism*. Cambridge, MA: Harvard University Press.

———. 1989. "The Rise of the 'Silent Majority.' " Pp. 243–68 in *The Rise and Fall of the New Deal Order*, ed. Steve Fraser and Gary Gerstle. Princeton: Princeton University Press.

Rimlinger, Gaston V. 1971. *Welfare Policy and Industrialization in Europe, America, and Russia*. New York: John Wiley.

Rivlin, Alice. 1971. *Systematic Thinking for Social Action*. Washington, DC: Brookings Institution.

Robins, Philip K., Robert G. Spiegelman, Samuel Weiner, and Joseph Bell, eds. 1980. *A Guaranteed Annual Income: Evidence from a Social Experiment*. New York: Academic Press.

Rodgers, Daniel T. 1974. *The Work Ethic in Industrial America, 1985–1920*. Chicago: University of Chicago Press.

Rueschmeyer, Dietrich, and Theda Skocpol, eds. 1996. *States, Social Knowledge, and the Origins of Modern Social Policies*. Princeton: Princeton University Press.

Ryan, William. 1971. *Blaming the Victim*. New York: Pantheon.

Schlesinger, Arthur M., Jr. 1965. *A Thousand Days: John F. Kennedy in the White House*. Boston: Houghton Mifflin.

Schneider, Anne, and Helen Ingram. 1993. "Social Construction of Target Populations: Implications for Politics and Policy." *American Political Science Review* 87:334–47.

Schorr, Alvin. 1966. *Poor Kids: A Report on Children in Poverty*. New York: Basic Books.

Schriftgiesser, Karl. 1967. *Business and Public Policy: The Role of the Committee for Economic Development*. Englewood Cliffs, NJ: Prentice-Hall.

Schwartz, John E. 1983. *America's Hidden Success: A Reassessment of Public Policy from Kennedy to Reagan*. New York: W. W. Norton.

Sears, David O., and Jack Citrin. 1982. *Tax Revolt: Something for Nothing in California*. Cambridge, MA: Harvard University Press.

Sewell, William H., Jr. 1985. "Ideologies and Social Revolutions: Reflections on the French Case." *Journal of Modern History* 57:57–85.

———. 1992. "A Theory of Structure: Duality, Agency, and Transformation." *American Journal of Sociology* 98:1–29.

———. 1999. "The Concept(s) of Culture." Pp. 35–61 in *Beyond the Cultural Turn: New Directions in the Study of Society and Culture*, ed. Victoria E. Bonnell and Lynn Hunt. Berkeley: University of California Press.

Shipler, David K. 2004. *The Working Poor: Invisible in America*. New York: Vintage.

Shulman, Bruce J. 2001. *The Seventies: The Great Shift in American Culture, Society, and Politics*. New York: Free Press.

Sitkoff, Harvard. 1981. *The Struggle for Black Equality, 1954–1980*. New York: Hill and Wang.

Skocpol, Theda. 1985a. "Bringing the State Back In: Strategies of Analysis in Current Research." Pp. 3–37 in *Bringing the State Back In*, ed. Peter B. Evans, Dietrich Rueschmeyer, and Theda Skocpol. New York: Cambridge University Press.

———. 1985b. "Cultural Idioms and Political Ideologies in the Revolutionary Reconstruction of State Power: A Rejoinder to Sewell." *Journal of Modern History* 57:86–96.

———. 1988. "The Limits of the New Deal System and the Roots of Contemporary Welfare Dilemmas." Pp. 293–311 in *The Politics of Social Policy in the United States*, ed. Margaret Weir, Ann Shola Orloff, and Theda Skocpol. Princeton: Princeton University Press.

———. 1992. *Protecting Soldiers and Mothers: The Political Origins of Social Policy in the United States*. Cambridge, MA: Harvard University Press.

———. 1995. "Targeting within Universalism: Politically Viable Policies to Combat Poverty in the United States." Pp. 250–74 in *Social Policy in the United States: Future Possibilities in Historical Perspective*, ed. Theda Skocpol. Princeton: Princeton University Press.

Skocpol, Theda, and Kenneth Finegold. 1982. "State Capacity and Economic Intervention in the Early New Deal." *Political Science Quarterly* 97:255–78.

Skocpol, Theda, and John Ikenberry. 1983. "The Political Formation of the American Welfare State in Historical and Comparative Perspective." *Comparative Social Research* 6:87–147.

Skrentny, John D. 1996. *The Ironies of Affirmative Action: Politics, Culture, and Justice in America*. Chicago: University of Chicago Press.

———. 2002. *The Minority Rights Revolution*. Cambridge, MA: Harvard University Press.

Somers, Margaret R., and Fred Block. 2005. "From Poverty to Perversity: Ideas, Markets, and Institutions over 200 Years of Welfare Debate." *American Sociological Review* 70:260–87.

Soysal, Yasemin Nohoglu. 1994. *Limits of Citizenship: Migrants and Postnational Membership in Europe.* Chicago: University of Chicago Press.

Starr, Paul. 1992. "Social Categories and Claims in the Liberal State." *Social Research* 50:263–95.

Steensland, Brian. 2002. "The Failed Welfare Revolution: Policy, Culture, and the Struggle for Guaranteed Income in the U.S., 1965–1980." Ph.D. diss., Princeton University.

———. 2006. "Cultural Categories and the American Welfare State: The Case of Guaranteed Income Policy." *American Journal of Sociology* 111:1273–1326.

Steiner, Gilbert Y. 1971. *The State of Welfare.* Washington, DC: Brookings Institution.

Steinmetz, George, ed. 1999. *State/Culture: State-Formation after the Cultural Turn.* Ithaca, NY: Cornell University Press.

Steinmo, Sven, Kathleen Thelen, and Frank Longstreth, eds. 1992. *Structuring Politics: Historical Institutionalism in Comparative Perspective.* New York: Cambridge University Press.

Steinmo, Sven, and Jon Watts. 1995. "It's the Institutions, Stupid! Why Comprehensive National Health Insurance Always Fails in America." *Journal of Health Politics, Policy, and Law* 20:329–72.

Stigler, George. 1946. "The Economics of Minimum Wage Legislation." *American Economic Review* 36:358–65.

Stone, Deborah. 1989. "Causal Stories and the Formation of Policy Agendas." *Political Science Quarterly* 104:281–300.

Sugrue, Thomas. 1996. *The Origins of the Urban Crisis: Race and Inequality in Postwar Detroit.* Princeton: Princeton University Press.

———. 1998. "Carter's Urban Policy Crisis." Pp. 137–57 in *The Carter Presidency: Policy Choices in the Post–New Deal Era,* ed. Gary M. Fink and Hugh Davis Graham. Lawrence: University Press of Kansas.

Sundquist, James L. 1968. *Politics and Policy: The Eisenhower, Kennedy, and Johnson Years.* Washington, DC: Brookings Institution.

Swenson, Peter. 2002. *Capitalists against Markets: The Making of Labor Markets and Welfare States in the United States and Sweden.* New York: Oxford University Press.

Swidler, Ann. 1986. "Culture in Action: Symbols and Strategies." *American Sociological Review* 51:273–86.

———. 2001. *Talk of Love: How Culture Matters.* Chicago: University of Chicago Press.

Teles, Steven M. 1996. *Whose Welfare: AFDC and Elite Politics.* Lawrence: University of Kansas Press.

Theobald, Robert. 1961. *The Challenge of Abundance.* New York: Clarkson N. Potter.

———. 1963. *Free Men and Free Markets.* New York: Clarkson N. Potter.

———, ed. 1966. *The Guaranteed Income: Next Step in Economic Evolution?* Garden City, NY: Doubleday.

Tilly, Charles, ed. 1975. *The Formation of National States in Western Europe.* Princeton: Princeton University Press.

Van Parijs, Philippe, ed. 1992. *Arguing for Basic Income: Ethical Foundations for a Radical Reform*. New York: Verso.

———. 1995. *Real Freedom for All: What, If Anything, Can Justify Capitalism?* New York: Oxford University Press.

———. 2001. *What's Wrong with a Free Lunch?* Boston: Beacon Press.

Van Trier, Walter. 2002. "Who Framed 'Social Dividend'?" Paper presented at USBIG Conference, City University of New York, March 8–10, 2002.

Weber, Max. 1930. *The Protestant Ethic and the Spirit of Capitalism*. New York: Routledge.

Weir, Margaret. 1992. *Politics and Jobs: The Boundaries of Employment Policy in the United States*. Princeton: Princeton University Press.

Weir, Margaret, Ann Shola Orloff, and Theda Skocpol, eds. 1988. *The Politics of Social Policy in the United States*. Princeton: Princeton University Press.

Wertheimer, Richard F. 1970. *The Monetary Rewards of Migration within the U.S.* Washington, DC: Urban Institute.

Widerquist, Karl. 2005. "A Failure to Communicate: What (If Anything) Can We Learn from the Negative Income Tax Experiments?" *Journal of Socio-Economics* 34:49–81.

Wildavsky, Aaron, and William Cavala. 1970. "The Political Feasibility of Income by Right." *Public Policy* 18:321–54.

Wilson, William Julius. 1987. *The Truly Disadvantaged: The Inner City, the Underclass, and Public Policy*. Chicago: University of Chicago Press.

Wright, Erik Olin. 2004. "Basic Income, Stakeholder Grants, and Class Analysis." *Politics and Society* 32:79–87.

Wuthnow, Robert. 1987. *Meaning and Moral Order: Explorations in Cultural Analysis*. Berkeley: University of California Press.

———. 1989. *Communities of Discourse: Ideology and Social Structure in the Reformation, the Enlightenment, and European Socialism*. Cambridge, MA: Harvard University Press.

Zaller, John R. 1992. *The Nature and Origins of Mass Opinion*. New York: Cambridge University Press.

Zelizer, Julian. 1998. *Taxing America: Wilbur D. Mills, Congress, and the State, 1945–1975*. New York: Cambridge University Press.

Zelizer, Viviana. 1994. *The Social Meaning of Money: Pin Money, Paychecks, Poor Relief, and Other Currencies*. New York: Basic Books.

Zerubavel, Eviatar. 1991. *The Fine Line: Making Distinctions in Everyday Life*. Chicago: University of Chicago Press.

Index

Aaron, Henry, 44, 187–88, 196
Abernathy, Ralph, 68, 105, 128
Ackerman, Bruce, 228
Ad Hoc Committee on the Triple Revolution, 42, 54
Affluent Society, The (Galbraith), 33, 35
AFL-CIO, 136, 145, 209. *See also* Meany, George
AFSCME, 209
Agnew, Spiro, 97, 114
Aid to Dependent Children (ADC), 14, 30
Aid to Families with Dependent Children (AFDC), 8, 30–31, 35–36, 39, 53–54, 59–62, 71–72, 80, 84, 94, 96, 102, 116, 154, 159–61, 172, 203, 220, 237, 240; growth in rolls of, 79, 89–90, 92, 97–98, 114, 142, 152; political vulnerability of recipients, 180, 220; retrenchment in 1980s and, 219–27
Alstott, Anne, 228
Amenta, Edwin, 7
American Jewish Committee, 138
Americans for Democratic Action, 137, 165
Anderson, Martin, 93, 119, 121, 160, 179, 216, 224, 241–42, 277n.118; his critique of FSS, 93–95
Arden House group, 68–70, 75, 86, 108, 132–33
Arendt, Hannah, 34

basic income, 228
Bateman, Worth, 88–89
Beame, Abraham, 199
Bennett, Wallace, 153–54
Berkowitz, Edward, 223
Berlin, Isaiah, 37
Beyond Entitlement (Mead), 225
Bowler, Kenneth, 270n.50
Brown, Michael, 38, 237
Bureau of the Budget, 87
Burns, Arthur, 88–89, 91–93, 102–3, 119, 134, 179, 239–42, 260n.91, 268n.5; his critique of FSS, 95–97, 110–11, 114; his critique of welfare rights, 95–96
business groups, 17, 145, 158, 209; concerns about urban problems, 91, 135; influence on social policy, 7–8, 241–43; interests of, 13, 15, 32–33, 67–70, 108–9, 130–35, 241–43; survey of business elites' attitudes, 135; views of GAI policy, 22, 64–70, 134–35
Business Week, 109
Butler, Lewis, 89

Califano, Joseph, 182, 186–88, 191–96, 200–203, 205, 209–11, 213, 216–18; announcement of preliminary plan, 198–99; centrality of, 186; his emphasis on comprehensive reform, 193; "monster-memo" and, 202
"California-style" reform, 21, 159, 169, 172, 183, 196, 218, 222–23
Canada, comparison with U.S., 2, 10
Capitalism and Freedom (Friedman), 36
Carleson, Robert, 172, 196, 204, 212, 223
Carter administration, 181, 245; competing welfare reform plans within, 191–93; compromise bill of, 211–12; and concerns about fraud, 205–6; conflict within, 189; legislative priorities of, 210–11; policy development process within, 187–94; triple-track proposals of, 189, 194–95, 201, 203, 206; two-track proposals of, 188; and welfare reform in 1979, 216; welfare reform principles and, 193
Carter, Jimmy, 2, 13, 18, 27, 181–84, 203–4, 208, 211, 217–18, 223, 275n.71; his disengagement from welfare reform, 186–87, 191, 211; his emphasis on comprehensive reform, 182–83, 185, 191–93, 206; his emphasis on cost containment, 191–95; as Georgia governor, 185; his governing style, 185; jobs and, 188; his policy principles announcement, 194–95; his support for categorical differentiation, 194; his view of welfare reform, 185; his view of working mothers, 200, 205; his welfare reform announcement, 206–7
categories of worth, 1, 3–5, 13–18, 25, 80, 116, 131, 143, 157, 161, 175–76, 183, 188–90, 194–95, 209, 212, 217, 225–26, 232, 245–46; and analytical issues, 234–39; flexibility of, 238–39; institutionalization of, 4,